KU-514-286

LEEDS POLYTECHNIC LIB

LEEDS BECKETT UNIVERSITY
LIBRARY
71 0138812 TELEPEN
DISCARDED

Costa-Gavras

The Political Fiction Film

Costa-Gavras

The Political Fiction Film

John J. Michalczyk

Philadelphia
The Art Alliance Press
London and Toronto: Associated University Presses

© 1984 by Associated University Presses, Inc.

Associated University Presses
440 Forsgate Drive
Cranbury, NJ 08512

Associated University Presses
25 Sicilian Avenue
London WC1A 2QH, England

Associated University Presses
2133 Royal Windsor Drive
Unit 1
Mississauga, Ontario
Canada L5J 1K5

Library of Congress Cataloging in Publication Data

Michalczyk, John J., 1941–
  Costa-Gavras, the political fiction film.

  Filmography: p.
  Bibliography: p.
  Includes index.
  1. Costa-Gavras, 1933–   I. Title.
PN1998.A3C79145   1983   791.43'0233'0924   81-72023
ISBN 0-87982-029-2

ᵐ138812 -2

LEEDS POLYTECHNIC
474579
AV
74600
21.5.86
791.43(495)GAV   791.4309495

Printed in the United States of America

To Albert M. Folkard—
From one *Homo politicus* to another!

Political cinema, then, for us, is cinema which proposes consciously and deliberately to deal with politics and dramatic material, and with content in a certain way related to reality. Taking this concept in the broad sense, it's not a question of last month's events, but of contemporary problems and concerns, which thus excludes the film that is historical only in *spirit*.

—COSTA-GAVRAS, 1970

Contents

Acknowledgments   9

Introduction   11

1. The Political Film   17

2. A Biographical Odyssey with Guiding Principles   29

3. *The Sleeping Car Murder* and *Shock Troops:* Doors to a Political Future 51

4. *Z:* A Greek Tragedy   76

5. *The Confession:* A Kafkaesque Political Tale   106

6. *State of Siege:* Ugly American or Good Samaritan?   143

7. *Special Section:* Vichy and the Reason of State   187

8. From *Clair de Femme* to *Missing:* Back on the Political Track   215

Conclusions and Epilogue   236

Notes   241

Filmography   255

Bibliography   260

Index   277

Acknowledgments

Although completed for the most part in creative solitude, this work of criticism reflects a score of rich personal contacts. For the first stage of this project, I am deeply indebted to the Reverend Joseph D. Gauthier, S.J., of Boston College, a personal mentor for more than fifteen years, for his many translations from the French, at times very complicated, and for the reading of the manuscript in its several phases; to Artur and Lise London for the two lengthy interviews which provided invaluable material for the chapter on *The Confession;* to Jorge Semprun and Franco Solinas for very useful information on their scriptwriting; to former Congressman Robert Drinan, S.J., for his continuous efforts through the Freedom of Information Act to procure important documentation for me from the Agency of International Development, the Central Intelligence Agency, and the U.S. State Department; to former Senator Enrique Erro (Uruguay) for his lengthy correspondence concerning the political crisis in Uruguay in 1970; to the staff of IDHEC film library, the Arsenal library, and Fédération des Organismes de la Communication Sociale in Paris, for documentation on Costa-Gavras and political film; to the Reverend Emmanuel Flipo, S.J., for his assistance with the research in Paris; to Françoise Bonnot for her firsthand information on the editing process for Costa-Gavras's films; to the Reverend John Willis, S.J., for the materials on the opera *Boris Godunov* for *Special Section;* to novelist Jean-Pierre Chabrol and historians of the Resistance Aimé Vielzeuf and René Bibault for their suggestions, references, and specifications with regard to the novel and film *Un Homme de trop* (Shock Troops); to the Honorable Barney Frank, for materials dealing with *Missing;* and to Dr. Harry Gavras for information concerning the family's background.

Several individuals must be mentioned who verified the content and proposed suggestions on style: the Reverend Francis Sullivan, S.J., Joseph Michalczyk, Angelo Andriopolos, Katherine and Stevan Kovacs, Alan Berger, and Patrick Baliani.

The Fondation Camargo (Cassis, France) provided the time and space necessary to rework the final draft of the manuscript.

I am grateful to Sister Florence Denoncourt and the Sisters of the Holy Union (Groton) and Claire Murray for the typing of the manuscript.

For the indispensable Index I am grateful to Susan Ross and for the attractive cover design to Carol Maryanski.

For the financing of the final part of the project I express my gratitude to the Mellon Foundation for its grant to assist further scholarship at Boston College.

Through this lengthy process I have received the continued support and encouragement from my family, friends, and members of the Jesuit communities at Boston College, Centre Sèvres, and 42, rue de Grenelle (Paris).

Introduction

More than a decade has elapsed since Costa-Gavras made his first political fiction film, Z, based on the assassination of a Greek deputy and alleged cover-up by the government. The film excited the politically aware public in 1969 but outraged the Greek military regime. Its immediate success was thus assured. Some producers and directors in France, Italy, and the United States were quick to capitalize on this box-office success drawing inspiration from the attractive style of the film. Soon another genre was added to the musical, western, romance, detective, and war film already exhaustively produced by the Hollywood dream factory. To create this innovative form of cinema referred to as the "political thriller" or "political fiction," the director would ordinarily plant a seed of politics in a tense, dramatic, and action-packed terrain. His aim would be to produce entertainment as well as a new consciousness in the viewer. For the most part, this new phase of filmmaking has been a successful attempt to distill intricate political issues for a large populace. The box-office receipts show it.

Costa-Gavras is the director most responsible for launching and popularizing the contemporary genre of political fiction and Z is the prototype. He merits being the focal point of this critical work since he is the cinematic pioneer with five significant political films among his eight features. His films are not situated in a vacuum but are concretized in a certain chronological period and sociopolitical milieu. We must first set his work in the general context of the political film, just as we would do if treating a Sergei Eisenstein or a Leni Riefenstahl in the framework of Soviet or Nazi ideologies of the 1920s or 1930s. Costa-Gavras's cinematic production, Z especially, comes at a critical moment in the history of political consciousness in society, witness the poignant subject matter and the ideological tone of films since the late 1960s.

We will then examine more specifically the environment in which Costa-Gavras made his films. He was influenced by personal exposure to international political crises, by rich relationships with friends and artists of the cinema world, and by recent technical developments in film. It is possible to grasp the colorful threads that bind together all of his films—there is a consistent style, an ensemble of actors and technicians, and an almost unvarying political optic.

The Sleeping Car Murder and *Shock Troops* were filmed before Z.[1] These two works of Costa-Gavras antedate his interest in the political thriller, but they do lay the groundwork for future dramatic and politicized fiction. They contain in

11

embryonic form what would mature by using the same actors, intensive action, and suspense, but with a larger budget and more politically controversial material. The two initial works indicated potential and promise to producers who were, at the time, anxious to attract new talent.

Costa-Gavras's five political films, *Z, The Confession, State of Siege, Special Section,* and his first English-language film, *Missing,* provide the focus for our critical analysis. Actual historical events following World War II gave rise to each of these films. We would like to present—as far as it is possible—an objective and detailed examination of the filmmaker's political approach to these events by documenting each event with government sources, press releases, interviews, and primary literary sources.

Ordinarily, a book used by the director as an initial blueprint for a film emerges from a historical incident, for example, totalitarianism in Czechoslovakia in the 1950s, as seen in the case of Costa-Gavras and London's exposé in *The Confession.* A study of the evolution from the historical situation to the book, and from the literary work to the script reveals Costa-Gavras's sensitivity to particular dramatic forms and sociopolitical concerns, as well as to the enriching collaborative relationships he shared with scriptwriters such as Jorge Semprun and Franco Solinas. This is the heart of the adaptation dilemma—how to dramatize a historical event found in a literary text and still make it suitable for mass consumption? Fidelity to the historical moment and to the text makes one set of demands; theatrical expression makes another. The controversy in Washington over *Missing* bears this out.

For Costa-Garvas the actual making of a film often raises difficult though not insoluble problems. With each film there are different challenges regarding permission to film, the need for realistic sets and actual locations, extensive financing—all usually skillfully resolved by the filmmaker and his team of technicians. Such was the case when the director attempted to film with some authenticity World War II Vichy of *Special Section* and Prague of the 1950s for *The Confession.*

Each chapter to follow constitutes an analysis of a particular film from an aesthetic and technical point of view. The analysis is reinforced by a wide sampling of film criticism emanating from France and the United States. The criticism will shed some light on the developmental process of Costa-Gavras in his art: public and critics alike have helped create the recent successes of Costa-Gavras in the genre of political fiction and have provided the classical sounding board for a director. Costa-Gavras mentioned on occasion the role of the public with respect to the ideological content of *Z:* "The film was not a political film. The public made it one." Jean-Patrick Lebel reinforces this remark in his Marxist-oriented *Cinéma et idéologie.* He notes the participatory role of the spectators in the dissemination of the political message:

> But the ideological thrust of a film is not expressed once and for all at the moment it is registered on celluloid (or on a magnetic strip).
> It depends concretely on the ideological impact of the film on the public. And this ideological impact is itself a function of the public's ideological formation.[2]

This type of political exchange is essential to the ongoing dialogue of the public and critics with the filmmaker, obliging the latter to assess his creative work constantly.

The present critical and dialectical study is designed to intensify this exchange. Its underlying purpose is to document the progressive stages of Costa-Gavras's political filming in a now commercialized genre, concomitantly to raise pertinent questions about contemporary directors' perception of social cinema for the masses, by comparing them with Costa-Gavras, the re-creator and popularizer of political fiction.

Costa-Gavras

The Political Fiction Film

1
The Political Film

> A political film is one which informs the largest mass possi-
> ble, people who are not necessarily militant. A militant film
> is totally tied to the activity of a party and is used for expla-
> nation or propaganda for the party's ideology.
> —Costa-Gavras

In the early 1970s there suddenly emerged on the national and international
scene a vast series of films with political themes and simultanesously a multitude
of studies to document them. How can we explain this phenomenon? Politics has
been in the air since the May 1968 events in Paris and the student rebellion at
Kent State, Harvard, Columbia, Berkeley, and many other American colleges
and universities. Given the widespread controversy in the United States about
the Vietnam war, politics has certainly not been a cloistered affair of the politicians in the Senate chambers. It has fallen into the hands of the public.
Sociopolitical problems have become living and concrete, says Christian Zimmer
in *Cinéma et politique*.[1] This is especially the case owing to the more recent impact
of television. From a comfortable living room one can watch a revolution take
place in a Third World country (for example, in Nicaragua) in serial form over a
number of months. The televised and widely publicized Watergate affair assisted
in the political awakening of the masses. Political films over the past ten years
have been attuned to the growth in ideological awareness among Americans and
Europeans alike, more so in Latin American peoples, as we will soon observe.

It is expedient at the outset of this study to pinpoint the specific characteristics
of this area of film; otherwise we may fall unwittingly into the trap of generaliz-
ing and stereotyping. The most elementary question that must be confronted is,
"What makes a political film?" Is it a particular genre, style, perspective, party, or
subject? We could further ask, "Is a film political because of the director's ideology?" His intention thus would be subliminal. These questions must certainly be
raised when considering the work of Costa-Gavras.

In *Cinéma et idéologie*, Jean-Patrick Lebel divides political films into two general
groupings. This division might be of some assistance as a starting point. The first
grouping consists of ideological films that develop a political theme but do not

17

engage the viewer to take action. The other type of films encourages and almost obliges direct political activity. These activist works are often created with a specific movement, meeting, or cause in mind.[2] Some of Costa-Gavras's films fit into the first category. They have also been used at political meetings, as for example Z,screened in conjunction with an international demonstration against the Greek military junta.

Guy Hennebelle and Daniel Serceau elaborate on different kinds of political film, placing them into three categories. The first corresponds to Lebel's non-committal cinema. Hennebelle and Serceau write:

> The first type had recourse to the "Z effect," so called because of Costa-Gavras' film on the Greek dictatorship. It consisted of taking up the Hollywood style of production with a simple insertion of a political theme. This commercial tendency gave rise in France, and also in Italy, to a new wave of "thrillers," characterized by an apparently immediate effectiveness, but whose flaws (cultural mimicry and ideological fuzziness) soon become more and more apparent.[3]

The French critics observe that the second type promotes a *telquelisme*, referring to the mentality of the contributors to the Parisian journal *Tel Quel* under the direction of Philippe Sollers. Formalism, intellectualism, and an ultraleftist perspective characterize this approach. The films of this group, best represented by the convoluted work of Jean-Luc Godard, manifest narcissism and snobbishness. Some critics say these films toy with Brecht's *distantiation* or estrangement principles of nonidentification of the theatergoer with the character. Hennebelle and Serceau quote Godard as claiming that cinema experiences innate original sin and the sin must be wiped away by a new form of film. The recent films are directed toward the politically convinced and are only seen in miniscule movie houses of the Latin Quarter or Greenwich Village. Godard's filmtract on the Palestinian question, *Ici et ailleurs,* would fit the above description. His *Comment ça va* is visually challenging even for Godard enthusiasts, for it approximates a type of cinema of alienation. The viewer must wade through confusing, recherché techniques in order to grasp the political message. Godard reacts to this critical response by stating that he makes films for himself, hence is diametrically opposed to the commercializing intentions of Costa-Gavras.

Analagous to Lebel's second style of political film is Hennebelle and Serceau's third category, militant film. This form of cinema is on the fringe of the commercial system, put together by nonprofessionals (and some professionals), with small budgets, using 16mm cameras and black and white film. The militant work becomes a weapon of political struggle. It is used in a political context, such as a rally or demonstration during which further polemical information is distributed. This cinema does not adhere to an art-for-art's-sake credo whereby the product is the end or goal. For a militant cineaste such as Chris Marker of the SLON film collective in France, film is a means to an end. It is in the service of an ideology, and takes up a specific cause, for example, human rights, the feminist movement, or housing injustices.[4] In the United States militant filmmakers have also used film as an ideological medium. They are well represented by the Pacific

Steel film collective and the San Francisco Newsreel, to name but two. The number of these film collectives multiplies as more and more funding becomes available.

The proletariat film has attracted some attention recently on both sides of the Atlantic, primarily from the many small audiences of workers in various interested factories or in closely related geographic areas, especially in France. In 1970, Costa-Gavras attended a session of the *cinéma ouvrier* (the blue-collar or proletariat film) with Chris Marker, Bernard Paul, and Edouard Luntz. It was not too long after the success of *Z* and about the time he was working on *The Confession*. The militant film in France was just beginning to make some headway. These filmmakers and others politically committed screened five or six films from Besançon and debated the essence of the worker-film. This type of noncommercial and nontraditional film deals with polemical labor topics such as the occupation of a factory, the abuse of human dignity, and the harsh realities of the worker's existence. Costa-Gavras's participation in this session indicated his openness to the militant film which supports a certain cause, yet he did not commit himself to this specific form.[5]

Further restricting or descriptive qualities can be added to the above schemas. The documentary or nonfictional film is, *grosso modo,* an educational and political instrument. It is deliberately designed to raise the consciousness of the viewer about certain social and historical problems, for example, Fred Wiseman's *Hospital, Titicut Follies, High School* or Alain Resnais's *Night and Fog.* The cineaste becomes chronicler, prophet, explorer, advocate, journalist, observer, and promoter, with the instrument of a documentary work.[6] Costa-Gavras will share in many of these characteristics while filming *The Confession* and *Special Section.*

For certain critics and directors, the semi-documentary falls into a separate, alluring category. Costa-Gavras's *State of Siege* provides a prime example of this aesthetic form. A historical event is scrupulously reenacted and recounted with an apparent objectivity, using documentary and cinéma vérité techniques—the hand-held camera, some nonprofessional actors, a tone of reportage. It is not documentary but *documented* cinema. Such was also the case of Pontecorvo's *Battle of Algiers.* The public at first believed that the final scenes in particular were actually filmed during the demonstrations for independence in the streets of Algiers. The intricate script, written by Franco Solinas after a study of thousands of documents, photographs, and testimonies, helped to give birth to a "historical" representation of the Algerian War.[7] The same convincing effect on the viewer came from Peter Watkin's totally staged *The War Game* (1965) on possible nuclear holocaust.[8]

In this semidocumentary approach there is a transformation of reality. Fact together with fiction helps create a cinematic hybrid, not unlike Truman Capote's novel *In Cold Blood.* The boundaries are blurred between documentary and fiction as a semblance of authenticity prevails. There is not the presence of absolute "fact." (A prologue to such a film will usually invite the viewer to consider the content of the work as an actual historical event.) In this style of film the director can take certain liberties and still maintain an atmosphere of veracity.

In pure fiction films, there exists a wide range of possibilities that depends on the political nature of the content and on the specific dosage intended in a given film. Sometimes the political ingredients are minimal—simply an excuse or a background—and the central thrust of the film is at best a sociopsychological study of government officials, a suspense or a spy story. Such would be the case of Ronald Neame's *The O.D.E.S.S.A. File,* a tense tale of Nazi hunting, or Jerry Schatzberg's *The Seduction of Joe Tynan,* a political and marital crisis in the life of a senator. Fiction, drama, and suspense fill the screen, not politics, in this type of film. For the viewer there is only a minor opportunity to consider the effects of politics on society or on a particular person in the film.

Joan Mellen's article on "Hollywood's 'Political' Cinema" diagnoses a recent glamorizing, capitalizing trend in political fiction. In her treatment of *Joe* (1970), *Drive, He Said* (1970), *Panic in Needle Park* (1971), *Billy Jack* (1971), *Sweet, Sweetback's Baadasssss Song* (1971), and *Johnny Got His Gun* (1971), she indicates how Hollywood reacts to certain popular themes:

> Of late Hollywood has become obsessed with the image of the radical. With the majority of film audiences between sixteen and twenty-four and the continuation of the war, the draft, and endemic poverty of blacks and poor whites, Hollywood has found it possible to ignore the new radicalization—despite the preference of the "dream machine" for themes which gently reconcile the viewer to the status quo.[9]

The critic then elaborates on the formula or mold used by Hollywood directors to commercialize and market this radical product:

> But Hollywood has discovered how to portray radicals, be they student, black, Indian, or in the case of *Johnny Got His Gun,* amputee, without conveying any political implications. Films dealing with students involved in radical causes, for example, are turned out according to a little-varying formula: the student radical and the youth culture are caricatured by the equating of physical degeneracy and incoherence with anti-war feeling or the dissident sensibility in general. The radical's ideas are thus easily dismissed as the neurotic outpourings of a psychological misfit whose discontent is reduced to personal *angst* independent of a society in need of change.[10]

Whether the political film is militant or entertaining, documentary, semidocumentary, or fiction, it is created to alter in varying degrees the viewer's perception of certain sociopolitical situations. It may capture social conflict, suffering because of oppression, or injustice in the legal system, as reflected in all of Costa-Gavras's films. It also may urge the spectator to take action immediately against oppressive forces, as in the multinational exposés, anti-Vietnam film tracts, elegies to the Farm Workers—all distributed by San Francisco Newsreel. Progressive government may welcome the commercial political fiction film, and only tolerate the militant film; repressive regimes may strike out ferociously against either or both when they touch one sensitive area, for example, political prisoners or torture. The latter films are then labeled "subversive" in Amos Vogel's sense of the term:

> The basis of politically and socially subversive cinema is the tension that

exists between society and artist. This expresses itself in forms and subjects that vary from country to country, resulting not from greater or lesser artistic sophistication or skill but from differing stages of societal development, from political pressure, from the absence or presence of democratic tendencies and the degree of sharpness of social contradictions. In each instance, however, the artist goes further than his particular Establishment wishes him to. This "going beyond" is the precise characteristic of all subversive art.[11]

At certain times the political film can be considered propaganda, especially when the director manipulates the viewer to side with a cause through a string of half-truths, stereotyping, selectivity of flattering or disparaging commentaries, emotional music, trick montage, or whitewashing. Critics were quick to point out that *Z* and *State of Siege* bordered on the propagandistic in their respective anti-junta and anti-American government views. The allegiance of the spectator was carefully drawn toward the director's partisan ideology.

When we consider the five major political films of Costa-Gavras, we find that they are not documentary studies of a particular subject; nor are they simply means of entertaining a quasi-politically oriented audience with a fragment of ideology. Yet his works reflect both tendencies, consciously. Concerning *State of Siege,* he and screenwriter Jorge Semprun indicate that they have verified everything, having worked with newspapers, interviews, and on-location studies. On the other hand, Costa-Gavras dramatizes the material to make it more appealing to a large international audience. Costa-Gavras justifies the distillation of political thought in a commercialized and popular form of entertainment in the following way:

> It is imperative that the political film be viewed since its purpose is, if not to transform reality, then to influence the viewer by apprising him. One must utilize the traditional type of production—with dramatic construction and use of actors—so that people may feel involved, and so that the film may have some useful purpose.[12]

Costa-Gavras, in his synthesis of two trends—the documentary and straight fiction—creates the new genre of popular political fiction or the political thriller. He goes one step beyond Pontecorvo's *Battle of Algiers* by making his own films more spectacular, by adding a commercial note to them, and then concluding them with an epilogue that leaves the public in a reflective state. His political films could be justly referred to as fictionalized politics or politicized fiction. Each of these films has a thesis, for example, social justice versus blatant injustice, but the message is couched in dramatically appealing terms. It is far from the primitive, hard-hitting, and at times propagandistic or partisan, militant film. The French critic Louis Seguin describes the popularizing intention of Costa-Gavras a bit more bluntly: "Z was made to soothe the conscience of the Saturday night, leftist filmgoer."[13]

We can say the works of Costa-Gavras are political in the broad sense of the word. They deal with such ideological topics as totalitarianism, imperialism, collaboration. They manifest unquestionably the leftist and anti-Establishment view of the director. Despite their apparent authenticity, they are not documentary, for Costa-Gavras's purpose is to *dramatize* the historical situation. The label "political fiction" is convenient for this genre although it does not get to the essence of it. Costa-Gavras will often reject the epithet from the mouth of an interviewer, but on occasion he will use the term to qualify his work during various workshops, interviews, or debates on "political film." In such cases he wishes to distinguish this genre from the militant film or the documentary.

To situate Costa-Gavras in a large historical and political context would require a condensation of a score of books on political film. This process would bring us into contact with a vast series of important but often unrelated films and subject matter, from George Méliès—whom Costa-Gavras considers the first political filmmaker with *L'Affaire Dreyfus* (1899)—through the Soviet, Nazi, and American propaganda films of World War II, to the contemporary revolutionary films of the Third World filmmakers.[14] As profitable as this may be, the survey would necessarily be superficial. On occasion, however, some of these political film classics made an impact on Costa-Gavras and these should be underscored.

Costa-Gavras acknowledges the debt of his generation to the Soviet filmmaker Sergei Eisenstein and to the leftist French novelist André Malraux, who wrote on the Chinese revolution and the Spanish Civil War. "An entire generation of militants, intellectual revolutionaries, has been formed by the viewing of *Potemkin* and the reading of *La Condition humaine* (Man's Fate)."[15]

The Italian neorealist film greatly interested and impressed Costa-Gavras. When he was asked of his opinion of foreign political films, he replied:

> The best is certainly the Italian film. All neo-realist films, especially *Bicycle Thieves*, are excellent examples of political film, and then, let me offer a few examples that come to mind—*Salvatore Giuliano, Battle of Algiers, Hands over the City,* and *Todo Modo.* The worst political films are without doubt American, for they are always made for commercial purposes.[16]

The contemporary political fiction film did not spring into existence fully "armed" as did Athena from the head of Zeus. It had its precursors, its inspirational forerunners. Costa-Gavras and other political filmmakers are in agreement that some type of political fiction film was already present in the United States as far back as the 1930s. The classical gangster, detective, or Film Noir works were certainly political in tone and content. The political fiction film continued on until the 1960s, with such films about political corruption as *Mr. Smith Goes to Washington* (1939), *The Last Hurrah* (1958), and *Advise and Consent* (1962). Europe has also witnessed precursors of the political-fiction genre. This type of film, however, has been the most popular in Italy recently, where politics is the bread and butter of social life. Witness simply the number of political parties, ideological newspapers, and changes within government—approximately forty—since the close of World War II.

Among the more noted Italian filmmakers with a political reputation is Gillo Pontecorvo. His *Long Blue Road* (1957) and *Kapò* (1959) paved the way for the international success of *Battle of Algiers* (1966). *Battle of Algiers* attracted the attention of Costa-Gavras; it was banned in France so he was not able to see it until he began shooting *Z* in Algeria.

In France, Alain Resnais and Jean-Luc Godard would be the heralds of this new wave of political fiction film. It is not very difficult to spot similar patterns in *La Guerre est finie* (1966) of Resnais and *Z* of Costa-Gavras, that is, collaboration with Jorge Semprun, screenwriter; the casting of Yves Montand, a soft-spoken but deliberate militant; and the topic of the challenge to a totalitarian regime. The Resnais film would antedate the exposé of the Greek situation by almost four years.

Perhaps more esoteric and political in intention is Godard's *La Chinoise* (1967). Godard's work was prophetic in style and content. It hit the Paris screens before the outbreak of the May 1968 events. Advancing a Marxist philosophy, the cineaste divined the student unrest of the late 1960s as well as major weak points in bourgeois society.[17] His other films, such as *Made in USA* (1966), referring to the Ben Barka affair in France, and *Weekend* (1967), a film that Amos Vogel refers to as "an apocalyptic vision of capitalist consumer society," also display a definite sociopolitical orientation.[18]

It is at this point in film history that Costa-Gavras puts a new face on political fiction film. Demonstrating basic leftist, anti-fascist principles, he discloses the corruption, injustices, and unethical, fascistic tendencies in the totalitarian government of Greece that provoked the assassination of Deputy Lambrakis in 1963. Screened at Cannes in 1969, the display window of the international cinema industry, *Z* officially began a new genre.

In France, the political fiction label is above all shared by Costa-Gavras, Yves Boisset, André Cayatte, and most recently Henri Verneuil. Costa-Gavras and Yves Boisset are often compared, for they both exhibit an interest in political fiction as well as a desire to attract a large public, unlike Godard, whose work is abstruse and introverted.[19] Boisset chose for his subjects the police in *Un Condé* (A Cop, 1970), the secret service and the Ben Barka case in *L'Attentat* (The French Conspiracy, 1972), the army in *R.A.S.* (1973), bourgeois racism in *Dupont Lajoie* (1974), and corrupt justice in *Le Juge Fayard dit "le Shériff"* (1976). His *Femme Flic* (1980) exposed corruption in municipal government, antifeminism in the ranks of the police, and a child-pornography ring clandestinely operated by the pillars of society.

André Cayatte has had a checkered career in political cinema. His works are normally thesis films with minimal political orientation emanating from his experience in law. He considers his most recent political fiction film on the international arms sale, *Raison d'Etat* (1978), a film pamphlet. Here a biologist studies armaments and finds unethical practices in sales. He is eliminated, and his colleague (Monica Vitti), in whom he confides the controversial research, shares the same fate.

Among the French filmmakers who have a penchant for the political genre we may list Philippe Labro (*Without Apparent Motive*, 1971, and *The Inheritor*, 1972), Jean-Pierre Mocky (*Solo*, 1969, and *The Albatross*), Frank Cassenti (*The Red Poster*, 1976), Michel Drach (*The Red Sweater*, 1979), Michel Deville (*Dossier 51*, 1978), and Laurent Heynemann (*La Question*, 1977).[20]

A film that bears a close affinity to the Costa-Gavras use of political fiction is Henri Verneuil's *I . . . comme Icare* (1980). Here Verneuil, after having read more than a hundred works on the John F. Kennedy assassination, points his finger at the Secret Service. He uses the Stanley Milgram studies concerning authority at Yale to support his debatable theory.

Just as Costa-Gavras's name is forever linked with the political fiction genre in France, that of Francesco Rosi is linked to the Italian political film. Rosi's *Salvatore Giuliano* (1961), a controversial account of a Sicilian bandit, marked his initiation into political film. In 1963, he directed *Hands Over the City*, which examined the exploitation of power by a Naples City Council member. *The Mattei Affair* (1972) treats the possible assassination of a leading oil industrialist by unknown forces—Mafia, Italian big business, or American oil magnates?

Rosi's *Extinct Corpses* deals with assassinations and a final cover-up to assure the correct direction of power. *Eboli* (1978), from Carlo Levi's classic *Christ Stopped at Eboli* (1947), paints the touching portrait of an anti-fascist doctor and amateur artist sent into political exile. The press release at the time of the American screening of *Eboli* considers Rosi's films more as personal statements than works of propaganda:

> I am not a professional politician. But I have always had a sort of political vocation which permits me to participate in one way or another in the political problems of Italy. I think the best way to do so is through my work. I will therefore continue to make propositions which will permit discussions about certain aspects of the reality of the country.[21]

To a certain extent this can also be said of Costa-Gavras but on an international scale.

Elio Petri is not far behind Rosi in his reputation as committed Italian political filmmaker. With *Investigation of a Citizen Above Suspicion* (1970), Petri closely parallels Costa-Gavras's style and content. It is a political thriller in which the head of Police Intelligence kills his mistress. The film concludes on the note that the intelligence officer will not be indicted since this would undermine the reputation of the police force. Petri's *The Working Class Goes to Heaven* (1972) holds a somber view of the social and political concerns of an average workingman.

Bernardo Bertolucci has also brought a rich flair for politics into his film work. The political questions of *Before the Revolution* (1965), *The Spider's Strategem* (1970), and *The Conformist* (1971) reflect the strong Marxist and anti-fascist leanings of the director. In the American-financed five-hour marathon *1900*, Bertolucci uses a panorama of Italian politics and war to delineate two friends of different classes. They develop in constant struggle for their own ideals, one communist, one bourgeois.

In 1973 Florestano Vancini filmed *The Matteoti Affair,* showing the kidnapping and assassination of an outspoken senator in 1924, presumably by his political competitor, Benito Mussolini. Giuliano Montaldo's *Sacco and Vanzetti* (1971) offers a disputatious view of the two Italian immigrants, avowed anarchists, presenting them as innocent of bank robbery and double murder. Bellocchio's *Slap the Monster on Page One* (1973) conveys the corruption of the press in the preelection period of February–March 1972.

Among the many other political directors in Italy, Lina Wertmüller is the most internationally well known. Her films have an ideological thrust that radically differs from that of Costa-Gavras. Her political ideas match her imaginative and provocative ideas in a nondocumentary approach. With the reversal of class roles in her more celebrated *Swept Away* (1975), she entertains the public with her favorite lead, Giancarlo Giannini, and offers food for political reflection. *The Seduction of Mimi* (1971), an earlier film, works with the political allurement of Mimi the metallurgist. *Love and Anarchy* (1972) presents a humorous political picture of an attempt to assassinate Mussolini. *Seven Beauties* (1974) graphically communicates a philosophy of survival during World War II. Her blend of parables and politics in these films puts her into a unique category of political film not specified as such by Lebel, Hennebelle, or Serceau.

The political fiction fever is contagious. The American film industry in the 1970s and early 1980s was soon affected by the new twist that the genre of political exposés and thrillers had taken over the past decade. Joan Mellen's earlier analysis did indicate, however, that the American cinema is not truly sophisticated in this genre.

American directors may be under the misguided notion that in order to sell, politics must be gift-wrapped in an attractive package. The political perspective or content must not be so strong as to ward off potential viewers. There is no American of the international stature of Costa-Gavras or Rosi who consistently films political subjects, although several directors' individual works must be acknowledged in this domain. Alan Pakula's *All the President's Men* (1976) is a tense and suspenseful adaptation of Bob Woodward and Carl Bernstein's literary revelation of the Watergate affair. Sydney Pollock admits that the political thriller *Three Days of the Condor* (1975) has its roots in the existence of individuals who secretly do research for the CIA. Antimilitaristic and very humanistic, Dalton Trumbo's *Johnny Got His Gun* (1971) shows the pathos of an amputee survivor of World War I. Following the death of the director of the FBI, *The Secret Files of J. Edgar Hoover* (c. 1977) by Larry Cohen reveals the tyranny involved in the almost fascistic leadership of this law-enforcement institution. Norman Jewison filmed *And Justice for All* (1979) to publicize the widespread corruption and injustices of the legal system.

In Stuart Rosenberg's *Brubaker* (1980), the freshly appointed warden (Robert Redford) tries to humanize the farm-prison system. He antagonizes government authorities and is necessarily replaced. On the surface he is an unfortunate failure, but he has won a moral victory that is recognized by the inmates at his departure.

Tony Luraschi's *Outsider* (1980), based on Colin Leinster's *Heritage of Michael Flaherty*, poignantly reveals the many-faceted philosophical and political problem of violence in the IRA's struggle to free Ireland of British influence.

In America as in Italy, the assassination film has been in vogue especially since the Kennedy and King deaths in the 1960s. Fred Zinnemann's *Day of the Jackal*

(1973) from the Frederick Forsythe novel fascinated the Americans with its ingenious solitary plot to execute De Gaulle. The film left the French cold. On the other hand, Alan Pakula's *The Parallax View* (1975) had the reverse reactions in the two countries. *The Parallax View* is a clever film that follows the hero (Warren Beatty) as he infiltrates a school for assassins, is set up, and then accused of attempted assassination of a political figure. As in the Costa-Gavras films, there is an epilogue that dramatizes the subsequent cover-up. *Executive Action* (1973) makes a feeble visual endeavor to get at the heart of the Kennedy assassi-nation of 1963, since the Warren Commission findings were not very conclusive and the theories were inexhaustible. The film, directed by David Miller from a script by Dalton Trumbo, appears implausible and self-defeating, says Joan Mel-len in *Cinéaste*.[22] It concludes with the customary epilogue to stir the conscience of the viewer further: Eighteen material witnesses "died" by 1967, one hundred thousand trillion to one odds, an actuary from the Lloyds of London insurance company determines.[23] *Brass Target* (1978) jumps on the assassination band-wagon in its depiction of the "execution" of General Patton. With little action, little tension, with greater improbability, the film cannot achieve the American success of Zinnemann's *Day of the Jackal* (1972), which hovers in the background as its apparent inspiration.

Marathon Man (1976) is a film that has several currents of political nuances flowing through the life of the student protagonist (Dustin Hoffmann). The themes of Nazism (The White Angel of Auschwitz returns from exile), the McCarthy period (the father supposedly committed suicide for political reasons), and secret agents (the big brother, an international agent, has been involved in contraband), are intertwined in an exciting fashion. Politics, however, comes in mild doses and is overshadowed by the torture and suspense surrounding the kidnapping of the naïve hero.

Blue Collar (1978), the first film of Paul Schrader, scriptwriter for *Taxi Driver*, may at first appear superficial and vacuous. A closer viewing would reveal that it offers a fairly honest rendering of the contemporary sociopolitical scene. The French critic Jean Collet finds this type of film more exotic than an American critic would. He observes that it marks a key date in film because of its prophetic quality in its treatment of workers, unions, and FBI.[24] As usual, a filmed epilo-gue concludes the study of political tensions in an automobile plant in Michi-gan—as the young black foreman and his white Polish friend verbally strike out at each other, then get in a fracas as the voice-off prophetically announces, "And they will turn Black against White," showing the true power of members of the Establishment.

Since the 1960s, the Latin American political cinema has daringly pushed political fiction in a new and dialectical direction. More political and militant than the Italian, and less commercial and entertaining than the American, the Third World cinema utilizes fiction and history to strike a blow at American imperialism, bourgeois domination of the proletariat, and dictatorial oppression in all forms.[25]

The Cinema Novo in Brazil sets itself up as a revolutionary arm, a ferment for true political action. Its best representatives are Glauber Rocha in *Antonio das*

Mortes (1969) and Nelson Pereira dos Santos in *Vidas Secas* (Barren Lives, 1963). Cultivating a confrontation attitude toward social issues in their films, these filmmakers aim to facilitate revolution. Their works closely approximate the type of militant film as described by Lebel, Hennebelle, and Serceau. In Argentina, Fernando Solanas's *The Hour of the Furnaces* (1969) documents Peronism over a period of years. Jorge Sanjines's Bolivian *Blood of the Condor* (1969), showing the systematic sterilization of women, is an anti-American statement. Miquel Littin of Chile is noted for his works *The Jackal of Nahueltoro* (1972) and *The Promised Land* (1973). The latter film, completed shortly before the coup of September 1973 in Chile, shows in a prophetic manner the annihilation by the army of a band of revolutionaries in the 1930s. While directing *Clair de Femme* (1979), Costa-Gavras had a renewed interest in Latin American film and co-produced Miquel Littin's *Viva el Presidente!* (Recurso del Metodo, 1978). Littin's study of a Latin American dictator reflects the balanced political fiction that Costa-Gavras sees as ideal.

Cuba has also turned out several political masterpieces—*Memories of Underdevelopment* (1973) and *The Last Supper* (1976) of Tomas Gutierrez Alea as well as Humberto Solas's *Lucia* (1969). In Cuba the film industry is government-controlled, and its aims will differ from other expressions of Latin American film. Born of pain and struggle, the Latin American cinema in general is a cinema of liberation and exists outside the system and against it. Although many directors such as Littin—presently in Mexico—have left their countries, the "remnant" filmmakers who stay home continue to rely heavily on folklore and tradition. Individually and collectively they manifest a leftist tendency that excites and inflames the citizens of the Third World and challenges the commercial political fiction directors of the First World.

The foregoing brief review of the contemporary political film cannot be so easily terminated. Other directors have developed this genre in England, Germany, Poland, and elsewhere. What once was considered box-office poison has now become an international cinematic elixir. We can observe in retrospect that the framework for many of these films, excepting the Latin American, has almost been standardized: a slightly romanticized or simplified exposé of some sociopolitical injustice, enhanced by rapid-fire parallel editing, a large budget, a cast of prominent actors, a conclusion with an epilogue or resolution that is far from optimistic. The politics injected into an already acceptable commercial genre may be diluted or it may be spiced with a vague humanism, yet the resulting film now purports to have the capacity to touch a large audience and to help spark some type of reflection.[26]

Epilogue:

Several years after the political film genre made some inroads, Guy Hennebelle has been able to put the film into perspective, claiming that this original French genre has been "Americanized" and has become the French equivalent of a "spaghetti Western," à la Serge Leone. His remarks serve as a good afterword to this survey of political fiction and as a starting point for a significantly nuanced study of Costa-Gavras's political work:

> In conlusion, the Z movies seem to me on the whole condemnable because of such hidden vices as the plagiarism of a foreign aesthetic, the illusion that forms can be innocent, the acceptance of an individualistic mythology based on a classless humanism, and an exaggerated reliance on questionable stylistic techniques. And if certain films of this type are nevertheless "recuperable" by the Left, "it is strictly insofar as they are characterized by a certain prudence in the uses of these effects, such as *State of Siege*."
> Finally, because it is a genre which lends itself more to denunciation than to incitation, it can only with difficulty avoid the limitations of the conventional "progressive" cinema and thus does not belong to that "third cinema" which, with Solanas, we hope for.[27]

It is now our challenge to determine whether the political fiction films of Costa-Gavras which have set the tone for the genre are condemnable, recuperable, or laudable.

2

A Biographical Odyssey with Guiding Principles

> I would like to try to explain the present in which we live by another moment in history, and this piece of the past by events which have since occurred.
> —Costa-Gavras, 1971

In his Spanish civil war novel *L'Espoir* (Man's Hope), André Malraux acutely perceived the myriad directions the life of an individual could take. "For the first time Manuel was hearing the voice of that which is more awe-inspiring even than the blood of men, more enigmatic even than their presence on the earth—the infinite possibilities of their destiny."[1] We may be equally struck as we consider the odyssey of Costa-Gavras from pre–World War II Greece to present-day France, a journey beset with multiple detours, dead ends, and eventual shortcuts to celebrity. One thing/event/person has led to another in a curious development of his biography.

Biographical Odyssey:

Panayotis Gavras, the director's father, originated in Odessa, Russia. In 1922, he left this port town made famous by Eisenstein in his revolutionary film *Potemkin* (1925), hoping to discover a new life in the promised land of America. En route, he stopped at the seaport of Piraeus in Greece. The father put aside his original intentions and stayed in Greece, assuming the position of a minor administrator in the Ministry of Finance. He married a Greek woman and had three sons, Tolis, a lawyer in Athens; Harry, a doctor in heart research in Boston; and Konstantinos (Costa), cineaste in Paris.

Costa-Gavras was born in 1933 in Klivia (Peloponnesus) and grew up in Athens in this cradle of democracy which would become a prison for some of his generation some thirty years later. During his youthful days in and around

Athens, cinema, dance, war, and religion would leave their impressions on him, some deeper than others.

At the age of eight, perched high in a tree near an outdoor summer theater, he watched films such as *Sabu the Indian*. This was the first film he recalls seeing. He also remembers documentaries of military parades that were impressive.[2] The young Konstantinos would soon be mesmerized by American films starring Errol Flynn, including *Captain Blood* (1935), *Gentleman Jim* (1942), and *Objective Burma* (1945). Gary Cooper was another familiar face on the silver screen, and Joan Fontaine became his favorite actress. The films of Charlie Chaplin, shown all over the world in the silent language of comitragedy, especially appealed to him as an adolescent. The young Konstantinos was thus exposed to a heavy dose of American film, and it was not until his arrival in France that he learned that there were many other important expressions of cinema of which he had been deprived. The only non-American films that he recalls viewing in Greece were Russian, but these were used solely as anti-Soviet propaganda.

As an adolescent, Konstantinos was under the constant religious guidance of his mother, a pious Greek Orthodox Catholic who almost suffocated the children with her strong beliefs. This would partially account for Costa-Gavras's later rejection of religion. Little by little the young boy grew disenchanted from seeing the fundamental contradictions of the Church and the application of its beliefs to everyday life.

From April 1941 to October 1944, the Germans occupied Greece. A resistance developed from the piecemeal noncooperation of the citizens to sabotage and serious political crimes. His father, Panyotis Gavras, joined one of the major branches of the resistance, the National Liberation Front or Ethniko Apeleftherotiko Metopo (EAM), very similar to the French resistance group Francs Tireurs et Partisans (FTP). The EAM was a clandestine anti-fascist organization of guerrilla fighters founded in 1941 on the initiative of the Greek Communist party. His mother, meanwhile, had the children safe in the Peloponnesus, but at one point, recounts Costa-Gavras, fought off a fascist patrol that tried to raid her larder.[3] The father's participation in the resistance would leave a permanent scar on the family. In the anticommunist regime following World War II, many members of the resistance were branded "communists" and thus were unable to find gainful employment. Although Costa-Gavras's father was never a communist, but simply an anti-royalist, says the director, he was cast into prison several times and never had the security of a position. A certificate of civic standing was obligatory for a job. The situation would briefly improve after 1954 . . . but not for long.

In the regime of the late 1940s and early 1950s, meanwhile, as the son of a resistance fighter, Costa-Gavras would be unable to attend the university, to hold any official position, or even obtain a driver's license. Life would be a cul-de-sac for him if he stayed in Greece. He would surely fall victim to the almost 50% rate of unemployment in the early 1950s. In 1952, still in his late teens, Costa-Gavras had intentions similar to his father's when the latter left Odessa. The son wanted to go to America, supposedly a land of limitless possibilities. However, once again because of his father's World War II record, he was unable to get a visa for the United States during this period which was deeply marked by Senator Joseph McCarthy's political paranoia.

Instead of going to America, Costa-Gavras went to Paris to pursue university studies. With a lively interest in reading and writing, he enrolled in a program of Comparative Literature at the Sorbonne. To complete a doctoral degree in this field a student could take up to ten years. His heart set on this degree, he began his academic program and resided at the Cité Universitaire, the international student residence. In this youthful melting pot he had an opportunity to meet students from all over the world, thus getting intensive exposure to various cultures. He learned French especially through his intensive reading and frequenting theaters and cinema houses. Later Costa-Gavras would become a naturalized French citizen.

In order to survive in the French capital he performed all types of odd jobs from washing cars to collecting old newspapers. Like many of the critics and cineastes of the French New Wave, he would spend much of this time in the Cinémathèque and the Left Bank movie houses. It would not be uncommon for him to watch two or three movies a day.[4]

Costa-Gavras's commitment to the Comparative Literature program at the Sorbonne lasted for slightly more than two years. As an active—almost restless—person, he did not have the patience, time, and reflectiveness to pursue the full program. The siren of cinema bewitched him, and so in November 1954, he enrolled in the film school of IDHEC (Institut des Hautes Etudes Cinématographiques).

In this school for the training of film technicians and directors, Costa-Gavras registered for two *cycles* or programs of two years, in *production-régie* (film production) and *réalisation* (film direction).[5] For production, the initiates had to pass through their own sacred rites, a series of courses dealing with the intricate system of the cinema industry, general orientation in film, and financing of a work. To apply their academic knowledge to filmmaking, they pursued practical exercises in film, usually for twenty-five days, under the supervision of M. Pierre Malfille, director and alumnus of IDHEC. In the second year of the program in production, the students learned the art of drawing up a manuscript, technical script, and working schedule—all culminating in a short film. The postproduction period involved synchronization, mixing, editing, and music, among other technical responsibilities. This was followed once again by six weeks of practical film exercises during which the students kept a dossier or journal of the production. Costa-Gavras and his peers were generally supervised by instructors such as Pierre Cardinal and Edouard Logereau.

The area of concentration for Costa-Gavras at IDHEC was film directing, which included theoretical and practical sessions on framing, technical scripts, choice of lens, and dialogue. In groups of ten, the students learned about the function and responsibility of the second assistant before, during, and after the filming. Other pragmatic courses in the program concentrated on acting, staging, and makeup. During the second year Costa-Gavras and his colleagues made 35mm sound films under supervision for six weeks, which were the culmination of both theory and practice mastered during the full program.

As part of his assignment, Costa-Gavras made two short films, a five-minute exercise and another eight- to ten-minute film that already hinted at his sociopolitical sensitivity. This short work dealt with three people of different classes and backgrounds who find themselves in a cowshed sharing their experiences, the young director's vision of a cinematic *huis clos!* In 1958, Costa-Gavras was also responsible for ten scenarios for Canadian and American television.[6]

From 1954 to 1958, Costa-Gavras fulfilled the requirements for the two programs. At the same time he was viewing countless films, learning more about the American film, which he had already encountered in Greece as a young boy. He especially began to learn more about the French and Russian classics. The Russian political films were certainly forbidden fruit in the anticommunist regime he knew in Greece. At IDHEC he also rubbed elbows with many creative individuals from various countries. Here he met the American James Blue, who would later direct the semidocumentary social study of the Algerian War, *The Olive Trees of Justice* (1963).[7]

After completing his training at IDHEC and trying his hand at scriptwriting for television, Costa-Gavras entered the concrete, practical phase of his film training. He first started out as a *stagiaire,* a type of apprentice sometimes called the "third assistant" in film. In 1959, he served as a second assistant director for one of Yves Allégret's films, *L'Ambitieuse,* for the director Jack Pinoteau in *Robinson et le triporteur* and J. Nahum in *Le Saint mène la danse.* When the novelist Jean Giono decided to film his own literary work instead of collaborating with Marcel Pagnol, as in *Angèle* and *Regain,* Costa-Gavras served as second assistant for his film *Crésus* (1960). That same year he accepted a similar responsibility for J. Cornu's *L'Homme à femmes.* He collaborated with René Clair in 1961 as second assistant for the production *Tout l'or du monde,* and in the following year as first assistant with Henri Verneuil for *Un Singe en hiver,* Jacques Demy for *La Baie des anges,* and René Clément for *Le Jour et l'heure.* In the latter part of 1962 he worked with Marcel Ophüls in *Peau de banane,* and then to conclude his apprenticeship in 1963, with René Clément in *Les Félins* and Jean Becker in *Echappement libre.*

The fertile period of study at IDHEC during which he learned to be a technician and his subsequent apprenticeship with several of the great French filmmakers laid the solid foundation for his filmmaking career. Costa-Gavras never discounts the importance that these role models/directors had for him. Others also inspired him through their works. The social politics of John Ford in *Grapes of Wrath* and Elia Kazan in *On the Waterfront* made a lasting impression on him. Several other American directors such as John Huston, Frank Capra, and Raoul Walsh also had the same effect. The Italian directors Francesco Rosi and Federico Fellini greatly appealed to him. Among the French filmmakers, the classic Jean Renoir, as well as Alain Resnais and Jean-Luc Godard of the New Wave, also left their mark on him. The documentarist Marcel Ophüls (*The Sorrow and the Pity* and later *Memory of Justice*) was a further influence on Costa-Gavras's formation. His work with the German-born director, however, preceded the two major social documentaries. Annette Insdorf points out the parallel between Costa-Gavras and Marcel Ophüls, "with whom he [Costa-

Gavras] subsequently shared a change of direction into films chronicling societal upheaval and social consciousness."[8]

In light of his international fame stemming from *Z*, Costa-Gavras was questioned as to which of the directors for whom he worked as assistant had the most influence on him. He replied:

> For me it was surely René Clément and Jacques Demy. I was impressed with Clément's technique, his rapport with the actors. Before that I had worked with five or six directors but Clément was the first one I met who really did direct the actors. Jacques Demy also . . . but they are different in their approach. Demy is very friendly and co-operative with the actors . . . they can change things around two or three times on the set. With Clément, he is . . . how do you say . . . a little "dictator," he imposes his view on them, not brutally, but very firmly; whereas with Demy it is real collaboration.[9]

Costa-Gavras stated that René Clément also gave him invaluable counsel that would help him in his future work. First the director advised simply, "Know how to write," and then also "Know how to edit." Costa-Gavras abided by both principles and constantly accentuated their importance in his filming career.

Soon after his training was complete, he went to Greenland, where he was to take stock shots for a feature film. The project, however, fell through and the film was never made.

While working as René Clément's assistant on the sociopolitical drama *Le Jour et l'heure* (The Day and the Hour, 1962), a film on the resistance in France in May 1944, Costa-Gavras had an opportunity to be on location with Simone Signoret. The French actress was playing Thérèse Dutheil, the wife of an imprisoned fighter who helps three fliers in their escape from the enemy. Simone Signoret would be the pivotal point for Costa-Gavras's first production, for she put him in touch with the right producer, Julien Derode, not too long after the Clément film. From this contact emanated Costa-Gavras's first film, a detective story, *The Sleeping Car Murder* (Compartiment tueurs), in 1964. After a remarkable success in his first venture, Costa-Gavras was invited by a major producer, Harry Saltzmann (known for his James Bond thrillers), to direct a World War II action melodrama, *Shock Troops* (Un Homme de trop).

One film leads to another, and in 1967 he was asked to direct *Le Fils*, about the return of a Corsican from America to his killer-infested homeland. *Film Français* for 14 March 1969 still indicated that he was to begin shooting *Le Fils* in Corsica in May 1969. With advance receipts he was able to visit Athens in April 1967, and it is there that he stumbled on the book that would change his life. In adapting *Z* of Vassilis Vassilikos, Costa-Gavras officially entered into the political arena. International success allowed him to drop the contract for *Le Fils*, which would be picked up in 1972 by Pierre Granier-Deferre, and continue in a political direction with *The Confession* (L'Aveu, 1970) inspired by the gruesome account of Artur London, a victim of the Slansky trial in Czechoslovakia.[10] With *State of Siege* (Etat de siège, 1973) Costa-Gavras pursued the same genre of political fiction. He reenacted in a quasi-documentary style the political assassination by guerrillas of an official of the Agency for International Development in Uruguay. The fourth political fiction film *Special Section* (Section Spéciale, 1974) on the judicial aberrations of the Vichy government of 1941 was not a "thriller" as such, and did not receive the acclaim that the others had earlier. To some critics the genre may already have been exhausted. His reputation suffered even though the film went to Cannes for international screening. *Clair de Femme* (1979) would be a hiatus in his film career. His most recent political film, *Missing,* made for Universal in 1982, would nevertheless re-establish him as one of the most prominent political fiction filmmakers. Costa-Gavras's work in Israel on a forthcoming film will also open new avenues in his artistic production.

Guiding Principles

The political perspective of Costa-Gavras primarily defines and determines the selection of subjects for his filmmaking. Costa-Gavras appears to have remained politically consistent, despite the comments of the critics who say that he changed camps from *Z* to *The Confession.* At the heart of his political fiction is the relationship of human beings to power. He battles against all forms of immoral, unethical, and unjust power behind whatever masks they wear—American imperialism, Greek totalitarianism, or Czechoslovakian Stalinism. He was dubbed an "agent provocateur" by the French press, according to Melton Davis in the *New York Times Magazine* for 21 March 1971.[11] Costa-Gavras normally detects a theme of social injustice that would lend itself to visual analysis, and then works out the details for a production. Hence, there abounds in his works a highly critical, demythologizing, negative perspective. He is antinuclear, anti-Stalinist, anti-fascist, anti-imperialist. He is in reality a leftist who espouses a profound humanitarian credo. His films, however, may be marked by a vague humanism that could tend to evanesce shortly after one views them. Perhaps we could say his works are more humanistic than political, for he strikes out against violence, repression, and especially against official injustice done to human beings in the name of justice.

Costa-Gavras's human and political concerns dovetail, as Franca Rovelli discovered in an interview for *Epoca:*

But I, too, have guiding principles—that of dignity for example, which I consider a basic necessity.

When Rovelli asked what Costa-Gavras meant by "dignity," the director replied:

Dignity for me means not being forced to beg for work, having things that others also have, not being rejected or humiliated by society, and being able to express one's own thoughts. I am absolutely convinced that an abuse of power above all tends to destroy human dignity.[12]

Although Costa-Gavras is sometimes dramatic or sensational in his projection of the world's problems, he is basically realistic. This trait is readily observed in his interviews where he expresses his opinions—mostly liberal—on Latin

America, the Arab world, immigrant workers in France, terrorism, drug problems among youth, and contemporary abuses of justice.[13] Although he is most conscious of these political ills, he stresses he is not a political activist, a revolutionary, a militant, or a party member. As a freethinker, he would feel restricted, for example, if he belonged to the Communist party, although some of his associates are or have been party members. In his early days in France someone told him, he said, "Look, but don't belong." He admits, therefore, he could not be a communist, for this would mean having a one-track mind, being obliged to follow a party line. For Greeks such as Costa-Gavras, independence is a cherished preference. He does not feel that either communism or Christianity, with their roots in social justice, is the solution to the world's crises. At the same time he refers to himself in purist fashion as a "Sartrean Marxist."

Costa-Gavras claims that he advocates a pacifist philosophy, as illustrated, for example, in *Z*. Yet he is attracted to portraying violence, attributable, he says, to his country of origin, where violence is an everyday affair. In most of his films, paradoxically enough, he uses violence—physical and psychological—to reflect the growth of this phenomenon in contemporary society. There are the mob scenes organized by the right wing in *Z*, brainwashing in *The Confession,* torture and assassination in *State of Siege* and *Missing.* These uses of violence nonetheless cause one to question his motivation.

For some critics Costa-Gavras's politics are harmless and are aimed at educating superficially or exalting romantically the bourgeois viewer who cannot be an activist. Censorship restrictions on his films prove that they are not totally innocent or devoid of political import. A film such as *Z* had screening problems in Greece during the rule of the colonels and also in a few Latin American countries. *The Confession* met with strong disapproval and hostile criticism from the French Communist party as well as from the Soviet satellite countries, especially Czechoslovakia. Costa-Gavras was unable to get a visa to socialist countries after this film was released in Europe. In America, tension mounted concerning the proposed screening of *State of Siege* at the American Film Institute Festival in Washington, D.C. Hence, Costa-Gavras's "sugar-coated bullets" (Godard) "made to soothe the conscience of the Saturday-night leftist filmgoer" (Seguin) are not so harmless as some people believe.

In his films Costa-Gavras attempts to get at the heart of a historical problem and read it with an eye to what has happened since. He runs the risks of anachronism and revisionism. For the most part he minimizes these risks by careful research on the script.

The director tempers his art with a political slant. The result is appealing and at the same time controversial. It usually polarizes audiences. Heinz-Dieter Rauchendorf, a cameraman and documentary filmmaker responsible for some of the photography of Leni Riefenstahl's *Triumph of the Will,* and for the Nazi campaign shorts *Baptism of Fire* and *Victory in the West,* discussed Costa-Gavras in terms of art and politics:

> Art can help create social values. I have been a champion of a specific set of values and have tried to create films to advance and ennoble those values. I

find Costa-Gavras interesting in this regard because he alone among the new directors has skill and politics.[14]

Nonetheless Rauchendorf is not blind to the weak points of Costa-Gavras's heroes with respect to their political causes:

> Unfortunately he is afraid of his own politics. His heroes are martyred tinsel. We don't care about their struggle. They seem born to die for their cause which is always a vague goodyism.[15]

As a political filmmaker, Costa-Gavras accepts responsibilities for his films. He and his scriptwriters Semprun and Solinas maintain that they have resisted the temptation to make use of sensationalized material. They may have failed a bit with Z, but always have in their possession documented proof for their cinematic statements and are constantly concerned about truth. To illustrate this, Costa-Gavras prided himself on having refused an offer to film *The Godfather*. He comments on his refusal as follows:

> When I was asked to direct *The Godfather* I told the producer that that film was the best thing that ever happened to the Mafia, for it made the Mafia look moral, and so I refused because I didn't want to assume that "ugly" responsibility. One responsibility that weighs on me very heavily is telling the truth.[16]

Personal Politics

Costa-Gavras's political awareness did not emerge on the scene fully developed with Z. His early exposure to the fascist government of Greece and the experience of the imprisonment of his father helped him to see social injustices from an eyewitness perspective. In an interview for the *New York Times* (22 April 1973), the director of *State of Siege* recalled that he first became interested in politics when he questioned the automatic succession to the Greek throne by a family member: King George died in 1947 and his brother Paul became king immediately. Costa-Gavras felt that there was something slightly corrupt about this procedure. Dictatorship, Occupation, Liberation, and civil and cold wars made the Greece of Costa-Gavras's early years perfect breeding grounds for political activists.

The personal harassments he received as son of a resistance member reinforced his political sensitivity, yet it was not until he came to Paris that he became conscious of the relationship of politics to society. Costa-Gavras maintains that his political vision was defined primarily between 1953 and 1956—during his early twenties—while at the Sorbonne, Cinémathèque, and IDHEC. In Paris he heard political ideas discussed on street corners, at jammed cafes, in university corridors. Hungarian students escaped to Paris in 1956. The Algerian War was dividing the French as the Dreyfus case had a half century earlier, as the Vietnam war would do to the Americans a decade later. At the Cité Universitaire he was surprised to find all types of political newspapers displayed on tables, for example, the communist and socialist press, something which he had not experienced in Greece. Besides his other general literary readings in Romain Rolland, Victor Hugo, and John Steinbeck, Costa-Gavras read Lenin and Marx. He attended meetings protesting the atom bomb organized by the French Communist party, but frequented by communist and non-communist alike. He also witnessed the vast rallies in support of the Rosenbergs convicted of espionage. Only later did he realize that injustices against this couple were very similar to those happening in socialist countries; witness *The Confession*. It was in this type of political environment that Costa-Gavras adopted France and France in turn adopted him as a naturalized son.

With such a sociopolitical background, the director embarked on his filmmaking career. His political viewpoint evolved over years, but not radically, for he gradually integrated the various ideologies and systems surrounding him. He would not want to use the cinema as a celluloid weapon. He claims it is not a gun. For him it appears to be more or less a political tool or instrument by means of which he could communicate and be convincing, but without preaching. He desired to use a commercial, nonmilitant form, realizing that the vast majority of viewers would not normally seek entertainment at a militant film on the occupation of the Lipp factory or on a Farm Workers' strike. To profit from the commercial market he would instead create appealing films. On several occasions he made the classic point, "You don't catch flies with vinegar." He believes that at the conclusion of one of his films a spectator should leave the theater with some knowledge of the particular problem and a sense of exaltation.[17]

As we have seen in the brief history of recent political fiction, the denunciatory spirit of the cineaste was already prefigured in cinema history in part by the Americans. Costa-Gavras infused a fresh breath of cinema life into this earlier, rapidly aging form. In the 1930s and 1940s in the United States the Film Noir (Black Cinema) or B series films with actors such as James Cagney, Humphrey Bogart, and Peter Lorre made compelling political, anti-Establishment statements. Some writers in this genre, for example, Dashiel Hammett, often expressed dissatisfaction with the workings of the American system. In an article on this genre Ed Rampell situated Costa-Gavras within the tradition:

> Costa-Gavras' ace in the hole was none other than—Film Noir! By placing this political work (*Z*) within the framework of the thriller, philosophy became combined with entertainment, thus enabling Costa-Gavras to reach a wide audience with his denouncement of the tyrants. The Greek-born director says that "those whom you call your 'silent majority' are the most important." Hence, through the use and exploitation of a popular form, Costa-Gavras speaks to many more than those who are already convinced. "I always try to speak of[sic] the general public, by the way, not just a few people on the left."[18]

Rampell notes that Costa-Gavras politicized this genre making more explicit the social forces that underlie greed and power. The director thus amplified, heightened, and clarified the somber implications of the black film, the film of dissatisfaction.

The political factors apparent in Costa-Gavras's works show up in a duality or a polarity that brings richness and tension to his films. He is an individual marked by two nationalities, cultures, and characters. He is thus a man of antitheses: Greek exuberance and French cartesianism; Christian youth and unbelieving adulthood; Greek totalitarianism and French democracy.[19]

Recognizing that the public's taste has changed, Costa-Gavras was able to take risks in his modifications of the older genres. He added some historical and sociopolitical depth to an otherwise entertaining and superficial narrative. He manifested some sensitivity to the historical process, as he explained at the time of the release of *The Confession* (1970). He said that his attempt was not to reconstruct the past with a historical fresco (which he would actually do, however, with *Special Section*), but to explain current events with a fragment of the past.[20]

With very good documentation from his own research and that of his scriptwriter, Costa-Gavras approximates the historical reality, but also telescopes the data, concisely putting fact together with fact until he has constructed a historical and dramatic work of art. What appears in newspapers, journals, books, and interviews in a piecemeal fashion over a long period of time is artistically condensed into two hours of intense drama. The ensemble of the data, if not carefully edited, could be long and drawn out, and thus boring to a film audience, which often chooses to be amused than instructed. With this type of documentation, for example, on the Tupamaro guerrillas for *State of Siege* and the cover-up of the assassination of Deputy Lambrakis in *Z*, Costa-Gavras achieved a realistic, semidocumentary effect in a nondocumentary genre. The director kept the material straightforward, above all with the intention of avoiding melodrama. A slight oversight might be the teary role played by Irene Papas, as the wife of Lambrakis in *Z*. Costa-Gavras has not succumbed to the temptation of the "happy ending" so common in the American film as late as the mid-1960s. The last shot in the epilogue is a jolt back to irresolution just after a problem of the ill-use of power appeared resolved.

The films of Costa-Gavras ordinarily introduce the viewer to a political problem that was formerly ignored, forgotten, or conveniently shunned. With *Z* the international public opened their eyes to the unjust government of the colonels and with *The Confession* to the grip of Stalinism in the Soviet satellites. The director sets in motion a dramatic chain of events that lead up to a particular injustice, and then furnishes a key to understand the present in light of these events. In this way the spectator gains insight into a rather complex political machine. The brilliant montage of quick-paced revelations obliges the viewer to use mind as well as heart. As in the Eisenstein model of editing, moreover, all the elements of the various series of images are painstakingly interrelated in the presentation of facts.

Despite the political and aesthetic impact of his films there are several negative factors which haunt the work of Costa-Gavras, factors perhaps inherent in this type of politicized fiction. Since he must telescope or condense the data, he runs the risk of stereotyping. The director in a short period of time must quickly paint the personality of the characters so the audience can more readily begin to understand the crucial problem at hand. Many have been the critics such as Stanley Kauffmann of *The New Republic,* who observed the black/white dichotomy in the characters of *Z.* On the side of the Good are the leftist pacifists, the lower class, the students, and the prosecutor; on the side of Evil are the police, the generals, the homosexuals, the lawless brutes, fascist crusaders, and the CIA. With some exceptions, there appears to be hardly any nuance of characterization. The director, however, responds to the charges of stereotyping:

> "I think I have been wrongly accused of a certain Manicheism, or black-and-white characterization. . . . While *Clair de Femme* is more obviously concerned with the subtleties and ambiguities of its characters than *Z* or *State of Siege,*" Mr. Costa-Gavras insisted that the difference is of degree rather than kind: "People forget, for example, that in *Z* the good guy—the judge—is in fact a man of the right. In *Special Section,* the most interesting characters are of the extreme right. So the Manicheism finally exists more in viewers' heads than in my films. I keep learning that the frontier between good and evil isn't as clear as one thinks, especially in politics."[21]

One can also come to the defense of Costa-Gavras in appreciating that in a vast fresco such as *Z,* the ensemble and general effect may be more important than the details of stereotyping. There is also something to be said about the occurrence of these archetypes. Carl Jung in psychology, for example, and Georg Lukács in philosophy both stress the need for archetypes.

Malraux's literary work is replete with war, adventure, and rebellion in which the characters are primarily male. There are parallels to this type of material in Costa-Gavras's films. Women, he readily admits, have often played roles of a second or third order. He observes that he treated their characters as if they were masculine. Only the wives of Lambrakis *(Z)* and London *(The Confession)* have any character development at all. He later compensates for this with *Clair de Femme* (1979), where he develops the character of Lydia (Romy Schneider) with fine sensitivity, and *Missing,* wherein he shows the true worth of Beth Horman (Sissy Spacek).

Besides being reproached for his supposed facile handling of characterization, Costa-Gavras is also criticized for the conclusions that he draws. Geoffrey Stokes makes this accusation:

> Given their preoccupation with power and its misuse, Costa-Gavras' films seem oddly innocent. It is not so much as they are wrong, as that they are short-sighted. Centralized political power is seen, vividly, as an evil, but it is not connected to anything beyond itself. It is as though the drive to accumulate power were some sort of human tropism rather than a function of competing societal interests.[22]

Closely related is the hermetic tone of *The Confession,* in which slogans of Titoism, Zionism, and imperialism are cast about without clarification of terms. The director may overestimate the political level of his audience.

Recurrent Elements

In the panorama of the five political films of Costa-Gavras, certain patterns and elements can be detected, especially in his three key political films. The protagonist played by Yves Montand (Lambrakis/London/Mitrione) is caught up in an unjust system created by a powerful and abusing Establishment. His life is in jeopardy. A trial is staged that brings the film to a pessimistic conclusion with an eye-opening epilogue. Throughout the film the various intrigues surrounding the innocent protagonist reflect the leftist political perspective of Costa-Gavras and his screenwriter. In each case, nonetheless, there are many and diverse nuances, variations on a theme of social injustice.

Several aspects of the legal and medical professions show up throughout his cinematic production, both professions not too alien from his family's interests. In each of the political films Costa-Gavras uses a judicial process, usually his means of revealing some injustice in the system. Ironically in *State of Siege*, the interrogation, trial, and decision of the Tupamaros to execute Mitrione appears most honest and democratic. Why this frequent portrayal of a trial in process? Costa-Gavras responds: "Because that is where authority, in the name of justice, uses its power; the impact on one's future is immediate."[23]

Medicine is also a thread that colorfully runs through the films of Costa-Gavras, represented by doctors, examinations, autopsies, and ambulances, all of which advance the narrative and are not extraneous to it. The medical reports during the operations on the fallen deputy and the subsequent autopsies, although self-consciously utilized with clever photographic effects and highly stylized cuts, nonetheless reveal the trauma of the death of Z. Slides about the biological mildew—in the film an analogy for the leftist elements in Greek society—and the blow to the cranium of the slain pacifist graphically fill the screen. The wives of American diplomats about to leave for Latin America in *State of Siege* undergo an illustrated briefing on the bacterial dangers in the food and water. Costa-Gavras plays the scene with subtle irony to show that the American families will be preserved from this problem because of their connection with the American State Department. The guerrillas of *State of Siege* sensitively offer the hostages in the People's Prison professional medical treatment in the prison itself as well as in the hospital. The use of the hospital sequence during which the wound of Santore (Montand) is treated demonstrates the extent of the network of Tupamaros, even to the top echelon of the medical profession. In *The Confession* the director accentuates the restoring of the thirteen witnesses on trial to some semblance of health after their rigorous interrogation. Sun lamps, dark glasses, injections, and medical examinations are all part of the sham for the predetermined trial after Gérard (Montand) has just been subjected to severe brainwashing. Beth and Ed Horman in *Missing* search for Charles among rows of bloodstained corpses in hospitals and morgues.

In his five principal political films Costa-Gavras situates a journalist/writer in a pivotal position. This individual is sensitive to a given injustice and takes risks to uncover it, very much like Carl Bernstein and Bob Woodward of the *Washington Post* during the Watergate affair. Among the various press men there will certainly be colorful shadings; they are not at all one-dimensional. The photographer/journalist (Jacques Perrin) in *Z* may be more ambitious to get the lead story for his paper than to stop moral injustice in Greece, but through his perseverance the authorities are implicated in an assassination, originally reported as "an accident." In *State of Siege,* the elderly reporter Carlos Ducas (O. E. Hasse) speaks candidly with the American authorities. He puts his finger on the sociopolitical pulse of his country as he openly accuses America of an all-pervasive imperialism:

> Be it when drinking beer, swallowing aspirin, brushing his teeth, cooking his food in an aluminum pan, turning on a radio, shaving, using his refrigerator, or heating a room, every citizen in my country contributes daily to the development of your economy.[24]

Lucien Sampaix (Bruno Cremer), the editor of the communist newspaper *L'Humanité,* in a well-articulated speech against the illegality of the German-directed court, helps put an abrupt stop to the corrupt machinery of justice.[25] Artur London of *The Confession,* through his postfactum exposé, reveals the oppression of the Stalinist regime. Charles Horman, in *Missing,* writes for a leftist journal. He disappears during the Chilean coup in 1973.

Costa-Gavras himself had ambitions of writing, especially while at the Sorbonne. He pursued this later with his scriptwriting for *Sleeping Car Murder, Shock Troops,* and more recently in the adaptation of *Clair de Femme.* During the process of creating a scenario, he worked very closely with either Semprun or Solinas. This procedure recalls the literary scrupulosness of Alain Resnais, who examined every word and comma in his collaboration with such literary figures as Jean Cayrol, Marguerite Duras, Alain Robbe-Grillet, Jorge Semprun, and Jacques Sternberg.[26]

The choice of the role of journalist or writer as the focal point of a film may appear commonplace, for reporters permeate the cinema world from *The Philadelphia Story* and *Ace in the Hole* to *The O.D.E.S.S.A. File* and *All the President's Men.* Yet, this type of character is integral to Costa-Gavras's films, someone professionally committed to the pursuit of truth.

In many of the films of Costa-Gavras, still photography is used to disclose some injustice or to supplement the data with artistic graphics. It is only normal that a cineaste would have a facility and fascination with still photography since the image is the life blood of his profession. Costa-Gavras, however, goes one step further in the use of photography, another recurring element. The photographer of *Z* uses his camera as a weapon in the struggle against the collusive military. His photos in the hands of the examining magistrate help expose the cover-up. The house in *The Confession* displays the famous Capa shot of the Republican soldier falling to the ground in the early stages of the Spanish civil war. This photo implies Gérard's background and his allegiance to the Republican cause while he was a member of the International Brigade. The pictures of Stalin, Gottwald, and Beria ironically take on a religious aura in the London home. They become political icons. Even more incriminating than the photos of *Z* are the snapshots in the hands of the Tupamaros in *State of Siege.* The guerrillas manipulate them to prove the inhumane tendencies of the American "diplo-mats" in Latin America by their involvement with torture. The photos show that Santore was more a police official teaching unethical interrogation procedures using torture than a traffic and communications controller. In reality the police used the Death Squad "to handle for good" any very difficult terrorist problems. They had the photographer Nelson Bardesio in their pay. The aggressors met regularly in his studio to plot the executions.[27]

At the heart of Costa-Gavras's political films there are what Paolo Freire in his *Pedagogy of the Oppressed* describes in detail as "generative themes." In these films the themes are the judicial, national, and police systems of power. There are recurrent elements such as the journalist, trial, still photography, and medical profession. They are aesthetically woven into the very fabric of each narrative in order to create a uniquely crafted object.

A World of Contacts

Costa-Gavras's naturalization in France, his literary studies at the Sorbonne, and his cinematic work at IDHEC expanded his postwar Greek horizons. He was affected also by the milieu in which he developed his interest and skills in film. Friends, family, and contacts with actors and technicians in the film world of-fered him a rich terrain on which to construct a professional career. Sometimes called "the clan," this group is akin to what Ingmar Bergman once achieved with his committed troupe—photographer Sven Nykvist and players Liv Ullmann, Max von Sydow, Bibi Andersson, and Gunnar Björnstrand; lasting friendships, mutual respect among artists, independence, and above all, creativity prevailed.

One constant support or tie for Costa-Gavras has been his wife, Michèle (Ray) Gavras. He has known her since 1963 and married her during the filming of *Z* in Algeria in 1968. She had been a House of Chanel model and a magazine corre-spondent in Vietnam during war there. In 1966, she was captured by the Viet-cong and held for three weeks. She filmed in 16mm some footage that was used in the collective film *Far from Vietnam* assembled by Jean-Luc Godard, William Klein, Joris Ivens, Agnès Varda, Chris Marker, Claude Lelouch, and Alain Res-nais. At the death of Ché Guevara in 1967, Michèle Ray went to Bolivia in hopes of acquiring his diaries but without success. When she went to Uruguay to cover its elections for French radio and television, she was kidnapped at gunpoint by an anarchist group, OPR 33, and held for three days.[28] Her journalistic en-deavors have continued. She served as the interviewer of Franco Solinas and Costa-Gavras for the dossier of *Etat de Siège* published on the release of the film in Paris in 1973. Prior to this, she and her husband intended to make a film on the May 1968 events in Paris, as noted earlier, but nothing came of the plan for many reasons. Although their interest and backgrounds may differ, they have in common the area of film and journalism . . . and the raising of their three children, Hélène, Alexandre, and Roman.

The first person one identifies in Costa-Gavras's professional troupe is Yves Montand, an integral part of his film production since 1964. "Why not?" says the director impishly in an interview for the *New York Times* in 1973: "John Wayne appeared in over 40 John Ford movies." In the American cinema Montand was often cast as the handsome and suave French lover, and in the French cinema as a political hero (*La Guerre est finie, Les Routes du Sud*), a police officer or commissioner (*Police Python 357, I . . . comme Icare*), a businessman (*César et Rosalie*), and occasionally a lover (*Le Sauvage*).

The actor's roots are in Mediterranean culture. Born Ivo Livi, Montand originated in Monsumano Alto, north of Florence, Italy, in 1921. His family emigrated to southern France when the Italian Fascists burned his father's broom factory. Alain Rémond situates him in history this way:

> Just line up a few words, like fascism, exile, human misery, factory, post-war, chanting proletariat, Appeal of Stockholm, cold war, Rosenberg, McCarthyism, Budapest, Moscow, Krushchev, Hollywood, Spain, Greece, Prague, Chile . . . or other words, like justice, commitment, entertainment, pleasure, politics. Montand is present at every stage, at every cross-road of those years which shaped us. (A unique case, it seems to me, of a star totally linked with his era.)[29]

Yves Montand entered cinema from the profession of cabaret singer, as did another emigrant to France, Jacques Brel, from Belgium. Before Montand had begun working with Costa-Gavras in *The Sleeping Car Murder,* he starred in approximately twenty films, many of them minor, and since then in more than twenty-five others, mostly box-office attractions, especially those directed by Costa-Gavras. On the team he works the closest and perhaps the best with Costa-Gavras, for they share a rapport of fraternity and confidence. The director, appreciating the dramatic skills of Montand, offers him great liberty of expression, and in return, the actor plays for the total effect of the picture, not only for himself. Montand also respects Costa-Gavras, understanding his temperament and political perspective, his fine qualities, his defects. Because of this mutual understanding, Montand played the lead role in five out of the director's eight features. The actor said of the director in retrospect after working with him on their first collaboration, *The Sleeping Car Murder:* "Then suddenly, with Costa-Gavras, something happened. I discovered him to be more than simply a director: I found him a perfect collaborator who revealed my true character."[30]

Montand received $60,000 or so for *Z* and $200,000 for *Stage of Siege,* but finances are far from being the motivational factor for their affiliation. There is a fraternal bond here that goes even beyond the filming. It showed in 1975 when Montand and Costa-Gavras went to Spain with Claude Mauriac and Régis Debray carrying signatures from Malraux, Aragon, Mendes-France, Sartre and others to procure the freedom of political prisoners . . . but in vain. For Montand, this would be simply one political gesture that he would make in a long litany of others, reflecting his controversial philosophy that was pro-Rosenberg, antinuclear (Stockholm), and anti-McCarthy. Some of the movements in which Yves Montand and Simone Signoret participated were organized by the Communist party. In her memoirs Simone Signoret discusses their political relations:

Neither Montand nor I was a member of the Communist Party, though we were in agreement with the majority of its opinions. A great many people believed we were card-carrying Communists. But it was a time when sending a denial to a newspaper that "claimed" you were a Communist—the quotes are intentional—gave the impression of denying an accusation. The Communists I had met during the war, when I didn't always know at the time that they were Communists, were people I respected enormously.[31]

The next ever-present source of creative collaboration is the Spanish-born Jorge Semprun. Like Costa-Gavras, he originated in a country temporarily beset with fascism and sought refuge in France. Ten years older than the director, Semprun matches Costa-Gavras's passion to express himself politically and aesthetically. At the outbreak of the Civil War he left Spain for asylum in France. His father in Spain, like Costa-Gavras's in anticommunist Greece, was a persona non grata because of his leftist, anti-fascist tendencies. Semprun was not one to accept the domination of the Fascists in his new home and entered the Communist party in 1941 and the resistance in 1942. The following year he was arrested and deported to a concentration camp. His first novel, *Le Grand Voyage* (1963), describes his experience en route to the camp. After his return from Buchenwald and Mauthausen, he served as a translator for UNESCO. In 1954, he was made a member of the Central Committee of the Spanish Communist party. For ten years he worked with a clandestine group of political militants in Spain. His scripts for *La Guerre est finie* and *Les Routes du Sud* show his own character refracted in the images of Diego and Larréa, respectively. In 1965, he was expelled from the Communist party in Spain for his divergent sentiments on the political action necessary during the Franco regime. While his literary production advanced with *L'Evanouissement, La Deuxième Mort de Ramon Mercader,* and *L'Autobiographie de Federico Sanchez* (his underground name in Spain), he worked at his adaptions for Costa-Gavras (*Z, The Confession, Special Section*), Yves Boisset (*The French Conspiracy*), Alain Resnais (*Stavisky*), Pierre Granier-Deferre (*Une Femme à sa fenêtre*), and Joseph Losey (*Les Routes du Sud*). His own film *Les Deux Mémoires* (1972–73) displays his constant preoccupation with politics in a sociohistorical context.

Jorge Semprun's leftist ideology is apparent throughout his scriptwriting for Costa-Gavras and Resnais, despite the fact that since the mid-1960s he has not belonged to the Communist party. In a debate among communist (and ex-communist) intellectuals in May 1978, Semprun vigorously exhibited a purist Marxist attitude in politics:

Today my opinion is that there is something completely contradictory and incompatible between the function of an intellectual and that of the communist system. I say "communist" in the strict sense used by the partisans. For I still continue to believe in the role of the Marxist intellectuals, beyond the narrow framework of the apparatus. Marx himself was not a Party member.[32]

The collaboration of Costa-Gavras and Semprun began with *Z*, when the director returned from Greece with the controversial novel of Vassilikos and asked the scriptwriter to assist him with the adaptation. In an interview for the *Christian Science Monitor,* Costa-Gavras commented on their rapport:

> It was not an accident that the meeting of both of us led to the explosion of *Z* . . . Moviemaking can be the business of a team—it is not by chance that (Elia) Kazan made his greatest film *(A Face in the Crowd* and *On the Waterfront)* with scripts by Budd Schulberg, or that (Vittorio) De Sica and (writer Cesare) Zavattini had excellent results.[33]

In the early 1970s, this team would do the same with *The Confession* and *Special Section,* sometimes taking up to a year to insure the authenticity or historicity of the scenario before filming.

Most important in launching Costa-Gavras into political fiction and into the international marketplace is Jacques Perrin, who first starred as a fair-featured adolescent in Costa-Gavras's *The Sleeping Car Murder* (1964), and then as a young partisan in *Shock Troops* (1966). Perrin then continued on with Costa-Gavras as the photographer in *Z* and the young liberal attorney Maître Lafarge in *Special Section.* They obtained financial backing from the nationalized Algerian film industry and from the French National Film Center. Perrin also helped in assuring distribution of the film and creating a market for the finished product. Later he assisted the director with *State of Siege* and *Special Section.* Assuming himself the great challenge of political fiction film, Perrin then helped to inaugurate the new genre and to convince other producers to take equal risks with nonestablished directors.

Editing

A permanent fixture in the cinema world of Costa-Gavras has been Françoise Bonnot, the editor responsible for infusing life into the Semprun-Solinas text and the Costa-Gavras filming. Françoise Bonnot's mother was pregnant with her while still editing (with George Grace) André Malraux's Spanish civil war film *L'Espoir* or *Sierra de Teruel.* Her mother also worked with other French directors such as René Clément in *This Angry Age* (Un Barrage contre le Pacifique).

As a young girl of twelve or thirteen, Françoise was already helping her mother at the editing table in the Paris studio. Once her plans for architectural studies did not appear to be working out as expected, she took up the profession of film editing. She already had much practical experience behind her. Her Oscar-winning editing of *Z* brought her international acclaim. She has offered her editing services to other directors such as Jean-Pierre Melville, Henri Verneuil, Yves Courrière, and Roman Polanski in France, Marco Ferreri and Serge Leone in Italy.

During our interview of 7 January 1980 at the Billancourt studio on the outskirts of Paris, Françoise Bonnot emphasized that the editor must work directly and closely with the director. She has found that her contacts with the directors enrich her work; this is especially true in the case of Costa-Gavras.

Although each editing task is different, she ordinarily follows the procedure of reading and discussing the scenario with Costa-Gavras, viewing the rushes and final product with him and showing him her preliminary results. They discuss other possibilities if necessary—he knows what he wants, Françoise Bonnot says. She never works directly with the screenwriter. Rarely does she go on location. One exception was *The Confession,* for which she spent several days at Lille. For *State of Seige* Costa-Gavras forwarded the rushes from Chile to Paris where Bonnot was supervising an assistant and a *stagiaire,* or apprentice. *Missing,* shot in Mexico, was also edited in Paris. In the three- or four-month postproduction phase she has often examined approximately 30,000 meters of celluloid to produce a film of 3,000 meters for which she sometimes has to share the responsibility for the sound editing.

Françoise Bonnot acknowledges that she follows her instincts and feelings more than principles of editing. These feelings, however, are a function of the material and the intentions of the director. She expounds on this in *Cinémonde* after her Oscar for *Z:*

> Montage is a question of rhythm, of sensitivity, of imagination, and of flexibility. Rhythm is of the utmost importance. Following as it does the plot of the film, the montage must never be thrust upon the viewer, but the change should appear at the very moment the viewer would want it to come. Lengthy shots must especially be avoided to prevent boredom. Choosing these shots is a stimulating aspect of this profession. In this stage there is almost a complete reconstruction of the film. The work of editing, moreover, is done in close collaboration with the director where flexibility plays a lead role.[34]

Costa-Gavras reiterates this: "Editing is the most important point in a picture, it is the director really writing the picture with his editing."[35]

The task of Françoise Bonnot is essential for the parallel editing and the recourse to flashbacks to advance the narrative with previous or simultaneous details. None of the plots of the Costa-Gavras's films unfolds in a perfectly chronological order. The flashbacks during the autopsy of *Z*, the Tupamaros's interrogation of Santore in *State of Seige,* and the trial in *Special Section* differ from each other and provide essential material for character development.

Annette Insdorf mentioned to Costa-Gavras that some critics accuse him of a manipulative use of staccato montages. The director disagreed:

> Editing is determined vis-à-vis the spectator. Film presents a monologue—it's false to think a film is a dialogue, and that you have to give the spectator time to think. The general public is not sufficiently trained to reflect upon a film while it is being projected. They have become accustomed to the rapid pace of American cinema, and I have to confess that I feel closer to this rhythm, too. It's only after the film that the spectator can truly reflect upon it. Or reject it.[36]

For some critics, such as Paul Vecchiali of *Revue du Cinéma,* the mold is too rigid and the results hackneyed or worn-out. Vecchiali maintains:

> Costa-Gavras's method remains constant throughout his works: from the

very outset he complicates the plot in a leisurely manner, by means of flash-backs or striking examples of parallel editing, placing the viewer in a kind of vise which he gradually releases as the narrative unfolds, thus clarifying the original situation with spectacular effects. . . . Towards the end, a Wagnerian redundancy adds a touch of lyricism to his didacticism to conclude in favor of the thesis he proposes.[37]

Music

The music of Costa-Gavras's films not only provides continuity to a battery of images rapidly flashing across the screen but also channels or directs the mood of the viewer. For the sound track of *Z* and *State of Siege* Costa-Gavras turned to a compatriot who also used art as a political tool, sometimes a weapon—Mikis Theodorakis, celebrated in the cinema world for his scores for *Zorba, Electra,* and *Iphigenia,* recognized in the political realm for his attacks on the regime of the colonels. While in his teens, he became politically oriented toward the Left. During World War II, Theodorakis was part of the resistance movement in the United All-Greek Youth Organization, an arm of the National Liberation Front, which had communist direction. Costa-Gavras's father also participated in the NLF, as noted earlier.[38]

In postwar Greece, Theodorakis gradually developed a Marxist philosophy, entering through the door of nationalism and patriotism. From 1947 on he was sporadically imprisoned for his antigovernment stance and exiled to the islands or to tiny mountain villages. In April 1963, he was jailed for his support of the illegal Marathon March to Athens mentioned in *Z* and was at the bedside of the dying Lambrakis following the lethal assassination attack.[39]

He is not far from the theories of Sergei Eisenstein concerning the relation-ship between art and politics. He is not, however, a "political" musician as such:

Although Theodorakis believes that true art is inevitably political, he does not consider himself a political composer except in the sense that his music expresses and interprets the feelings of the Greek people. Nevertheless he concedes that his music can be divided into distinct periods and styles, each corresponding to an essentially political experience.[40]

Among the technicians, besides film editor Françoise Bonnot, Raoul Coutard assumes a prominent position and greatly contributes to Costa-Gavras's films with his photography in *Z* and in *The Confession.* The special issue of *Focus on Film* on "Great Cameramen" furnishes an insight into the role of the chief photogra-pher:

The director of photography needs no apologia for his contribution to the art of film-making. Sufficient to say that he is responsible for the overall visual style of a film (as opposed to the content) as dictated by or worked out col-laboratively with the director.[41]

It is only fair to say, however, that Costa-Gavras diminishes the role of the cameraman, whom, he claims, the Americans unduly deify. In *Filmmakers News-*

letter for February 1976, he says he personally assumes the full responsibility of the lights and angles and tells the cameraman to execute them.

Of the photographers associated with the New Wave, Sacha Vierny and Raoul Coutard have established the finest reputations. Vierny worked especially with Resnais *(Night and Fog, Last Year at Marienbad, Muriel, La Guerre est finie)*, while Coutard assisted Truffaut *(Shoot the Piano Player, Jules and Jim, The Bride Wore Black)* and Godard *(Breathless, Le Petit Soldat, Les Carabiniers, La Chinoise)*. In *La Chinoise* Godard's self-conscious camera captures Coutard on celluloid.

Needless to say, each film requires different camera techniques. Melton Davis remarked at the time of the shooting of *The Confession* that the hand-held camera of *Z*, which created an on-the-spot sensation, gave way to telescopic shots in *The Confession*. "Costa wants the spectator to follow the story and not be encumbered by trick shots," Coutard mentioned to Davis.[42] Coutard did not continue with Costa-Gavras after making his own film *Hoa Binh* (1970), a type of film document about the plight of a boy in Vietnam surrounded by misery.

In the films of Costa-Gavras, political and less political, a pleiad of other stars besides Montand and Perrin brightens the screen. Simone Signoret, by now *la grande dame* of French film and theater, has been in the acting profession for more than thirty years. An Oscar for *Room at the Top* in 1959 was a crowning achievement in her career. Her roles in *Ship of Fools* and *Is Paris Burning?* were also laudable. Signoret's exceptional acting in *Madame Rosa,* adapted from Emile Ajar's *La Vie devant soi,* has further convinced the public that her ability to create a character has not diminished.

Even as a young girl Simone knew the political world. Her father was Jewish, working in Wiesbaden, Germany, in the French occupying force. She was born there in 1921. Her father read such things as *Candide* and *Gringoire,*literary weeklies politically oriented toward the Right. Her mother was romantically leftist. During the occupation of France by the Nazis, the young Simone changed her family name from Kaminker to Signoret and began to work in cinema. In Paris, she was acquainted with the existentialist world at the Café Flore, where Jean-Paul Sartre and Simone de Beauvoir enlightened the world. She married Yves Allégret, in whose films she also starred. Simone Signoret then met Yves Montand while he was singing at St. Paul-de-Vence on 19 August 1949 and married him two years later. It was with Montand that her interests in art and politics merged. Together they played the Proctor couple in *Les Sorcières de Salem* (The Witches of Salem, 1957) adapted for the French production by Jean-Paul Sartre from Arthur Miller's play *The Crucible*. This allegory of the 1950s set in Puritan times was a poignant reflection of the witch-hunting era of Joseph McCarthy. A year later, Montand, accompanied by Simone Signoret, traveled throughout the Eastern European countries performing in factories and music halls. In 1959, they visited the United States only after great difficulty in obtaining a visa because of their political orientation. Once in the United States, they frankly explained their problems with the American policy concerning communists and fellow travelers, just as they did with reference to Soviet policies after they were in Moscow.

Through her association with Costa-Gavras in René Clément's *The Day and the*

Hour she entered into the director's political-film world, drawing with her both husband and daughter. She played the glamorous actress on the decline in *The Sleeping Car Murder* and Lise London, the wife of Gérard, in *The Confession*. Cathérine Allégret, her daughter by her first husband, became the coquettish Bambi in *The Sleeping Car Murder*. Cathérine was still in her late teens when she began her career in cinema following studies in Paris and at the French Lycée in New York. After studying acting with René Simon, she officially began her film career with *Lady L*—from the novel by Romain Gary—in which she performed with Sophia Loren and Paul Newman. Fifteen years after *The Sleeping Car Murder* she appeared on the screen as a prostitute in Costa-Gavras's *Clair de Femme*.

Other faces are immediately recognizable in Costa-Gavras's repertoire as they graduate from one film to another. Jean Bouise, who plays Ramón, the political exile, in Resnais's *La Guerre est finie*, becomes the deputy Georges Pirou in *Z*, Lise London's sympathetic boss in *The Confession*, and the ethical Judge Linais in *Special Section*. In Costa-Gavras's films he always retains a leftist or anti-Establishment posture toward the political events occurring at the time. Bruno Cremer advances from being the partisan leader Cazal in *Shock Troops* to Sampaix, the aggressive editor of the communist paper *L'Humanité* on trial in *Special Section*. Among many of the other films he starred in are William Friedkin's *The Sorcerer* (1977), in which he plays a Parisian banker, and *La Légion saute sur le Kolwezi* (1980) of Raoul Coutard, assuming the role of an outspoken mining official caught by the rebels. Renato Salvatori, one of the assassins of *Z*, enters a "cleaner" profession as the Police Captain Lopez in *State of Siege*. His accomplice in *Z*, Marcel Bozzufi, continues in the role of villain. He plays the first killer in *Le Fils* of Pierre Granier-Deferre. Pierre Dux, the simpleton fascist general in *Z*, appears as the attorney general in *Special Section*. Costa-Gavras uses these actors as a recurring motif in a colorful moving painting. He knows them and can work well with them, for the professional respect of the director and actors is mutual. The same actors will soon become commonplace in "committed films," in which art and politics merge, adding richly to each film. Critic Pauline Kael has another explanation of this crossbreeding in cinema:

> The world of political movies has been incestuous—partly, I imagine, be-cause some committed actors have been eager to work on these projects, and partly because the actors could confer their own movie backgrounds on the shorthand storytelling methods of these fast, complicated, information-packed thrillers. The actors have commuted from one revolutionary situation to another, and to other kinds of political films, and to commercial thrillers.[43]

Be it by cinematic crossbreeding, incest, or shorthand, these people have reenacted Costa-Gavras's perception of history with sensitivity, compassion, and skill.

Epilogue

For some critics Costa-Gavras has created a genre: the political fiction film. For others he has merely injected some leftist, anti-Establishment politics into an already existing genre such as the Film Noir. Throughout his films the recurrence of elements such as still photography or medicine, the same actors or technicians, techniques or themes, provides continuity, while the actual political situation of each film differs and the country and period vary. Costa-Gavras has felt that he has been very narrowly labeled and no longer feels free. His critics who tired of his political melodrama immediately reacted when he departed from that carefully crafted genre with *Clair de Femme*. To appease them, he had to explain the film as "politics of the heart," or the couple as the smallest, "most political unit." After these four political films he admitted he longed to do something else—western, musical, melodrama! We will later see that his adaptation of Romain Gary's *Clair de Femme* was just the right distance he needed from the political fiction genre to get a healthy perspective on it.

3

The Sleeping Car Murder and *Shock Troops:* Doors to a Political Future

A first film is extremely difficult. I had to have a subject that was not too easy. The New Wave directors did other kinds of things as their first films. My situation was different. I was a foreigner. *Sleeping Car Murders* was a solid film that could open doors to the future.

—Costa-Gavras, 1969

In my film *[Shock Troops,]* the idea of justice, which was secondary in the book, takes precedence over whether the end justifies the means. I don't believe that it does. The end is always the good of man. Therefore it is important not to crush man for his own good.

Costa-Gavras, 1971

The Sleeping Car Murder (Compartiment tueurs, 1965)

When you take a berth in a sleeping car, be wary of chance meetings.
When a strangled woman is found in your compartment, be wary of your
   neighbors.
When your neighbors are eliminated, one by one, be wary, period.
If you yourself are not the assassin, it could be rather annoying.

So reads the enticing jacket for Sébastien Japrisot's novel *Compartiment tueurs*. This classic mystery adventure serves as the rich source for the cinematic murder-on-the-Marseilles-express thriller made by the thirty-one-year-old Costa-Gavras, who only a decade earlier was beginning his training at IDHEC. This work was the first personal, cinematic step of a lengthy but fascinating journey. He wished to begin his film career very pragmatically with a police thriller because this genre usually insures a reasonable number of tickets at the box office, very necessary for a novice filmmaker in convincing his producer that he has potential. Costa-Gavras also admitted he always liked film adventure anyway. *The Sleeping Car Murder* thus fulfilled some of his expectations for his first film

51

project.[1] The director remarked he had a strong interest in and respect for the American police thriller, a component of the detective genre, observing that the American cinema soon after its birth became a social cinema.[2] Although his initial work was not political, it was still germinal in the sense that the technique, actors, suspense, and realistic themes of this film would continue through all of his production.

In 1962, Jean-Baptiste Rossi, under the anagrammatic pseudonym of Sébastien Japrisot, published *Compartiment tueurs* in Denoël's Crime Club collection following his debut at the age of seventeen with *Les Mal Partis*. *Compartiment tueurs* would be the first of many Japrisot novels that would reach the screen, such as *Piège pour Cendrillon* and *Le Passager de la pluie*. Japrisot's novels and scripts readily provided tense plots for the cinema, combining psychology, mystery, and action.

Shortly after the publication of *Compartiment tueurs*, Costa-Gavras came upon the book and had an opportunity to meet the author. Costa-Gavras was also familiar with Japrisot's *Piège pour Cendrillon*. He liked the psychological depth of the plot of *Cendrillon* but not the characters and so was not interested in undertaking this adaptation. Cayatte already had an option on *Compartiment tueurs,* but this mystery story fascinated Costa-Gavras considerably. Despite Cayatte's option, Costa-Gavras attempted his own scenario of the novel and would eventually obtain the rights. Drawing up a suitable script took him almost two months.

The next hurdle to jump was that of finding a producer. This required a bit more time since Costa-Gavras had no commercial expertise or name to fall back on. He showed his results to Simone Signoret, whom he had known since their work with Clément a few years earlier. She felt that it had possibilities and suggested Julien Derode, who eventually took the risk with this unknown and inexperienced director. Derode agreed to finance the filming itself but could not afford to pay the actors. They would be obliged to finance it as a cooperative venture and subsequently share in the profits.

What Costa-Gavras actually handed to Signoret could be considered the film in an embryonic stage, for modifications invariably had to be made during the filming. Japrisot also accepted Costa-Gavras's invitation to write the dialogue for the adaptation. The final plot that the director decided upon was a close parallel to the mystery novel in content, tone, and technique.

Narrative

On Le Phocéen night express from Marseilles to Paris, the debonair Mlle Benjamine Bombat, known as Bambi (Cathérine Allégret), enters her second-class compartment at Avignon. Here she encounters Eliane Darrès (Simone Signoret), an actress returning from southern France, where she has been on location for a film. Rivolani, a gas-company employee, also occupies the compartment but is almost nonexistent, for he quickly falls off to sleep. Between the two other occupants—the seductive Georgette Thomas (Pascale Roberts) and the lecherous René Cabourg (Michel Piccoli)—a flirtation and, later, a confrontation take place. She is representative of the Barlin Perfume firm, and he, an office worker for a company that specializes in modern kitchens. Into the sixth berth, reserved by a Mme. Garaudy, who never arrives, Bambi slips her awkward young friend, Daniel (Jacques Perrin), who has no ticket.

Early next morning the train arrives at the Gare de Lyon in Paris and quickly spews its human contents along the quay. When Daniel slips back to the compartment to fetch his valise, he discovers the body of the strangled Georgette Thomas, but says nothing about it. The sympathetic Bambi then invites him to her apartment as she initiates her new career as secretary in the French capital.

The investigation by the flu-afflicted inspector Grazziano or Grazzi (Yves Montand) gets underway. His boss, Commissioner Tarquin (Pierre Mondy) gives all the orders and the team of Grazzi and assistant Jean Lou (Claude Mann) executes them, starting with an examination of all the details of luggage, address book, and purse of the victim. They reject the motive of theft since her purse still contained 300 francs after the murder. They conclude that the crime must have been the work of a sadist.

Through a notice in the newspaper, Grazzi alerts the other occupants of the compartment to contact the police immediately. René Cabourg is the first. He stumbles on Georgette Thomas's picture in the paper and recalls their encounter. He phones the police and, while relating his experiences of that evening, he plays with the erotic graffiti on the wall of the telephone booth. Cabourg leaves the booth on the run to attend a boxing match. It will be his last, for he is liquidated in the men's room during intermission.

Grazzi and Jean-Lou arrive at Eliane Darrès's apartment to question her as Eric Grandin (Jean-Louis Trintignant) silently slips out. The actress mentions to the duo that she recalls having heard the voice of a young boy in the compartment of the train. Further questioning of this witness will have to take place later. Not long after this visit, however, she is trapped between floors in the open elevator and brutally shot in the chest. Shortly afterwards, Rivolani received similar treatment, shot six times with the same type of heavy-caliber weapon. The bullets appeared professionally filed down for a more lethal effect. The murderer apparently stalks and eliminates the possible witnesses one step ahead of the police.

Bambi, of course, is the proposed next victim. However, Daniel supplies the key to the series of crimes. When he phones Grazzi, Jean-Lou intercepts the call and bolts off to meet the young lad. It is now obvious that Jean-Lou is the villain and Eric Grandin, his associate. Jean-Lou attempts to kill Daniel in the phone booth, but the frisky youth escapes with Jean-Lou in hot pursuit. A wild motorcycle and auto chase ensues, the police in feverish pursuit of Jean-Lou. The cornered Jean-Lou surrenders. As he hands over the machine gun he pulls the trigger on himself.

In closing the case Grazzi learns that the homicide of Georgette Thomas was to be part of a crime without any apparent motive. As in the novel and film *Compulsion*, about the Leopold-Loeb case, Jean-Lou and Eric had concocted a plan to commit a perfect crime. The extra murders of the other travelers in the compartment were arranged to throw off suspicion from the real crime—the death and robbery of Eliane Darrès, whom Jean-Lou did not appreciate and who had a large bank account.

Adaptation

Japrisot's novel provides a solid basis for the film, but Costa-Gavras's script and film understandably differ from the original work. In an adaptation it is most important not to translate one scene into another, for the media of literature and film are distinct means of expression, although they overlap. The general nature of the book is that of a detective thriller and will thus necessarily include suspense, mystery, corpses, and at times humor. It is certainly more contrived and dense than a dime run-of-the-mill whodunit. Yves Montand said that the book for him was practically unreadable because of the complexity of the plot. Japrisot documented his adventure very well, knowing both the Marseilles and Paris scene, having originated in one and spent time writing in the other. His documentation borders on the journalistic—dates, times, and events lend a sophisticated air of precision.

The work of adaptation can be considered as an arithmetical task—Costa-Gavras referred to this one as *une exercice*. The script is full of additions and subtractions, divisions of scenes and multiplication of dialogue for clarity. In this process, Costa-Gavras wanted to make the adaptation result in a more personal film, distinct from other types of detective films.[3] It was to be more than entertainment. One of his first concerns was to tighten up the work, to streamline it. He had to clarify certain parts of the text that succeed as literature but do not succeed as good cinema, for instance, certain geographical or psychological descriptions that are at times too minute and complex.

Basically, the director retained more than just the nucleus of the novel. He kept the detective atmosphere that shows the influence of the American Film Noir or B film of the 1930s and 1940s on the cineaste.[4] Costa-Gavras also utilized a cubist perspective: Each of the characters offers his or her reading of an incident, thus presenting several views of the same incident. This technique will be perfected in *Missing* as witnesses try to describe the arrest of Charles.

For comic relief—already present in the novel—the director accentuated Daniel's awkwardness. The youth accidentally tears Bambi's nylons four times in the film. The repetition typecasts him and also adds a touch of humor.

Costa-Gavras had Japrisot redo the dialogue of the novel. In the literary work, the dialogue is ordinarily absorbed into the narrative. For example Grazzi, afflicted with a cold, sniffles his way through the investigation on the train:

> He was about to say something else, but instead he shrugged and just said, damn it, he'd caught a bad one [that is, a cold]. He looked down at the man with the pearls and said, I'll see you at the office about noon, *ciao*. He went out without closing the door.[5]

The Sleeping Car Murder: Commissioner Tarquin (Pierre Mondy) and Inspector Grazzi
(Yves Montand) discuss brutal murder of another passenger.
(Permission of Audio-Brandon/Macmillan Electronic Media)

Japrisot also sculpted rapid-fire dialogue, crisp one-liners, to correspond to the
pace of the film. At times, however, the verbal exchange was too syncopated.

To the novel Costa-Gavras added more suspense, à la Hitchcock. In the middle of the night, for instance, following several bloody murders, someone approaches Bambi's bed with a pointed object in hand. Startled, she finds it is only clumsy Daniel holding a broken faucet. The tension reaches a climax when Jean-Lou is on the verge of shooting Daniel trapped in the phone booth. Suddenly the intended victim bursts out of the booth and past the assistant, who follows in pursuit. As in *Bullitt, French Connection,* and early American gangster and western films, there is an exciting chase sequence. The leather-jacketed motorcycle gang could have come right out of *The Wild One* (with Marlon Brando). Costa-Gavras tightened up the film's ending by creating a better sense of unity of place. He has Daniel remain in Paris—where he is almost killed—instead of having him take the train south, as in the novel. The director injected the suicide of Jean-Lou, which brings the film to a startling conclusion instead of its being the lengthy, anticlimactic interrogation of Eric and the anticipation of Daniel's arrival found in the novel. Costa-Gavras eliminated the questioning session as such during which much of the criminal motivation is divulged by Jean-Lou's accomplice. In one respect, this does bring the film to a more dramatic close, but in another it leaves the viewer literally in the dark with a complicated resolution.

To make the plot unfold more evenly and naturally, he transplanted some of the flashbacks into the normal chronological order of the film. The scene of Daniel and Bambi in the toilet of the train avoiding the ticket collector occurred as a flashback beyond the midpoint of the book. Costa-Gavras inserted it in the beginning, soon after they get on the train separately, in order to indicate the logical course of events in the couple's first encounter.

Editing and Photography

To fabricate a quick-paced rhythm Costa-Gavras relied on the right dosage of provocative material, telescoping scenes, rapid cutting. He believes that the key to good editing is cutting at the precise moment when the spectator is about to lose attention. When the director does this, he can manipulate the suspense until that crucial moment. With the ellipse or jump cut, the director forces the viewer to fill in the blanks and then put the scattered pieces of the puzzle together. The rhythm achieved by these techniques in *The Sleeping Car Murder* is compared by some critics to an express carrying the spectator speedily along without his or her realizing how or why. The editor, Christian Gaudin, supervised by the director, was responsible for the physical aspect of the editing.

Japrisot's text is not lacking in flashbacks, and Costa-Gavras is clever to imitate and rework them visually. This is noticeable in the scene in which René Cabourg spots the picture of the murdered woman in the paper:

> It was the photograph above the headline that really startled him. In spite of the fuzzy quality of the newspaper picture, it had the slightly shocking reality of a face you think you have seen for the last time, thank God, and then find again on the next street corner.
> Beyond the gray and black of the ink, he could see the color of her eyes, the thickness of her hair, and the warmth of the smile that had brought on everything at the very beginning of the trip last night—the unreasoning hope he had felt for a while, and the shame and disgrace of a quarter after twelve.[6]

Costa-Gavras takes his inspiration from a scene such as this. In the photograph seen in the film, the legs of Georgette Thomas immediately catch Cabourg's eye, and there is a flashback to the train and her sensual pose with her legs exposed toward him. The legs are the connecting link of the two scenes, just as water will be a few minutes later, although not in a flashback. Cabourg is shot, and the water in the bathroom sink continues to flow. A quick cut brings the viewer to the apartment of Bambi, who is taking a shower. These types of flashbacks and cuts are carefully constructed and could be considered parallel to good transitional phrases introducing new paragraphs. They also create the effect of telescoping time frames of past, present, and future. As in Resnais's *La Guerre est finie* of the following year, there is an occasion to use the novelty of a flashforward which recreates the actual psychological process of daydreaming. Cabourg, walking down the street, has a fleeting thought about what he would be doing that evening. Moreover, his sexual fantasies are stylized; they destroy time zones and add an oneiric tone to the film.

The photographer Jean Tournier, using a hand-held camera, was able to work out a cinéma vérité effect; it gives the sensation of on-the-spot testimony or witness to the action. Much later, after Costa-Gavras's political triumphs, the director felt that this style was too primitive and did not add anything to the film.

Compositions using mirrors in the film are aesthetically appealing, for example, in the bathroom on the train and in Eric's apartment, which resembles a curious museum. These shots not only provide new perspectives to the image but also serve as framing devices. A subjective camera technique puts the viewer into an actual scene. With a loud detonation, a high-caliber pistol is fired directly into the face of the spectator/camera. On the wild motorcycle ride, one shot is taken from the cycle itself, creating the effect of the viewer's being involved in the actual chase. When Daniel peers down the staircase of Bambi's apartment, the camera also leans over the edge of the railing to disclose a cleverly framed staircase.

Music

The nervous atmosphere of *The Sleeping Car Murder* is partially the result of Michel Magne's music. Just as in a Hitchcock thriller, music reinforces the suspense. Magne composed the score for this film after previously collaborating with Henri Verneuil (*Un Singe en hiver* in 1961, and *Mélodie en sous-sol* in 1962), Christian Marquand (*Les Grands Chemins*, 1963), and Yves Allégret (*Germinal*, 1963).

Characterization and Acting

Costa-Gavras had the good fortune to work with talented actors and actresses who met his expectations and conformed to his view of the ensemble of the film. They, in turn, no doubt helped shape his political and aesthetic views. Since the highly involved narrative manifested some complex psychology and called for many diverse roles, the players had to typify ingeniously the characters they played with gestures, dialogue, tics, and intimate reactions that would immediately express what the character essentially was.

Still in her late teens, Cathérine Allégret, daughter of Yves Allégret and Simone Signoret, plays Bambi with charm and apparent ease. She is a minuscule version of her mother, and shares in her talents. Her baby-faced features make her perfect for a character who is somewhere in that nebulous age of no longer being an adolescent and not yet being a woman. Her mother, still celebrated for her previous astounding film and theater role in *The Witches of Salem*, incarnates perfectly the "middle-aged road-show actress" on the decline, as Bosley Crow-

The Sleeping Car Murder: Bambi (Cathérine Allégret) and Daniel (Jacques Perrin) have a
relationship of peril.
(Permission of Audio-Brandon/Macmillan Electronic Media)

ther put it.[7] Yves Montand, her husband, had recently completed a series of
films in America with George Cukor (*Let's Make Love*, 1960), with the British
director Tony Richardson (*Sanctuary*, 1960), with Anatole Litvak (*Good-Bye
Again*, 1961), and with Jack Cardiff (*My Geisha*, 1961). In his early forties and
after three years' absence from the screen, he returned to cinema with a new
dynamic style of acting, a desire for different roles, and a more serious tone to
his character. Montand comments on the fresh direction his life took with his
work in *The Sleeping Car Murder*:

> It was with *The Sleeping Car Murder*, that my real career began—my total
> commitment to film. . . . Up until then my forte was the one man show onstage,
> which required absolute concentration, no distractions. I did play in some
> films, but more or less as an amateur. Then suddenly, with Costa-Gavras,
> something happened. I discovered him to be more than simply a director; I
> found him a perfect collaborator who revealed my true character.[8]

Directed by Costa-Gavras in *The Sleeping Car Murder*, Montand plays Grazzi, the
Marseilles-born Paris cop who goes from a type of nonhero in the first part of the
film to becoming the pivotal point in the resolution of the crime with Daniel's
assistance at its close. For twenty years, confessed Montand, he had tried to get

rid of his Marseilles accent, which was characterized by nasalization and a pro-
nunciation of every syl-la-ble. In this film he had to cultivate the long-lost accent.
Michel Capdenac of *Les Lettres Françaises* compared Montand to Humphrey
Bogart, while Jean-Louis Bory of *Arts* likened him to the famous French stage
and screen actor Louis Jouvet in *Quai des Orfèvres,* another detective film.

Jean-Louis Trintignant, whose roles in *A Man and a Woman* and *Z* would soon
catapult him into international fame, assumes a Don Juan role with Eliane
Darrès, but also the role of boyfriend and accomplice of Jean-Lou. As the incur-
able libertine Cabourg, Michel Piccoli does artistically reveal his pitiable character with his fantasies, his furtive glances at women, and his interest in obscene
graffiti. Jacques Perrin in the 1960s was often cast as a fair-skinned, naïve youth,
before he advanced with age and experience to more sophisticated roles. As the
destitute and sleuthing Daniel from the provinces, he possesses charm and dramatic skill. Pierre Mondy, in the minor role of Grazzi's boss, successfully and
quickly develops the character, pretentious, authoritarian. Pascale Roberts as the
enticing murder victim has but a few moments to reveal her personality. Obviously no depth of character can emerge in such a short space of time. The
flashbacks, however, help to develop her character. Charles Denner as Bob
Vatski, the loud-mouthed critic of the police, is cast in a more negative role than

The Sleeping Car Murder: Eric (Jean-Louis Trintignant) cultivates the wealthy actress
Eliane Darrès (Simone Signoret).
(Permission of Audio-Brandon/Macmillan Electronic Media)

in *Z* (leftist lawyer at the side of the pacifist leader Lambrakis). The villain himself—played by Claude Mann—manifests a more silent presence. The book more so than the film characterizes him as a calculating killer for whom murder is second nature. He is of the philosophy that it is rather easy after your first victim, a sentiment shared by Eric during the interrogation.[9] Jean-Lou's fellow conspirator recounts their series of criminal acts as gratuitous violence not too different from that of Kubrick's protagonists, the Droogs, in *A Clockwork Orange*.

This was the family of actors and technicians who co-created the film with Costa-Gavras at the Studio de Saint Maurice on the banks of the Marne. The director trusted their judgment and offered suggestions. At the same time, since this was his first major film, he was assigned a technical assistant to insure a professional job. To prove himself, Costa-Gavras stayed up all night to work out the shots for the next day. In the long run this was a wise and crucial investment. The film worked out successfully and was influential in his attracting other producers for his subsequent films.

Criticism

The critics offered a wide range of responses to *The Sleeping Car Murder*. In the United States it had a profitable run, especially in New York. Bosley Crowther of the *New York Times* praised the brilliance of the actors and the breathless pace achieved through the editing. In *Film Quarterly*, James Michael Martin situates the film in the historical context of the detective-gangster type of film and sees it as a finely finished product. He then concentrates on the sexual side of the film, describing the fantasies of the lascivious Cabourg and the relationships of the eternal triangle—Jean-Lou, Eric, and Eliane. John Simon later puts the film in perspective:

> His first film, *The Sleeping-Car Murder*, was trivial hokum, but even into this gimmicky and attitudinizing murder story, Costa-Gavras was able to sneak some politically gilt-edged stances, and introduce marvelous performances from actors sometimes cast against type, sometimes more famous than their parts would warrant and yielding stunning results.[10]

Richard Davis, in the British journal *Films and Filming*, observes that *The Sleeping Car Murder* is directed with cool and efficient heartlessness, "a direct harking back to the vintage years of French whodunits."[11]

The French critics, closer to the scene of the crime, show the full gamut of reactions. In *Cahiers du Cinéma*, several critics give it the grade "*Inutile à se déranger*," equivalent to "Don't bother!" Others suggested seeing it, but "*À la rigueur!*"—"Proceed with caution!" In the same journal, Jean Eustache emphasizes the fact that this film had been made by someone who has seriously reflected upon this medium, while Luc Moellet refers to the work as simply a "*succès mineur*." Samuel Lachize of the communist paper *L'Humanité* speaks favorably of the production, stressing its close resemblance to the American gangster-detective film. Henry Chapier in *Combat* associates the diabolical machinery set in motion by Costa-Gavras with that of Hitchcock. The *Parisien Libéré* applauds the new blood in French cinema, while Pierre Ajame of *Les Nouvelles Littéraires* refers unfavorably to the film, labeling it *"Premiers (faux) pas"* of the director.

In general, the critics in France usually give Costa-Gavras's pedigree (from IDHEC to his apprenticeship with the leading French filmmakers) in order to expand the consciousness of the reader of film criticism and provide the historical film context of this debutant. They are also quick to compare him to Hitchcock for the tension, to Clouzot for the darker side of human nature, to Simenon/Maigret for the crime and suspense, and to Wyler for the subject matter (*Detective Story*, 1951).

Shock Troops (Un Homme de trop, 1966)

Following the success of *The Sleeping Car Murder* in America and the mixed but hope-filled reactions in France, Costa-Gavras was approached by Harry Saltzmann, producer of some of the James Bond classics, to film a World War II drama based on a novel by Jean-Pierre Chabrol, author of *Les Fous de Dieu, La Chatte rouge,* and *Le Canon Fraternité.* Working with a large production company could prove a dangerous venture for the novice filmmaker, for in such circumstances he could possibly find himself victimized by the system or manipulated through a multitude of compromises. Costa-Gavras accepted the challenge and wrote an adaptation of *Un Homme de trop* (Gallimard, 1958). He completed the film in 1967; it was later screened at the Moscow Film Festival, where it merited a prize. Although ideally it would make exciting film viewing material in the United States, it was slow in making its way here. It arrived two years later.

Narrative

The film begins: 1939, Berlin. A swastika, represented on a map as in Capra's *Why We Fight* series, becomes larger and larger: the growth of fascism! By 1943, it covers a significant portion of the European terrain. Resistance against this malady becomes more and more organized. A group of partisans under orders from London attacks a Nazi prison compound in the south of France to liberate comrades important to the resistance movement. With split-second timing, the commandos storm the prison, free the prisoners in death row, and quickly escape in two trucks. Unfortunately they happened to have released thirteen instead of twelve men. Who is number thirteen, a certain "Robert" (Michel Piccoli)? A planted informer? A traitor? A common criminal? An innocent simpleton? All of the above or none of the above?

After the partisans' attack on the prison, the Nazis seal off the nearby town. Disguised as laborers, the underground unit takes a tense bus ride through the security check and arrives safely at their secluded mountain encampment. En route they find the thirteenth man more mysterious. Eventually he discloses his pacifist philosophy. He has no liking for war; he does not believe in being harnessed to ideas. Still suspect, he is held prisoner by the partisans while the three leaders Cazal (Bruno Cremer), Jean (Jean-Claude Brialy), and Thomas (Gérard Blain) discuss his fate. In the meantime, an old shepherd, Passevin (Charles Vanel), stumbles upon the camp and is forced to remain with the group for the sake of security.

Once again the partisans act with deftness. They take a local town which is more closely aligned with Marshal Pétain than with the resistance. The group holds up the police station and robs the bank. A fascist *milicien* (Pierre Clementi) is seized after he wounds one of the partisans, Philippe, in a sniper attack. Just as the Nazis arrive, the partisans hastily leave town. The suspect prisoner helps them out of the perilous situation, driving the escape truck and later helping to give necessary injections to the wounded Philippe, who nonetheless dies of the gunshot wound. Kerk (Jacques Perrin), in retaliation for the death of his companion, shoots the *milicien* in cold blood. Cazal officiates at a memorial service for the fallen partisan Philippe.

A message from the regional directors of the resistance arrives with Jeanne (Julie Dassin); there is "one prisoner too many," implying that the thirteenth man must be exterminated. Jean strongly agrees, but Thomas rejects the idea. Thomas, however, reluctantly accepts the task of eliminating the prisoner. Learning that "Robert" is a deserter and not really a criminal, he hesitates, and then allows him to go free. Later that evening "Robert" returns to the partisan camp in order to inform them of the Nazi encirclement. He escapes again next morning. His brusque departure jeopardizes the existence of the resistance network. Jean and Cazal in pursuit of "Robert" are caught by the Nazis along with him, but Cazal manages eventually to break away from his captors. In the meantime, the partisans defend the mountain with all the forces and equipment they can muster. Their plans to blow up the pass to prevent further Nazi movement succeed, but at great cost of life. Meanwhile, Jean and "Robert" are to be hung from the viaduct by the Nazis to serve as an example. Prematurely, Jean jumps and takes one Nazi soldier with him to die at the bottom of the ravine. The enigmatic prisoner miraculously and ironically escapes the execution squad by climbing through the beams of the viaduct. He never revealed any secrets to the Nazis.

Novel versus Film

The literary work itself comes from the actual experiences of the maquis (French underground) in the Cévennes area of southern France. The operations of the resistance movement are vividly depicted by Chabrol, who originated in this area and fought with the partisans. For his screen adaptation, Costa-Gavras maintained the basic plot and characterization of the novel, but also took some liberties with the text in order to make it a more commercialized and appealing work for a large audience.

Costa-Gavras first situated the story in its historical context. More than twenty years had passed since the end of World War II, and the public, especially the international public, needed some type of reference point for the narrative.

Hence, Costa-Gavras opens with the symbolism of a Nazi swastika intensifying with power from 1939 to 1943. He then filmed the action mostly on its original site in the Cévennes Massif, where hills, mountains, and shrub provided excellent cover for the many resistance efforts.

The film soon bursts into action. The attack on the prison provides instant excitement and adventure, and furnishes the background on the release of the curious prisoner. Costa-Gavras imaginatively recreated this incident, only alluded to in the literary work. The action in the novel begins the day after the Sarlande prison escape—20 July 1943. In fact, the attack on the Nîmes prison that inspired this episode occurred 4 February 1944. Aimé Vielzeuf offers an exciting historical reconstruction of this attack in his most engaging literary work, *On les appelait "les bandits."* Vielzeuf records that, led by Marty (Rémy Sauer), on the night of 4 February, three small groups (attack, protection, security) of Operation "Centrale" took over a regional prison that held 850 prisoners. With the complicity of one of the guards, Louis, the attack group penetrated the prison and freed twenty-six men. A few common criminals infiltrated the liberated group, among whom were Ange-Marie Salicetti (29), Abrumdio Sanchis (34), and Adolphe Ross (35). In their escape the partisans took with them four local police who were alerted during the prison break. The group missed the rendezvous with the truck because of several delays and was forced to travel on foot 130 kilometers, approximately eighty miles. The liberated prisoners marched in bare feet or in worn-out socks. They made their way north toward the Lozère region, where they finally found refuge among fellow partisans in Les Bouzèdes after six nights in frigid February temperatures.[12]

Shortly following the film sequence of the liberation of the prisoners, the director inserted the nerve-wracking ride of the twenty-seven partisans disguised as workers as they pass through the Nazi barricade. They are almost detected, but are eventually successful.

To relieve the tension, there are a few details that are blended into the narrative. The anarchist Groubac (Claude Brasseur) supplies comic relief with his libertine gestures and comments, at the house of Menjou (François Perrier) and in the town. He assumes part of the characterization of Chambranle of the novel. When the partisans receive an arms supply from the British, one of the bazookas accidentally fires. It causes alarm which changes to humor, just as in the case of "Robert," who first escapes his guard but only to relieve himself outdoors.

Only a few very minor feminine characters appear in the novel. Julie Dassin, the daughter of the director Jules Dassin *(Never on Sunday, Topkapi)*, plays the role of Jeanne in the film, a part that was written into the script by the director.

Costa-Gavras made changes in certain events and characters, transforming the original work, but not to such an extent that the literary material becomes unrecognizable. He took the text, interpreted it visually, and accentuated certain traits in order to make it over into a commercial film production. The first significant change is in that of the thirteenth man (number twelve in the book). In the novel he is mentally deficient and monosyllabic, except when faced by Thomas and the SS officers. The old shepherd Passevin in the text dispels some of the mystery surrounding the prisoner by recounting this man's early years in

Shock Troops: "Robert" (Michel Piccoli), the one "shock trooper" too many.
(Permission of Terrafilm/United Artists Corp.)

Shock Troops: Kerk (Jacques Perrin) takes revenge on wounded fascist sniper (Pierre Clementi).
(Permission of Terrafilm/United Artists Corp.)

their native village. The news clippings about his crime—rape and strangling of a woman—provide more details about his personality. Chabrol's work furthermore casts him as a more disturbed figure than in the film, and as a milder, less convincing pacifist. Relying on testimony from eyewitnesses to the events, we would say that Chabrol's interpretation would be closer to the reality than Costa-Gavras's.

The names of the characters and their roles shift from novel to film. Paulo, the leader, becomes Cazal, and the wounded Cheminée, Philippe. The execution of the *milicien*—Jean-Paul Moulinay of the novel—is effected quietly outside of the camp. In the film adaptation, the impulsive Kerk in a rage of anger and retaliation fires the lethal shots inside the camp. The memorial service for the dead partisan is ritualized, though not with the ritual of institutional religion. Paulo stammers out a simple farewell to the young man (18) who loved life. "The future is costly." The film version is more solemn. Cazal's eulogy here is touching: "Some people can't understand why others die, why people are willing to die [for a cause]. We will try to understand. Our nature will not be that of our enemies." It is not difficult to see parallels with the cult of the heroic dead in other films such as in Eisenstein's epic *Alexander Nevsky,* Malraux's anti-fascist *Espoir,* or the short Nazi eulogy of the putsch martyrs, *For Us.*

The rapport between Thomas and the extra prisoner is strengthened in the

Shock Troops: Jeanne (Julie Dassin) delivers message to Cazal (Bruno Cremer).
(Permission of Terrafilm/United Artists Corp.)

film by a more intimate dialogue and by Thomas's prolonged hesitation to eliminate the pacifist. The latter has an opportunity then to exonerate himself, consciously or unconsciously, so that the sympathetic Thomas can truly understand his reasoning. The novel does not allow sufficient exchange between the two of them, so that the true character of the prisoner still remains deliberately cloaked in ambiguity.

Whereas the novel enters into rich, philosophical discussion on ends and means with respect to the execution of "Robert," the film is forced to limit it to a sketch. The deliberations are kept to a minimum in the screen version since any lengthy debate would slow down the tempo of the film. Dropping some of the philosophical questioning—not enough for some critics—allowed Costa-Gavras to tighten up the structure of the material. As a result, the film is more episodic and action-oriented.

The attack on the town and on the ammunition train are at the heart of the narrative of the novel. The town—Pradeilhes in the book—is still under control of fascist sympathizers. Polemics about party politics and about the ethics of killing accompany both attacks. Costa-Gavras in the film proposes a triptych of guerrilla activities—the storming of the jail, the robbing of the town bank (to "borrow" some money for the resistance operations), and the blocking of the mountain pass during the Nazi attack at the conclusion of the film. Costa-Gavras made these three moments the pillars upon which the rest of the plot rests. He peppered all three with violent deaths, as at the opening of the film (the slashing of a soldier's throat) and at its end (heroic fraternal gestures of rescue during the Nazi siege).

The novel concludes with the hanging from the viaduct of the two partisans Jean and Thomas as well as "Robert" during the Nazi encirclement. This is changed in the film to the sole execution of Jean, for Cazal managed to escape earlier; at the last moment the enigmatic prisoner eludes his captors by slipping through the beams of the viaduct as he is about to be executed.

Under the direction of Costa-Gavras certain elements of the novel were discarded. One that would have provided exciting material for the audience is the ambush of the ammunition train. This attack displayed the vast coordination of the underground from different camps in the realization of the one operation. It would have been a costly filming venture given the amount of material and extras necessary to reenact the assault.

In Chabrol's work, the appearance of comrade Francis, a calculating stoic, is far from incidental. It serves to introduce questioning about an ethical approach to handling "Robert." The security of the local resistance movement is at stake. Should they hesitate to execute one man? In the film Francis does not appear to be this type of controversial figure, but this style of ethical reasoning is certainly present in the attitude of the Marxist Jean.

Filming

Before undertaking this commercial enterprise, Costa-Gavras met at length with Jean-Pierre Chabrol.[13] A native to the Cévennes region and a member of the local resistance during the war, Chabrol offered the director invaluable, precise details that could not have been discovered by just reading and studying the novel. Costa-Gavras and his crew then went on location in the region slightly north of Nîmes in southern France. For seven weeks in the Cévennes Massif they filmed *Shock Troops*.

To shoot certain sequences required taking a three-hour ride into the mountains and then a half-mile walk loaded down with material to Le Mas Perdu (literally, "the lost farm"). They filmed primarily between Alès and Saint-Flour, and especially in the latter area for the opening sequence of the prison break. They also shot on Mt. Bouquet near Brouze-les-Alès. Three weeks were then necessary to film other scenes, making it in all a ten-week project.

Acting and Characterization

During the shooting, Costa-Gavras had the opportunity to direct a large group of actors with varied talents. Playing the weathered shepherd was Charles Vanel, a veteran of the crew at seventy-three years of age. With his rustic personality and attachment to nature, Passevin could easily have emerged from a Jean Giono novel. Francesco Rosi later cast him in the role of a similar aged peasant in *Three Brothers* (Tre Fratelli), 1981. Bruno Cremer has often been selected for war or adventure films—*317ème Section, Objectif 500 million*, and the colossal *Is Paris Burning?* as the late Colonel Rol Tanguy. He admitted that after *Un Homme de trop* he would prefer to star in other genres besides the war film. Here he plays a sound and respected leader who takes the initiative. In the novel the character he plays, Cazal, appears slightly harsh especially during the interrogation of "Robert." The model for Cazal was René Bibault, a leader of one group of partisans in southern France and known by the name "Capitaine Jean." It was he who recounted the episode of the prison break to the novelist Jean-Pierre Chabrol. In retrospect, Bibault felt that the character of Cazal reflects "all the problems and debates that I had known and which were, in the long run, well presented."[14]

Gèrard Blain conveys perfectly the character of the undecided and sensitive Thomas. To show the other side of the coin, Costa-Gavras casts Jean-Claude Brialy (later director of *L'Oiseau rare* and *Les Volets clos*), as the strong-minded and cold-blooded resistance member. The Marxist Jean feels that any action is warranted in order to protect "the Cause," even the killing of a man who may be innocent. Jacques Perrin plays a very impetuous Kerk, who takes revenge on a wounded sniper for the slaying of his comrade in arms. Pierre Clementi, as a credible fascist sympathizer, is often typed as a villain in European films. Because of his dark, sharp physical features and cold gaze, he can readily incarnate an evil force.

Michel Piccoli's ambiguity as the one prisoner too many is most convincing in the film. His willingness to help the partisans when they are in difficulty and his desire to escape at certain times and remain prisoner at others, make his character impenetrable. In contrast to the part in the novel, the character remains more heroic in the film and he warns the partisans of the arrival of the Nazis, thus endangering his own life. He does not succumb to the questioning of the SS who capture him.

The dialogue of these characters may at times be too minimal to support the original theme and plot for the novel. Yet, the conversations can be confusing in some instances as Costa-Gavras attempts to retain the dense material of the literary work. The exchanges are not revealing enough to develop the characters, which results at times in stereotyped characters.

Technique

From the point of view of technique, the film stands on its own fine qualities and requires that it be judged apart from the novel. The editor Christian Gaudin, working with Costa-Gavras, employs feverish quick-cutting to shift rapidly from one scene to another. The technique carries the spectator rapidly along as in *The Sleeping Car Murder*. The vignettes may appear a bit scrambled and demand reflection, but the furious pace present from the initial shots of the liberation of the detainees to the bombing of the pass leave little time for reflection. Generally the spectator proceeds from one episode of the resistance action to another at breakneck speed, except when weighed down by the quasi-philosophical dialogue mentioned earlier. The freeze shots during the credits are especially colorful and appealing. The constantly moving camera does not have adequate time to penetrate the psychology of each of the many characters, thus, the film becomes deliberately more action-oriented than psychological or reflective. Parallel editing of the final sequence of the Nazi chase of Cazal, and cutting from the detonation of the explosives at the pass to the hanging scene on the viaduct create high-powered tension and drama.

Richard Jameson in *Film Quarterly* lauds some of Jean Tournier's photographical skills, suggesting the participatory effect of Tournier's camera action. The viewer and the camera become one:

And when, from an aerial vantage, we watch a truck full of guerrillas wind down a mountain road, while a German convoy approaches on a lower level, the camera plane turns with the truck into a handy cul-de-sac a split second before the convoy rounds the last bend. Few are the viewers who do not hold their breath during the long, lovely, intricate shot that makes us all involuntary partisans.[15]

Besides the aerial shots from the helicopter, there are telescopic shots of the Nazis attacking a partisan camp; the spectator watches the action through field glasses. The night shot of "Robert" escaping through the countryside with his solitary lamp also adds a touch of lyricism to the film. Eastmancolor brings out the richness of these scenes set in the picturesque Cévennes Massif, but it also has the unfortunate effect of glamorizing or romanticizing the actual reality. The music of Michel Magne, an earlier collaborator for *The Sleeping Car Murder*, reinforces this richness.

Shock Troops: "Robert" (Michel Piccoli) is seized by the Nazis.
(Permission of Terrafilm/United Artists Corp.)

Generally speaking, the technique exhibited here by Costa-Gavras shows promise. It will be even more skillfully applied in his later films.

Criticism

Costa-Gavras should be the first to offer his critical appreciation of the film:

> I would like to see *Un Homme de trop* again now and analyze what are the problems with the film. I'm sure that looking at it again now [1970], two or three years later, they could be solved. But I still like it very much. I'm very attached to it . . . it's like with children, it is often the odd one out that becomes your favorite.
>
> I was young and somewhat inexperienced. There is perhaps not enough motivation of the characters . . . or perhaps too much action, and it is in the action that central concerns of the film are lost. People would see the film and then afterwards they would say, "so what?" . . . that was very frustrating for me. Action sequences are fun to make, but in films they are only secondary to what it says, it is the subject that must always come first.[16]

The film elicited varied reactions from those who participated in the actual events in 1944. The novelist Jean-Pierre Chabrol states that in the liberation of the prison there actually was "one man too many"—"*un gangster.*" In his book he freely enlarged upon these events. Viewing Costa-Gavras's adaptation of his rendering of the story brought on this reaction: "At the first screening I was indignant [*outré*], then I got accustomed to it. As a film enthusiast, I eventually was able to consider it an original work—somewhat different from my novel—and really appreciate it."[17]

René Bibault speaks of Chabrol's novel as a literary work based on a marginal aspect of the historical fact of the prison attack. Bibault's response is valuable since he was one of the leaders of the resistance fighters of the FTP (Francs Tireurs et Partisans) in the areas Le Crespin, Les Bouzèdes, and Le Bougès. Some of his men participated in the release of the prisoners under the direction of "Marty" (Rémy Sauer). Bibault assisted some of the escapees later on after their many trials and tribulations. He observed:

> There really was one man too many who no longer was a young man (forty-five perhaps), a pander, and perhaps a murderer (should be verified). I never knew his real name. He should have behaved properly. Instead he chose to try to corrupt some of the maquis. It was necessary to come to some decision on the regional level.
>
> I must admit that the work of Chabrol (who participated in the nearby maquis under my leadership) brought together many souvenirs and that his text was difficult for someone [like myself] who had lived through these experiences . . . just as it was difficult to watch the film where I appeared in the role

Shock Troops: Kerk (Jacques Perrin) succeeds in blowing up the pass.
(Permission of Terrafilm/United Artists Corp.)

of B. Cremer with all the problems and debates of conscience that I had known and which were, in the long run, well presented.

Costa-Gavras's film, in my opinion, is a good film but not a masterpiece. He has certainly made better ones.

I feel he sacrificed too much to the commercial in certain scenes (in the opening sequence where a truck crashes through the door at the finale of the maquis's attack, and also in the scene at the viaduct).

Other scenes are excellent—the attack of the small city relates very precisely to the one I directed at "le Grand Courbe." We held the city for an entire morning in order to acquire arms, food supplies, and money. You can see that Chabrol was there and offered advice to C[osta]-G[avras]. But the episode of the *milicien* was added. The scene of the viaduct is completely fictional, if not, I would not be able to write to you. It was filmed at Garabit.[18]

The decisions and debates of conscience underlined in the book, film, and Bibault's letter were very much a part of the day-to-day wartime experience. Jean-Paul Sartre in *Existentialism and Human Emotions* (and earlier in *L'Existentialisme est un humanisme*) illustrates this with the example of his student coming to see him to help resolve his conscience—to stay with his mother to help her survive after the loss of her other son in 1940, or to leave to join the Free French Forces. The young man had the choice on one hand to follow an ethics of sympathy or personal devotion, and on the other a broader ethics, one whose efficacy Sartre says could be more dubious. Sartre's advice was that this young man was free and that no book of ethics, no doctrine could help him. He must invent his choice.[19]

A historian of and participant in World War II, Aimé Vielzeuf communicated his sentiments about *Un Homme de trop:*

Reaction to the film: The original idea of Chabrol was distorted. I prefer—a 100 times over!—the book to the film. As much as I appreciated *Z, La Guerre est finie* [of Resnais], *L'Aveu,* I find this film mediocre; it is far from the truth. Costa-Gavras should have gotten some good advice from former *maquisards.*[20]

Costa-Gavras's perception of his results echoes that of the French critics at the release of *Un Homme de trop*—too much action in the film at the expense of the motivation in character and the central idea of the work. The critics, however, were a bit more severe with the director at that time since this was his second work and a more commercial undertaking with more substantial backing. Damning it with faint praise, they compared it to a western in the great American tradition. Georges Charensol of *Les Nouvelles Littéraires* gave it a very mediocre review, stressing the weakness of Costa-Gavras for *le grand spectacle* and humorous gags. Jean de Baroncelli, writing for *Le Monde,* shows the same degree of critical opinion, and adds that, though the work is respectable, it leaves the viewer cold and indifferent. For a critic such as Henry Chapier of *Combat, Un Homme de trop* recalled *La Longue·Marche* of Alexandre Astruc, while others compared it to *Is Paris Burning?* It is not an original scenario nor does it express a personal style, reflected Chapier; it represents established cinema. Not far from this approach is Louis Chauvet of *Le Figaro,* who maintained that, although Costa-Gavras possesses great talent, it is a bad choice of subject and scenario.

Shock Troops: Jean (Jean-Claude Brialy) takes his Nazi executioner with him to the bottom of the ravine.
(Permission of Terrafilm/United Artists Corp.)

Samuel Lachize of *L'Humanité* stated that the film is certainly not a complete failure, but it is simply insufficient. More positive in their critiques of the work are Eric Leguebe of *Le Parisien Libéré* and Robert Chazal of *Le Soir*. They are laudatory in their judgment of the film and feel that, although the work is not original, it is very effective just the same. Of the French critics, only Jean Rochereau of *La Croix* goes to the painstaking trouble of actually comparing and contrasting the novel and film.

The importing of the film into the American marketplace created its own problems. The dubbed version did not have the same impact as the original French. It had a similar effect that one gets from watching John Wayne speak impeccable French in an American western shown in Paris. Costa-Gavras was displeased with the American title—*Shock Troops*. It shifted the thrust of the original—*One Man Too Many*—from the psychological and ethical discussions of the extra prisoner to the war film genre that is primarily designed as an action-filled piece of entertainment.

The film drew mixed reviews in America. Writing for the *New York Post* in 1969, Archer Winsten speaks highly of the editing, the general pace of the film, and the characterization. Also in a positive light, Richard Jameson in *Film Quarterly* analyzes the action, characters, and above all the photography. For its "frenzied vitality and photographic expertise," Howard Thompson in the *New York*

Times also believed the film was worthwhile viewing. He was, however, quick to point out the flaws in the development of the first half of the film, basically its hesitancy and lack of unity.

Epilogue

Although *The Sleeping Car Murder* and *Shock Troops* do not fall into the category of the political film genre, nevertheless Costa-Gavras asserts that they already possess the essence of his philosophy of film and political thought.

In *The Sleeping Car Murder* there is a general anti-police tone showing that not even this sector of society is exempt from criminal tendencies. Originally Costa-Gavras wanted to make a police officer guilty of the crime, but the protests from the censors obliged him to use a different culprit, an apprentice. The police tended to be rather sensitive about their image, not unlike the negative feelings evoked by Sidney Lumet's filming of *Serpico* in 1974. The Préfecture de Police did not want the director to film in Paris, but the reluctance on their part was eventually overridden. Throughout the shooting, however, the crew was obliged to have a police representative on hand. Costa-Gavras had difficulty in shooting where he wished and had confrontations with the police on a few occasions. The film itself reveals a very controversial character in Bob Vatski (Charles Denner), who is quick to share his negative reaction to the police force. Early on in the film Vatski shows himself to be hostile toward the authorities, snidely remarking that the police disgust him. His words in the film are harsh: "Beware of a jackass behind you, or a monkey in front of you . . . or a cop anywhere." This anti-Establishment tone will be developed in Costa-Gavras's more mature political later works as he takes on the police, government, army, and the U.S. State Department.

Some of the later political concerns of the director are also evident in his first works. In an interview for *1000 Eyes* he discusses *Shock Troops* and his original intentions. He observed that in this film he tried to mix a bit of "politics," for want of a better word. He wanted to show thus that during the Occupation it was difficult to stay neutral, not to take a position.[21] Costa-Gavras succeeds in expressing this omnipresent tension especially as it surrounds the figure of "Robert," who is persecuted by the Nazis as well as by the resistance. Because of his noncommitment and pacifist ideas, prisoner number thirteen finds himself in an existential no-man's-land.

Costa-Gavras dramatically reveals the inner machinery of the resistance in its struggle against the mesmerizing forces of the fascists. The general tone of the film is obviously anti-fascist. Costa-Gavras has one of the commandos tear down the picture of Marshal Pétain, "the guardian of peace," in the Free Zone of southern France, indicating where his sympathies lay. His negative reaction toward Pétain will be more developed in *Special Section*. Very briefly he alludes to some of the tension among the partisans themselves, that is, the communists against the noncommunists. Nonetheless, the director raises a human question of greater importance—is it ethical to sacrifice a man's life for a cause if there is a chance that he may not be guilty? In peacetime or war, does the end ever justify the means?

The Sleeping Car Murder and *Shock Troops* did not show Costa-Gavras to be a cinematic genius. Nor did they indicate that he was wasting his time in the filmmaking profession. In 1967, despite some of the weaknesses of these first films, the critics saw in him solid potential, artistic sensitivity, and technical expertise. He soon coupled this with a very expressive political perspective to create some of the more powerful films of contemporary cinema.

4

Z: A Greek Tragedy

The idea of Death haunts me. How fortunate are those who have hope; as for me, I cannot accept a hope in another life better than the present one. And yet, I believe that the just and the thoughts of the just cannot die.
                                                           COSTA-GAVRAS, 1969

If Costa-Gavras considered his first two films as his door to the future, with *Z* (1969) he crossed the threshhold to technical cinematic maturity, deep political consciousness, and international fame. After his second film, *Shock Troops,* he received several offers to make films. He had already been in search of a historical situation that would serve as a solid basis for a next project. He considered John F. Kennedy's assassination, the Ben Barka affair in Paris, and the events surrounding the possible rehabilitation of Seznec, accused of murdering his friend following World War I. A political current ran through all these events.

Robert Dorfmann (producer of *Jeux interdits* and *Papillon*) and Bertrand Javal agreed to sign Costa-Gavras to make a film about a big-time operator, Ange Orahona, who returns from New York to his native Corsica to be with his dying mother. Costa-Gavras received an advance for the film in spring 1967 and thus took the opportunity to return to Greece to visit his family. During Costa-Gavras's stay in Athens in March, his brother Tolis, an attorney, suggested to him a book that would interest him. It was the freshly published novel *Z*, written by the young author Vassilis Vassilikos, already celebrated for his trilogy, *The Plant, The Wall,* and *The Angel.* The novel *Z* dealt with the assassination of a pacifist deputy or representative of the Greek parliament and its extensive cover-up by the government, something that excited the Greeks as Watergate would the American public several years later. Costa-Gavras read the book intently. Then, on 21 April 1967, less than a week after his departure from Greece, the country was politically and psychologically paralyzed by the coup of a group of approximately fifty of the military. Sensing some type of causal connection between the assassination and the arrival of the junta, Costa-Gavras decided that this must be the raw material for his next work. Dorfmann and Javal released the director from his obligation to shoot the film in prospect, *Le Fils* with Yves

76

Montand, a task undertaken a few years later by Pierre Granier-Deferre. The producers did not forget their contract that easily, and later asked Costa-Gavras to do *The Confession*.

Costa-Gavras's first step was to obtain the rights to adapt the novel *Z*. Vassilikos, who loved his country deeply, was already in self-imposed exile, in Rome and then later in Paris. When Costa-Gavras met with the novelist, they agreed that Costa-Gavras transpose the novel to the screen. The writer knew Costa-Gavras's earlier films and also had great trust in the Greek-born director's sensitivity to the subject. Because of his origins and personal political embattlements in his youth, Costa-Gavras felt closer to the material than would a foreign cineaste with more film experience. He then received the rights to make a documentary as well as a fiction film on the assassination, for at this early stage he was uncertain which direction he would take; he would always have the possibility of another film later on, if it was financially feasible.

When Costa-Gavras first read the novel given to him by his brother, it made a dramatic impact upon him. He saw here that Vassilikos took the historical event of May 1963 and lyricized it. Costa-Gavras would develop the death of Lambrakis even further. To appreciate the nuances of the novel and the film, it is fundamental to observe the evolution of events that led up to the assassination and the government cover-up.

Historical Background

Most outsiders have only a romanticized or classical view of Greece—that of a tourist's utopia where one listens to bazooki music, takes boat trips to the islands, or basks in the sun, sea, and ouzo; or that of a scholar's paradise, with the historical monuments, priceless icons, and precious manuscripts in this cradle of democracy. Fewer in number are those who have taken time to penetrate the other strata of Greek society—commerce, internal politics, and international relations. Since World War II, the political tension in the country, and especially with the government itself, increased with the growth of communism.[1] Former resistance members on the Left, like Costa-Gavras's father and the militant musician Mikis Theodorakis, always faced the danger of going to prison for their political views. On the Right, it appears that many pro-Nazi collaborators had a tendency to enter the domain of law and order, in either the police or the armed forces. The stubbornly held political beliefs of Left and Right polarized the Greek politicians as well as the citizens, and this tension continued until recently except for a brief calm in the 1950s.

From World War II to the filming of *Z* in 1968, there were more than forty changes of government, and each ruling body had to decide upon the necessary force or political strategy to utilize in order to maintain its position of power. Early in the 1960s, a new form of political consciousness was developing in Greece, manifest in a concern about the right-wing government in office under Constantine Karamanlis. A deputy and leader in the opposition party, the communist-oriented Union of the Democratic Left (EDA), Gregory Lambrakis was reportedly a politician in no one's pocket. Although of the Left and sympathetic to the communist cause, he differed with some of the policies of the Soviet Union. He equally opposed American involvement in Greek affairs. According to Costa-Gavras's implications in the film, this opposition would be one of the underlying reasons for his assassination.

Since the end of World War II, American and Greek relations were very close. The British, once deeply committed to Greece politically and economically, eventually abandoned their financial investment in the fight against communism. President Truman quickly responded to the challenge of preventing the octopus of the Soviet Union from wrapping its tentacles around yet another unsuspecting country and offered immediate aid to Greece in March 1947. An Agency for International Development report indicates that between 1946 and 1970, American economic aid to Greece amounted to $1,887 million, while military aid reached $2,020 million.[2] Both figures are significant, but especially that of military assistance. Pauline A. Mian, analyst in Western European Affairs, offers a background to the reason that outspoken pacifists in the Greek Parliament such as Lambrakis were against American involvement:

> The links between the U.S. and Greece have grown stronger since Greece became a member of NATO in 1952. The United States has provided military assistance to enable Greece to improve its defense posture and meet its NATO commitments. In return, Greece has made available installations and facilities considered vital to U.S. and NATO forces in the Eastern Mediterranean.[3]

The Greek government in general was in agreement with the direction in which this relationship was developing and welcomed the technical advantages of such collaboration. Lambrakis and others did not share these sentiments.

Lambrakis was a true humanitarian. He had a dream. His plan was to build a brave new world not with bombs but with medicine and education. Besides manifesting his concern about possible nuclear holocaust through the build-up of arms—as seen in the protests in *Z* against the American polaris missile base in Salonika—as a doctor he contributed his service twice a week to the poor before becoming a deputy. He was also associate professor at the Athens Medical College. On 21 April 1963, less than a month before his death, with parliamentary immunity he made a peace march from Marathon to Athens with a few colleagues. Other doctors were intimidated by the authorities and did not participate. He primarily believed in parliamentary procedures, although he did not hesitate to defy the law. The authorities were deeply troubled that with his background as a popular figure (athletic hero of the Balkan Games), incorruptible politician, committed man of medicine, and outspoken, daring leader, he and the United Democratic Left might win the next elections. They believed in taking the necessary measures to prevent this from happening especially since it would endanger international relations.

On 22 May 1963, Gregory Lambrakis, with the assistance of the Friends of Peace, organized an antinuclear rally in Salonika, the second largest city after Athens, and protested the presence of American missiles in the country. It was a double protest in fact, for the demonstration was scheduled on the same evening that the Bolshoi Ballet was performing in the city. Lambrakis wanted to highlight the ambiguity of the government rapport with the Soviet Union—on one hand the officials and royal family fostered cultural ties with the U.S.S.R., but on the other hand, were ferociously combating the communists since the end of World War II. Lambrakis would like to have seen Greece freed from the domination of communist and capitalist blocs.

After speaking at the rally, Lambrakis was blackjacked by a figure in a moving vehicle. His skull was crushed. Other pacifists involved in the demonstration were allegedly hit with crowbars. Another deputy was brutally bludgeoned during the counterdemonstration. For Lambrakis, it was a 100-hour struggle for life. He died on 25 May without regaining consciousness. The funeral cortege of close to 400,000 mourners followed the slain political idealist to his grave. The authorities were quick to refer to the incident as "an unfortunate traffic accident." The driver of the small three-wheel vehicle, Spyros Gotzamanis, was arrested shortly after the demonstration, while his accomplice, Emanuel Emanouelidis, was arrested a few days later. Opposition leader George Papandreou publicly accused President Karamanlis for being morally responsible for this incident. The authorities appointed an examining magistrate, Christos Sartzetakis, to appease those who protested. The officials felt that they could manipulate the young Sartzetakis, but were sorely mistaken. When he began to study the accident, he discovered that something was amiss. He learned the act was premeditated and carried out through the assistance of an extreme right-wing organization controlled by the authorities. The investigation covered all the evidence, but witnesses to the "accident" would disappear mysteriously. A wounded deputy, Piroukas, "died of a heart attack," officials said. Others sympathetic to the Lambrakis cause were deported to the islands. The trial lasted from October 1966 to September 1968, almost two years. The general came to trial armed with a pistol, threatening suicide. Only the two civilians received sentences—Gotzamanis, to eleven and a half years and Emanouelidis, to eight and a half years in a farm prison, where each year counts double. The officers involved in the cover-up were released from their positions, but not prosecuted, and were rehabilitated in September 1968.[4]

The conservative government of Constantine Karamanlis fell on 11 June 1963. The Center Left of George Papandreou assumed the power, but by an arbitrary act. The king removed the government. On 21 April 1967, a core of colonels and other army officers organized a bloodless coup and seized the government, closed the airport, took control of the radio, and arrested opposition and resistance. Former Premier Karamanlis went into exile, where he remained until he was sworn in as prime minister in July 1974. During the military regime under George Papadopoulos with former Prosecutor-General Kollias as president of the council, General Mitsou and Colonel Kamoutsis of the gendarmerie, once relieved of their duties, were cleared of all charges and rehabilitated by government decree. Judge Sartzetakis was no longer allowed to practice law and was arrested, evoking a sharp cry of protest from French lawyers. It was only after the Cyprus crisis in the summer of 1974 that he was restored as appellate judge.

Confronted with the assassination and cover-up, various individuals and groups, as expected, reacted differently. The Lambrakis Youth Movement, an arm of the United Democratic Left with membership hovering around 50,000, took up the cause of the dead deputy and offered resistance. These Antigone-like youths were crying out for justice against their powerful Creons. The musician Mikis Theodorakis led the organization as president and himself took an active part in the resistance to the government which brought about his arrest and imprisonment following the coup. The United States took a wait-and-see attitude after the junta came to power, temporarily cut back on arms sales, and then resumed military aid in September 1970, during Richard Nixon's presidency.

Z—The Novel

When the thirty-year-old Vassilis Vassilikos was in the process of writing his novel Z, based on the assassination of Lambrakis, he had access to more than 5,000 pages of the investigation.[5] He had relative freedom to examine this material during the Papandreou government, for the colonels had not yet come to power. From the immediate aftermath of the incident through the first stage of the trial, Vassilikos committed himself to his art. He was well prepared to paint an icon of Z that would not fade.

Raised in Salonika, he possessed an intimate knowledge of the city and the details involved in the assassination plot. As a member of the Lambrakis Youth Movement, he had a partisan perspective; in conscience he could not side with those in authority. With his experience in law and journalism he readily understood and communicated the political nuances of the affair. For Vassilikos, the cause of Lambrakis took on a special hope for future justice.

Vassilikos published Z in Greece in 1966 with the Themelio Press while the trial was still in progress.[6] Although remaining true to the details, he had to fictionalize the material in order to publish it. He changed the names of the characters involved in the conspiracy and created a montage of these individuals' thoughts and actions. The transposition resulted in a toned-down, lyrical version of the unfortunate "accident." The form that the novel took was poeticized fiction, highly stylized, for Vassilikos was partially influenced by the French New Novelists. Michel Butor was his professor at the French *lycée* at Salonika, and left his literary imprint on the Greek author. With Z, Vassilikos did not create artificial barriers between politics, journalism, and poetry. Instead, his purpose was to go further in order to create poetic fiction with a sound basis in reality. Politically, he explains his primary intention in *Le Monde* for 29 May 1969:

> An imperious priority orders me to unmask the evil that reigns in my country, to express myself in the name of those reduced to silence, to alert the others, those innumerable optimists who, falsely, believe that they benefit from fascism.[7]

When the reader confronts the literary version of the crime, he or she is struck by the curious blend of concrete historical fact with lyric poetry that simultaneously evokes a response of anger at the authorities and sorrow for the widow and the disciples of the slain deputy Z, as he is referred to in the novel. To recreate the assassination of Z, Vassilikos arranged his material in five parts: "An Evening in May from 7:30 to 10:30," "A Train Whistles in the Night," "After the Earthquake," "Apologias," and "One Year Later."

Scenario

Once Vassilikos consented to Costa-Gavras's directing the film, the next important question was "Who would write the scenario for this political intrigue?" The novelist would have been the perfect person to do it, but he declined since he was still caught up in the literary forms of novel and poetry, a far cry from the technical precision and compartmentalization necessary in drafting a scenario.

Costa-Gavras turned to the screenwriter who had worked extremely closely with Resnais in *La Guerre est finie*, Jorge Semprun, the Spanish-born literary militant, working in Paris. Semprun acknowledged that his work with the French director had prepared him more than adequately for this undertaking. Vassilikos's characterization of the noble, stoic hero; his techniques of flashback to indicate constant shifts of chronological order; his support of a political cause on the Left—all of these elements soon reappeared but modified under the pen of Semprun. United Artists financed the new collaboration. For reconstructing the basic material that inspired Vassilikos, Costa-Gavras went to the Institut d'Etudes Politiques in Paris to document the trial. At first he thought that the novelist had invented the string of incredible characters. There, however, in a liberal Greek journal, he found the proceedings of the trial, with a day-by-day description of the actual investigation. With this supportive evidence concerning the early phase of the trial, he was able to develop detailed characterization for his film.[8]

For two and a half months Costa-Gavras and Jorge Semprun struggled over the scenario. Each character and event that they resurrected had a basis in reality. Semprun and Costa-Gavras had a significant advantage over the novelist. They had a better historical perspective a few years after the publication of the novel, and could interpret the events in light of the April 1967 coup. The form that the scenario and film took was that of political fiction as opposed to political documentary.[9] The account of the assassination would be well documented but also dramatized to attract a larger viewing public. At times the results of the collaboration of Semprun and Costa-Gavras bordered on the semidocumentary, especially in the highly researched detail seen in the final part of the film. Costa-Gavras and Semprun later insisted that they tried to show what was essential to revealing the political mechanisms at work and therefore dropped accidental or accessory material. In the film there are few traces of the lyricism of the original novel, although Vassilikos would defend the poetry of the visual image, stating that one tear in the eye of the widow on the screen could be the equivalent of four pages of text. Nor does the reader of the script or film spectator witness the novelist's powerful philosophical and religious musings about death and liberty.

Despite these so-called deficiencies, the director and screenwriter were able to capture the *état d'âme* or psychic state of the soul of their characters.

The two collaborators moreover developed striking continuity between isolated events that later formed into tragic patterns. In a two-hour action film they carefully and honestly condensed the lengthy novel—376 pages in the English translation. They extended the parameters of the literary text which concludes with the opening of the trial. The film thus covered the four years from the event through the military junta and through the conclusion of the trial.

As the director and screenwriter planned their film, politics were already in the air. Godard's *La Chinoise* made the prophecy of the forthcoming May 1968 upheaval in Paris, as we said earlier. In the process of writing the screenplay, the creators of *Z* wanted to give their material about a local assassination in Greece a much broader application. They thus fabricated a political parable with application to any totalitarian country, be it Brazil, Argentina, or Franco's Spain. Semprun wanted to alert the viewer to this global phenomenon: "Let us not try to reassure ourselves, this type of thing doesn't only happen elsewhere, it happens everywhere.[10] Moreover, instead of the usual disclaimer that correspondence to any person or event seen in the film is coincidental, they claim the opposite at the outset of the film: "Any similarity to actual events or persons living or dead is not coincidental. It is intentional." Allusion to the Greek political scene is there, but the film also opens up recently closed wounds inflicted on people by the assassination of the Kennedy brothers, Malcolm X, Ben Barka, Humberto Delgado, Patrice Lumumba, and Enrico Mattei, names mentioned by Costa-Gavras as if in a litany of saints. The intention of Semprun and Costa-Gavras was to make a courageous plea for liberty and human dignity on the international scale.

The collaborators originally felt that they wanted to take the raw material and make of it a suspense-filled story showing first the murder and the hunt for the criminals, then finally the discovery of how vast the political plot really was.[11] They included an original subtitle to define their study further: "The Anatomy of a Political Assassination," recalling the Otto Preminger film greatly appreciated by Costa-Gavras, *The Anatomy of a Murder* (1959). Eventually they dropped the subtitle and simply kept the more enigmatic final letter of the alphabet to represent the fact that the deputy lives on after his death. Following the assassination of the deputy, Greek students wrote "Z" on every wall and street corner for the third person singular of the verb for to be alive, *zei*, or *he lives!* Semprun and Costa-Gavras decided moreover to take the Vassilikos novel and film it almost in chronological order, and allow flashbacks to reveal the necessary material of the past. These flashbacks help characterize the persons involved and give political color to the government machinery in the assassination plot.

The novel provides a large fresco of characters carefully designed by Vassilikos. Semprun had to eliminate some of them in order to be able to concentrate on the unethical apparatus functioning under the guise of legitimate power. He fused some characters into one, for example, the journalist. In the text there are several mentioned who played out their part in the 1963 tragedy.

They represented the omniscient, probing media that helped bring to light the conspiracy. In the scenario Semprun consolidated them into a journalist/photographer who assumed the functions of the vast troupe of courageous and outspoken reporters.

To make the film action-oriented, the dialogue had to be clear and precise. As in the adaptation of *Shock Troops*, many of the longer discourses that could slow down the pace of the film were eliminated. Rich allusions of a religious, classical, or philosophical nature also fell by the wayside. The accelerated camera action broke up those which were retained. According to Costa-Gavras and Semprun, some of the dialogue also had a contemporary political ring to it, for the two artists wanted not only to show the universality discussed above, but also to have some direct bearing on the events of the present-day reality, at that time, 1969— the military government in Greece. History and actuality thus merge under the skillful pen of the screenwriter. By the time the crew got to filming on location in Algeria, the director was also able to evoke something of the May 1968 events in Paris. The student-police confrontation in *Z* harks back to these events, for example, the caricature of the police cutting the hair of students. In Greece in the 1960s such slogans as "Homosexuals back to Peking" and other anti-Left catch-words were already being bantered about.

Just a few years prior to writing the scenario, an exiled African leader in Switzerland was lured to Paris, where he was executed by his opponents. This was the Ben Barka case alluded to earlier which fascinated the director and screenwriter, and later inspired Yves Boisset's *The French Conspiracy*. Many of the Parisian critics and public watching *Z* instinctively associated it with the Ben Barka execution, while the American critics and public could not help but relive the Kennedy assassinations. Clarifying his purpose in making *Z*, Costa-Gavras pinpointed his choice of the available material dealing with assassinations in the 1960s:

> The main reason for making *Z* was my Greek origins, of course. I can't see how anyone without those origins could possibly have made such a film. I had been concerned about the Lambrakis murder ever since it occurred in 1963, but after the military coup of 1967, I wanted to do something concrete against the dictatorship. I had also been troubled by the murder of Ben Barka in Paris during the fall of 1965. There were many parallels with Greek events, but the Lambrakis murder had all the classic elements of political conspiracy posed most clearly. It had the police complicity, the disappearance of key witnesses, corruption in government—all those kinds of things. There was the additional question of the way some men make culprits of others. Most important for me was that the Lambrakis affair had a conclusion. There was a trial which produced concrete testimony and evidence. This was not so in the case of Ben Barka or some of the assassinations in the United States.[12]

These assassinations were seen as part of a global picture of political conspiracy and would significantly influence the scriptwriters.

Costa-Gavras and Semprun did not wish the film to become sentimental, so they eliminated some of the actual events that would recall the Kennedy assassinations. For American readers of *Z*, for example, the solemn train cortege of the deputy's body from Salonika to Athens furnished a sad parallel to the Robert F. Kennedy escort from Washington to New York in 1968. Costa-Gavras may have wanted to recreate this powerful experience, but the financing of 400,000 or 500,000 extras to record it as it actually happened would not have been feasible. In the filmmakers' estimation this material also lies outside of the scope of developing the political intricacies of the crime. John F. Kennedy sent a telegram of condolence to the widow of Lambrakis, but the director and screenwriter chose not to include this note in the film since Kennedy himself would be dead exactly one-half year later. From the historical events they dropped the general's threat of suicide with a pistol at the trial. This would make the authorities look even more ludicrous than they appear in the film. Some of the anti-Semitic incidents were omitted, although these slogans were shouted by the demonstrators against the Friends of Peace. In the film, the general also was wont to make anti-Semitic remarks. When asked by a journalist, following the deposition, if he were a victim of injustice like Dreyfus, the general replied, suffering from faulty history or deliberate anti-Semitic conviction, "Dreyfus was guilty!"

When Vassilis Vassilikos read the scenario, he was completely satisfied with Semprun's work. He felt that the screenwriter had scrupulously respected the tone and character of the original literary piece while simultaneously injecting the creative note required by an adaptation to another medium. When the film finally made the history of the assassination come alive, the effect was a moving pointillist painting of finely placed dashes and colors of novel, script, and celluloid.

Plot

Costa-Gavras arrived at a political consciousness-raising, action film using this script and making certain modifications in the course of the filming in order to update the political statement. Although the film was first subtitled an *anatomy* of a political assassination, its plot unfolds more like that of an *ancient Greek tragedy*, in which blind Fate is the only victor.

Prelude—The Assemblies of the Right and the Left

The tragedy begins with a government meeting in an undesignated country. An undersecretary of agriculture (Bob de Bragelonne) describes the need to take precise measures to prevent mildew in the vines, boring his captive audience with irrelevant details about farming. Planes dropping flyers will help inform the farmers about the means to control this problem. Borrowing the same terminology, the general of the gendarmerie (Pierre Dux) shows that the real mildew that must be combatted and prevented is ideological. The growing mildew of communism is caused by lethal germs and parasitic agents that must be eliminated at all costs, nipping the problem in the bud—during adolescence, university training, and military service. The conference terminates on this note.

In the meantime, the committee members of the Friends of Peace, Manuel (Charles Denner), Matt (Bernard Fresson) and Pierre (Jean-Pierre Miquel), a pacifist group with leftist orientation, are refused one hall after another for their meeting. The authorities have pressured the proprietors into refusing. Even the procurator (François Perier)—the equivalent of a district attorney or public prosecutor—appears helpless and ineffective. The organizers still have no meeting place when Z, the deputy-doctor (Yves Montand) arrives from the capital. At police headquarters the colonel, the head of security (Julien Guiomar), condescends to offer them an absurdly minuscule union hall with seating for 150 to 200 persons.

The first dose of preventive medicine aimed at the ideological mildew is directed at a handful of Friends of Peace who are leafletting in preparation for the assembly that evening. The leader of the extreme right-wing group CROC (Combattants Royalistes de l'Occident Chrétien—Royalist Combatants of the Christian West) sends his lackeys to break up the orderly group of youth. It is only a foretaste of the blind and brutal force of CROC. It will become more apparent that evening during the major rally, scheduled for the same time as the Bolshoi Ballet's performance of *Romeo and Juliet*.

That night the young journalist/photographer (Jacques Perrin) chooses to cover the demonstration instead of the cultural event and becomes an objective witness to rightist oppression of the nonviolent demonstrators of the Friends of Peace. As Z leaves his hotel to attend the meeting, he is struck from behind, staggers, and barely makes it to the hall. He summons up the necessary courage and energy to address the assembled partisans. Calmly and deliberately, he points out the need for nuclear disarmament, for the transfer of military funding to the construction of hospitals and schools, and for PEACE among all peoples.

Act One—The Assassination

The general, in civilian clothes, does not wish to put down the bloodthirsty rightist counterdemonstrators. The furor of the crowd swells. As Z leaves the hall, he is struck by a light three-wheeled vehicle crazily driven by Yago (Renato Salvatori) with Vago (Marcel Bozzufi) riding in the rear. The procurator is alerted to the "accident" as the ballet ends and initiates the investigation since the incident could have grave political repercussions. To the case he appoints a young examining magistrate, a type of criminal investigator (Jean-Louis Trintignant).

While the unconscious Z is being operated on by specialists, the general obtains from the authorities' carefully kept files/dossiers on the committee members of the Friends of Peace. He systematically attacks their communist and Semitic backgrounds. When Z dies, the autopsy reveals that his skull was crushed by a blow from a solid object. For his wife, Hélène (Irene Papas), it is a deep psychological blow. She cannot be easily consoled. The general in the meantime becomes infuriated that the magistrate has taken things into his own hands in ordering an autopsy.

Z: Members of the fascist organization CROC disrupt a peaceful demonstration. *(Permission of Cinema 5 Ltd.)*

Act Two—The Investigation

The examining magistrate methodically gathers his data from bystanders. The real witnesses are harassed, or mysteriously die. The false witnesses are legion, all carefully agreeing to each other's alibi. We are in a viper's tangle. The ambitious journalist, with objective proof from photographs, assembles sufficient evidence to demonstrate that the accident was indeed an assassination. Difficult to destroy, however, is the many-handed Hydra—of CROC, fascist leaders, henchmen, the colonel and the general, army, and police. With the aid of the docker Dumas (Guy Mairesse), the journalist builds up a sizable dossier on the organization which he then hands over to the examining magistrate. With this incriminating information, the magistrate picks holes in the testimony of the authorities and false witnesses, but not without pressure from the higher authorities to abandon the case. He persists at the risk of losing his position.

Act Three—Deposition and Trial

With a brilliant display of intelligence and sangfroid, the magistrate inculpates all those involved in the assassination game from the pawns to the major pieces of the plot. The photographs of the journalist provide a basis for the investigator's conclusions. The guilty police and military officials storm from the magistrate's office.

The results of the trial are broadcast on television by the journalist. The deputy public prosecutor who worked closely with the magistrate "died" of a heart attack, according to official reports. Seven other persons died and could not testify—death by automobile accident, suicide, gas explosion, and so on. Yago was sentenced to eleven years in a farm prison where each year counts as double, and Vago to eight years under the same conditions. The four officers involved were given sanctions that were not publicly revealed.

Epilogue—Reactions and Interdictions

With the citizens highly disturbed by the comportment of the corrupt authorities, the government resigned. A few weeks before the elections, the military took over the government and released the examining magistrate from his functions. Georges Pirou (Jean Bouise), the deputy wounded in the melee, died of an embolism, stated the police. Matt, committee member of the Friends of Peace, was deported to the islands; Manuel died when he fell from the seventh floor, attempting to escape, said the police. The journalist himself received four

Z: The deputy (Yves Montand) with his assistants Manuel (Charles Denner) and Pierre (Jean-Pierre Miquel) during the antinuclear rally.
(Permission of Cinema 5 Ltd.)

years in prison (three years according to the published script) for having distributed official documents. The real blow to freedom comes as the list of interdictions set by the military appears on the screen:

Euripides	Modern music/Popular music (Mikis
Sophocles	Theodorakis)
Long hair, miniskirts	Freedom of the Press
Lurçat	Sociology
Tolstoy	The Bar Association
Mark Twain (in	Beatles/Albee
part)	New Math
Russian-style toasts	Writing that Socrates was homosexual
Aragon, Trotsky	Learning Bulgarian
Labor Unions	Gorki, Dostoevski
Ionesco, Sartre	Peace movements
Learning Russian	And the letter Z, which means, HE
Beckett	LIVES![13]

Filming

For almost a year and a half a string of producers turned down the script of
Semprun and Costa-Gavras. United Artists, which had originally intended that
Costa-Gavras make two or three more films with them (after *Shock Troops*), and
had offered the director advance funding for the scriptwriting, refused the
scenario. The work was too political. On one hand, they feared the usual "box-
office poison" that repels the general public. Alfred Hitchcock shared the same
sentiments with Montand when the actor turned him down for *Topaz* to make *Z*.
Hitchcock felt this type of political film would not interest anyone. On the other
hand, the producers expressed concern that all United Artists films would be
banned in Greece. Diplomatically they turned down the production. Warner
Brothers, Columbia, and Twentieth Century–Fox followed suit. In France,
Gaumont would not undertake the risks either. Costa-Gavras said the Italians
were afraid of handling this political dynamite, the Yugoslavs refused, the
Rumanians never answered his request.

In the meantime, in order to have more leverage with the financing companies, Costa-Gavras drew up a profile on each potential actor and actress for
the production. Montand, Papas, Perier, and Trintignant would be good drawing cards. These players agreed to participate in the film, yet by the fall of 1967
Costa-Gavras did not have a producer. He kept the actors informed of the delays
and promised to include them if a producer came through with the funding. On
the verge of abandoning the project, he spoke with Jacques Perrin, to whom he
promised the role of the journalist. Perrin was just assuming the directorship of
Reggane Films, already eight years old. If possible, he would use *Z* as publicity
for the new management and direction of the company. As a final possibility for
raising money, Perrin said he would try to request funding from the Algerians,
whose industry had become independent six months earlier and had already

made financial commitments to eight films. The Algerian company read the scenario and within three days agreed to co-produce *Z*.

With an advance from the Centre National du Cinéma in Paris and financial backing from Hercule Mucchielli, distributor of Valoria Films, and other French sources, Perrin was able to help raise approximately $750,000 for the film. It was the Algerians who rescued the film and also provided invaluable aid in its production. Costa-Gavras explained the Algerian assistance in this way:

> They didn't give much money but they helped with extras and in giving us locations. It may seem strange that a semi-police state like Algeria would allow us to make such a film. Perhaps it was partly luck. They didn't know the film would be so good or so popular. They wanted to have good rapport with the French intellectuals. They want to show that they are the most advanced Arab nation in the Mediterranean. I want to make it very clear, however, that if they had not taken part in the production, *Z* probably would not have been made.[14]

Algeria was the best site for the production, Costa-Gavras believed, since, for the most part, it resembled the climate and geography of Greece. Although *Z* was filmed in North Africa, right from the outset the viewer senses that the film really deals with political repression in Greece. There are specific clues to the identity of Greece: a sign for FIX beer; the deputy's arrival on Olympia airlines; a picture of the king and queen of Greece; the Theodorakis music in the background; the ban on his music in the epilogue. There are references to people deported to the islands. The camera passes by a portrait of the communist Nikos Belloyannis, a Greek political hero executed in 1952. Greece is never mentioned, nor is Athens. All references are deliberately kept vague and universal— "national interests" or "the capital."

Costa-Gavras began filming *Z* on 31 July 1968. He used Quai de Brest in the port of Algiers for some of the locations. Once there, he had to simplify some of his elaborate ideas because of the physical and financial conditions of production. Yet the director did not want to resort to stock shots or newsreels of the funeral or of demonstrations. For twelve nights the intersection of Place Maurice Audin in Algiers was closed off to traffic. During the Left/Right clash, the participants got very involved in the reenactment, which resulted in serious injuries at times. The uniforms worn by the military were a compromise between the NATO forces and the Greek military. There were some difficulties using women as extras, for Arab women could not pass before the camera.

For seven and a half weeks Costa-Gavras and his crew filmed in Algeria. Ten more days of interiors at the Paris studio were necessary to complete the filming. Despite its complexity, the production went more or less according to schedule.

Actors and Characterization

The troupe of actors who agreed to work with Costa-Gavras on the film was impressive. The director told Gérard Langlois of *Les Lettres Françaises* of his concept of actors: "And so, if the film is a kind of circle, the actors are the radii [*rayons*] which converge at the center."[15] As in *The Sleeping Car Murder,* the actors participated in the financing of the film and shared in the receipts.

Yves Montand worked prodigiously in 1968–69 making *Z, Un Soir, un train,* and *Le Diable par le queue.* In *Z,* he plays the stoic deputy who appears in the early part of the film, is assassinated, and reappears in intermittent flashbacks. Poise, dignity, and courage characterize his leadership and dialogue with the officials. Like his predecessor, Socrates, he is accused of introducing new gods (pacifist goals) and corrupting youth (especially leftist university students). In the role of the assassinated deputy, Montand said he felt like Kennedy entering Dallas. Costa-Gavras responded thus to a question concerning the choice of Montand for the principal role:

> I knew from the beginning that Montand was the only one who could play Lambrakis. . . . Today political figures are as well-known as stars, and we had to have someone with whom audiences could immediately identify. Neither Montand nor I was bothered by the fact that he would have to be killed early in the movie.[16]

Jean-Louis Trintignant was already known internationally for *A Man and a Woman* (1966), *Is Paris Burning?* (1966) and *Trans-Europ-Express* (1967). *Z* would crown his acting career of the late 1960s. Peering from behind tinted glasses, Trintignant is objective and calculating as the incorruptible examining magistrate. He cannot be intimidated by the Left or the Right. Costa-Gavras describes his character in this manner: "At any point he was free to halt his investigation. He was quite crucial to the exposé of the police. He was a man of the Right, a man of the Establishment, but he was an honest man." This criminal investigator who becomes central to the second half of the film and takes up the torch from Lambrakis after his assassination has a crystal soul; but it is unbreakable.

Irene Papas, after playing many classical roles in theater and film, incarnates the grief-stricken widow of Z with extreme emotion. Many Americans saw in Papas some vestige of Jackie Kennedy after the presidential assassination. Costa-Gavras discusses with Guy Flatley her affiliation with the film:

> It was also tremendously important for me to have Irene Papas in Z. She is the only Greek in the cast, you know, and she is used as a symbol of Greek suffering. Irene is passionately opposed to the military regime. She was at the funeral of Lambrakis. And she is a great friend of Mikis Theodorakis.[17]

Jacques Perrin at twenty-seven had already made approximately twenty films, some in Italy, and many in France with such directors as Marcel Camus *(Vivre la nuit)* and Costa-Gavras *(The Sleeping Car Murder* and *Shock Troops).* As the reporter/photographer, he appears more ambitious and solicitous of accumulating sensational material than of fighting for the cause of justice. He is opportunistic and aggressive. His tactics are unethical as he mercilessly invades the privacy of the grieving widow. In one sense this journalist is a young, socratic gadfly who dares to provoke the authorities by exposing the gangrenous elements of political life in the country. In another, he is the chorus of a Greek tragedy—identifying characters, clarifying issues, and discussing the motivation of certain individuals.

Charles Denner worked with Costa-Gavras in *The Sleeping Car Murder,* in which he played Bob, the cynical mocker of the police. In *Z,* as the deputy's right-hand man, Manuel, he is no lover of authority and is almost eliminated in the sensational car chase supposedly arranged by the powers that be to prevent him from continuing his pursuit of justice. Denner plays well the high-powered, tempestuous committee member of the Friends of Peace. Manuel is half-Jewish, so he is referred to by the general as the worst kind of Jew: Half-Jews feel themselves superior to the Jews, observes the officer. Aside from the Dreyfus allusion at the end of the film, there are only a few references to Jews, whereas the anti-Russian ones abound, especially in the mouth of the general. During the filming of *Z,* Costa-Gavras, who originally related closely with the idealistic Z, gradually began to identify with the lawyer Manuel. Costa-Gavras felt that Manuel was more realistic and enterprising in his approach to life and politics.

Marcel Bozzufi plays Vago, the person who actually strikes the deputy. Vago is a sinister creature, as his eccentric mannerisms, his brutality, and his lecherousness reflect. He is a rabid anticommunist, pederast, and manipulator. A pawn in the corrupt system, he will be destroyed by it. He must accept a prison term while high-ranking officials manage to escape the sanctions of justice. The character of Vago may appear to reek of exaggeration in the film, yet the director stated that he and Semprun actually had to tone down the other worse characteristics of the real individual in order to make him more credible. It was important that they depict him as a homosexual, said Costa-Gavras, for this makes him the lackey of the police, who could readily manipulate him.

The spectator quickly grasps the true nature of Julien Guiomar as the head of security. The colonel incarnates evil as only his beady eyes appear over the top of the large red dossier during his encounter with the Friends of Peace. To accomplish his dirty work, he bribes his pawns with a license or a truck. He is another key link in the chain of responsibility for the assassination of Z and the subsequent cover-up.

Renato Salvatori has acted in both Italian and French films over the past two decades. As Yago, he embodies the scum of society. Yago is trapped by the police. He has to pay for his small pickup truck and will resort to anything to own it finally. For this reason he belongs to the para-state security corps of CROC with the likes of Vago.

François Perier as the public prosecutor portrays the character as outside the system of the assassination plot yet uncomfortably caught between his superiors in the capital and the local army officials. He falls prey to the more powerful corrupt forces at the close of the film.

All of these secondary characters are extremely important in the casting. One would think that the stars, the big names, would be able to carry the production alone. Costa-Gavras feels that these minor characters add indispensable depth to a work, and that the director should not cut expenses by using weak actors in these roles.

Once these major or minor characters are set in motion on the screen in *Z*, after a few moments they are almost immediately recognized—on the side of good (leftist, humanist, idealist) or on the side of evil (authoritative, racist, deceptive, brutal). Some of this polarizing, of course, is drawn from the novel as well as the actual historical situation. Costa-Gavras nonetheless further provides each individual with characteristic colors that would identify the person quickly and precisely, and with some depth. Designating someone with easily recognized lines for rapid identification has its disadvantages. Some critics feel that it is too obvious a play, and that it is a black-and-white or Manichean perception of characters, as we noted in chapter 2. Without additional nuances, this manner of stereotyping abuses the intelligence of the viewer. In *Z* there is no need for characters to wear white hats or black hats as in the traditional western. Character shaping has evolved greatly since the birth of western film, yet the stereotyping seen in *Z* is on occasion similarly trite. The simplification of the actors' essential characteristics in the film tend to reduce the depth of the work and to discourage further discussion after the screening. In *Z*, the target set up by the director and screenwriter is wide, an enemy that is generally typed as salacious, fat, balding, fascist, sharp-featured, or ugly. The enemy is automatically reduced to a lower level of existence. Costa-Gavras nonetheless believes that he has portrayed these individuals, especially the rightists ones, in a realistic and non-stereotypical manner. The Right in the film was evil because that was how it was in Greece, he insists, in fact ten times worse.[18]

However, the characterization borders on caricature at times. The director portrays the CIA agents as lurking behind dark glasses, having close-cropped hair, constantly watching the Friends of Peace either from behind the cover of *Look* magazine or, in an American Ford of the 1950s, following Z and his disciples. The same caricaturing occurs during the meeting of the Friends of Peace with the colonel at police headquarters. The colonel peers suspiciously over the dossier at the intruding pacifists.

To direct our sympathies toward the deputy Z, Costa-Gavras utilizes the traditional cinematic device of apotheosis.[19] Z's character is streamlined. The hero wears a nontarnishable halo. His triumphal arrival at the airport is supported by rich, emotional music; his disciples surround him; he greets the masses, who are in awe of him.

Generally speaking, each actor and actress handles his or her part admirably, being concerned about the individual role as well as the overall effect of the film. In some cases the characters they play are stereotypes; that is the way they appear in the novel. Besides the obviously good and evil characters, there is a whole level of other individuals who cannot easily be classed or typed. There is a witness Nick (Georges Géret), whose only real concern is soccer, but who feels he must do his duty as a citizen and report what he knows about the assassination plot. His sister, played by Magali Noël, is married to a rightist and depends on his position and politics to survive. They are legion who must please the unprincipled police in order to receive a license for their business. The careful orchestration of all these characters in the film gives it a sociopolitical dimension, for it reveals all those involved in the political machinations as well as those who innocently fall victim to it.

Tone/Technique

Through the performance of the actors and by elaborate cinematic technique, Costa-Gavras is able to play his cinematic instrument simultaneously in several registers. From the viewer he evokes strong reactions that are far from neutral. The spectator senses anger and hostility toward the various forms of repression set in motion by the legitimate authorities. When the deputy disembarks from the plane, there is an aura of exaltation—the saving hero is in our midst! The ensuing assassination quickly produces pity and fear in the filmgoer—pity for the innocent sufferer who is caught in a web of conspiracy, and fear that this could become more widespread and encompass the spectator with it. When the authorities are challenged, the viewer breathes a sigh of relief that justice has been at last meted out—a true catharsis—only to be quickly struck in the face with further corruption. The epilogue proves that truth and justice do not always prevail, and the viewer is abandoned by Costa-Gavras in a state of shock and frustration.

With this type of playing on different levels and with deliberate shock effect, the director acknowledges some influence from American films of the 1930s and 1940s which have a social thrust. Like Stanley Kubrick in *Dr. Strangelove*, Costa-Gavras combines various genres and approaches. With the western and detective film, *Z* shares their clear and distinct characterization. Basically, good falls on one side of the fence and evil on the other. The concrete facts and the reporting in the last part of the film imply a documentary approach. The occasional grainy shots add historical, factual dimensions to the work, though Costa-Gavras did not revert to total documentary and use newsreels for such events as the deputy's funeral. The anti-Establishment tone of the film, directed primarily at the police, military, and judicial systems, makes it a film of political nature. Caricature, satire, and humorous incident provide a comic, sardonic atmosphere to the work. Gordon Gow of *Films and Filming* calls this aspect of the film "black satire."[20] Like the films of Alfred Hitchcock, *Z* has its moments of suspense, a car chase, and threats that make a psychological thriller of it. The attempt to eliminate Manuel with a car parallels the pursuit of Thornhill (Cary Grant) by a crop-dusting biplane in the solitude of the prairie in Hitchcock's *North by Northwest*. All of these elements from various genres are present in *Z*, yet orchestrated cleverly so that they do not cancel each other out.

Similar to the multiple perspective found in *The Sleeping Car Murder*, *Z* also represents a cubist approach. Each witness recounts his or her vision of the events, coloring them in the telling, while these events are replayed in flashback for the examining magistrate. At every turn, some new detail in the assassination is brought to the viewer's attention and that of the magistrate. The journalist, friends of Z, and the magistrate also have their own perspective which is equally limited, as Andrée Tournès points out in *Jeune Cinéma*.[21] In some respect the result is similar to viewing the Zapruder film of the Kennedy assassination in Dallas screened for the Warren Commission.

Although Costa-Gavras is ultimately responsible for the total production of any of his films, he has to have good technicians, just as an established conductor must have talented musicians performing for him. The photography of Raoul Coutard makes the script come alive and introduces a rich dimension to the film. Coutard's professional link with the New Wave gave him the depth of experience that allowed him to work intimately with the director, but yet permitted something original of his own personality and aesthetics to enter into the compositions. He was no marionette. For *Z* he was to Costa-Gavras what Sven Nykvist was to Bergman. In Coutard's hands the camera not only documents but also vivifies and interprets. It captures, for example, the aesthetic composition created by four or five oval discs on the wall; it meanders about the room, peering at the pictures of the king and queen. With telescopic vision, it watches the landing of Z's plane. Moving frenetically, the camera translates the moments of terror into memorable events, such as the pursuit of Manuel in the city streets. It brings a touch of caricature to the portrayal of the military, zooming in on their ribbon-laden chests or capturing a close-up of the bored colonel picking his teeth with a match at the government meeting. The choice of shots aids in the characterization of the various individuals. In a few the subjective camera becomes the individual, as in the swooning Z with blurry vision, after being struck on the head by a demonstrator en route to the meeting. Through a fish-eye lens the faces of the people surrounding him suddenly become rubbery. With close-ups interspliced with long shots of the demonstration, the photographer and the editor create from the ensemble the effect of the viewer's participation in the fray. Costa-Gavras coordinated the movements of these crowds with a megaphone while Coutard was there to record the situation, deciding along with the director the proper lighting and camera angle. John Simon praises the work of the photographer:

> Raoul Coutard is a magnificent cinematographer, and his work with light and shadow, sunburst and brooding nightscape, treacherously lovely exteriors and morose interiors is always exciting without falling into mere prettiness. The images remain just a little grainy—the true texture of history on film; and there is brilliant use of large expanses of white against which a little black or red or both can work miracles of coloristic poignancy.[22]

At times the camera work may be too self-conscious and destroy the feeling of authenticity. The use of flashbacks, scrupulously structured and restructured during the editing process, can seem to be purely contrived.

Jorge Semprun's penchant for the flashback, dating to his early literary works and to his film collaboration with Alain Resnais, and Costa-Gavras's brilliant use of this technique in *The Sleeping Car Murder* paved the way for its use in *Z*. The flashback visually translates the literary tool used astutely by Vassilikos. Some flashbacks in the film *Z* reveal the past relationship of the deputy and his wife. They add brief, enigmatic material concerning Z's rapport with other women. At certain moments the device helps recount events of the crime as seen by the witnesses. Through flashbacks Z lives longer on the screen, for his assassination takes place early on in the film. If flashbacks are too long, numerous, or complex, an audience becomes lost, bored, or frustrated, something Costa-Gavras knows from experience and from his own reflections on the use of this technique. In Z, the risk was warranted, and Costa-Gavras overcame it. Though the film is slightly convoluted, the quick-paced action in the work is not destroyed.

In the final physical structuring of the flashbacks, Françoise Bonnot was most important. It is a remarkable feat to maintain a serious tone and political depth for Z and still to keep the film action moving at a rapid tempo. The final challenge was to make the ensemble a work of art and not merely entertainment. Her close collaboration with Costa-Gavras helped her to achieve these ideals. Besides the general intricate play of flashbacks throughout the film, several examples of editing furnish striking results. The examining magistrate asks one person a question, but a quick cut switches the spectator to the response by another. It is a brilliant shorthand device. Another quick cut uses darkness as a technical link. Yago is detained by a policeman in the hallway where an automatic time switch casts both into darkness every few minutes. Another quick cut leads the viewer to the shadowy theater and the end of a performance of *Romeo and Juliet*. This type of link relates closely to the dialogue as each of the false witnesses in reporting his description of the events parrots the same contrived expression, "*souple et féroce comme un tigre*," that is, "lithe and fierce as a tiger." The parallel editing during Z's speech rings with tragic irony. The deputy pleads for international peace while outdoors Baroné mercilessly beats Deputy Pirou, mistaking him for Z. Françoise Bonnot's Oscar for editing in 1969 was well deserved and her first work with Costa-Gavras in Z merited her a permanent place on his team.

Music

The musical score provided by Mikis Theodorakis warrants some discussion, for it adds a political and aesthetic dimension to the film. When Theodorakis's close friend Deputy Lambrakis was assassinated in May 1963, the politically committed musician took up the cause. Given his previous anti-fascist activities during the resistance and during the political unrest following World War II, Theodorakis was already *engagé*, or "committed." In 1963, almost twenty years after the war, he drew on his national and international reputation in music and his political consciousness to help organize and head the Lambrakis Youth Movement, a group numbering at one time more than 50,000 who were resisters. Like his colleague, he was elected to parliament to represent the same geographical district, Piraeus. In parliament, as a member of the E.D.A., he continued his quest for political, social, and cultural reforms, as he recounts in his *Journal of Resistance*.[23]

Because of Theodorakis's reaction to rightist oppression, his music was banned by rightist law in January 1966. It was forbidden to be played by army order number 13 following the April 1967 coup. The junta banned all of Theodorakis's works, even those which had no sociopolitical reference. During the military regime, his music could not be played in public, written about in the press, or purchased from record stores.

After the military takeover, Theodorakis went underground, but was arrested in August 1967. He spent five months in prison and then was released in January 1968, only to be forced into exile with his family in the desolate mountain village of Zatouna in central Peloponnesus, once described by Vassilis Vassilikos as a village of thirty homes, with a population of 200, and a police force of 400.

Costa-Gavras wanted his countryman's music to be in the film. Theodorakis represented repressed cultural and ideological expression. His music, internationally known since *Zorba*, would immediately situate the viewer in Greece, although no mention would be made of this country in the film. The acquisition of the film score reads like cloak-and-dagger. Jacques Perrin was to visit Mikis Theodorakis still imprisoned in the village of Zatouna. Costa-Gavras recounted the episode to Guy Flatley:

> He [Perrin] met with Theodorakis's wife and lawyer secretly in a hotel near the house where Theodorakis was being held. Afterward, outside the hotel, Jacques was stopped by the police, put into a car and driven to the airport. "It would be better for you not to come back to Greece," they told him. And that was before they knew anything about the movie having been made.[24]

Eventually a message with the request for the film music was slipped to Theodorakis. He composed two songs and recorded them on a cassette. The songs were smuggled out for use in *Z*. In the film we hear one of the original compositions sung by Theodorakis in the background while the journalist tries to learn more about the membership of the CROC organization. The remainder of the musical sound track was also composed by Theodorakis but recorded commercially at an earlier date. Still other music theretofore unpublished was used. Bernard Gérard rearranged all of the material for the film.

In his *Journal of Resistance*, Mikis Theodorakis recounts how the scenario for *Z* was examined by the police in Zatouna and eventually by the officials of General Security in Athens. The latter recognized it as the story of Lambrakis and did not wish to arouse public sympathy over what they considered the plight of a dead communist deputy. General Velianitis denied Theodorakis's lawyer permission to have his client receive the scenario. The musician writes:

> So I was not able to read the scenario. I gave my consent to my music being used in the film, without my being involved. I merely indicated some of the songs I had written between 1962 and 1966 which bore some relation to Lambrakis. For example the song about "The Child Who Is Smiling," which was based on the poem by Brendan Behan. Our people had associated it with the memory of the deputy from Piraeus after his assassination. The tune became the theme of *Z*.[25]

Dan Georgakas of *Cinéaste* and *Film Society Review* comments in the latter journal on the levels of irony and meaning in the sound track that would normally escape a non-Greek filmgoer:

> A song which mocks the Nazi wartime practice of playing concert music during executions (and which attacks the indifference of the "good" Germans to what was happening in their nation) is played as background as an elegant black tie audience leaves a performance of the Bolshoi Ballet—at almost the same moment Z is being killed elsewhere in the city.[26]

This same irony and emotion can also be found as Z is being operated on in the hospital:

> The lyrics of the song heard ("Who can bear to say it, that half are found beneath the earth, the other half in irons") are from a series about the fallen guerrilla-revolutionaries of the Resistance. The official song of the Lambrakis Youth Movement is among the other songs played, all employed with exceptional effect.[27]

The music of the film creates a full gamut of moods. In the attempted elimination of Manuel during the car chase, the breathtaking tempo of the music suggests simultaneously a rapid heartbeat and hurried steps. The "cafe rock" music accompanies heel-clicking Vago as he races to the pinball machine in the cafe where he will gradually and coyly try to seduce the youth playing the machine. This contrasts with the gentle and tragic (but also sentimental) melodies played at the arrival of Hélène and the momentary triumphant and exalting music at the depositions.

Although still in prison when *Z* burst on the international scene, Mikis Theodorakis represented "the voice of liberty." He was eventually liberated in April 1970 through the efforts of Jean-Jacques Servan-Schreiber of the Radical Socialist party in France and the protests of the public after the success of *Z*.

Epilogue of the Film

Attaching an epilogue to the conclusion of the narrative in a film is usually an effort to chronicle what occurred in the aftermath so as to create a historical consciousness. Epilogues are now an international film phenomenon—*Parallax View* of Alan Pakula, *Le Pull-over Rouge* by the French cineaste Michel Drach, and *Death of the President* by the Polish filmmaker Jerzy Kawalerowicz all include this final form of political enlightenment. Most of the time epilogues are used for shock effect or to incriminate the Establishment, as in the case of Michel Drach's study of the recent guillotining of a twenty-two-year-old youth, Christian Ranucci, the alleged abductor of a young girl. The epilogue here states that the most important pieces of defense evidence for the accused Ranucci "disappeared" in the course of the investigation. In discussing the epilogue to *Z*, the American critic John Simon indicates the various registers on which Costa-Gavras plays in the finale of the film:

> The last part of the sad tale appears in the film only as a brief, bitterly ironic epilogue: the body of *Z* concerns itself with what looks and feels like the arduous triumph of justice, and is meant to instill in us elation and hopefulness. . . . Then, however, comes the epilogue, in which with a casualness that deliberately verges on the sardonic, we learn of the complete reversal of the just ending, the systematic destruction of truth and goodness, and a reversion to conditions even worse than the initial ones.[28]

This epilogue is obviously not a part of the novel, since the trial was just beginning when the book was published, and the junta would take control of the government almost a year later. While filming in Algeria, however, Costa-Gavras learned that a key journalist had been imprisoned and other witnesses were "disappearing." The director honestly felt that he should include this with the Vassilikos material to clarify what he saw as the correlation between the Lambrakis affair and the coup of the colonels.

During the military regime, manipulation of information was absolutely essential to control thought. Classical and modern plays were "modified" so as not to "undermine the healthy morals and customs of the Greek people," according to the censorship law of 1967. The ban included plays of Sophocles and Aristophanes. In 1967, the censors also issued an index of forbidden books that could not be displayed, purchased, or discussed. Vassilis Vassilikos was obviously on the blacklist among other controversial litterateurs. On the same index could be found a Greek-Bulgarian dictionary, a translation of Tolstoy's life of Peter the Great, and a Russian grammar. The ban extended to the press. *Avghi* (Dawn), the newspaper of Lambrakis's party, the E.D.A., was forbidden. Radio and television became instruments of the military propaganda machine. After three or four years of military rule—but *after* the release of the film *Z*—some of these interdictions were dropped or mitigated.

An anonymous member of the rightist regime stated in an interview with Pierre d'André for Réseau d'Organismes Culturelles that these interdictions were film exaggerations—or lies—for Chekhov was played during the regime of the colonels; smashing glasses in a Russian toast was never a custom in Greece anyway; and that those who believe that all Greek philosophers were homosexual are very naïve. What we see here is that Costa-Gavras caught the tone of the political interdictions invading a citizen's life. He then juxtaposes them all dramatically at the conclusion of the film. The director skillfully mounts the evidence against the regime. His point is solidly made.

Politics

Because of the political orientation of the director and his films, it is necessary to make several distinctions with regard to political film. Claude Veillot in *L'Express* calls *Z* "the first French political film."[29] Melton Davis of the *New York Times* refers to Costa-Gavras as an "agent provocateur."[30] Is *Z* a political work because of the real-life ideological perspective of Costa-Gavras, because of the insight of the director, or because of the nature of the material? Some critics might say that in the case of *Z* all three factors make it a political film. Others, notably Marcel Martin, believe that it is more a film about politics than a political film—it has a political subject as its focal point, but it is not designed purely as a militant ideological weapon.

Costa-Gavras comes from Greece, where he was accustomed early to breathing the political air of Greek resistance. His political perspective over the past decade or so has been certainly leftist, anti-Establishment, but not party-affiliated. For many other leftist intellectuals in Paris—Semprun included—to adhere to the Communist party was to endanger one's personal freedom. Costa-Gavras may be considered in a minor fashion a "fellow traveler," amenable to presenting communists sympathetically in *Z* and later *Special Section,* but he claimed no party membership.

The director's primary intention in making *Z* was to show how political power is manipulated for selfish and nonhumanitarian ends. The original subtitle showed his interest in the political nature of the events. He called it "Anatomy of a Political Assassination." Frustrated with the developing Greek situation in the late 1960s, Costa-Gavras wanted to use this film as a political weapon against the junta. For him, it would not be simply a film about politics as Marcel Martin claimed. "I always meant the film as a political act. And the proof that it succeeds is that everyone recognizes the situation as the one in Greece, even though Greece is never once mentioned."[31] Much later, with a greater historical perspective, he would say of *Z:* "Basically *Z* is less a political film (what is a political film anyway?) than a political act."[32]

Costa-Gavras in 1970 reproached the American government for involvement in Greek affairs as he did concerning AID assistance in Latin America shown in *State of Siege:*

> The day America understands that the people of Greece *must* be free is the day that there will be hope for Greece. Because on that day America will stop helping the military government—a government that could not stand for one week without her help. But Mr. Agnew has been saying that Greece has been *saved* by the military government, that he considers it the best government Greece could have. A strange concept of democracy.[33]

The content of Costa-Gavras's film deals with politics, and more specifically, with the insidious inner doings of an oppressive rightist regime. He strikes out against the military and their abuse of power, against the manipulation of the people by police and government over obtaining licenses, political favors, nuclear weapons, American military aid. Costa-Gavras refers to this manipulation as "white-collar terrorism." The director shows the complex influences at work in all the sectors of a citizen's life. Costa-Gavras launches his campaign against intolerance in general and in particular around the heroic Lambrakis/Z. Racism and fascism manifest in the dialogue and behavior of the military also become his targets.

Costa-Gavras reacts to critics' labeling his works "political films," for he feels that this is to pigeonhole a free artistic creation. To Yvonne Baby he remarked:

The word "political" is an unfortunate one, a word which drags along in its
wake many evil things. "Political" makes one think of politicians, of those very
people who had a hand in the assassination of Lambrakis. Z is above all a film
about the difficulty of overcoming certain obstacles so that truth may come to
light, as well as about the difficulty that some genuine political figures experience in existing and asserting themselves.[34]

Costa-Gavras cautions the French critic Robert Grelier about the use of the
expression *film politique* because it includes too much mythology. Apropos of Z,
he offers a nuance: "It is a film which gives free reign to reflection. If reflection is
synonymous with politics, then Z is a political film."[35]

In Costa-Gavras's thinking, Z and his other films are really supposed to be
more humanitarian than political. They are to serve as an argument for struggling for human rights and for the betterment of the human condition, against
torture and repression. This battle should transcend ideology; politics is, however, one means of achieving the removal of contemporary social evils. The film
Z is a concrete way in which to raise these human questions. The director points
out the essence of the film in the following manner:

> The theme of this "adventure film," which is represented for me by the
> letter "Z," is not a plea in favor of a political party, but a plea in favor of a Man
> and an Idea (even before this Man became identified with "Government" and
> the Idea had a "political label").[36]

The humanitarian overshadows the political in the address of the deputy who
speaks as a doctor at the peace rally. The doctor states that there is insufficient
medical care while the government sets military goals as absolute priorities. The
deputy offers horrifying statistics—each rocket costs as much as four universities; each long-range bomber, seven schools; and each long-range teleguided
interception missile, as much as 9,800 tractors. All across the world there are
many militarists with their finger on the trigger ready to fire, Z says.[37] Jorge
Semprun and Costa-Gavras used as a basis for the deputy's words the actual
speeches of Lambrakis. Vassilikos puts these words into the mouth of Z:

> I am speaking to you at this moment primarily as a physician. Every day I
> am brought face to face with the deplorable condition of our country. There
> are not enough doctors. The mountain villages are isolated. The land that
> gave birth to Hippocrates lacks so much as a public health system worthy of
> the name, and it claims to be living in the twentieth century. And when these
> elementary essentials are absent, how can civilization exist? How can people
> live under such conditions? If instead of half the government's budget going
> for military expenditures, it went into education, athletic fields, medical care,
> and industrial investment, wouldn't we live better?[38]

The glorification of the deputy and his peace-loving ideals reaches its apogee
when Z becomes a martyr for the cause. His death takes on mythological proportions. Costa-Gavras evokes the cult of the heroic dead when he portrays the
students' taking up the cause. There is something profoundly religious or sacred
to the memory of Z's death; although the deputy's body is dead, his spirit lives

on. The students design their own icons of the fallen hero and parade them through the street. As the young are beaten back by the police in their peaceful demonstrations, they draw great sympathy from an audience who sees them as the underdog. Omnipresent police armed with clubs (and scissors) cudgel and shear the long-haired pacifist demonstrators. This scene is but a portent of things to come as forces of the nether world are unleashed in the military coup of April 1967.

In the blend of lofty ideals, realistic political beliefs, and pure entertainment, Costa-Gavras draws our attention both to a national cause (military disarmament in Greece) and to an international cause (world peace). *Z* provokes discussion, clarifies issues, raises the veil on political machinations, and encourages humanitarian causes. Furthermore, the film challenges unethical processes, for example, the totalitarian state, which believes that the end (law and order) justifies the means (the brutality of the CROC militants).

There are some weaknesses in the depiction of the political scene in *Z*, given the nature of the film genre—adventure or thriller. Gavras also says he got subjectively involved, that he could not be wholly objective since he grew up in the repressive environment. The film shows that his version of the truth is, asserts Stanley Kauffmann of the *New Republic*, only the partial truth of both sides who think that each has all of the truth and the other none.[39] Costa-Gavras's caricatures of the police and army are humorous, but they detract from the solemnity of his message. He pushes them to the point of buffoonery.

In the presentation of his case, Costa-Gavras very much resembles his Greek forebear, the far-traveling, clever-tongued Odysseus, who knew many tricks and pulled a variety of them out of his bag. Both have an exciting sense of tale-telling, express strong ideas, and wish to please the public.

The political causes in the film are simplified. The liberal humanitarianism of *Z* is vague, expressed as a platform for peace through nuclear disarmament and more extensive education and health care. Nothing is very specific. Costa-Gavras's whipping boys are the fashionable ones of the 1960s—government, police, and military. John Simon outlines the broad targets of Costa-Gavras:

> With whatever difficulties, at the cost of martyr's blood and every kind of suffering, the body politic goes from the sickness of warmongering, elitism, religious fanaticism, racism, and despotism to the health of Leftism, pacifism, democracy, freedom, and justice for all.[40]

Some critics consider the link of the coup of the colonels with the assassination of *Z* as politically inaccurate. Andrew Sarris feels that linking these two incidents would be like discovering a logical connection between the assassination of Bobby Kennedy and ascension to the vice-presidency by Spiro Agnew. There is, however, a greater connection than meets the eye in the Greek situation, given the fact that the prosecutor general who came from Athens to Salonika to squelch the investigation of the assassination became the president of the council at the time of the military coup.

Vassilis Vassilikos, who knew the case well from his presence in Greece at the time of the assassination and his scrutiny of the documents, saw the film and put his stamp of approval on it, implying that the film does not do an injustice to either the political reality or to the aesthetic recreation in the novel. He remarked that the adaptation was done magnificently, that the actors truly represented the real individuals, and that he himself finally understood more clearly all the political nuances and interconnections in the Lambrakis affair. Vassilikos states in the press release for Z:

> The film Z closely following the book Z, and the book being faithful to the true story, provides the path for the document becoming Art. For my part, I believe that the suspense and the politics intermingle in the film as they intermingled in the press, and the path towards Truth appears, with as much difficulty in the film as with the actual events.[41]

At the release of the film, the novelist described the government and cancerous elements that are referred to in the film in this way:

> The film Z is an accusation against the usurpers, showing with exactitude the climate created before their coming to power. A climate of rot and corruption in the ruling class, where the voice of the people couldn't be heard any further than the widow's window.[42]

Vassilikos concludes his sympathetic observations on the political and humanitarian concerns of the creators of Z:

> The film, free of any elements of folklore, shows an underprivileged class dependent on the police, the police dependent on the ruling class, the ruling class dependent on foreign capitals, and how these elements led to the brutal murder of a man who only wanted peace between his brothers.[43]

Criticism

As many French and American critics point out, the time, 1969, was politically ripe for a film such as Z. The film elicited a plethora of discussions, critiques, and lengthy articles.

The slow, unprepossessing start that Z made in Paris left the creators anxious. The first few showings drew a very mediocre response. Then the message got around by word of mouth. The audiences grew in numbers. Additional publicity helped create a national and international attraction. The film began to have a shock effect on the public, enlightening them to the repressive situation in Greece. In France the criticism was favorable for the most part; it praised the acting, dramatic thrills, consciousness-raising thrust, brilliant editing, and rich composition. Each reviewer, however, often picked at flaws in the organic structure of the work.

The actors were generally given high marks, but the characters whom they represent were called stereotypes or caricatures in the American and French press, and "cardboard saints" by Lawrence Loewinger of *Film Quarterly*.[44] Jean Collet in *Projets* notes that this type of characterization results in a "transparent allegory."[45] Collet balances this with the observation that Sergei Eisenstein condescended to use stereotypical characters in *Strike* and *Potemkin*. Dan Georgakas is for the most part positive and sympathetic with Costa-Gavras's approach to the material. In discussing the characterization of Z for *Film Society Review*, he admits that "ill-defined motivations become increasingly important, for the film's events take place in a social vacuum. Aside from a few minor street scuffles there is no sense of a nation in convulsion."[46] Some critics view Irene Papas as too emotional and weepy. John Simon makes her the sole exception to the otherwise "remarkable" cast: "Only Irene Papas, as the victim's wife, is content to walk through her part with a face frozen into an easy tragic mask. It may be that the part does not permit much more."[47]

Thomas Quinn Curtiss of the *Herald Tribune* calls the film an ably acted melodrama and a good allegory. Some critics consider Z unique. Pauline Kael in the *New Yorker* reproaches the film for its lack of originality. She feels it derives from American gangster and prison films as well as from earlier anti-fascist melodramas. Kael enumerates its parallels in *Cornered, Brute Force, Crossfire,* and *All the King's Men.* She notes that political films during the McCarthy era also used melodrama as their primary vehicle.[48] The problem with genre and style is further raised by Charles W. Brooks of *Commentary:*

> The essential ambiguity of Z is that it is too serious—in intention at least—to thrill, and tries too hard to thrill to be taken seriously. Costa-Gavras wanted Z to show the true history of the Lambrakis affair. But he tried to hedge it by telling it like a detective story. The reason he did so goes a long way toward explaining Z's serious structural weakness.[49]

Jean Narboni of *Cahiers du Cinéma,* a journal with a more serious political orientation since 1968, feels that Z resembles the American heroic film, for example, *High Noon,* in which good usually triumphs, only in this case, justice triumphs but momentarily.

Most of the significant negative criticism of Z by national and international critics is related to Costa-Gavras's political perspective in the development of the content of the film. Paul-Louis Thirard of *Positif* calls Z a message film and Jean d'Yvoire of *Télérama,* a thesis film. Along the same lines, in *Panorama Aujourd'hui,* Olivier Galande states that Z is not only a historical reconstruction but also a *film-cri,* a type of political tract. Like Georgakas earlier, Charles Flynn writing for *Focus* pinpoints what he views as a major difficulty: Costa-Gavras has failed to analyze the structure of society or to present any vision of humanity in general. The film is deceptive, concludes Flynn, for it pretends to make a complex moral statement about the situation in Greece. Andrew Sarris in the *Village Voice* goes further and labels it a mendacious view of Greek history especially because of the telescoping of the four years' events to serve its own purposes. In that respect, Sarris believes the film becomes manipulative propaganda, an opinion shared by the American critic John Simon and the French critic Jean-Louis Bory of *Le Nouvel Observateur.* Vincent Canby's critique in the *New York Times* disappointed Costa-Gavras. Canby finds Z manipulative, melodramatic, a clever ruse to ennoble sheer entertainment.

The positive elements of the film are especially accentuated by the French reviewers, and they far outweigh the negative ones mentioned above. Where the first wave of criticism is perhaps overly enthusiastic, the second wave, following other political films by Costa-Gavras, is more objective and balanced. It is most capable of setting Z in its context of film history and politics.

Henry Chapier of *Combat* remarks that in the last twenty years of film history there has not been a political film as beautiful and as pure as that of Costa-Gavras's Z. Michel Capdenac, writing in *Les Lettres Françaises*, speaks with optimism about the film and praises it for its semidocumentary effect. In *Le Nouvel Observateur*, Jean-Louis Bory writes that Z is not the end of the alphabet but the beginning of a struggle.

For an equitable view of Z, it is important to see the weaknesses and strengths of the film, to judge it in its historical context, to take note of the intention of the director. Let us consider John Simon's perspective as a conclusion to our treatment. Simon added his own list of grievances to those of the international critics, but he could still conclude: "Let it be a message film, oversimplified, and propagandistic. It is taut, humane, intelligently constructed, sharply executed, and it is against those colonels who have plunged Greece into barbarism."[50]

Epilogue

Z proved successful but also highly provocative, containing the right mix of politics and adventure. The film does not end with the epilogue of interdictions. The consequences for the film itself continued for another several years:

• It accumulated one prize after another: At Cannes, the Jury Prize and one for Jean-Louis Trintignant as best actor; in Hollywood (representing Algiers, since *Ma nuit chez Maud* was France's entry), an Oscar for best foreign film and another to Françoise Bonnot for best editing; the film also merited the New York Critics' Award and the Christopher Award.

• In Paris, the film had an extensive first run of thirty-six weeks; smoke bombs were thrown into five Parisian theaters, however, in order to protest the screenings.

• Subsequent to the May 1968 events, Costa-Gavras said that if he were eighteen, he, too, would be in the streets, but since he was thirty-six, he made Z instead.

• In France, only one line of the film was censored, concerning the para-state organization CROC used as an auxiliary force when De Gaulle visited Greece.

• A group of political prisoners in Athens clandestinely made a collage and sent it simply to "Z," Paris. It arrived safely in the hands of the addressee.

• The film was banned in other countries besides Greece, for example, Spain and Mexico. Costa-Gavras also mentioned bannings in Morocco, Brazil, Portugal, and India—where America apparently has the greatest influence, he claimed.

• Z was first screened in Costa-Gavras's native country in late 1974. After the first four weeks 350,000 people had seen the film with intense exhilaration.

• The reaction to Z in Greece in 1974 was: the Left said it does not go far enough to reveal CIA involvement while the Right said it insults the monarchy and military. Premier Constantine Karamanlis stated that he was not guilty in the events depicted.

• Following the coup of the colonels, General Mitsou, Colonel Kamoutsis, Commander Diamandopoulos, and Lieutenant Capelonis were rehabilitated, as we discussed previously. General Mitsou (played by Pierre Dux in the film) was then recalled to active service, offered a promotion, and when retired later, given a large pension and honorary citation. Spyros Gotzamanis and Emanuel Emanouelidis were released in 1970, after serving only part of their prison term. At the same time, the examining magistrate Christos Sartzetakis was arrested on Christmas Eve 1970 with no regard for habeas corpus.[51] The truth was more dangerous to the regime than bombs. When Sartzetakis saw the film for the first time at its release in Greece, he offered this reaction: "I can only tell you that the film covers only a small part of the reality—it barely touches the surface. The real case was a thousand times worse."[52]

• Z was used as a tool of political consciousness-raising in rallies around the United States; the Black Panthers at one time seized a copy of it.

5

The Confession: A Kafkaesque Political Tale

> I made this film because Stalinism is not just a thing of the
> past; it is forever present. Every single day it begins anew,
> and not only in Czechoslovakia.
> —COSTA-GAVRAS, 1970

"Someone must have been telling lies about Joseph K., for this morning, without having done anything wrong, he was arrested." So begins *The Trial*, the celebrated novel by the Czech writer, Franz Kafka, replete with its own maze of long corridors, overpowering bureaucrats, and absurd situations through which the innocent victim helplessly meanders in the dark.

Kafka's novel of the absurd reads like *The Confession*, the autobiography of a fellow Czech, Artur London, one of the fourteen victims of the Stalinist regime during the Slansky trials in Prague. London, undersecretary (or vice-minister) of foreign affairs in the Czech Communist party, was secretly arrested on 28 January 1951, imprisoned, interrogated, tortured for twenty-two months, then forced to confess to crimes against the state. Following the interrogation, he and his fellow "conspirators" became the focal point of the international press during the Prague trial of 20–27 November 1952, a microcosm of the so-called show trials and of countless other purges by Stalin in Eastern Europe. The film of Costa-Gavras, *The Confession* (L'Aveu), made in 1970, uses Artur London's testimony to recreate the political mood of the 1950s, a time when the two major political blocs, capitalist and communist, went on separate witch hunts. In light of the political density of the film, certainly the most complex of the director's to that date, it is important first to uncover its solid historical foundation.

Historicopolitical Context

The pillars of the Soviet society were shaken on 21 January 1924 when Vladimir Ilitch (Lenin), the father of the revolution and the founder of Bolshevism, passed away. Joseph Vissarionovitch Djougatchvili, alias Joseph Stalin, the villain in London's autobiography *The Confession* and Costa-Gavras's adaptation, was quick to move into position to determine the political direction of the country. As the Russian Bolshevik party's secretary-general, Stalin aimed at constructing a power base following Lenin's death, envisioning a "socialism in one country." He did not stand unchallenged. It soon became a battle, Leon Trotsky versus Joseph Stalin. Trotsky was a theoretician, advocating the principle of permanent revolution. Stalin followed another ideological star. He had his opposition radically undermined by banishing Trotsky in 1928 and later (1940) by having him assassinated in Mexico. Trotsky's banishment was Stalin's first major step toward the assumption of total power. The great machine got underway, and anyone who was not one in mind with the leader's policies, be he a member of the Trotsky-organized Red Army, theoretician, or politician, was soon sent off to the camps or executed. Alexander Solzhenitsyn's *First Circle* and *Gulag Archipelago* and Arthur Koestler's *Darkness at Noon* are powerful accounts of this clever but not too subtle process of elimination.

With World War II, German fascism banged loudly on Russia's door, as Sergei Eisenstein prophesied in the film *Alexander Nevsky* (1938). With great loss in population and land, Russia staved off the Nazi sweep from the west, then helped the Allies carve up the Third Reich. In the aftermath of the war, those countries liberated by the Russian army—Hungary, Poland, Rumania, Bulgaria, and East Germany—were incorporated into the economic and political sphere of the Soviet Union. In February 1948, the Czech Communist party, the largest political faction in the government, gained control of the country. At approximately the same time, Yugoslav guerrilla leader Marshal Tito, feeling no great dependence on the U.S.S.R., decided to dissolve his relations with the Soviet bloc and to follow a separate road to socialism, a national one. This was a bold and delicate balancing act, which Tito performed until his death in May 1980.

Everything that Stalin had hoped for in a united political front could dissolve if any of the other satellite countries took the same independent steps as the heretical Tito. The subsequent trials—at the heart of London's autobiography and Costa-Gavras's film—would be Stalin's means of keeping his tightly knit system in operation. These trials were public theater, but most of the real action was in the wings—gruesome gulags or echoless tombs. To understand these trials we must go back in time. The process started in Russia in the 1930s with the Great Terror encompassing Zinoviev and Kamenev along with fourteen others accused of wallowing in Troyskyism.[1] In 1937, eighteen victims of suspicion, among whom were Piatakov, Radek, and Sokolnikov, were put on trial. Executions followed. In March of the following year, Boukarin and Rykov and sixteen "traitors" were tried and executed. By 1939, of the 139 members of the Central Committee of the party, 98 were arrested and liquidated. Thus, Stalin, with his thorough administrative violence, systematically eliminated the Bolshevik old guard, a lurking threat to his power. London was in Moscow during some of the purges, and he, somewhat like Saul at the execution of Stephen in the Acts of the Apostles, gave his silent approval.

Once the political scene was under control at home and the war over, Stalin looked across the borders to attain the same fidelity to the absolute policies he engendered. Lavrenty Beria was then given the commission to cure the political malady in Hungary, Bulgaria, and Czechoslovakia, which meant any political figure who was "a danger, a problem, an obstacle," testified London in an important lengthy interview he granted us in Paris on 21 September 1979.[2]

From 16 to 24 September 1949, former Hungarian Foreign Minister of the party Laszlo Rajk and seven other prominent officials were tried and found guilty of espionage and conspiracy to overthrow the government, to cite two of a long litany of other charges. Rajk was executed 15 October 1949—the example was set. Two months later in Bulgaria, the same proceedings began anew—arrests, interrogations, confessions, guilt. This time, Traicho Kostov, former deputy premier, and ten leading political figures were charged with the same crimes as Rajk. The scapegoat Kostov was executed on 16 December 1949.

Stalin's paranoia increased, and the well-oiled machine was kept in motion for the purging of the Czech ranks.[3] In *The Confession* Artur London offers us firsthand testimony of this exorcising of political enemies. One after another, he recounts, the old, crusty Czech Bolsheviks with international experience, sound leadership, and dauntless courage were arrested, tried, convicted, and executed. Albania, Rumania, and Poland would soon have their heretics eliminated. From 20 to 27 November 1952, fourteen Czech defendants from the party, held incommunicado up until then, were put on exhibit at a trial rigged to make them confess their conspiracy against the state. They were to serve as deterrent examples to any independent thinker. The atmosphere is chillingly described by London:

> How unjustly and brutally the Party members had been treated. Suspicion had been systematically cultivated in our ranks. The cadres had been judged by police methods. An atmosphere of distrust, fear, and then terror, developed in the Party and the country. It was produced by this monstrous, all-powerful cancer, which, under cover of state security, ate into the Party and into socialism itself by applying the Stalinist concept of accentuating the class struggle during the construction of socialism.[4]

This was all happening as Dwight D. Eisenhower began his presidency, with John Foster Dulles as his secretary of state. Senator Joseph McCarthy, communist hunter par excellence in the United States, was concurrently exerting more and more pressure on the American public to cough up party members or fellow travelers. The House-Committee on Un-American Activities would become a fine parallel to the undemocratic process of the purge trials, as concretely reflected in the films *Hollywood on Trial* and *The Trials of Alger Hiss*. McCarthy's probings usually terminated in a loss of reputation and career for the victim, while Stalin's show trials terminated in a destruction of health, family, reputation and, often enough, life itself.

Artur London's Testimony

A participant in the Slansky trial, one of the fourteen accused, one of the three survivors (with Eugen Loebl and Vavro Hajdu), Artur London made a personal record of the sordid machinery in operation in Czechoslovakia. He writes as a faithful disciple in the political religion of socialism, as a firm believer in the infallibility of the Central Committee of the party. London reveals a human side to his socialism, showing his ideals and health as almost destroyed, but not his optimism for the future of the international movement.

By means of a first-person narrative, London constructs and reconstructs his personal political biography for his interrogator, for himself, and for the reader. In a series of flashbacks and associations carefully edited to offer a literary and psychological dimension to the report, he narrates how he rose like a meteor in the governing of the Communist party in Czechoslovakia, next how he was labeled a Judas, and then how he was kidnapped by order of the Soviet security agents or advisors. The record of his interrogation at the Koldeje castle near Prague and then at Ruzyn, brings together the disparate experiences of his youthful days. Influenced by his socialist father, he began his struggle for revolutionary ideals in the Communist Youth at the age of thirteen, a few years after Lenin's death and Stalin's ascendency to power. In his late teens, during the revolutionary 1930s in Russia, London witnessed socialism at its home base. He shared with the masses a personality cult of Stalin. He viewed Moscow as a sacred site and watched the shadows of revolutionary salvation history pass before him. "We were full of faith and optimism: tomorrow the revolution would be everywhere."[5] Little did he suspect that Stalin's Great Terror would soon catch up with him and his comrades.

Motivated by his leftist ideals, he and countless other militants of Eastern Europe made their way to embattled Spain as part of the International Brigade not long after the outbreak of war in July 1936. When London left this rehearsal in Spain for the forthcoming international martial drama of World War II, he had had the experience of a heroic struggle for a revolutionary cause pitted against fascism. Following the invasion of Poland in September 1939, Europe began to tremble. In France, in 1940, London worked in the French underground. Chosen as one of the leaders of the Immigrant Workers (Main d'Oeuvre Immigré), a section of the Communist party dealing with immigrant laborers in France, London worked with this group until he was arrested. He was sentenced to ten years of forced labor and deported to Neue Bremme and Sarrebruck, Gestapo punishment camps, before being transported to Mauthausen. At Mauthausen, too, London organized for socialism until he was released from the camp through the efforts of the International Red Cross in April 1945.

His health ravaged by the subhuman conditions of the camps, London was forced to seek medical care. In 1947, he went to Geneva for treatment of tuberculosis. Here he first met Noel Field, an American working as the European director of the Unitarian Relief Service Committee. For three months Field assisted London until the latter's salary arrived from the Czech cultural attaché in Geneva. This meeting between the two later proved to be an unfortunate encounter for both individuals.

His health somewhat restored, London returned to Czechoslovakia and requested a visa for France in order to undertake a new post in Paris. In February 1949, while he waited for his visa, London was offered the position of undersecretary of foreign affairs in Prague during the presidency of Klement Gottwald. He accepted. Meanwhile the Laszlo Rajk trial began in Hungary, during which Field's name was associated with espionage. Other political individuals arrested at the time happened to drop the name of London. The kindling that was later to cause a vast political bonfire was lit. Allusions, implications, suspicions ran rampant through upper echelons of the party, reaching a climax, for London, in his arrest. Long-standing comrades ignored him. He now could understand the plight of Kafka's Joseph K.

It was on 28 January 1951, after less than two years in office, that he was secretly apprehended by the security police:

> After three hundred yards, as I was entering the lane behind the Tuscan Palace, one of the cars overtook me and stopped dead in front of me. Six men rushed up, pulled me off my seat, handcuffed me and threw me into the first car, which drove off at full speed. I struggled, and demanded to know who they were, but they blindfolded me and shouted: "Shut up! No point in asking questions! You'll know who we are soon enough!"[6]

This was just the beginning of the dehumanization process used to break London and his communist peers. The brainwashing would be long and systematic, more thorough than even the Gestapo's methods. The brainwashing began by stripping the individual, clothing him in rags, forcing him to eat and take care of his hygenic needs like an animal.[7] Just as in Korea and later Vietnam, in this type of process London was reduced to a number and isolated from the rest of his comrades in the Koldeje castle on the outskirts of Prague.

For eighteen to twenty hours a day, the interrogation ran on, leaving little time for food and sleep. What further reduced the prisoner was exposure to the cold and to senseless beatings by the guards and by Soviet-directed interrogators. These cross-examiners came from the ranks of the secret police, who were above the Central Committee of the party and were here to expose the "traitors" of the party. The shadow of Lavrenty Beria's policy lurked along the corridors. With ridiculous lies, with half-lies and half-truths, the interrogators tried to turn London and the other prisoners against each other and admit to a plot against the state.[8] The charges, made to bolster current party ideology, were repeated over and over again and could be schematized in this way:

> Trotskyism—swayed by the false ideology of Stalin's archenemy; Titoism— sympathetic to the overly independent Yugoslav socialist; espionage—linked with Noel Field, "an American spy"[9]; bourgeois Western influence— corrupted by capitalism and cosmopolitanism; Zionism—contaminated by "the number one enemy of the working class."[10]

In the film these invectives will be shouted hostilely and constantly at the victims, making the nuances of the accusation somewhat difficult to absorb for the viewer. With the assurance that the party needed a trial and not heads, London gradually gave in to his examiners. In the book (and film) we watch the tragic evolution of a self-confident party official, totally in charge of the situation, to a self-doubting, and then acquiescent, broken victim, who is reduced to sign confessions heavily seeded with lies. The scientific and diabolical questioning succeeded privately. Now the show of force had to be arranged to bring the accused to party loyalty publicly. Rehearsal for the trial required time, during which the fourteen accused were especially cared for in order to create a favorable impression. In November 1952, after more than two years of preparation, the Slansky trial took place behind closed doors while the public awaited the results.[11] It was a parody of justice; the Czech marionettes were manipulated from far-off Moscow. The drama went off as planned. First, three hours of indictments were read against the accused. Each defendant in turn rattled off his memorized confession word for word. The results of the trial showed that eleven of the men whose heads the party supposedly did not "need" were hung on 3 December 1952, while the others—London, Loebl, and Hajdu—were given life sentences. Many of the convicted men had approved of the Rajk trial and, like Slansky, helped keep in motion the machinery that swallowed up the others. Now they fell victim to the same machinery turned on them.[12]

London, remaining faithful to the party, even during the twenty-two months of brutal and degrading interrogation, discovered himself in prison. There he found time to reflect on his painful past. His hell was the moral torture that his own party inflicted upon him, the members of the same party that he had loyally served for more than twenty years! In prison he decided that if he ever survived this ordeal, he would have to tell the world about this abuse of socialism, of justice, of humanity. His wife, Lise, whom he had met and married in Russia in 1935 and who stood by him through all of the revolutionary action of the Spanish civil war and World War II in the struggle against fascism, hesitated and questioned her husband's loyalty to the party. After his case was reviewed and he was released, she said that for two years she did not know the whereabouts of her husband. When she heard his public confession broadcast, she really believed he had turned traitor to the cause to which they dedicated their entire lives.

Lise London eventually saw through the sham trial. With the fiery spirit of a La Passionara, she fought for his release. Maurice Thorez of the French Communist party helped in the struggle. The death of Stalin on 5 March 1953 and of Klement Gottwald on 14 March 1953 slowed down the oppressive political machinery enough for the still incarcerated London to begin the excruciating process of public revelation.[13] Writing his notes on thin sheets of paper and smuggling them out to his wife, London was able to provide an accurate account of the proceedings. In 1953, a special commission published a 550-page account of the trial with his assistance. The year of the Twentieth Party Congress— 1956—marked simultaneously Krushchev's denunciation of Stalin and London's long-awaited freedom. He and other deeply committed members of the party had hopes that the party congress would clean the Augean stables of Stalinism.

Twelve years later, in May 1968, while Alexander Dubcek was at the helm, all fourteen defendants in the Slansky trial were fully rehabilitated and exonerated—a bit too late for the eleven who were immediately executed in 1952. With a historical perspective and making use of the rough draft of the lengthy special commission report, letters from friends, and personal observations, London was able to write his own understanding of the process that brought him to death's door. He came from France to Czechoslovakia to publish it with the blessing of the Communist party. The spring turned to winter, however, for as he arrived in Prague, he witnessed on that 20th of August 1968 the invasion of his country by 600,000 men and 6,000 tanks of the countries of the Warsaw Pact—Russia, Hungary, Bulgaria, Poland, and East Germany. It was a crushing blow, the reversal of the ever-renewing phoenix. London and others on the sidelines sympathetic to the Czech cause, such as Yves Montand and Simone Signoret, saw hope in the spring thaw of Prague, but were heartbroken to watch this sudden chill three months later.

For some time London had had the idea to publish his book before the actual printing took place, but felt he did not want to give ammunition to anticommunists. In 1968, Gallimard published the collaborative results of Lise and Artur London under the title *L'Aveu: Dans l'engrenage du procès de Slansky,* which could be graphically translated as *The Confession: Caught in the Machinery of the Slansky Trial.* A year later, a Czech account appeared through the efforts of the publishing house of Czechoslovak Writers, and 30,000 copies were sold the first day. An English translation by Alastair Hamilton appeared in 1970, but with approximately forty pages eliminated from the original manuscript. This material primarily dealt with London's wife. London felt that the editing for the publication in English made the narrative more of a *policier* than a human story.

The author said that it was important to see the book as a *cri,* as a protest not against Marxism, not against the Communist party, but against the abuses of Stalinism. In prison he told himself, "If I survive, I must say it," and in Prague's springtime, "Now more than ever I must say it." He published it in 1968 *for* communists, not *against* them, to tell them that despite the weaknesses of the system, they must have faith, just as a Christian who continues to believe— London said in the course of our September 1979 interview—despite the Inquisition and the Crusades. The strong must keep vigilance against perversions of the system. For London in 1968 it was important to tell the whole truth since for him socialism was an affair of the masses and not of small, secretive committees.

London stressed his purpose in a dialogue with the film critic Robert Grelier:

> Since my book was, above all, a witness to the despotic tendencies, to the abuses, and let us pronounce the word, to the crimes of the Stalin era, its purpose was to alert all the followers of socialism to the possible dangers and traps in which they could fall. It was a warning to them to be aware lest terrible distortions unknown to socialism be repeated. But the book was also the undertaking of a militant. It was written as a contribution to the "Prague Spring" and it must be understood in that context. The "Prague Spring" moved in the direction opened up by the Twentieth Congress of the Communist Party of the Soviet Union.[14]

In this manner Artur London made public his ordeal, but while still in the bosom of the Communist party and with its benediction, unlike Victor Kravchenco *(I*

Choose Freedom) and Arthur Koestler *(Darkness at Noon)*, who wrote from outside the pale. For London this process was a therapeutic self-revelation, curing the political sores on the body of socialism, and not a vile attack of revenge.

In August 1968, while Costa-Gavras was still in Algeria filming *Z*, and Warsaw Pact tanks were churning up the streets of Prague, Artur London arrived in the Czech capital with his manuscript. He was obliged to return to France with it. As Gallimard was on the verge of publishing the work a short time later, another ending to it was necessary so as to offer the total picture. When the political memoirs appeared in Paris, the West became instantly aware of the interconnected series of events that led from the Slansky trial to the Soviet invasion of Czechoslovakia.

Scenario and Production

At Christmastime 1968, while Costa-Gavras was attending a soirée at the residence of the actress Françoise Arnoul, he came across the London bestseller. After some reflection, he decided to adapt it for the screen. He had one stumbling block, however, his contract to film *Le Fils* for producers Robert Dorfmann and Bertrand Javal. The producers were not very anxious to undertake this new project proposed by Costa-Gavras, since *Z* was not yet completed and would not be released until February 1969. The Oscars and the Cannes jury prize were still to come. Costa-Gavras's political film genre had not yet been established, and this undertaking would be a serious risk. Javal nevertheless read *The Confession* but was still reluctant to accept the challenge.[15]

Several things happened that concluded with Costa-Gavras's becoming the director of the film. Jorge Semprun, the screenwriter for *Z*, was involved very early in the process. Semprun's first intention was to write a play from the material, but he was also willing to go along with Costa-Gavras's desire to make a film. The screenwriter, like London, curiously enough, had the name of Gérard in the resistance. They had met at a political gathering, remarked London in our lengthy 1979 discussion. Semprun, on the other hand, knew London for his work since 1942 with the movement MOI during the resistance. London had read and appreciated Semprun's novel of deportation, *Un Grand Voyage*. When Semprun presented Costa-Gavras to London, the Czech author initially felt that it would be impossible for Costa-Gavras to film *The Confession* since the Czechs themselves were interested in adapting the work. London believed that a Czech would best understand the political nuances of the period. The politically sensitive Costa-Gavras was in agreement with that. London also mentioned to the French cineaste that he once promised the Czech director Milos Forman (*One Flew Over the Cuckoo's Nest* and *Hair*), now living in New York, that if ever the book were to be made into a film, he would be the person to direct it. (London knew Forman personally, for he was a friend of his daughter Françoise, a film editor in France.) He then wrote to Forman in New York explaining the situation. The Czech director replied that he would be unable to undertake the project since he was presently occupied with other filming plans, presumably *Taking Off*, which was completed in 1970–1971. The door to this Kafkaesque world was thus still ajar.

The Czechs were indeed planning to adapt the provocative work. When they heard of Costa-Gavras's interest, they encouraged him to make it a Czech-French co-production with Javal and Dorfmann as producers. In April 1969, with Alexander Dubcek still in power, the Czechs invited Costa-Gavras, Javal, and Semprun to Prague. An agreement was signed with a view to a Czech-French collaboration. London mentioned in our September 1979 interview that it was about this time or even earlier that Costa-Gavras was slightly concerned that Jorge Semprun, excluded from the Spanish Communist party for divergence from party policy in Spain, would not be acceptable as a screenwriter for the film. London reassured the director that there would be no problem.

At the Cannes film festival in May 1969, the Czech-French co-production was announced, and the project was gradually getting underway. Yves Montand had been contacted by Costa-Gavras in Hollywood, where the actor was working with Barbara Striesand on the film *On a Clear Day You Can See Forever*. Costa-Gavras sent Montand a copy of the book to give him some basis for a decision. Montand admitted to nightmares and insomnia after reading parts of the horrifying book. He agreed, however, despite the objections of Simone Signoret and Colette Semprun, wife of the screenwriter, to undertake this controversial work. Montand was to play the lead role of Gérard, and eventually others including Signoret and Jean Bouise were added to the cast.

At a stroke, everything collapsed. In August 1969, there was a change of management in the Czech film industry, and the contract of Javal and the Czech film company was not respected. But by this time, *Z*'s fame had attained international proportions, and it was not too difficult to create another type of financial liaison. The Italian film industry became interested in the project and created a Franco-Italian co-production.

Scenario

In the writing of the scenario, Semprun and Costa-Gavras wanted to remain as faithful to the text as possible without betraying either the political import or the dramatic structure of the work. Semprun mentioned this in the course of our 9 March 1981 interview. They sought more than an adaptation, however, in an attempt to raise the initial account to a greater visual and reflective level. The director would not make any concessions to the commercial film market as he did with *Z*, often citing excesses of the American film, the traditional whipping boy. There would be no happy ending—*à l'américain*—that would be an artificial and senseless conclusion to the film. After *Z*, Costa-Gavras cut the umbilical cord with the American film, liberating himself temporarily from this popular and commercial venture in cinema. At the same time, nonetheless, he would not go so far as to make the type of militant film which he respected but felt would not get beyond the student or leftist ghettos.

On the political side, Semprun and Costa-Gavras wanted to help the communists to demythologize the party, following London's intentions. As with his other political films, Costa-Gavras's purpose in undertaking *The Confession* was to show an individual caught in the machinery of power—already implied in the subtitle to the French publication—which grinds away and eventually pulverizes its victim.

In adapting the work, Semprun and Costa-Gavras found that there was an overabundance of material, enough for a film of six hours, or perhaps three of regular length. What criteria would they use to choose the necessary elements for a sound political fiction film? They decided to exclude any suspense, although certain traces remain in the initial sequences of the suspenseful trailing of Gérard by security forces. Elimination of distracting material would keep the viewer on the right political track. Along with the original testimony of the trial, which they were able to verify from the stenographic court account, they retained the anti-Semitic elements of the book. Costa-Gavras discussed this pervasive anti-Semitic tone with Ginette Gervais of *Jeune Cinéma:*

> On the other hand, it seemed necessary to us to reproduce the scene in its entirety where Smola hurls out anti-Semitic invectives, because the police never speak by themselves; they know what those in charge want to be said. That is what gives intensity to Smola's violent anti-Semitism.[16]

Semprun and Costa-Gavras wished to reproduce this gradual passing down of orders from Stalin through Beria to the Soviet secret service in Czechoslovakia, to the guards and interrogators—all resulting in the destruction of the designated scapegoat. Antonin Liehm in *Le Passé présent: Le socialisme oriental face au monde moderne* describes the type of pyramid or chain of command in the Stalinist regime as one in which the authorities send down orders through an entire military, political, and police system. The orders are to be carried out without the slightest modification. In this system all the citizens are considered employees of the state and the functioning of the pyramid becomes an end in itself.[17] One critique that could be made of Costa-Gavras on this issue is that he only sketches the bottom part of the pyramid without developing the links upward to the top of the Soviet bureaucracy.

The artists had to make other sacrifices to tighten up the material they wished to present. They used the typewriter and dossier 3225 to link together various parts of the interrogations. They dropped the experiences as a young communist in Moscow, when he was bursting with revolutionary romanticism and ideals. To show this idealism, then follow it by the harshness of scenes with him in the hands of Stalinist brutes would dampen the spirit of young revolutionaries, believed Costa-Gavras and Semprun. They did not include the role Maurice Thorez played in France for the release of London. This would require a whole new avenue of exploration into the relationship of the French Communist party with the Czech events. The same principle held for not developing the role at the trials of the correspondant from the French communist newspaper *L'Humanité*. The audience might find the torture in the film difficult to support for two hours, yet the two artists deliberately wished to reduce the torture described even more extensively in the book. London heartily agreed to the elimination of some of the actual torture scenes.

Semprun told his interviewer Robert Grelier that he and the director submitted the material in the script to London at various stages of development. London in turn offered his remarks, corrections, and general opinion. He suggested in fact the typewriter and the file cabinet mentioned above that were used to connect the periods of questioning. His absolute approval was a sine qua non before the first day of filming, said Semprun.[18]

Costa-Gavras and Semprun eliminated certain aspects of the book that were not physically possible to film or did not correspond to their cinematic vision of the material. At times the director slightly modified the dialogue or scene which the screenwriter had furnished, but he relied primarily upon the blueprint approved by London. The epilogue was conceived later. Given the amount of material, Costa-Gavras and Semprun felt limited, restricted, but they used the two hours of film time in the best possible manner.

With the Prague locale out of the question because of the dissolution of the Czech-French co-production, it was necessary to choose sites that resembled Prague of the 1950s. Lille was decided upon. On 15 October 1969, the initial day of filming, that northern French city became Prague of 1951. The streets became Eastern European; the underground corridors of an old hospital morgue became London's prison, and the Bois de la Deule, the park.[19]

Film Narrative

The Confession begins with haunting music in the background as Noel Field is introduced, a key figure in the espionage charge against London and others:

> A Harvard graduate, Field served with the United States State Department. During and after World War II he directed Unitarian relief centers in Marseilles and Geneva, aiding anti-Fascist refugees and Nazi concentration camp survivors; among them were former International Brigade volunteers who had fought Franco in the Spanish Civil War.
> Field disappeared in Prague in 1949. He reappeared in prison in Hungary, accused of being an American agent who had lured Foreign Minister Rajk and other Communist leaders into treason and espionage for the U.S.A.

Then we receive our historical bearings—"Prague, 1951." Gérard (Yves Montand)—the name that Artur London had in the resistance and which his wife used during our 1979 interview—is followed by security vehicles. No one knows who assigned them to tail Gérard. His wife (Simone Signoret) receives a threatening phone call. His friends, also International Brigade veterans, voice concern about his safety as well as their own.

He is mysteriously kidnapped one day by the secret police and whisked off to a secluded prison. There he is stripped, numbered (dossier 3225), tortured, in short, totally dehumanized. His wife is worried. She cannot locate him. Agents arrive to make certain she is not concealing anything and thoroughly search the residence. They prevent her from phoning the secretary general of the party.

The Interrogation

Gérard is questioned mercilessly about his political doings. During the interrogation we hear Gérard, voice-off, "At first you try to help the Party . . . see more clearly. . . . You search yourself as to why you're there . . . what error led you there. You're ready for self-criticism . . . to admit mistakes . . . detrimental to the Party. Years of struggle, discipline, training had us convinced the Party is never wrong, the USSR always right." Then a bit later, "Better be wrong inside the Party than right outside of it."

The brainwashing process begins. The guards scream their commands. Gérard, in isolation, does not know what time it is, night or day. No sleep. Little or no food. The guards and interrogators are inhuman in their questioning. In between sessions he is told by his interrogators: "Your duty is to help establish the truth."

The examiners begin implicating Gérard with Trotskyites in Spain, with Titoists in Yugoslavia, with American espionage agents such as Noel Field in Geneva and Allen Dulles, and with the convicted Rajk in Hungary. They break his solidarity with his comrades, trying to turn them one against the other. Voice-off, Gérard reflects: "Abandoned by the Party, by friends, and the comrades. No one can have any doubt that I'm guilty. I myself reacted that way to the Moscow and Rajk trials. What Communist wouldn't be shaken? How could his Party which he reveres and considers infallible make innocent people confess? But confess what? And why?" Meanwhile, Gérard is under constant surveillance. The anonymous eye in the spy hole watches him—Big Brother of *1984*, thirty years ahead of its time!

The prisoner begins with a report about his past, giving details about his origins to his interrogators. He informs them of his father's political and cultural leanings—an antireligious socialist who worked for a time in America, liked Paine and Jefferson, on and on he discusses him. Many of Gérard's family died in the concentration camps because of their Jewish heritage. His brother was shot by the Gestapo.

To spring a "confession" from Gérard more quickly, the guards take him outdoors and fake hanging him. He refuses adamantly to confess to all the trumped-up charges. He says he is not guilty. His voice-off mutters, however: "A person in anguish not over being guilty, but being *thought* guilty, becomes guilty." His physical and psychological condition deteriorates radically, but he still maintains faith in the party and in his own total innocence. He babbles in Spanish: "Es imposible de pensarlo. El Partido . . . Stalin sabe lo que hace, seguro!" (It is impossible to think of it. The party . . . Stalin knows what he is doing, certainly!)

From the series of interrogations of Gérard and the others, there is a cut, a flashforward to sunny Monte Carlo where Gérard projects himself. He sees himself meeting with comrades affiliated with the French Communist party to

The Confession: The interrogators of Gérard (Yves Montand) fake hanging him.
(Permission of Paramount Pictures Corp.)

discuss the publication of his book. He asserts that in 1952 the French Communist party did not help him, did not speak out on his behalf. The facts, however, only came out in 1956, three years after the death of Stalin.

In the meantime, London's wife, Lise, is still unsure about her husband's fate. She is forced to resign her radio position to take a menial job in a factory. The party moves the family from their modest residence to a dismal apartment. Lise has no one in office to whom she can turn. She and her husband have become political lepers. Everyone is afraid of being contaminated and inculpated. The secretary general himself, Rudolf Slansky, responsible for the arrests of many party officials, is himself arrested. He will be designated the ringleader in this conspiracy. Lise's boss at the factory (Jean Bouise) counsels and consoles her, a breath of fresh air in the suffocating political atmosphere of Prague.

The Confession

The interrogation intensifies. Kohoutek (Gabriele Ferzetti) takes up the questioning in a soft, gentle manner, the opposite approach to that of the barbaric Smola (Michel Vitold). Kohoutek tells Gérard they have plenty of time, and cleverly attempts to get him to admit to espionage activities with Field in Switzerland and Hungary, Zilliacus in Great Britain, and Trotskyite and anarchist groups in Spain. A young interrogator in the film puts his finger on the irony of the situation: "The past must be judged by the truth the Party established today." They prepare a confession for him in order to save time; it is only a working document, they say. They remind him: "Confession is the highest form of self-criticism, and the spirit of self-criticism is a Communist's chief virtue."

After twenty months of interrogation and brainwashing, Gérard, like the other thirteen "traitors," is ready to confess his crimes. He rehearses his part. His mind flashes back to the Sacco and Vanzetti march, to Nazi banners, to a Russian flag, and to a child running—his last image of normal life before he is abducted. This cheerful shot is followed by another flashforward, the ashes of the victims being strewn on an icy highway.

The Trial

One after another the extensive charges mentioned earlier are read in court and piped into Lise's factory. It is heartbreaking to hear her husband admit that all along he was a spy. A new bit of information is added to the ceremonial of the trial as each individual gives his testimony by rote. Hearing the confession of her husband, Lise writes a letter to the president of the Republic stating that her husband was truly a traitor to the party, and demands a severe judgment for those on trial.[20]

During the testimony the trousers of one of the defendants, Otto Sling (Jacques Rispal), slip to the floor because of his drastic weight loss in prison. Hysterical laughter breaks out among the whole assembly. An ironic cut is repeated—the ashes of the executed men are tossed on the road. Kohoutek says that this pants incident was a trick and that Sling will suffer worse consequences. When the sentence for conspiracy against the state is read, and eleven get the death sentence, three life imprisonment, each defendant rhythmically parrots: "I accept my sentence."[21]

Epilogue

The last part of the film contains a series of related events in a type of extended epilogue. In 1953 Stalin died; in 1954, Beria was executed for his part in organizing the trials; in 1956, Gérard was liberated; in 1963, the group of fourteen were rehabilitated and exonerated. One day Gérard, returning from beyond the Soviet tomb, meets his interrogator Kohoutek in a public square in Prague. Kahoutek tells Gérard that those who gave orders are still in power, and he, too, has become a pawn. Ironically he invites Gérard to have a drink. Gérard walks away dazed by this encounter.

In April 1968, during the freshness of Prague's political springtime, Lise and Gérard are working away at the manuscript of his own personal testimony. A cut to 20 August 1968 reveals a tragic shift of political winds. As Gérard arrives in Prague, he witnesses the Soviet invasion. He is surprised and shocked. He feels betrayed. Newsreels and stills show the actual incidents on the streets of Prague. The film ends with political scribbling on a nearby wall: "Lenine, zobud se oni se zbaznili." (Lenin, awaken, they have gone mad!)

Actors and Characterization

Stripped of suspense, anecdote, and incidental action, the film is down to an absolute purity. In terms of characterization, Costa-Gavras uses Gérard as the focal point of the action, as he was in the book. The success of the character of Gérard is dependent on three factors—a physical condition, dramatic skill, and political perspective. To portray the calvary of London, Montand took drastic measures to lose weight. He looked emaciated during the filming and on occasion he lost all sense of time and place. London himself had lost forty-two pounds during the twenty-two-month ordeal. Montand lost more than twenty-five over six weeks. The rough conditions of filming in the underground cell in Lille helped him to experience the anguish and physical discomfort of London to the point where he identified with his character between takes, offstage, and at night. Nightmares of the walls closing in on him disrupted his sleep. His wrists were raw and bruised from the handcuffs. Toward the end of the filming his weary face was drawn and creviced—like the political map of twentieth-century Europe, observed Kauffman.[22]

With respect to Montand's acting, Jacqueline Michel of *Télé Sept Jours* noted:

> It is insufficient to state that Yves Montand embodies Artur London. The identification is so complete and so painfully exact that one dares not call it an actor's performance. What he achieved surpasses a performance. Little by

little, from Resnais's *La Guerre est finie*, to *Z*, then to *The Confession*, Yves Montand ceases to be an actor and becomes a tortured and anguished militant in whom we place our faith.[23]

It is difficult not to be impressed with Montand's dramatic power as we see him evolve from a self-possessed, confident party official to an outraged but ultimately accepting victim tortured by members of his own party. When he becomes self-doubting, losing his grip on his own humanity, he evokes our sympathy even more. His last moments of acquiescence are the most excruciating—he is now totally broken by the same party he has faithfully served since he was thirteen. This evolution of character, evident in the book, makes even more of an impact on the screen through Montand's skill—conveyed more through painful gestures and attitudes than through dialogue. Montand admitted that he would never attempt this again, for the physical and psychological effort was overwhelming.

Costa-Gavras's choice of Montand arose from their long-standing friendship and his acting ability, but perhaps more essentially, from their common political leanings. In an interview in New York in 1971, Costa-Gavras commented on the role that Montand played in *The Confession*, saying that he did not think an actor who had never had any relations with socialism, communism, or politics could have played the part the way Montand did. Everything that resulted from his acting was really part of his political past, confirmed the director. Costa-Gavras is correct in assessing Montand's success as resulting from his political experience. Montand's father's struggles against fascism in Italy and misery in southern France, provided the basis, but the 1950s gave him the opportunity to be an activist. He participated in the Movement of Peace, signed the 1950 petition in the Appeal of Stockholm, protested against McCarthy's witch hunting, demonstrated in favor of the Rosenbergs, and traveled and sang through the socialist cities of Moscow, Kiev, Warsaw, and Belgrade. During the Indochinese War he used his music as a weapon of protest with songs such as "Le Dormeur du val" of Arthur Rimbaud or "Quand un Soldat." He thus used his art in the service of humanitarian and/or political causes.

This was also true in 1956, when he and Simone Signoret played the Proctor couple in the French adaptation of Miller's drama, *The Crucible*. Proctor signs a confession of his supposed complicity with the devil, then tears it up—unlike London, who was forced to play his role to the end. There is an irony to Montand's making *The Confession*. It dates back to the scene in Prague in 1952. Montand and a host of other important literary and political figures signed Paul Eluard's petition supporting the Slansky trial. Eluard phrased his sentence thus: "I've got too much to do with the innocent proclaiming their innocence to spend time on the guilty [that is, London et al.] asserting their guilt."[24] Fifteen years later, with a more historical overview of the Stalinist regime, Montand put things back into perspective. During his interviews after the release of *The Confession*, he often quoted Gramsci, "Truth is always revolutionary." He spoke out against the abuses of the Stalinist period. He did not look naïvely at the past and accept it.

The words of the politically involved theater director Bertold Brecht were also on his lips during the interviews: "The one who is ignorant of something is an imbecile, but the one who knows and says nothing is a criminal."

Perhaps playing in *The Confession* was for Montand a release of the guilt that he as well as prominent political figures had felt in being deceived during the Stalinist purges. Simone Signoret says in her memoirs:

> I can't think of anyone who could have played the character of London as he did. You had to be absolutely torn apart, internally as he was. He, too, had signed Eluard's text at the time. You had to feel a very strong measure of guilt in yourself in order to act the part as he did.[25]

In several interviews, Montand admitted that for him it was a difficult decision to make the film; in fact the whole group—Signoret, Semprun, and Costa-Gavras—in a sense would have preferred not to have made it, but that would have been an easy way out of the situation. Montand and his peers could not go on voicing leftist, progressive ideas and still have remained silent in the face of the shocking events that took place in Czechoslovakia in the early 1950s.[26] Costa-Gavras, Semprun, and Montand did not claim to be providing any kind of a lesson, moral, or conclusion. They said they simply wanted some truths out in the open.

In our 1979 meeting with the Londons, they stated that they had not known Montand and Signoret personally but genuinely respected their acting. In the role of Gérard and Lise, the couple represented convincingly their real life counterparts. London himself felt that all of the actors had something to say about that political situation in the 1950s and projected their opinions through their acting. They made every attempt to recreate a personal testimony to the injustice, protesting this fanatic abuse of power.

Like Irene Papas's role in *Z*, that of Simone Signoret in this film may seem minor. Nonetheless, it was crucial to mirroring London's ideals and to obtaining his release. Even though the character she plays is not on the screen for an extensive period of time, her presence is constantly felt through letters, contacts with officials and friends, through her doubts and reactions during the course of the trial. In the film Signoret truly captures the character of Lise London, the staunch communist schooled in Moscow at the dawn of Stalinism, who wavers between fidelity to her husband and fidelity to the almighty party in whom she has put all her trust. Although Signoret had initially hesitated about seeing the film made, she agreed to it, realizing the importance of letting the truth be known. She, too, played her part because of a sense of political commitment. She was incapable of lending her acting skills to an enterprise that went contrary to her most profound convictions. These same leftist convictions, as noted earlier, created difficulties for her in obtaining a visa to come to the United States in the 1950s.

The other actors in the film richly portray the characters (fewer in number than in the book). The spectator comes to hate Gérard's interrogators with a passion, and to sympathize with the Londons with the same degree of emotion.

Gabriele Ferzetti (Kohoutek) and Michel Vetold (Smola) almost destroy every possible bit of humanity left in London by their half-lies and insinuations, by their brutal physical treatment of him. They are nothing short of diabolical on the screen. Yet, London feels that the two barbaric interrogators are not caricatured by Costa-Gavras. During the actual brainwashing sessions they behaved even more harshly. In trying to extract confessions, Kohoutek at times appears as a soft, mild-mannered gentleman, but he is as insidious as Smola, who stops at nothing to break London's stubborn will.

The one ray of hope inside the party is the factory manager later eliminated from his position. He is played by Jean Bouise. With incredible independence and insight, he advises Lise at the time of the trial, saying that he does not believe in or trust this type of trial. Bouise arouses our sympathy for the character who is willing to accept a demotion for his political beliefs. As in other films of Costa-Gavras, Bouise plays the secondary role of the committed individual who cannot be swayed from his strong, pure ideological feelings—in *La Guerre est finie* as the Spanish comrade of Diego, in *Z* as the deputy's close associate, and later in *Special Section*, as the honest judge.

As for the other actors, we sense their vital presence despite their minimal roles—the young interrogator, the hard-nosed Soviet guard, the comic-tragic Otto Sling, played by Jacques Rispal. London remarked that in the case of Sling, he did wave to the assembly at the conclusion of the verdict of the Slansky trial, but it was slightly more discreet than in the film.

Rudolf Slansky, local executioner for the Moscow bureaucrats, was shortly eliminated himself. In the film we never see him close up. As the secretary general of the party in Czechoslovakia, he is the faceless pawn caught in a vicious circle of political experience. His reddish-orange hair is the sole factor identifying his enigmatic presence throughout the trial scene.

Stalin floats through the film worshiped by the Soviets as their messiah, their redeemer. The photos of Stalin in the film show him being religiously revered. The newsreels at his death record the lines of mourners filing past his bier with a sense of eternal loss. Costa-Gavras underlines the ambiguity in the image of Stalin at the time of his death in the early 1950s—a man responsible for the death and exile of thousands of Russian citizens, a man wept for like a lost father.

Tone and Technique

Through a combination of toned-down color, slow-paced, then quick-paced cutting, stark composition, and irritating sound, *The Confession* grinds away slowly, catching up London, his comrades, and eventually the spectator in its gears. With no gimmicks, no caricatures, no suspense, no entertainment, and no happy ending, *The Confession* is a gruesome experience. There is a psychological and physical tension that holds throughout the film. Only the humor created by one of the defendants and the idyllic scene at Monte Carlo break the spell. The progressive ensnarement lets up near the end, but only momentarily.

Sets

Bernard Evien's sets are reduced to an absolute minimum—a typewriter, a dossier, a bare lightbulb for the interrogators' sessions, a dismal, empty cell for the incarceration. Evien and Costa-Gavras's reduction of the accessories to pathetic starkness creates a nearly pure abstraction. Their purpose was to make the privileged moment and place be the dialogue of torturer and tortured. On the other hand, the long, damp corridors are even more convincing than were the sets in Orson Welles's *Trial*. The viewer of *The Confession* feels trapped in a Sartrean *huis clos*.

Photography

As with other films of Costa-Gavras there is an iconography that helps situate the characters in time and space. In semiological terms, these elements become the *signifiers* of political *significance*. The pictures of the idolized Stalin, of President Gottwald, and even of the executioner Beria take on an aura of icons for party adherents such as Lise and Gérard. The Capa photo of the Republican soldier and Thaelmann banner in the London's residence allude to the past struggles against fascism.

As noted in our discussion of *Z*, Raoul Coutard has a concept of camera work that, although not independent of the director, manifests his personal approach. He does not have to depend upon Costa-Garvas for every detail but goes about his work professionally, having the confidence of his director. David Denby in the *Atlantic Monthly* comments on tone that can be created with a camera: "Raoul Coutard, who photographed *Z* and many of Godard's greatest movies, keeps the restlessly moving London . . . in extremely tight frame, a technical skill in the handling of the camera that produces the effect of tension and claustrophobia."[27] By prolonging the tension with a close-up of the confused Gérard in his cell or of one of the browbeaten individuals during the questioning, Coutard forces us to enter the psychological state of the victim. When an interrogator of Gérard guzzles beer and stuffs himself with sausage, the close-up of his face from the perspective of the starved Gérard is overpowering. We come to detest this outrage against humanity in the person of the interrogator. Occasionally a zoom shot catches a close-up of the chair and table—the tools of the inquisitors—and underlines their importance in the process, though it may seem overly aesthetic and artificial. Gérard's glance through the rearview mirror at the mysterious car trailing him heightens the dramatic tension. Although there is a repetition of certain images and shots from diverse angles, Costa-Gavras and Raoul Coutard primarily use only one camera. Unlike some of the American productions, they choose not to use a full, rich Technicolor to romanticize the image, something Costa-Gavras had learned with *Shock Troops*. Color is toned down in *The Confession*. With somber shades accented, the ambiance is one of gloom, pain, and death. The harsh tones reveal a state of feeling, says Stanley Kauffmann in *The New Republic*. They do not just provide a background.

Joan Mellen in *Cinéaste* rightly considers the employment of color here as "judgmental," perhaps one step beyond the "revelatory" function remarked on by Kauffmann. Mellen observes:

> That Costa-Gavras chose to do the story of grey bureaucrats in a grey landscape in color was a superb choice. The absence of color in the presence of Eastman color further reinforces the moral judgment we are meant to make on Stalinist society. The bright blue sky of the bay in Southern France from which London is shown to be telling his story in 1965 imparts the spiritual relief of London's final escape from the torture of the crumbling grey walls of the Czech prisons.[28]

Parallel to the camera work of Coutard is the still photography of Chris Marker, who is a master of the image, as can be seen in his assembly of still photos for a political projection of the future in *La Jetée* and in the historical review for *Le Fond de l'air est rouge*.[29] For the production of *The Confession* he was the set photographer. From his experience with the crew, he also made a short film on the making of *The Confession, Le Deuxième Procès d'Artur London* (The Second Trial of Artur London).

Throughout the film Costa-Gavras inserts newsreels. When Gérard catches sight of the red star on the cap of the Soviet guard, he is immediately taken back into history. Scenes of the October Revolution and the anti-Nazi struggle are superimposed on the star. Directly prior to the trial there is a flash to the newsreel of the Sacco and Vanzetti march—two other supposedly innocent victims executed in the name of justice in 1927. As part of the epilogue actual newsreels of the Prague invasion in 1968 are included. Speaking of the blending of newsreels with realistic fiction film, Costa-Gavras recounted to his interviewer Glenn O'Brien:

> The use of footage in *The Confession* is very short and it's only related to images we all have in our minds. It really relates to what I said before about the Soviet Union. The images of the Nazi flags thrown in front of Stalin—is an image extremely important for us Europeans. And most people over ten or twelve years old in 1945 do remember this. So in fact they are not documentary images—they were in fact pieces of memory that I was bringing back. I was inciting the memory to return to these images.[30]

Whereas Jorge Semprun and Costa-Gavras deliberately chose not to include newsreels in *Z* to avoid sentimentality, as at the funeral of the martyred deputy, in *The Confession* they wisely decided to use them to recreate the London flashbacks of the book, but above all, to render a more historical dimension to the situation of the victim.[31]

Besides furnishing historical depth to the film, Costa-Gavras further utilizes newsreels to express the psychological confusion of Gérard as Joan Mellen points out:

> Costa-Gavras's juxtaposition of newsreel footage with his narrative is an attempt to clarify through visual means the political issues which he has left undefined. On the night before the trial, London recalls marching in the fight

to save the lives of Sacco and Vanzetti. He remembers scenes such as Soviet soldiers burning Nazi flags. The use of newsreels to represent human memory is imaginative. But in this particular instance the memories of London show only his continuing confusion: on the eve before eleven men, no more guilty than he, are to be condemned by the state, he is still associating the Soviet Union with freedom, symbolized by the fight against fascism. The hammer and sickle and the red star on the hat of the prison guard recall to London the triumphant figure of Lenin. Combined with the many newsreel clips of Stalin, at work and at play, these images set up once again the terms of London's dilemma. In what meaningful terms can he continue to call himself a Communist, as he understands the term?[32]

While these newsreels or memory banks serve as historical recapitulation, Costa-Gavras employs the flashforward several times to launch the characters and the spectator into an uncertain future. This device, somewhat imaginative and daring, breaks the natural flow of the narrative. As Osvald Zavrodosky, minister of state security, is being interrogated, there is a flashforward—he is executed in 1954 (two years later). As already developed, after the laughter of the court at defendant Sling's embarrassment at last subsides, there is the ironic flashforward to the remains of the eleven executed men being sprinkled on the roadway to provide traction for the vehicle.

The most audacious and significant use of flashforward technique is the Monte Carlo episode depicting an event of 1965. In the film Gérard faints from exhaustion during the interrogation. He is revived by a bucket of water tossed on him. The scene moves in slow motion. A quick cut to Monte Carlo with its blue water and sky comes as a visual shock. Costa-Gavras deliberately uses the Brechtian technique of a flashfoward to create the effect of *distantiation*. This pulls the spectator out of the normal course of chronological narrative in order to spark his or her reflection on the actual events of 1952. Costa-Gavras comments on his purpose in using this technique:

> This method of interrupting the narrative is anti-cinematographic in the sense that all idea of suspense is shattered by a flashforward. The character whom we have been following and who we may imagine will be executed, is discovered to be very much alive. It was important to do this so that the viewer might pause for a moment and reflect.[33]

This projection into the future may appear artificial, but it corresponds totally to what was happening in London's psyche during the interrogation. London confirmed it in our 1979 interview. Such hallucinations were common to London and to the other prisoners with him, just as starving inmates of the concentration camps used to fantasize about food. This usage of flashforwards may be partially the idea of Semprun, who worked with Resnais. The New Wave director was most sensitive to this type of mechanism, already conveying the correspondence of cinematic technique with psychological tricks of memory in *Marienbad, Hiroshima, Providence,* and more recently in showing the experiences of Dr. Henri Laborit in *Mon Oncle d'Amérique*.[34]

Editing

A director ordinarily has full control over the editing process and can encourage or veto certain shots or juxtapositions proposed by an editor. Costa-Gavras, however, creates a symbiotic relationship with Françoise Bonnot, who edited *Z* and earned a Hollywood Oscar for it. For more than three months in early 1970 Costa-Gavras supervised the editing of the footage at Billancourt, working with four editors and assistants. Costa-Gavras commented on the relationship of director to screenwriter and editor in the following manner:

> In France and I think now in the U.S., the director does the editing. I think the director has control of the film in all its aspects. Jorge Semprun wrote the scenario but if he had written it for another director he would have written it differently. Obviously the director does the shooting but most of all the montage. It's the real writing of the director. The director cannot just give orders to an editor and tell him to go ahead and edit. Personally, and I think all my generation in France, the director does all the editing. He spends eight hours a day with the editor and we say we have to cut here and here—and so really he is in complete control.[35]

The editor, just like the director of photography—for example, Coutard—lends personality and experience to the cutting, although the director supervises and determines the tone. This is obviously the case with Françoise Bonnot. The editor must bear a large part of the responsibility for the actual physical task of cutting, choosing the length of shots, and planning the juxtapositions, which creates the tone and rhythm. Much depends, of course, on the original scenario and on the footage at hand from the filming. Several factors must be discussed with respect to the editing in *The Confession*. First of all, the overall tone of the film is necessarily heavy, dense, and solemn, as determined in advance by the subject matter. Only the humorous incident at the trial and the Monte Carlo flashforward lighten the work. The newsreels maintain the same serious tone, adding a historical as opposed to a human, psychological dimension to the film. The interrogators move along ploddingly at times, as one half-truth is added to another until the final confession is ready after almost two years. Occasionally the extensive interrogation—a daily affair of almost eighteen hours—was broken up in the film by a quick shifting from one interrogator to another, a procedure Costa-Gavras used in *Z*, having the examining magistrate rapidly question a long series of witnesses.

After the viewer has entered slowly into Gérard's physical and psychological condition over the long period of interrogation, the tempo changes to a quick pace—very much like the conclusion of *Z*. We view quickly the trial, sentence, acceptance of the punishment, and the series of incidents that make up the epilogue. The viewer is almost euphoric at the end, when justice has been at last established. Yet the final images return the spectator to the harsh, concrete reality of August 1968, the Soviet invasion.

As noted earlier, quick cutting produces the psychological effect of association of images. There is a cut on a certain clue—the water splashed on Gérard or the red star on the cap of the guard. There is one flashback that shows Gérard at a dinner with his wife, in which she says, "The Party is always right." There is a cut back to Gérard's cell, where his voice-off agrees: "The Party is always right. It's a misunderstanding. Truth will prevail, if we observe the rules, however hard they are, as proof of our faith."

The juxtaposition of the trial scene with the incident of the ashes may appear on the surface as cruel and ironic, but it is no more so than the actuality. In 1968, London learned from the Czech press the fate of his comrades:

> When the eleven men had been executed the interrogator D. happened to be in the Ruzyn prison in the office of the (Soviet) adviser Galkin. The chauffeur and the two interrogators who were supposed to get rid of the ashes were also there. They said they had put them in a potato sack and had made for the suburbs of Prague, hoping to leave them in a field. Seeing the icy road, however, they decided to throw the ashes on it. The chauffeur laughed. He said it was the first time he had driven fourteen passengers in his Tatra, three alive and eleven in a sack.[36]

In general, the editing techniques of Françoise Bonnot are very sophisticated. Critics such as Vincent Canby are less appreciative of the editing and the flashy style of cinema. Canby and others claim that the extraordinary zoom shots, flashbacks, and close-ups mitigate against the message—a classic case of form opposing content. Whereas this may be true for some of Costa-Gavras's other works, for example, *Z*, the devices appear less obvious and contrived in *The Confession*.

Sound

Part of Françoise Bonnot's work also included sound editing. Her skill is evident in the trial sequence in which there is a dramatic repetition of the phrase "of Jewish origin" and later the meek mutterings of "I accept my sentence." In *The Confession* the dimension of sound is creative and revolutionary. William Sivel was the sound engineer and Daniel Couteau was responsible for the unique effects. Costa-Gavras discusses the conscious manipulation of sound in the film:

> It is in order to accentuate the solitude of the character. This individual has lived twenty-two months with the same noises, the same sound of closing doors, of footsteps—all associated with the recurrence of the interrogation sessions. As soon as a man begins to live in an isolated world, as London did, with little sleep and minimal food, every little noise automatically assumed greater proportions.[37]

To achieve the sense of solitude as well as to recreate the dehumanizing process, the sounds in the prison are exaggerated. The gurgling of filth oozing up from the floor of the cell becomes revolting for London and for the spectator. The voices of the interrogators are fraught with violence as they bully Gérard into submission—"*Marchez*" (Walk!), "*Mangez*" (Eat!), "*Confessez*" (Admit!). The penetrating screams of the other victims undergoing torture make a house of horrors of the prison.

The now common cliché of a spastic heartbeat, used in Z during the deputy's operation, is repeated twice in *The Confession*. As Gérard is being followed by the ominous Tatra, his heartbeat quickens. He feels tense. Gérard senses greater anxiety later when the interrogators take him to a park and pretend that they are going to hang him. There is a close-up of Gérard's ear listening to the birds chirping, an alien but welcome sound of nature, of freedom, of life. This use of the close-up of Gérard's ear occurred at the outset of the film as he listened to chimes, while blindfolded by his captors.

Sound was used to introduce irony into the situation. As the curtain is about to rise on the well-rehearsed drama of the trial, a farce, one defendant strikes the traditional three knocks of the French theater to indicate the opening of the performance. While the hunted men soon to be apprehended meet in one room, the sound of children spontaneously emitting bursts of laughter can be heard from the next room—another ironic juxtaposition. One of the most powerful uses of sound occurs in the epilogue during the protest of Prague youth against the Soviet invasion. As the images of the struggle unfold on the screen, the sound track is silent—a symbolic gesture of the embattled, but also a silent protest against this domineering move by the U.S.S.R. Joan Mellen suggests that the absence of sound in this final sequence could be a symbol of the impotence of these youth, but it could also be a symbol of the silent resistance that the Czechs would have to take for the time being.

For the most part music does not play a major role in *The Confession* as it did in Z. That makes the film all the more unusual and noncommercial. When music does appear, it is lush and haunting. Just as the sound track of Z had its own history, so, too, does that of *The Confession*. London mentioned to us that, while on location in Lille, Chris Marker discovered the music later used in the film. The simple melody is the work of a Czech composer and gives an added dimension to its use in the film. There are only approximately three minutes of music in the two-hour film. Several individuals encouraged the director to insert more music in the sound track to accelerate the momentum of the film. He refused since he had a different purpose in mind and did not feel it was necessary.

Because of the innovative use of sound in the amplication of natural noises, mechanical sounds such as grinding doors, human screams and orders, enigmatic music, in the reflective voice-off of Gérard, Vincent Canby of the *New York Times* calls *The Confession* "one of the most aurally resonant movies" that he has ever seen.[38]

The Film's Epilogue

As in Z, there is an epilogue to the film. Just as everything is resolved and one sees Gérard and the others triumphing with their rehabilitation, Costa-Gavras deals the filmgoer a final blow. Several events that followed the trial are used in the epilogue and are worth noting. When London chances to meet his torturer Kohoutek in the Prague square, and the latter shrugs off the guilt and responsibility of the executions, Gérard is stupified. The freeze shot captures this reaction perfectly. When Kohoutek wonders what London can make of all this and mentions that he, too, has become a victim of the powers that be, the director underlines the fact that abusers of power eventually become the abused. Colin Westerbeck comments on the implications of this chance meeting: "What a superb irony this is! All men are trapped by the necessity of history after all, no matter how wisely or warily they try to move with the times."[39] London mentioned to us that this encounter between him and Kohoutek did not actually take place, but between another victim, Eduard Goldstücker, and Kohoutek. The intrinsic value of the scene in the epilogue is not destroyed, London insisted in our lengthy interview.

A second irony to the epilogue is London's arrival in Prague to submit his manuscript to the Committee of Czech Writers, which agreed to publish it. He arrived on the day of the invasion, 20 August 1968. The shot of a perplexed London, staring before him into the Prague square (actually shot in Amiens), destroys any hope in the mind of the viewer that justice will really be restored. As he stands there, he witnesses the Czech resistance against the Soviets. The subsequent shots of Prague during the invasion by the tanks were actually taken by a group of French cineastes who were on location in the city at the time to document the supposed political thaw. The police harassed them and prevented them from filming. Nonetheless, they were able to come away with some excellent footage of the invasion. Costa-Gavras contacted them and got permission to use their material in his film. The result of the projection of these incidents is to create a powerful message of resistance.

The last irony of the epilogue, the concluding note, is the political inscription the youth wrote on the walls of Prague: "Lenin, awaken, they have gone mad!" It expresses the young people's revolutionary desire to return to the pure sources of revolution represented by Lenin, to protest against the Stalinist abuses of power, and to rebel against the present Soviet regime. London explained that the original graffiti read, "Lenin, awaken. Brezhnev has gone mad!" The slogan was altered to avoid possible problems with the censors and with international relationships. The modified inscription is more ambiguous and impersonal, but the point is well made.

The epilogue was later severely criticized by the Communist party. It accused the director and screenwriter of stacking the cards against the party with the shots of the Soviet invasion as a false, shocking finale. London defends the film artists by stating that Semprun and Costa-Gavras did not cheat or prostitute his own interpretation. As a witness to the historical events, London explains:

> It was not possible to end the film without showing scenes of August 1968, without mentioning the occupation of Czechoslovakia by the Warsaw Pact armies. These incidents take up two pages in the book and five minutes in the film, but their insertion was absolutely indispensable. To conclude with my rehabilitation would have implied that these events never happened. The invasion and occupation of August 1968 were the answer to the "Springtime

The Confession: "Lenin, awaken, they have gone mad."
(Permission of Paramount Pictures Corp.)

of Prague" during which my countrymen had affirmed their determination to put an end once and for all to this Stalinist period and to pursue the political battle.[40]

Coming fifteen years after the death of Stalin, the Soviet entry into Czechoslovakia reveals that the spirit of a man lives long after his passing away. We sense that Stalin's death did not mark the end of party totalitarianism, aggression, or racism.

Politics

After the widespread popularity of *Z* as a political thriller, a Unifrance film interviewer asked Costa-Gavras if he feared the label of "director of political films." Costa-Gavras replied, "Not at all. Today this genre is the only one that really interests me. . . . It is my personal means of crying out, of revolting."[41] He understood realistically that cinema would not radically change society, causing someone either to occupy a factory or overthrow a government.[42] For Costa-Gavras a specific film—such as *Z* or *The Confession*—is meant to reflect a universal reality and to symbolize a type of situation to which it is necessary to attract attention.

To this genre of fiction film Costa-Gavras added the ingredients of history, law, and politics, the kind already evident in London's literary testimony. *The Confession* thus made the politics of Stalinism more comprehensible and actual. Because the film is a vivid audiovisual medium, it makes a more significant impact than the book, and is concomitantly open to more criticism from a vast and varied public, as we will later see.

In general, Costa-Gavras's film stirred up massive political waves because it was not the usual anticommunist attack by the Right, but a serious, soul-searching document by two artists of leftist leanings: Costa-Gavras in March of 1971 referred to himself as a Sartrean Marxist; Semprun was a former member of the Spanish Communist party. In the past any reaction by political conservatives to Soviet abuses was normally considered partisan propaganda. Now the liberal Left joined the battle against these antihumanitarian indignities, and the voice of their protest becomes loud and clear. Following *Z*, *The Confession* shifts the target from the totalitarian Right to the totalitarian Left. The latter film does not contradict the earlier one but complements it.

The issues in *The Confession* are more complex than in *Z* and in other Italian, French, or American political films. They require some careful scrutiny. Costa-Gavras insists that in *The Confession* he wishes to go beyond politics to something deeper, to treat of a man, his problems, and his psychology. In his films, he stresses that the human being is always more important than the state. That credo obliges him to develop the conflict of the one with the other. Costa-Gavras, with Jorge Semprun and Artur London, sought a kind of socialism with a human face. Above all, the director did not want a human being destroyed by a political party. Costa-Gavras realized that *The Confession* would be a disturbing film and would cause serious repercussions, but he questioned whether someone should lose all traces of human dignity because of loyalty to a party and to an ideological discipline.

Costa-Gavras hoped to unveil the inhuman and insidious Stalinist regime, beyond dealing with the interior struggle of London to survive the anonymous horror of the party, beyond stressing his blind religious faith in the revolutionary cause. In his other films the director showed the innocent, heroic individual trapped by an all-persuasive and destructive mechanism—Greek fascism, American imperialism, or French collaboration. The human being is victim of political repression, caught in this machine that only history or fate can expose. The bureaucracy for which these convicted individuals work eventually consumes its own employees, the die-hard militants who dedicated their lives to the cause which now turns on them.

The political machine gone haywire in *The Confession* is socialism, manipulated to serve Stalin's personal and perverse purposes. The film, like the book, is not meant to be antisocialist or anticommunist, but anti-Stalinist, an important distinction that must be made, if one is not to fall into the trap of political ignorance as some of the French and American critics have done. The film is primarily a denunciation of the various and multitudinous crimes that Stalin committed in the name of party purity. Semprun reiterated this distinction: "Our film is not anticommunist. It is communist. We have remained totally within the sphere of the communist world."[43]

To make a further distinction, Semprun and Costa-Gavras's purpose was to bring to light the aberrations from Lenin's original policies without tarnishing or challenging the original idea. They wished to indicate how these political obscenities of "Uncle Joe" should be avoided in the future, just like the latent fascism of *Z*. Within the film they can offer a historical hindsight. They can put the sociopolitical picture into focus by juxtaposing the dual image of Stalin—the anonymous executioner on a headhunting mission for freethinking Czech party officials; the humanitarian involved in civic good deeds. The villain becomes the paternal figure who is sorely missed when he dies, as the newsreels show. This suggests the twofold perspective of the Soviet leader—the hidden reality and the deceiving image.

David Denby in his critique "Stalinism on Film," indicates that, since *The Confession* is made by a celebrated leftist director, the sense of the great historical betrayal that it conveys cannot be simply dismissed as right-wing or obscurantist propaganda. When Denby spoke with Costa-Gavras about the film, the director mentioned that, in the past, filmmakers who approached this topic feared being labeled "anticommunist" or "anti-Socialist." Costa-Gavras developed this further, "As a result, inadmissable things were done in the Communist world, and no one on the left made a film about it. My film has been experienced as a catharsis because it expresses criticisms and doubts that had been repressed."[44]

We will shortly examine in closer detail the criticism launched by political figures, public, and film critics on this cinematic "catharsis." Politically speaking, for many people involved in the party, the screening of *The Confession* was obviously painful to endure. Party members were particularly sensitive to the treatment of the film since it was not just past history that was starkly exposed, but uncomfortable current events. The Soviet invasion took place less than two years before the release of the film.

Costa-Gavras chose to accentuate in the film a fiendish Stalinist anti-Semitism that was a divergence from the original ideology of the Communist Party. Stalin was waging his own racist war one decade before Hitler and Goebbels ideologically and systematically decimated the ranks of the Jewish people throughout Europe via tracts, posters, government policies, and formation of public opinion that resulted in the establishment of the extermination camps in the 1930s. By the early 1950s, the anti-Semitism of the Soviet government was spreading malignantly. Stalin closed Jewish schools and other institutions and disbanded the Jewish antifascist committee in order to eliminate the Jews from any positions of power and influence. In *The Origins of Totalitarianism* Hannah Arendt addresses these policies of the Soviet Union:

> The most dramatic element in this last purge which Stalin planned in the last years of his life, was a decisive shift in ideology, the introduction of a Jewish world conspiracy. For years, the ground for this change had been carefully laid in a number of trials in the satellite countries—the Rajk trial in Hungary, the Ana Pauker affair in Rumania, and, in 1952, the Slansky trial in Czechoslovakia. In these preparatory measures, high party officials were singled out because of their "Jewish bourgeois" origins and accused of Zionism; this accusation was gradually changed to implicate notoriously non-Zionist agencies (especially the American Jewish Point Distribution Committee), in order to

indicate that all Jews were Zionists and all Zionists "hirelings of American imperialism" (John A. Armstrong's words). There was of course nothing new in the "crime" of Zionism, but as the campaign progressed and began to center on Jews in the Soviet Union, another significant change took place: Jews now stood accused of "cosmopolitanism" rather than Zionism, and the pattern of accusations that developed out of this slogan followed ever more closely the Nazi patterns of a Jewish world conspiracy in the sense of the Elders of Zion.[45]

Throughout the interrogation of London presented in the book and film the label "Zionist" is cast in his face. In the film it is repeated with great disgust and venom. London is condemned for having *returned* from the Mauthausen camp despite his Jewish origins. Irony of ironies! The trial brings out the spirit of anti-Semitism poignantly. As the name of each of the accused is read off, the epithet is attached—"of Jewish origin." A stab in the back for eleven of the Jews. To implicate them further, simultaneously linking them with the bourgeois and separating them from the working class, there is also added "son of a businessman" or "son of a merchant." The last sacrilegious act to humanity is the scattering of the ashes of the executed at the close of the film. Costa-Gavras thus understands the historical fact of anti-Semitism and puts it into historical perspective.

Politics and Art

In merging politics with art, Costa-Gavras and Jorge Semprun create a dialectic process on the screen that obliges the viewer to produce a synthesis. Sergei Eisenstein, who greatly influenced Costa-Gavras's generation by his revolutionary content and technique, paved the way for this modern dialectic approach. Semprun and Costa-Gavras follow in the tradition of having art become the vehicle of an ideology that evokes a response, a reflection, a reaction.

In Robert Grelier's interview with London, the Czech author notes that he was impressed with the politico-aesthetic ideas of a fellow Eastern European, Miklós Jancsó:

> As a film director, I have done my best through my art, the art of the masses as Lenin defined it, to communicate to our friends, our comrades who are struggling to create a socialist atmosphere in the West, the tragic experience that we have lived along the way in the establishment of socialism. This is to prevent them from making the same errors, stumbling into the same pitfalls.[46]

The caveat fell on deaf ears behind the Iron Curtain.

Criticism

The ink spilt over the film *The Confession* in France and also in the U.S.— although to a lesser degree—was certainly more voluminous than that spilt over Z. Most French and American film critics compared and contrasted the two, underscoring especially a suspected shift of political perspective in Costa-Gavras and Jorge Semprun from one film to the other. In Czechoslovakia, however, *Rude Pravo,* the official newspaper of the Communist party, referred to the film as "a hate campaign against Czechoslovakia, against the U.S.S.R., against all the socialist countries, in fact against socialism." *Izvestia* in Moscow published a violent attack on the film and on all of the collaborators, especially after the Yugoslav officials took a positive stand toward it.

As could be expected, the language of the critics was imaginatively couched in imagery taken from the political sphere—Left, antisocialist, totalitarian, and so on. Occasionally there would be a literary reference in their critiques, for example, to Kafka or the realm of the absurd. Most often, especially in France, religious language prevailed. A compilation of their criticism shows that Stalin and the Muscovite *pontiffs* try to *exorcise* the *evil spirits* of Czechoslovakia during their political *Inquisition.* Stalin, fearing the *schism* of Titoism, thus *excommunicates* the *high priests* of the party, while certain *believers* such as London remain *loyal* in their *profession of faith* in the *infallibility* of Stalin. London—a *Judas, scapegoat,* or *heretic*—thus becomes a *martyr* following his supposed *departure* from *orthodoxy.*

At the time of the release of the film of *The Confession* in the United States—a time distant from the Cold War of the 1950s, a geography distant from Mother Russia—the criticism was less heated. Apart from Joan Mellen's detailed study of the political nuances of the film, American criticism was often shallow and less penetrating than its European counterpart. It was pointed out in the local criticism that the political climate resembled very much the one represented in the film *The Prisoner* about the plight of London's fellow countryman, Cardinal Mindzenty (which followed the film *Guilty of Treason* on the same subject). The American Communist party, perhaps one-thirtieth the size of the French Communist party, could not make headway against the film as did the French critics and party members. In France, where memories of the Slansky trial still painfully lingered on, and where individuals who signed their affirmation of the Soviet trials were still in the party or were fellow travelers, the reaction to the film was often partisan and hostile.

In general, criticism of the film was addressed to four aspects—adaptation, cinematic technique, acting, and, above all, politics. Anyone who knew the political scene of the 1950s or who read the account of Artur and Lise London in the French Gallimard edition, could immediately sense that it would be impossible to impart the complexity of the actual events in any one film. The written text conveyed not only the twenty-two-month interrogation and trial, but also sweeping phases of history—Russian socialism in the early 1930s, antifascism in the International Brigade in Spain in the late 1930s, the resistance movement in France during the 1940s, the Czech Communist party activities in the late 1940s and early 1950s. Newsreels did help to remind the viewer of the historical context, but it was physically impossible to construct adequately the true, political atmosphere unless the film had the scope of a production such as Bertolucci's *1900,* a cinematic marathon five hours long.

Artur London's response to the film was most crucial, since he is the protagonist of both the book and the film. In a sense he is partially responsible for the accuracy of the film production, for at every principal step of the writing of the scenario, he was aware of the director and screenwriter's intentions. His suggestions and guidance about specific details of the interrogation and the trial provided what was necessary for its authenticity. When the film was first projected in Paris, he was interviewed on several occasions to determine his appreciation of the adaptation.

In Bernard Féron's article in *Le Monde*, London affirms that Costa-Gavras and Jorge Semprun scrupulously respected the spirit of the book. They simplified the material, London admits, but did not eliminate anything that was absolutely essential. In fact, London confirms that they restored the truth of the book.[47] He also remarks that, in schematizing the essentials of the literary account, they condensed the true tragedy. For artistic reasons changes were made, but ordinarily with London in agreement. An artist involved in an adaptation must make a selection and exercise a judgment, he notes.[48] London concedes that for dramatic purposes, it is important to reinterpret an original work. London has seen the film several times, and on each occasion he finds it an enriching experience, discovering in it something new each time, he mentioned to us. What would London have liked to have seen in the film? He remarked that there should have been a greater development of the role of his wife, who was crucial to his survival. This also points up the difference between the French and English editions of the text. London further added that it would also have been most advantageous to present the historical climate more clearly and in greater detail, but at the same time, he said he understood the limitations of film production.

On another level, most of the film criticism underlined the technical skills of the entire crew, praised the acting, script, photography, color, sound, staging, and overall direction. Few critics mentioned the editing of Françoise Bonnot, which they took for granted, and yet her work was a significant factor in the success of the film.

There is almost unanimity in the press about the incredible power of Yves Montand to recreate London's existential situation. London himself was impressed and felt that it was a perfect rendering of this ordeal. Montand was never more emotionally committed to a role, and his convictions were most intimately conveyed. The critics attribute Montand's realistic and convincing portrayal of Gérard to his weight loss, seclusion from the crew during the filming, to his sleeping on the floor at night, but above all, to his intellectual and psychological grasp of the plight of London in the 1950s. Mark Goodman in *Time* says that it is not "possible to fault Montand's performance as a Camus figure cast into a dialectic inferno."[49] Most critics are positive in their assessment of Montand, calling his acting "total identification," as did Jacqueline Michel of *Télé Sept Jours*. There were three notable exceptions. François Maurin of the communist newspaper *L'Humanité* fails to appreciate Montand as actor or appreciate the character he plays, judging the film in a caustic and polemical fashion. In the *Herald Tribune*, Thomas Quinn Curtis speaks of Montand in somewhat derogatory terms—"The Don Quixote of the Left." Patrick McFadden in *Film Society Review* suggests more cruelly that the actor is suffering "from an ennobling form of dropsy—looking both hurt and surprised like an artificially inseminated cow."[50]

The critics see Simone Signoret as excellent in her reduced role. Mark Goodman in *Time* reports that Signoret "is relegated to the unhappy role of two-dimensional superfluity."[51] The secondary figure of a Michel Vitold (Smola) was occasionally considered a caricature; witness the review of Paul-Louis Thirard in *Positif*. McFadden comments on the other actors:

> There are two outstanding performances: Gabriele Ferzetti as Kohoutek, the interrogator who conducts his sessions with the kind of uncertain authority one finds in lapsed priests; and Jean Bouise, who makes a splendid little cameo out of a factory manager who bears the quiet integrity of one who knows these things will pass.[52]

In general, in this film there is a correlation of characterization and ideology. Joan Mellen says:

> Prison guards and interrogators are always cruel and hateful. Harassed and suffering innocent victims are invariably martyrs with whom we can identify. But the dilemma is that these stereotypes could describe the inquisition, the Dreyfus trial or that of Angela Davis equally. The task of *The Confession* was to inform these contemporary participants in the eternal drama of punisher and punished with their specific historical, intellectual and social reference. Without this, as in Z, the melodrama, the excitement, the easy moral righteousness of the participants in *The Confession* mitigate against the successful alliance of image and idea.[53]

It is in the aspect of Costa-Gavras's politics—revisionist or reformist in the mind of some critics—that *The Confession* evoked the most impassioned discussion. Costa-Gavras realized that the film would spark a controversy. He anticipated it by first screening the film for a group of French Communist party members—Andrieu, Aragon, Daix, and others—to solicit their reactions. At this session, and continuing for the next several months, there was a multitude of mixed reactions, to say the least. The crusty old Stalinists (who do not admit to being so) were embarrassed and at times hostile. The liberal leftists certainly applauded. A large group of traditional communists fell in between the two positions, but among themselves had a varied response; many were open and sensitive to the purpose of Semprun and Costa-Gavras and to the cinematic treatment of the subject. Some did not like the Monte Carlo sequence. Others felt that including the Soviet invasion in the epilogue might be putting a new weapon in the hands of the unsympathetic bourgeois press, which could use the Cassandra attitude, "See, we told you so!" Thierry Maulnier, drama director and member of the Académie Française, reflected a similar viewpoint when he said that the Right had been condemning the Siberian labor camps and the fear and terror of a police state for fifty years before this film came along, and very few people listened.[54] Montand in *L'Express* is quick to mention that it was not the fault of the creators of *The Confession* that Russia invaded Czechoslovakia!

Jean de Baroncelli of *Le Monde* for 2 May 1970 testifies that the film powerfully recreates a nightmare, shakes our nerves, and wounds our conscience at the same time. Despite many hostile attacks by the French political press, Jean Limoursin of *Valeurs Actuelles* for 18 May 1970 calls it a "rare proof of the objectivity of the cineastes." These critics reflect the positive in their approach to the film.

The sharpest attack comes from the heart of the French Communist party. It was published in an article by François Maurin (*L'Humanité*) on 29 April 1970. Although the party did accept the publication of London's text, it did not look kindly upon the release of the film. Maurin first of all charges that Costa-Gavras made of London's communist text a basically anticommunist film. (Semprun, Costa-Gavras, and London would repeat, *anti-Stalinist!*) This is evident, Maurin wrote, in the portrayal of the brutality and unsavory character of the Soviet agents, of the stacking of evidence against the Soviets with the polemical epilogue dealing with the invasion. In this sense Costa-Gavras distorts history, and deliberately sets out to provoke the Communist party. Maurin also notes that the Twentieth Party Congress is not mentioned in the film. (London wrote back to say that it is.) Maurin's accusations continue. The role of Maurice Thorez in London's release is deliberately omitted, and the *L'Humanité* reporter at the trial apparently showed complicity with what was going on by his mere presence. The critic also feels that the film (perhaps like the book) does not show London acknowledging his responsibility for these crimes as a child of the socialist machinery. The last salvo that Maurin aims at Costa-Gavras is an accusation that the director demonstrates a Manichean conception of the world and a romanticized vision of the revolutionary struggle. To be fair in recording Maurin's reaction to the film, it must be said that the book appealed to him, for here he could perceive a man in his totality—body and soul—committed to the party. The critic could also see the quest for truth and the value of exposing these crimes as a violation of socialist legality. Nonetheless, this is where he stops.

Les Lettres Françaises, whose editor is London's son-in-law, Pierre Daix, helps redeem the film in the 13 May 1970 issue. Here, the critic Michel Capdenac views it not as a didactic or historical work, but as one that expresses truths difficult to accept but important. It is like open-heart surgery—risky but saving for the health of the body. Capdenac observes that the most significant value of this film is to warn us of what can happen in the future if we are not careful.

The debate does not end here. Several of London's comrades refused to speak to him after the appearance of the book. The film intensified their silence. Although the case did not attain the proportions of *L'Affaire Dreyfus*, it did divide the ranks of the communists. Certain communists campaigned against the film. Others tolerated the barb. Noncommunists questioned how London could proclaim his innocence when he himself was responsible for the inner workings of the Czech regime and had nodded his approval in the execution of Hungary's scapegoat, Laszlo Rajk.

Inside and outside the party, criticism snowballed, primarily aimed at the political aspect of the film. Judith Crist of *New York* writes:

> *The Confession* is the first movie to rise above the simplistic and sophomoric political mouthings of the dismally youth-oriented kiddie-level fictional movies and documentaries that have flooded the screens. . . . Initially gripping, inherently grueling, it becomes wearing and wearying. Nevertheless, it is a fascinating film in its detail.[55]

The negative press is just as articulate and almost as voluminous. Much of the criticism surrounding the politics of the film also raised the charge that it lacked historical perspective. Although the scenario was supplemented by London's precisions for the interrogation and the trial, and though newsreels helped fill in the details, all this was still insufficient for many critics. They spoke of the film taking place in a vacuum. Albert Cervoni of the communist weekly *France Nouvelle* accused Costa-Gavras of taking one aspect of socialism and forgetting about the rest.

Addressing the political weaknesses of the film, Joan Mellen comments:

> Likewise, in *The Confession,* he [Costa-Gavras] deals with the mechanics of the Stalinist purges without probing their dynamic, without exploring motive. Never once does this film effectively explain what was meant by "Trotskyism" or "Titoism" or why these men haunted the dreams of Stalin, why he assassinated the one and tried his best to isolate the other once he was beyond his control.[56]

Mike Prokosch in *Film Quarterly* questions why Costa-Gavras does not provide London with greater motivation for remaining in the party than the sentimental reasons provided by a few photographs (and newsreels) and a few friends. Patrick McFadden is less gentle: "Hence he [Costa-Gavras] settles, as he did in *Z*, for a preachy humanism, packaged for the popcorn radicals of the Film Generation."[57]

In *Le Figaro Littéraire* for 17 August 1970, Claude Mauriac intelligently places the film in its ideological and historical context, touching upon the resistance, the Prague events of 1952, the methodology of forced confessions, and the role of the Communist party through it all. Mauriac enumerates the various details that Semprun and Costa-Gavras suppressed, for example, London's Communist Youth activities, his crusade in Moscow in the 1930s, and his suicide attempts, but despite these and other lacunae, the critic feels that this film has the power to make a previously known and tolerated situation totally unbearable.

In *Films in Review*, Henry Hart strikes out against the political bearing of *The Confession*, perhaps misunderstanding some of the essentials:

> *The Confession* is the same sort of inept propaganda that *Z* was, and it was directed by the same inept director (Costa-Gavras). This time the political propaganda is anti-Communist, or more exactly, anti-Soviet, but it's so double-talking, and secretive about its primary propaganda purpose, the USSR is rarely if ever mentioned by name.[58]

Pauline Kael in the *New Yorker* of 21 December 1970 objects that there is too much data given and insufficient reflection upon it. In the *Herald Tribune* of 2

May 1970, Thomas Quinn Curtiss refers to the film as a "political melodrama." Gaston Haustrate's approach to the film in *Témoignage Chrétien,* 7 May 1970, is also negative, calling it a "little inspired political *spectacle,*" one that is too schematized and too archetypal. In the *Village Voice* for 17 December 1970, Andrew Sarris admits, "*The Confession* lingers in my mind as one of the most boring experiences I have endured since I began reviewing films. . . . [It is] stupefyingly dull and obvious, and idiotically belated . . . a facile political film." Jean Collet of *Télérama* of 17 May 1970 attacks the film as he did *Z* for "its unfair methods which are ever so many low body blows—an organized bludgeoning of the public."

Mark Goodman in *Time* of 4 January 1971 strikes a balance. He observes that *The Confession* has enough individual merits to redeem it from its overall flaws; however, "*The Confession* fails as a film because it is at base a stenographic document, meticulously recounting the liturgy of political confession without regard for its drama."

Epilogue

Costa-Gavras, Jorge Semprun, and Artur London undertook a significant risk in making *The Confession.* Their decision was not made in a vacuum, yet they did not fully realize all of the repercussions the film could cause, surpassing the international repercussions of *Z*. As the criticism accumulated on both sides of the Iron Curtain and within and without the Communist party, a series of incidents occurred indicating that the film was far from a neutral and innocent object on the international cinema market.

• In March 1970, *Variety* reported that Costa-Gavras went on his own to Spain to record reaction to *The Confession* of the Spanish public during the Franco regime. In a press conference he discussed censorship. "When you forbid a film it's because you're afraid of it, because it applies to the country where it's barred." *The Confession,* however, was shown in its entirety in Spain, although London mentioned that almost twenty minutes (the conversation at Monte Carlo) were cut in a private screening for Franco.

• *Variety* of April 1970 noted that while Costa-Gavras was in Chile preparing his next film, he discovered that right-wing opposition parties there had turned *The Confession* into a major issue for the forthcoming elections. The communist daily *El Siglo,* like *L'Humanité,* published two articles attacking the film. Costa-Gavras saw the right people, appeared on television to explain his original intent in making the film, and suggested to the Warner Brothers distributors in Chile to postpone the opening of the film until after the elections.

• In the same month of April, *Les Lettres Françaises* published an interview with Costa-Gavras by Gérard Langlois in which the director mentioned that the European success of *The Confession* was due to an antifascist spirit. In America, the film was popular primarily on university campuses. One student newspaper translated the Stalinist situation into an American problem using the names of U.S. government leaders, said Costa-Gavras. He ended the interview with, "In any case, it is about time that the political film has come into its own. There should be at least ten produced a year in France."

• In May 1970, the vice-president of Soviet cinema, Vladimir Boskakov in his visit to Paris stated pointblank that *The Confession* was anticommunist. He hadn't seen it and didn't plan to!

• *The Confession* was screened for the first time in a socialist country of Eastern Europe, at Zagreb, Yugoslavia, in July 1970. It was a private, noncommercial screening arranged by the weekly *Vus.* Artur London was invited but could not attend. Lise London went, accompanied by Costa-Gavras, Jorge Semprun, Yves Montand, and Simone Signoret. It was touching to hear Lise London discuss this trip during our interview in 1979. She described the gathering of the old and young at the session, many recognizing in the film what they had already seen or sensed close up. In the question-and-answer period Lise had discussed the bourgeois implications of the film—the coupons found on London's person at his arrest and the fact that her children were never taken to school in the ministry's car but walked the one mile every day. At the end of the screening, according to *Combat* of 2 July 1970, Lise London said, "I look forward to the day when one will be able to see this film in Prague, in the Soviet Union, in Bulgaria, everywhere. . . . Then we will be able to say that our cause has triumphed!"

• On 5 August 1970 London was stripped of his nationality for the second time, for his collaboration in the film. He had experienced the same excommunication in 1952 in the course of the trial. The Hussak regime of 1970 struggled to reduce the impact of the film by having certain newspapers in Prague and Brno publish the most repulsive allegations against London from the files of the Slansky trial as if they were all established fact. The award of Order of the Republic granted him by President Swoboda in May 1968 was obviously reversed. The "Amicale" group of the Mauthausen survivors in Paris protested against this treatment, saluting London as a humanitarian and citing his bravery and intelligence in organizing resistance during his internment in the camps.

• At one point during the regime of the colonels in Greece (1967–74), Costa-Gavras was asked to screen *The Confession* in his native country. He would agree, he said, only if the government permitted the same distribution liberties to *Z*, which was only allowed in 1974.

• The film was banned in Czechoslovakia, although many Czechs saw it, for it was broadcast by Viennese and West German television, which could be received in Czechoslovakia.

• In 1971, the film won the United Nations prize of the British Film Academy; in the same year Costa-Gavras became president of the Société des Réalisateurs Français.

• French television had a special screening of *The Confession* in December 1976 as part of the series "Dossiers de l'Ecran," on the topic "The Trial in the Eastern European Bloc: A Socialist Malady." The participants were the Londons, Pierre Juquin and Jean Kanapa of the French Communist party, Laurent Scwartz, a mathematician, and the former director of Radio Prague, Jiri Pelikan. Six years after the premiere of the film in Paris, Jean Kanapa tried to play down the antagonism of the party in 1970 toward the collaborators in the making of the film, much to the dismay of the Londons. At the conclusion of the program, said Lise London, the technicians applauded her and swooped down to congratulate her.

• After the release of the film in Paris and at the time of his sixtieth birthday, London proudly claimed to Nicole Chatel for *Le Monde:* "For forty years I have been faithful to myself. Today, just as yesterday, I feel proud of all those who, in Vietnam, in Greece, in Latin America, in Africa, in the United States, everywhere, fight injustice and foreign domination, in order to build a socialist society where Man can totally fulfill his every aspiration." As our interview of 1979 concluded, Lise and Artur London expressed the same optimism and fervor that they shared more than forty years ago in Moscow when they first met. Never cynical, they maintain an inner possession of the "truth." Their deep and unchanged faith in the socialist movement, despite their physical, psychological, and political ordeals, continues.

• London, Semprun, and Costa-Gavras wrote and filmed *The Confession* to bring to light the perversions of Stalinism and to encourage other communists to keep the faith, for it could happen again. On 22 October 1979 a similar tragedy did reoccur. In Prague, six signees of the Charter 77 for human rights were brought to court in a secret state trial on charges of a liaison with the CIA and other Western agents. The trial was considered the most significant and abusive since the Stalinist trials. Then following the well-established pattern from the days of the 1968 Prague takeover, the Soviet army invaded Afghanistan on 27 December 1979. Curiously parallel is Fritz Lang's conclusion to his antifascist film *Hangmen Also Die!* (1943), about the political situation of Czechoslovakia: "NOT THE END"!

6

State of Siege: Ugly American or Good Samaritan?

> Today, *State of Siege*, which I am about to complete, concludes a trilogy. Now that I have made these three films, I sense a great weight lifted from my shoulders. I feel better. Now I am anxious to go on to something else.
>
> —COSTA-GAVRAS, 1972

With *State of Siege* (Etat de Siège, 1973), Costa-Gavras felt that another period of his controversial film career drew to a close. His first two films, *The Sleeping Car Murder* and *Shock Troops,* may be considered a rite of passage. *Z, The Confession,* and *State of Siege* clearly reveal a more perfect development of cinematic technique, a creation of strong ties with the established film industry, solid friendships among actors and technicians, but above all, a more profound political astuteness. In numerous interviews dating from 1972–1973 Costa-Gavras reflects a deep consciousness about many sociopolitical problems that are harmful to the health of the individual, the country, and the world. The director began to detect and point out to his international audiences certain unfortunate patterns in fascist rightist governments in totalitarian leftist regimes and in imperialist policies of large countries. This global view was added to his perspective on problems of political assassinations, repressive police forces, and legal systems that could hardly be called legal.

In the third part of his trilogy, Costa-Gavras touches upon a sensitive and contentious topic—political and economic relations of the North American government to countries currently undergoing economic development. The specific target of his cinematic wrath is the use of systematized torture in interrogation allegedly initiated by an American official from the Agency for International Development (AID) acting under the appearance of technician of public safety and communications. This agent, Philip Michael Santore (Dan A. Mitrione in reality), is ultimately caught between duty to American governmental policy and the Tupamaro guerrillas' hostile reaction to the unethical means of interrogating and eliminating the Latin American revolutionary group. Costa-Gavras pene-

143

trates the core of the political problem at hand by portraying this embarrassing example of American imperialism in Uruguay in 1970, although Uruguay will not be specifically named. He indicts Mitrione through the character of Santore for his implementation of institutional torture into the process of the questioning of subversives. For Costa-Gavras, this man is only a symbol of the larger inhuman beast of imperialism that runs savagely and freely throughout Latin America. Making *State of Siege* meant freezing its image on the screen momentarily for a vast public to see.

Inspiration and Scenario

With the facility of a talented and experienced tale-teller, Costa-Gavras narrates the history behind the film in an interview included in the published text of *State of Siege* and in an article in *Cinema* in 1974. His insight for the film about Mitrione really came when he was researching another sample of what he considered "imperialist America":

> For a long time I had been thinking about making a film like this. The first inspiration, if it can be called that, came to me many years ago when I was still in Greece, and the U.S. ambassador in Athens was somebody by the name of John Peurifoy. Some guy this Peurifoy. He was the one actually deciding Greek politics. Peurifoy was a real expert, a travelling salesman of imperialist America, a man who arrived in a country and determined its politics. After having established the Karamanlis administration—an administration of the right which lasted eight years—he left Greece and where did he go? To Guatemala, where, shortly before, the progressive Arbenz administration had been elected. There this Peurifoy, who toted a Colt .45 at his waist, got in touch with all the most reactionary elements, the Heads of the Church, the Apostolic Nuncio, the old generals.[1]

Costa-Gavras went on to explain that the leftist administration of Guatemala was eventually forced out through the efforts of John Peurifoy, who was linked with the United Fruit Company, the owner of most of the country's fertile land.[2] Thus, after almost three years in Greece and after a short time in Guatemala, in 1955 Peurifoy went on to a third country with his cultivated skill in economic and political negotiations, Thailand. Here he and his nine-year-old son were killed in an automobile accident under very mysterious circumstances.

This American ambassador greatly intrigued Costa-Gavras. After the director had completed *The Confession* in 1970, he began seriously to study Peurifoy's diplomatic career, especially his political role in Guatemala. Costa-Gavras prepared approximately 300 pages of notes, almost a scenario, he noted. For further documentation, Costa-Gavras headed off to Mexico, where the Guatemalan Jacobo Arbenz Guzmán was living in political exile. The former leftist leader had resigned in 1954 when the United States, fearing communist influences in his regime, helped support a revolt against him. Arbenz died "accidentally" before Costa-Gavras had the opportunity to meet him to discuss the Guatemalan-American political relationship during his regime.

State of Siege: Philip Michael Santore (Yves Montand)—ugly American or good Samaritan?
(Permission of Cinema 5 Ltd.)

The more he studied the history of Guatemala, the more Costa-Gavras
realized that times had changed. The policy of direct military intervention,
which he refers to as "the politics of the big stick," was no longer operative,
especially in America's relationships with Latin American countries. He felt that
the mechanism of intervention was more subtle, less observable, work done by
advisers who used politics and technology, not cannons, as weapons. The anticommunist crusade that fostered this sophisticated style of intervention is described by A. J. Langguth in his study of Mitrione's career in Latin America:

> Police advisers like Mitrione were the foot soldiers in Latin America; the
> CIA officials were the officer corps; the ambassadors, the ranking military
> attachés, and the CIA station chiefs from the upper echelons of each U.S.
> embassy were the field commanders.[3]

Around February 1971, Costa-Gavras decided to extend his travels to South
America, and to Chile in particular, where *The Confession* was about to be released. In the turmoil of the new socialist government, each political party was
trying to use the film as a propaganda instrument for itself until the director
intervened. Costa-Gavras thus got a close-up view of Latin American politics.

The director explained how he finally decided upon the specific subject for the
film:

It was during my stay of six weeks in Montevideo that I began thinking of making a movie about the Tupamaros, or rather about urban guerrilla methods as a means of political action. What fascinated me about the Tupamaros was their political maturity, their ways of analyzing a situation in terms of the country's real conditions, the perfection of their technique, their effectiveness on both the military and political levels, and finally their complete lack of "revolutionary hot air."[4]

On 21 February 1971, the Brazilian consul Días Gomide, held hostage by the Tupamaros, was finally released. He had been kidnapped along with Mitrione on 31 July 1970. The American agronomist Claude Fly was kidnapped just a short time later. Costa-Gavras, in Uruguay at that moment, was curious about the fate of the other official, Mitrione, who was executed instead. When Costa-Gavras returned to Paris, he phoned Franco Solinas near Rome to see if Solinas would be interested in writing the script for this proposed film.

Costa-Gavras also explains chancing on his subject in another way. He read in *Le Monde* of early August 1970 about the execution of Mitrione by the Uruguayan terrorists. In the first edition the notice stated that he was a U.S. official, the next edition of *Le Monde* read a policeman; and the third, a diplomat. This puzzled the director, seeing that the news item ascribed three different functions to Mitrione. He wished to pursue the true reason for the death of the person. He felt he could do so in conjunction with Franco Solinas.

Since Jorge Semprun was occupied with a script for Yves Boisset's *L'Attentat* and was writing his own book, Solinas, who was living in Fregene outside of Rome, was Costa-Gavras's next choice. The director lamented the fact that other than Semprun there was not another French screenwriter who could undertake the challenge of the political film that Costa-Gavras envisaged. Costa-Gavras did not know Solinas personally, nor did he realize that he was a communist. However, he was most familiar with the radical scripts of the screenwriter from the past decade. With Francesco Rosi, Solinas had written *Salvatore Guiliano* (1961) and with Gillo Pontecorvo *Kapò* (1959), *Battle of Algiers* (1964), and *Burn!* (1970). In the latter two works, observes Costa-Gavras, Solinas developed a dialectical-materialist approach, yet still tried to reach a large audience, not unlike Costa-Gavras's own ideal. Solinas discusses his inclination toward political films in this manner:

> I write scenarios which generally deal with political themes because in my opinion politics is a fundamental matter. I'm not interested in psychological stories; I have no use for literature in the traditional sense, the continual repetition of the same old patterns turned out with varying degrees of taste and intelligence, and presenting problems that are always personal and in the end uninteresting. This sort of story can only serve to shock and confuse the audience and cannot give it a key for understanding reality.[5]

When Costa-Gavras phoned him in Italy, Solinas had just completed a scenario for Sam Peckinpah, *La Vie c'est comme un train*, and he was just about to go on vacation. He did know Costa-Gavras through his films, but had not yet seen *The Confession*. He had followed the polemical reactions to this film in the newspapers and felt that the film was anti-Stalinist, and even, in his mind, possibly anticommunist. Costa-Gavras spoke to Solinas of the Latin American project. It intrigued the screenwriter, but also made him apprehensive. As a member of the Communist party, Solinas believed strongly not in armed revolution, as was the case of the Uruguayan guerrillas, but in peaceful socialist politics through work with the masses. The ideologies of Semprun and Costa-Gavras differed and had to be reconciled before they could cooperate on the enormous project of this film. Costa-Gavras recounts some of the tension that they experienced and how they began their collaboration:

> At the beginning, Solinas and I had some problems; we did not get along well. He felt we should not lean toward one side or the other. He didn't want us to be pro-Tupamaro; I could be more understanding to their way of seeing things. On the other hand, Solinas did not want to be sentimental or romantic; I didn't either, where we show how a poor man who has been kidnapped (Mitrione) has problems. Finally we learned how to know each other, we decided what we really wanted to do.[6]

Once there was basic agreement between them on presenting the political situation faithfully—an absolutely necessary condition for Solinas—Costa-Gavras left Paris for Fregene to launch the project. Every day he and Solinas met for long discussions about political perspectives, essential details, about fresh ideas with respect to the film. Then Solinas would write down the results of their sessions. If they were not in harmony on a certain element in the text that Solinas was writing, they would discuss it and modify it, remarked the screenwriter in our interview of 4 May 1981.

Costa-Gavras found these three months of collaboration an enriching experience not only because of the scriptwriter's personality and insight into cinema, but also because of his perspective on life. This would also be a unique cinematic moment for Costa-Gavras, for it was the first time that he would construct a film *ex nihilo,* unlike adapting an established literary piece. In this situation he resembles the French director Resnais with his intensive collaboration with the scriptwriters/*littérateurs* Duras, Robbe-Grillet, Semprun, Cayrol, and Sternberg, where each script element was weighed for its political and aesthetic value.[7] An original script for Costa-Gavras would above all eliminate comparisons of the book with the film, as had been done to his works from the very beginning, *The Sleeping Car Murder* and more recently *The Confession* when he was accused by François Maurin of *L'Humanité* of making an anticommunist film from an anti-Stalinist book. It took six months to a year of additional work, but the result was greater control by the director over the ingredients. At the conclusion of their collaboration, Costa-Gavras and Solinas published the text of the script, for the director felt it had evolved into a literary piece.

The director and screenwriter required elaborate documentation in order to write a politically astute scenario that would have some credibility. They spent six weeks in Latin America accumulating data. Both went with the intention of being open-minded journalists, although Costa-Gavras, according to Solinas, was still caught up in the heroic and revolutionary image of the guerrillas. They would include some of this image later, but first they basically agreed on one major factor—American imperialism exists and exerts a controlling force over Latin American politics and economy. This was especially true for a country such as Uruguay which grew up under the tutelage of Spain and then England, finally receiving its independence in 1825.

In August 1971 they began their odysssey by searching for facts that would verify some of their hypotheses about the political scene in Uruguay. They arrived very discretely in Montevideo. There they gradually developed a consciousness of the character that was Mitrione, for Costa-Gavras the "imperialist agent" who symbolized the actual mechanics of political oppression worked by a large capitalist country. Ironically it was one year exactly from the day Mitrione had been assassinated. On the first anniversary of his death, there was a special memorial mass for him at the Sacred Heart Church and memorial prayers at the Holy Trinity Episcopal Church in Montevideo. Officials dedicated a plaque to commemorate Mitrione's service:

> To the memory of Dan A. Mitrione, 1920–1970, Chief Public Safety Adviser USAID Mission to Uruguary: He died that democratic institutions might live. Placed by his friends and colleagues. Montevideo, August 10, 1971. Charles W. Adair, Ambassador.

Another plaque at Montevideo Police Headquarters—dedicated the same day Solinas and Costa-Gavras arrived—referred to him as the Chief of Public Security Services in Uruguay, victim of terrorism in this country. It was erected by his *compañeros de lucha,* his embattled comrades in the struggle against revolutionary forces.

The cult of the fallen hero continued in Uruguay as well as in Washington, D.C., and in Richmond, Indiana. President Jorge Pacheo Areco authorized the issuance of 100,000 international first-class air-mail stamps commemorating the first anniversary of Mitrione's death, stating that he had "fallen in the service of freedom and democracy." In the State Department ceremony attended by AID officials, various State Department members, and the Uruguayan ambassador, U.S. Undersecretary Irwin presented the Secretary's award posthumously to Dan Mitrione. Mitrione's wife and children accepted the bronze plaque, which read: "For dedication to the cause of a more democratic way of life for the people of Uruguay, for which he gave his life, 1970." The award is usually offered in recognition of sacrifices of personal health, including life, in the performance of official duty. Meanwhile, Mitrione's daughter, Mrs. Linda Tarter, attended a memorial mass at the Holy Family Church in Richmond, Indiana, Mitrione's home town.[8]

This is the type of hero worship that surrounded the figure of Dan Mitrione when Costa-Gavras and Franco Solinas arrived in Montevideo in August 1971. They had further clues, however, to indicate that there were some ghosts in Mitrione's diplomatic closet that the two governments were trying to keep there. Thus for six weeks they struggled to unravel the mystery behind this character and to document the American imperialism solidly entrenched in this South American country.

Costa-Gavras and Franco Solinas were able to piece together information about Mitrione's family life as well as his professional work. They learned that in the late 1960s the Uruguayan government and the Montevideo police turned to the U.S. for assistance in their antiguerrilla program. The perfect choice for a coordinator of this program was Daniel A. Mitrione, who could work in the country as "public safety and communications expert." An Italian-American police officer, Mitrione, turning fifty, father of nine children, had a background and extensive experience that would be invaluable in this struggle against terrorism that was destroying Uruguay. After his World War II term in the Navy, Mitrione had returned to Richmond, Indiana, to join the police force, where he eventually became chief in 1956. He held the position for four years before being attracted by the State Department's recruiting of advisers for foreign police forces. In a three-month course in Washington at the FBI Academy, he learned about the modernization necessary for police work to keep up with rising crime and politically related problems, that is, guerrillas.

His first Latin American mission was to Belo Horizonte in Brazil. There he established training programs for the police and did public relations to improve their image. Disciplined and professional, he wanted to teach what he believed best and essential for a policeman in a modern urban society. Mitrione worked in Belo Horizonte for two years and was then transferred to Rio de Janeiro. He then returned to Washington, where for two years (1967–1969) he taught police elite from various Third World countries. He then went back to South America to undertake the same type of police-modernizing work.

Costa-Gavras and Solinas learned that Mitrione's work in Uruguay began in July 1969. As police adviser he followed the same directives as earlier—to streamline the police force, instill discipline, learn the political situation, uncover the revolutionary forces (read "Tupamaros"), and then take action against them. Mitrione still worked for AID within the State Department, but he was assigned to the Montevideo police headquarters. From July 1969 to July 1970 he built up a solid law-enforcement body in Montevideo. He carried a .38 Smith and Wesson revolver and worked in a bulletproof office, characteristics more of a police officer than of an American State Department aide.

When Costa-Gavras and Solinas interviewed Carlos Quijano, editor of *Marcha*, they had a new insight into the somber side of American involvement in Uruguay. *Marcha* published a special issue that dramatically uncovered the use of systematic torture on political prisoners. It was the report prepared by members of the senate—presented in condensed form in *State of Siege* by the woman senator. The report stated that during intensive questioning by the police, detainees had electric needles placed under their fingernails and electrical shocks applied to different parts of the anatomy, especially in the genital area. From the *Marcha* material and the senate report Costa-Gavras and Solinas were able to document the series of tortures, some having exotic names (such as the parrot's perch, roast chicken, the hydraulic, dragon's chair, and Chinese bath). The more common tortures inflicted by the interrogators under American supervision were cigarette burns, sexual harassment, sodium pentothal, and solitary confinement.[9]

State of Siege: Santore (Yves Montand) with his family.
(Permission of Cinema 5 Ltd.)

The thesis of Costa-Gavras and Solinas was that this systematic torture of political prisoners dated from Mitrione's arrival in Montevideo. A published interview with Alejandro Otero for *Jornal do Brazil* supported their hunches. The former police commissioner under Mitrione specified that U.S. advisers in particular had introduced scientific methods of torture in the interrogation of Uruguayan political prisoners, men and women. Later in August 1978, a Cuban "agent," formerly with the public safety division of the AID office in Montevideo, charged that Mitrione personally tortured four beggars to death as part of his interrogation course for the Uruguayan police in 1970. This condemning statement of Manuel Hevia Cosculluela is apparently the only published one that links Mitrione physically and directly with torture. Hevia Coscullela clarified, however: "This [talk about Mitrione] is wrong because it suggests that his behavior was the excess of an individual. Mitrione represented the program of the American mission, and Mitrione was only carrying out policy."[10]

Another challenge that Costa-Gavras encountered in the course of documentation was a direct contact with the militant members of the Tupamaros as he had had on his earlier Latin American trip. In order to insure its absolute security, the revolutionary movement had set up a protective shield around the organization, as one of the leaders pointed out in an interview in 1970:

> We could say that the compartmentalization and discretion are, to the urban guerrilla, what the secret path is to the rural guerrilla. The system of not

knowing any more than one should know, not commenting on more than what one should comment on, not knowing any places other than those needed to carry out one's own actions, and not knowing any names other than those which one must necessarily know—not even those of the comrades in one's own cell—and the use of *noms de guerre* instead of one's true name are a guarantee that, any time one of the cadres is captured, the damage to the Movement is slight or practically nil. Let us say that all these things constitute our protective shield.[11]

Costa-Gavras and Solinas were cautiously allowed to penetrate this protective shield of the Tupamaros. The urban guerrillas knew Solinas's work in *The Battle of Algiers,* and some had seen or heard about *Z.* They favored the film project but expressed some skepticism about it. They were also extremely cautious about aiding this type of public venture, given the clandestine nature of their organization where a leak in communications could endanger some of the members. The cineastes learned more and more about the movement, but now from within.

Costa-Gavras and Solinas learned the history of the Tupamaros. The genealogy of the Uruguayan guerrilla movement—the National Liberation Movement (Movimiento de Liberación Nacional)—went back almost four centuries. Their name originates in that of the Inca leader Tupac Amaru I, who spearheaded an Indian revolt in Peru against the Spanish *conquistadores.* He was captured and quartered in the square of Cuzco in 1572. Almost 200 years later José Gabriel Condorcanqui (1741–1781) claimed to be a direct descendant of the revolutionary leader and took the name Tupac Amaru. He fought the Spanish colonialist exploitation of the Incas. The Latin American struggle went on into the next century. In Uruguay, in 1811, José Artigas, whose name was often on the lips and in the communiqués of the Tupamaros, finally rallied forces that would result in the liberation of the country.

By the time Costa-Gavras and Solinas met with the Tupamaros, the terrain of their warfare had long shifted from the country to the capital city. The extreme leftist organization had its roots among rural cane-cutter groups. The radical socialist Raúl Sendic in 1962 was most influential in the political gestation of the movement. From a small number of thirty union members and extreme leftists the Tupamaros grew to 3,000 with 4,000 sympathizers.[12] Costa-Gavras and Solinas discovered that the membership of the guerrilla movement did not consist of wild, alienated, anarchistic youth. The members came primarily from the middle and upper classes. They were from all walks of life—university professors and students, intellectuals, attorneys, soldiers, priests, police, artists, doctors, and other professionals. Costa-Gavras later remarked, "They are everywhere and nowhere."

The political thought of the National Liberation Front which perhaps did not directly find its way into the film, showed a long-range general vision to create a socialist society that would touch every sector of human life in Uruguay. The ideal of the Tupamaros was to liberate their country from foreign influence, especially American with its all-pervasive industrial, financial, and business investments. Their particular plan called for socializing large factories, initiating land reforms, and offering legal, medical, and educational benefits to the poor and needy. The guerrillas aimed to fight for human rights, to improve the standard of living primarily by eliminating poverty and unemployment. Their ideals sound reasonable and humanitarian. Their means, however, were revolutionary and controversial.

The Tupamaros felt that the law benefited only the wealthy and influential, and that it was only the poor who suffered from the sanctions of the law. They reasoned, therefore, that they must act outside the law in order to remedy the situation. They began with action, not theory: "Words divide us, actions unite us." Armed terrorist activity became their modus operandi—robbing of banks, hijacking food for the poor, requisitioning cars and trucks, stealing police uniforms, and, on occasion, sabotaging with dynamite.

Of the various actions of the guerrillas, Costa-Gavras was most fascinated by the kidnapping of officials. From September 1969 to February 1972 there would be thirteen major kidnappings of individuals, including Geoffrey Jackson, the British ambassador to Uruguay, and Nelson Bardesio, a member of the Death Squad reportedly secretly organized by the authorities to eliminate terrorist elements in Montevideo. Eventually the terrorist weapon of kidnapping would be the key to the structure of the film.

In the Montevideo press—*El País, El Diario,* and *El Día*—Solinas and Costa-Gavras were able to study the evolution of events from 1 to 10 August 1970. We took a similar approach in our own research. Not all the evidence was in the open during the first few days of Brazilian consul Gomide and Mitrione's kidnapping. Only later would information leak out about Mitrione's real function in Uruguay. In fact, the first few days the local press discussed Mitrione's role as a type of American diplomat who had been there with AID for only one year. This view was gradually nuanced to show his real work was as an adviser to the police department. The two items mentioned earlier that incriminated Mitrione and fed the imagination of the Left in 1970 and Solinas and Costa-Gavras a year later were the police and FBI cards forwarded by the Tupamaros on 6 August 1970 and the Aymore-Otero interview of 14 August 1970 for *Jornal do Brasil*.[13] This last bit of information—later disseminated by a Reuters cable—turned the tide of evidence against the supposedly innocent U.S. State Department official and furnished supportive documentation for the filmmakers' case.

A year after the release of this information on the true character of Mitrione's work, Costa-Gavras and Solinas found that the material had grown enormously. One clue led to another. They soon discovered that AID had a branch dealing with security, basically police work, and that there was an international police training center in Washington at the "old car barn" in the Georgetown section. In *Hidden Terrors* Langguth outlines at length the program of this AID-sponsored endeavor, perhaps in a more balanced fashion than Costa-Gavras and Franco Solinas in the documents of their work. Where the filmmakers bitterly attack the academy for teaching torture techniques, Langguth, from his research, shows that some officers saw torture of a prisoner as cowardly and immoral, but others saw it as the best way to save lives of others.

Costa-Gavras procured a brochure of the International Police Academy from a former participant in the academy who was involved with the Tupamaros while still maintaining his police position, a type of double agent. This evidence appeared in the film during flashbacks to Santore's selection of police officers to attend the academy. Costa-Gavras went so far as to include in the film one of the police officers under his true name, Inspector Fontana (Mario Montilles).

In his research Costa-Gavras discovered that once the carefully screened group of promising police officials arrived in Washington, they were put through a very demanding program. They had lectures dealing with geography, political science, internal security with the technical use of intelligence equipment, with police protection for dignitaries. They learned about subversive groups flourishing in Third World countries. These lectures were supplemented by films with commentaries on the Algerian and Vietnam wars. They were also given FBI instructions and rifle-range practice. The filmmakers learned that these first four weeks dealt with the normal police methods utilized internationally during a time of growing terrorist activity. It was the last week of the course that indicated to Solinas and Costa-Gavras that there was something awry in this business of police training.

Some students of the IPA specialized in explosives and were sent to Los Fresnos, Texas, where they learned not only to defuse bombs, but to construct and use them in simulated political situations. This instruction was referred to as Investigation of Terrorist Activity. The course was held in complete secrecy, carefully supervised by Green Berets, who kept the police students under permanent guard. It was thus that these police novices learned the scientific background of explosives and then the use of such weapons against revolutionary forces. They were diligently taught so that they could effectively train others when needed in their respective countries. Langguth observes that at the conclusion of a course on the use of explosives, one student inquired about the purpose of such a course. He was told, "The United States thinks that the moment will come when in each of the friendly countries, they could use a student of confidence—who has become a specialist in explosives; that is why the different governments have chosen their favorite persons."[14] This particular program at the police academy proved to be a bit embarrassing to the AID organization, for it implied a type of subversive and illegal activity that was just as unethical as that used by the Tupamaros and other guerrillas.

The dossier on Mitrione kept growing. Solinas and Costa-Gavras amassed testimony from different sources to prove that the American advisor had brought Uruguayan interrogation into the technological age by means of U.S. materials sent by diplomatic pouch. They had access to the speech on torture, the one delivered emotionally in the film by the woman senator. They also got an original address given by the head of the police academy. They procured several photos, so that in the film the reconstructed photo with which Santore is challenged by the Tupamaros is an authentic and incriminating item. In both photos we see Mitrione/Santore at a banquet in Brazil surrounded by police officials, receiving a gift of a Rolex watch. The decor is most realistically recreated.[15]

The guerrillas offered Solinas and Costa-Gavras another valuable piece of documentation for their research—a tape recording of Mitrione's voice during the interrogation in the People's Prison. Solinas stated that the tape—with its hours of material—was indispensable, for it was a firsthand testimony to the way the questioning went. On the tape Mitrione came across as a self-assured, confident individual who felt superior to his captors. He truly believed he would not be harmed. Solinas and Costa-Gavras did not use very much of the content of the tape, but profited from the tone and atmosphere of the interrogation in order to recreate what Mitrione's incarceration was like. The *Baltimore Sun* reported in September 1970 that, after being tipped off by an anonymous call, a Reuters correspondent in Montevideo picked up a similar tape recording that appeared to be authentic. In *Hidden Terrors* Langguth mentions that U.S. government officials supplied a copy of a tape of the interrogation to Mitrione's brother, Ray, in Richmond, Indiana. Most recently Mitrione's voice comes back from the grave in Allan Francovich's documentary *On Company Business*. It deals with the involvement of the CIA in Latin America. On tape Mitrione claims to know nothing of the CIA.

Franco Solinas and Costa-Gavras thus spent almost six weeks in Uruguay clandestinely gathering documents, interviewing former police officers, speaking with members of the Tupamaros, meeting with foreigners who knew Mitrione's earlier activities. At one point Solinas went to the Dominican Republic to try to obtain further documentation on Mitrione. He made several efforts to meet with members of the Communist party but was unable to make any important contacts. Nonetheless, he learned more about torture techniques in interrogation allegedly initiated by Mitrione. Further research took the filmmakers to Argentina, Chile, and Cuba. Prior to returning to Europe, Costa-Gavras stopped over briefly in the U.S. He was curious about Mitrione's birthplace, so he visited Richmond, Indiana, to see if the family was still there. They were not, so he visited the local newspaper to see how the press treated his death. He learned about the Frank Sinatra and Jerry Lewis benefit in Richmond which brought Mitrione's widow and children $20,000. If he did take the time to read the reactions of the local citizens, he would have grasped their anger and bitterness toward the Tupamaros whom the director would portray in a favorable light as idealistic Robin Hoods of the Uruguayan society.

Costa-Gavras then continued his research in Washington. He worked at the Library of Congress, where he was able to get concrete facts on AID as well as other items which he used for the background of the film. He learned of the large number of AID personnel in Latin America, for instance, and obtained more documentation to sustain his thesis. Although much of this additional material was superfluous and could not possibly be woven into the fabric of *State of Siege,* it gave the writers a solid basis from which to proceed when dealing with the American grant program.

With all of this material in hand—Costa-Gavras estimated it to be approximately 300 pages after several months of work—the next task was to decide what would be the line of action in the film. Solinas and Costa-Gavras were obliged to streamline the data in order to give a synthetic, simplified view of the problems of U.S. involvement in Latin America as they had uncovered them. Robert Grelier's interview with Solinas and Costa-Gavras highlighted their triple purpose in creating both the scenario and the film—to show the operation of an American empire and to reveal another side to U.S. investments; to dissect the forms and means by which repression takes place; and to show how one force grew to act against this repressive violence.[16]

Costa-Gavras and Solinas finally settled on the structure of the ten-day imprisonment of Santore/Mitrione as the action line. At the same time they decided to treat quickly several years in the life of Mitrione, his stay in Brazil, his teaching at the International Police Academy in Washington, and his arrival in Uruguay. These would be treated by flashbacks inserted into the ten-day chronological framework of the main action. Solinas explains their point of departure:

> But at the same time we hadn't wanted to make a suspense film. We tried to put our question to the public, not on the classic level—is he going to die?—but rather, is he or isn't he responsible? And his culpability was also not the classic sort—as if he had killed or stolen—but much broader, a responsibility of a political order. Our point of view is not "romantic." We do not make a moralistic speech. We do not try to find out whether Mitrione was "good" or "bad." Mitrione interested us because he represents a system that is bad for the majority of people.[17]

Solinas is partly correct in stating that they suppressed the suspense aspect of the film, although not totally, for dramatic reasons. At the outset of the film the spectator realizes that the protagonist is dead, but does not know how or why. Dramatic tension does arise when the very house that harbors the People's Prison is being searched by the police; when the Tupamaros in the ambulance with the disguised Santore are stopped by security forces; when a police officer gets on the same bus as Este, the Tupamaro leader.

Solinas and Costa-Gavras tightened the narrative they had written, to show the continuity in the life and travels of Santore/Mitrione, using his arrival in each country as the symbol of American imperialism. Costa-Gavras had noticed the same symbol in John Peurifoy: the "traveling salesman of American imperialism." Costa-Gavras said something similar to Solinas in an interview in the *Washington Post:*

> We constantly avoided any compromise of taste or style. We avoided completely any type of traditional suspense. It would often have been handy to put in episodes not 100 per cent true in order to help the story, but we just left them out.[18]

Some of the details were modified in the process. Several facts were telescoped.

The papal nuncio's homily in the film, however, corresponded basically to the actual one of the memorial mass of 19 August. The newspaper version reads:

> Dan Anthony Mitrione, may you rest in peace. May the Lord receive you and offer you the reward of the just, and that to us, after this tempest, may peace return. May your wife and children live in your memory, following your example and seeking always to serve others with love. Amen.

In the homily Costa-Gavras underlines the papal nuncio's sympathetic view of Mitrione and his work. The nuncio refers to the American official as a sacrificial victim.[19] The director also underscores the fact that the local archbishop, Obispo Coadjutor Monseñor Carlos Partelli, did not celebrate the mass because he opposed American intervention and torture during interrogations. Many of the Church hierarchy were present at the memorial mass on 19 August, including the former bishop, rector of the seminary, as well as American and Uruguayan officials. By blending this mass in Uruguay into the actual funeral mass in Richmond celebrated by the Reverend Robert Minton, the director and screenwriter streamlined the narrative, simultaneously making a statement about various reactions to Mitrione's death, especially the reaction of the archbishop.

The extensive documentation from which the scenario springs affords an authentic but rapid glimpse of the Church, police, American and Uruguayan governments, and of the Tupamaros. The material requires a documentary-realism approach to the work. Yet one has the same apprehension that Franco Solinas had at the outset, that is, showing war as a legitimate means of revolution. Solinas finally acquiesced to Costa-Gavras's decisions about guerrilla warfare in the body of the film, that it was an integral factor in opposition to American imperialism.

According to Yves Montand, the film was originally to be entitled *Amerikan,* with a "k," an adjective used by the revolutionary Left in the U.S. in the late 1960s. With this title Costa-Gavras wished to differentiate a negative type of American investment and imperialism in Latin America from a more positive view of the influence of America and its people.

The reconstruction of the scenario, film, and dossier cannot be called "objectively historical," for it is obvious that only one side of the material is shown. All of the documentation that makes a case against American imperialism, torture techniques taught by the police, unethical training in explosives is thoroughly presented. The other side is not included, for example, the need of a government to insure security for its citizens or AID's contributions to the fields of medicine and education in Latin America. Hence there occurs a lack of a balanced perspective. The scenario and film may thus be judged to be products of a subjective interpretation of materials. In an interview with Costa-Gavras and Franco Solinas, Donia Mills of Washington's *Evening Star and Daily News* received two different opinions on this—Costa-Gavras admitting that all moviemaking is necessarily subjective, Solinas stating that it is entirely possible to present an objective case study in a film. Mills concludes that both director and screenwriter eventually agreed that the documents of the film were objectively factual, but that they both applied their own personal and subjective interpretation to those documents. As a result, Louis Chauvet of *Le Figaro* states that the scenario is a victim of doubtful purity of intention, that is, that under false appearances of being constantly impartial, Costa-Gavras can scarcely hide his sympathy for the brutal action of the execution of the hostage. When we discuss the image of the Tupamaros in Costa-Gavras's political perspective, we will be able to bring this criticism into a clearer light.

Production and Filming

To support this supposed anti-American venture, Costa-Gavras received fifty percent of the required funding for the film from American sources. The two American producers who had the most invested in *State of Siege* were millionaire Max Palevsky and President of Cinema V Donald Rugoff. Jacques Perrin in Paris provided further financial support for the film project. Costa-Gavras, learning from his experience with *Z*, invested his own money in the production.

Just as with *Z*, a proper location had to be discovered to recreate the Uruguay of 1970 realistically. To film in Uruguay itself was out of the question. The director decided upon Chile. Climatically it is on the same latitude as Uruguay. He also chose the country because the Chilean government under Allende offered the crew full liberty in filming. Another advantage was the presence of the film equipment needed for the production. The preceding Frei government had established a national cinema organization, so Costa-Gavras could rely upon this system in his film production. He began it at the end of May 1972.

Costa-Gavras once said that actually Chile only tolerated the presence of his film company. From the outset the crew was beset by political difficulties. The entertainment industry journal *Variety* reported that an unexpected attack came from the Left, despite the presence of the communist Franco Solinas, after he showed a copy of the script to the Communist party:

> The weekly *Ramona* (Communist Party) featured an unshaven and sinister looking Costa-Gavras on its cover and headlined: "A Film Against Chile." The cover story accused the director of simply making a film for profit, without really caring about the revolutionary movement in Latin America; other points brought up were that there were anti-Communist strains in the film and the agent Mitrione was presented in too favorable a light. The tabloid *Puro Chile* was even more violent, while *El Siglo* (the party flagship daily) was formally more moderate, but also strongly against the film.[20]

Variety went on to explain that the tension surrounding the film derived from a split within the Left—the new Left and the traditional Left. The Communist party felt that the film moved too strongly toward the new Left in its approval of violent action to attain socialism as opposed to attaining it by constitutional means. This accounts for the smear from the Communist party in the press and for the resignation of six actors, requiring the scenes shot with them to be redone. The Right—but not the extreme Right—appeared a bit more favorable to the filming. Perhaps this was a result of Costa-Gavras's anti-Stalinist film *The Confession*, which provided the Right with ammunition against the Left and thus brought the director into more positive light.

To resolve the political tension, Costa-Gavras went right to the top. He spoke with President Salvador Allende. Costa-Gavras recounts the meeting:

> "Once I had dinner with him," the director says, "and he said he didn't find any political reasons to criticize the script. He read it like a detective novel. Once when he received a protest from the Uruguayan embassy in Chile, he

told them, 'This is a free country with no censorship, and they can shoot whatever they want.' "[21]

In the Grelier interview with Costa-Gavras and Solinas, the director quoted Allende as saying, "There is no problem, Chile is open to you, and it will continue to be. Make your film."[22]

Further problems arose when weapons were needed for the production. The Chilean Army, trying to remain neutral in this pitched political battle, refused to loan any arms. Eventually, the crew had to import them from France. Apart from these political details, the crew was left in relative peace to shoot the film. For eleven weeks they shot in Santiago, Valparaiso, and in a hallucinogenic desert where entire cities had been abandoned since the end of World War I. By a vote in Parliament they were also allowed to film for one day in the hall of Congress. The last part of the filming was done in France.

Narrative

The film begins: "The events actually took place in a Latin American country."

It is August, winter in South America. As with Z we are once again in a universal situation. It could be any Latin country.[23] Even so, clues throughout the film indicate that it is Montevideo, Uruguay, in 1970, and that it is the Mitrione case.

Police turn up the body of a man in the rear seat of a 1948 Cadillac with Montevideo plates. It is that of Philip Michael Santore (Yves Montand), age fifty, an American AID official kidnapped ten days earlier (on 31 July). His death startles the nation. The Parliament, with thirty-two leftist seats vacant, declares a day of national mourning. Santore's funeral at the cathedral is attended by key American and national figures. A eulogy is preached by the papal nuncio (Robert Holmes). In the course of the nuncio's message there is a double flashback to the Foreign Service Institute in the U.S., where Mrs. Santore and other diplomats' wives are being briefed on health precautions in Latin America. The speaker, however, assures these women that they will never have to worry about this problem, for they will be among the privileged.

The principal action of the film takes off from the third flashback during the nuncio's homily. Santore en route to his office on Tuesday morning—according to the journalistic titles—is kidnapped by a group of young armed revolutionaries (the Tupamaros of MLN), in a carefully organized ambush. In the process, a nervous and inexperienced guerrilla accidentally wounds him. After requisitioning a large number of cars for their action, they also kidnap the Brazilian consul Fernando Campos and Anthony Lee (Jerry Brouer). The latter will shortly escape.

A press conference given by the Minister of Interior (Maurice Teynac) does not satisfy the journalists' questions, especially those of the veteran Carlos Ducas (O. E. Hasse) concerning the functions of Santore and AID. The director of AID (Douglas Harris) is equally vague about the duties of Santore. Ducas criticizes American presence and influence in their country.

State of Siege: The elderly reporter Carlos Ducas (O. E. Hasse) gathers details about the kidnapping of Santore.
(Permission of Cinema 5 Ltd.)

Captain López (Renato Salvatori) of the local police force later adds details about Santore's position in public safety and communication, alluding to the official's previous work in the Dominican Republic and Brazil. A brief flashback reveals Santore's activities in the Dominican Republic.

Meanwhile, interrogation of the kidnapped Santore commences in the clandestine People's Prison, directed by the young Tupamaro leader Hugo (Jacques Weber). Point by point and with precise documentation, Hugo draws out the true identity of this public-safety expert. When the terrorist questioner speaks about Santore's work in Brazil, there is a flashback to a demonstration of torture with electric wires. It shows a police student becoming nauseous and dashing out.

Then with a series of "proofs," Hugo establishes Santore's link with torture: a *New York Times* article offering incredible statistics about Brazilian police officials trained in the U.S.; a photo of Santore at a banquet with Brazilian police officials receiving a watch; the same Rolex watch with the inscription, "A souvenir from his Brazilian friends." "Coincidence?" asks Hugo.

A doctor inspects the prisoner's wounds and recommends an X ray. The drugged Santore, with hair tinted black and a mustache for the false passport, is taken by ambulance through police lines to a hospital. Later, a communiqué of the Tupamaros provides an update on the health of the two prisoners Santore

and Campos, and specifies the conditions for their release—the liberation of 150
political prisoners and a considerable ransom.[24]

The interrogation continues, concentrating on Santore's mission to the
Dominican Republic from 1965 to 1967. A scene at the Parliament shows the
Left-Right tension with Deputy or Representative Fabbri (André Falcon) repre-
senting the Left, intensely critical of American involvement in the country. A
flashback shows the spectator the arrival of Santore in the country a year earlier.
He was greeted by López and Romero (Robert Navarette).

Another flashback during the interrogation introduces us to the International
Police Academy in Washington, to which many countries sent their leading
officers for training. There are several representing this country. Captain López
is among the more conscientious.

Back at the People's Prison, Hugo produces further proof of Santore's link
with the police—a class photo with López and Romero in the Washington group,
and then the major embarrassment for Santore, the program of the police
academy described in great detail. There is a cut to the university, where the
police are at the gates. To Ducas, the dean of the law school (Maurice Jacquemont) laments the fact that the police trample on the rights not only of the
university but of all citizens, and that the president of the country is helpless.

The police almost discover the People's Prison. Following the tension involved
with the search, the interrogation progresses. A flashback furnishes a glimpse of
torture equipment arriving from Brazil in a diplomatic pouch.

A woman senator (Yvette Etiévant) dramatically produces the results of a
commission to uncover torture used officially and systematically in questioning
detainees, especially students and union leaders. Hugo and Santore discuss these
tortures. Referring to the courses in the IPA, the Tupamaros document its
unethical activities with Xerox copies of confidential materials. The use of explosives, for example, is taught in Texas—a flashback to the deserted airport. The
results of the IPA tactical lessons are found in the work of Enrique Macchi
(Alejandro Sieverina) and his fascist organization, as parallel to the Death Squad
of Brazil, which was responsible for the assassination of communists and other
revolutionaries.

There follows a series of rapid scenes:

—The president makes a statement: no negotiations with criminals. It is in the
hands of the police now. Later he feels he should resign.

—Mr. Snow, an agronomist, is also kidnapped.

—The ministers assemble for a high-level discussion; all have large financial
holdings; there is a conflict of interests.

—The police raid a Tupamaro meeting place and capture Hugo and key
leaders, but Este (Jean-Luc Bideau) escapes the trap and assumes responsibility
for the hostage Santore.

—A fourth communiqué from the terrorists gives the government twenty-four
hours to fulfill guerrilla demands before Santore will be shot. The government
does not budge.

Following the necessary move of prisoners to avoid detection and the further
questioning of Santore by Este, a vote is taken "democratically" among some of

State of Siege: A woman senator (Yvette Etiévant) makes a passionate statement against torture.
(Permission of Cinema 5 Ltd.)

the rank and file of the liberation movement aboard a bus. Shall Mitrione die or not? Este tells each individual that with respect to Santore's fate, it is not a sentimental situation, but a political problem. The vote goes against the hostage.

Like a grandiose parenthesis, the principal flashback closes, and we return to the cathedral for Santore's funeral and then to the airport for the shipping of Santore's body to the States. At the same precise moment another plane arrives with Santore's replacement, who is greeted by López and Fontana (Mario Montilles). A pair of Tupamaro eyes surveys the reception of the new official.

Actors and Characterization

Once again there is an international cast—French, American, Italian, German, and Chilean. For the leading character, Costa-Gavras had several possibilities lined up, thinking first of all to have the role played by an actual American or English-speaking actor. He considered Marlon Brando, Richard Burton, Gene Hackman, and George C. Scott. He went so far as to make an initial but superficial contact with Scott's agent. The director then felt that an American playing the role would come across too harshly, especially if he had leftist tendencies. He preferred instead someone who could play a low-keyed Santore.

To complete a third panel of a political triptych with Costa-Gavras, Yves Montand accepted the invitation to play Santore. This would be the first time in a Costa-Gavras film that Montand played the role of an antihero. In the dossier he relates his reasoning for accepting the part:

> I agreed to make this film because once more I was moved by the fact that it denounces and condemns intolerance, wherever it originates, and I am always sympathetic to this position.[25]

Mitrione's personality intrigued Montand, for he and Mitrione both had Italian roots and emigrated early from Italy. Montand and Mitrione were both two years old when they arrived in France and America respectively. The actor says that all physical and moral resemblance stops there!

Montand lived up to the expectations of the director, playing the role in a calm, assured, and low-keyed manner. The tape of the actual interrogation that Costa-Gavras procured from the Tupamaros furnished Montand with an idea of the temperament of the American hostage. Costa-Gavras chose Mitrione/Santore to represent a personal image of American imperialism, for he was a fine blend of the Good Samaritan and the Ugly American. Since the original character was comprised of good and bad characteristics, the presentation is not Manichean. At first one is very sympathetic toward Santore as he is kidnapped, for earlier we see him happily involved with his family. (Communists attacked Costa-Gavras for this curious juxtaposition in the character of Santore, for they wanted a Jack Palance, villain-type actor in the role.) Then as the film unravels and the protagonist is shown more and more condoning torture, more and more affiliated with teaching modern techniques of interrogation, viewer sympathy gives way to puzzlement and at times to hostility. In the final part of the film he still stoically maintains confidence that the cause that he supports is right, although his eyes are shown to well up with culpability. During the interrogation he comes across as a crusading anticommunist, justifying his actions:

> You are subversives, Communists. You want to destroy the foundations of society, the fundamental values of our Christian civilization, the very existence of the free world. You are an enemy who must be fought in every possible way.[26]

In the *Philadelphia Tribune* of 9 October 1973 Harry Amana speaks of Montand as a credible example of a career diplomat who is reasonable, conservative, and loyal to his country. Amana observes that Santore's cold analysis of the crisis in which he finds himself recalls for the American public images of the key Watergate officials such as John Dean.

In general, Santore's character and Montand's acting are more complex and subtle than Lambrakis's part in *Z* and Gérard's in *The Confession*. The Santore character is fraught with inner contradictions—gentle family man and disciplined policeman, believing Catholic and professional torturer. Although we do not hear the inner ticking of his mind and heart, the flashbacks, interrogation, and proofs reveal his true character to the Tupamaros and the filmgoer. For his performance, *Movietone* calls Montand charismatic, while the *New Yorker* in Penelope Gilliatt's critique is very harsh on him, criticizing him first of all as a Frenchman playing the role of an American in Latin America, and then as never losing the jaded, intellectual, left-wing European look:

> Hopes unfulfilled by events seem to be lying emptied in the dead air of his head. Montand can make idealism and radicalism look like habits of long ago. Nothing new here, he seems to be feeling, but still nothing to be given up. Life is full of a taste like sour wine, and of sleep lost on the undertaking of missionary tasks with vanished purposes.[27]

In her negative review of Montand, Gilliatt stands almost alone among the critics in France and the U.S. Most of them appreciated the nuances of the role and Montand's acting whether they agreed or not with Costa-Gavras and Franco Solinas's political ideology represented here.

The German veteran O. E. Hasse (*The Doctor from Stalingrad*), playing the journalist Carlos Ducas, seems to be the classical Greek tragic chorus, commenting on the action, introducing the characters (ministers), delineating the political problems. Costa-Gavras says more precisely that he is the Coryphaeus, the leader, and the other journalists are the chorus players.[28] The reporter in *State of Siege* is more finely drawn than the journalist/photographer in *Z*. Franco Solinas comments on this character:

> We also wanted to show, using the character of an old journalist, the sort of traditional democratic awareness and feeling which exists in the country. Although he did not accept violence as the solution to the problem, he was not, in view of the situation, opposed to it.[29]

Another important character who, like Ducas, challenges the oppressive government is Deputy Fabbri, forthright member of Parliament. In his interventions before his rightist opponents, he dramatically exposes the recent history of American imperialism in Latin America through various organizations such as the American Health Organization, the U.S. Public Health Service, and the American Institute for Free Labor Development.

The character of the deputy is modeled on the political figure of former Senator Enrique Erro. In recent correspondence with us, the senator confirms that Fabbri's frank statements in Parliament were very consistent with his own political philosophy—anti-imperialistic since his youth. Erro was Minister of Industry and Work in the government of the Partido Nacional (from 1 May 1959). In 1962, he broke with the party, and when the Unión Popular was formed with the socialists, Catholics, intellectuals, and leftists, he was elected national representative for the coalition. He served in Parliament from 1962 to 1966. In 1971, the Frente Amplio came into being, comprised of Christian Democrats, socialists, and communists, and Erro was elected senator. With Senator Zelmar Michelini, he denounced torture, prisons, and the military. In 1973, he was accused of being in complicity with the Tupamaros. He sought political refuge in Argentina. Once there, he was cast into one prison after another for two years. In

State of Siege: A government press conference on Santore's situation.
(Permission of Cinema 5 Ltd.)

December 1976, he went into exile in France, where a Uruguayan military com-
mando attempted to assassinate him. In many ways Erro and Fabbri's ideologies
are one.[30]

The acting of Renato Salvatori evolved from the fascist henchman of the
Greek military regime of *Z*, to one of the directors of the semi-fascist police force
of *State of Siege*. He convincingly plays the role of the Latin American connection—Captain López, a police official sent to the police academy in the U.S. to
learn, among many other lessons, how to "properly interrogate" a prisoner. His
background and personality are not very far from those of the actual policeman
Juan Maria Lucas. Penelope Gilliatt characterizes Salvatori in this manner: "He
is a goonish A.I.D. hireling of forty called Captain López, flawless in hypocrisy,
evasive under journalists' catechisms, and impeccably sad at official funerals."[31]
It is difficult not to dislike the character as he is cast by Costa-Gavras in his
torturing of a young woman and his greeting of Santore's replacement.

Yvette Etiévant plays the woman senator who denounces torture in a voice
vibrating with indignation. This character, according to Senator Enrique Erro,
has as its inspiration Doctor Alba Roballa, who presided over the commission to
investigate torture. She was then the only woman to preside in the Uruguayan
senate and general assembly and was the Minister of Education and Culture
during the presidency of Jorge Pacheo Areco, but resigned when she could no
longer tolerate the policies of the government.

Among the revolutionaries, only two catch our attention—Hugo and Este. Jacques Weber plays Hugo, the young, handsome interrogator of Santore in the People's Prison. A forceful, fiery idealist, he fights a battle of wits against the very confident Santore.

> You're not an ordinary official, Mr. Santore. You're neither a minor em-
> ployee nor a simple specialist. You are a man who controls things. You di-
> rected the Belo Horizonte police in Brazil, the police of Santo Domingo, and
> our own. You do it directly and also through the men you send to Washing-
> ton—where they learn, among other things, to betray their countries. You say
> you're defending freedom and democracy. . . . Your methods are war, fascism,
> and torture. . . . Surely you agree with me, Mr. Santore?[32]

There are some traces of Raúl Sendic, founder of the Tupamaros, in the character of Hugo, but Sendic would be ten to fifteen years older than the present
leader. Sendic, like Hugo, was actually captured on 7 August 1970 with other
guerrilla leaders—Jorge Candal Grajales, Raúl Bidegain, and Luis Martínez Platero. At one point during the filming of the interrogation in the People's Prison,
things were not going as planned. Behind his cloth mask Jacques Weber began to
sob. Despite the fact that the lights and technical aspects of the set were not ideal,
Costa-Gavras decided quickly to shoot the scene in order to capitalize on Hugo's
own human feelings.

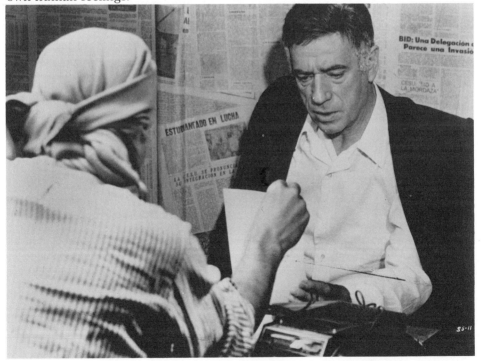

State of Siege: Hugo (Jacques Weber) hands Santore (Yves Montand) proof of the latter's
unethical activities.
(Permission of Cinema 5 Ltd.)

State of Siege: Este (Jean-Luc Bideau) notifies Santore (Yves Montand) that there is no
hope left for him.
(Permission of Cinema 5 Ltd.)

Este, played by Jean-Luc Bideau *(La Salamandre)* appears as a troubled but
sympathetic leader. Este backs into his role as leader when Hugo is captured
during a raid. Human in his approach to the situation, he asks Santore if he is
warm enough or if he would like to write to his family (Mitrione actually did
write his wife a letter from the prison shortly before he died). Este, caught in the
dilemma of executing or releasing Santore, admits: "If we execute him, the
entire press, all the television and radio stations will talk about his seven kids. . . .
But if we don't kill him, all the Governments will become a little stronger, and
the revolutionary movements weaker."[33]

Many critics feel that in his description of the Tupamaros and the members of
the Right, once again Costa-Gavras resorts to a black-and-white stereotyping or
Manichean characterization. This may especially be noticed in the one-
dimensional delineation of opposing forces that one sees immediately in the
film. The Tupamaros are young, idealistic, attractive, and full of revolutionary
zeal.

By contrast, we have the police and the established Church. The police are
caricatured as semi-fascist using repressive means against students, as completely
fascist when they create the Death Squad. In *State of Siege*, the portrayal of the
Death Squad—later named D.A.M. after Daniel A. Mitrione—is slightly anach-

ronistic. It is used as a type of flashforward to 1971 showing an execution of several communists at the Twentieth Division headquarters. According to the witness interrogated by the Tupamaros, Nelson Bardesio, the squad did not fully function in Uruguay until December 1970, almost four months after Mitrione's death.[34] In general, Latin American police come across as stupid, disorganized, sadistic, and destructive—no match for the disciplined, organized revolutionaries. The American police instructors are opposite to the Latin Americans—efficient, technologically advanced, though they use their technology to abuse their prisoners.

The papal nuncio (Robert Holmes in the film and Augstín Sepinski in actuality) in shown elegantly vested and conservative. By his presence at the funeral mass and by his eulogy, he reveals that he implicitly backs the Uruguayan and American collaboration and considers Santore/Mitrione an innocent victim of his abductors. The newspaper account of the mass indicates that Costa-Gavras and Franco Solinas are faithful to the character of the papal nuncio. In all fairness, Costa-Gavras does present another side of the Roman Catholic Church, linked more with the oppressed people than with the Vatican. More knowledgeable and liberal, the archbishop is absent from the mass. Like several other liberal Latin American bishops, he protests American involvement in the dehumanizing techniques of torture. The chancery refuses to lower the flag to half-mast in mourning over Santore's death. Hence the Church is portrayed as having different readings of the political scene in this Latin American country in 1970, and in this instance, Costa-Gavras nuances his characterizations.

Government officials are all cut from the same cloth—all cast in negative light. We can say this even though much is drawn from the characters of the actual political scene of Uruguay in 1970. The characters are rarely individualized. So the cards are heavily stacked against the U.S. Latin American government officials, police, and the bourgeois—again, all the traditional whipping boys of the late 1960s.

Theodore Sorensen, Special Counsel to President John Kennedy, in speaking about the controversy that would soon develop over the film, maintained that Kennedy would have disagreed with much of the film's contents but would still see it, reflect upon it, and like it. Sorensen, however, is critical of the characterization:

> No shades of gray, no lingering doubts or exceptions intrude. . . . With the possible exception of one wise old reporter-narrator, there is no one in the middle, no one to suggest that urban guerrillas may be as brutal and terroristic as the police department's unofficial execution squad, no one to suggest that the Alliance for Progress and A.I.D. might, for all their imperfections, have done some good, or that Latin-American resentment of the United States would rightly and greatly increase, not diminish, if all the United States aid and investments were ever in fact to be withdrawn—which the film implicitly favors.[35]

Many critics find that this type of casting is the Achilles heel of Costa-Gavras in *State of Siege* as in his other films.

Dialogue

The film is often heavy with political dialogue in which the viewer could readily get lost. For the North American viewer, the Latin American scene appears most complicated. The parliamentary speeches, communiqués, interrogations, and government notices do present the political situation but in a burdensome manner. At times the characters become tape-recorded ideologies in dialogues disconnected from their human bodies. They become the mouthpieces of various political stances in the senate (Left and Right), in the police (Right and extreme Right), in the president (nonhuman, hard-line, non-negotiating), in Santore/Mitrione (crusading, with a law and order mentality), and in the Tupamaros (extreme Left, idealistic, terrorist).

These individuals nonetheless bring about a dialectical process in a viewing audience, obliging it to begin by asking, "What do *I* think about this political dilemma? What is correct? What is ethical?" Because the film has used the authentic tape of the interrogation of Mitrione by the Tupamaros and of interviews with various representatives of political and governmental philosophies, the audience can ascertain the tone of the original dialogues. For some critics the dialogues of the urban guerrillas appear too idealistic, far from the realism of the true socioeconomic scene. Louis Chauvet in *Le Figaro* for 11 February 1973 refers negatively to the dialogue as emanating from a manual of the perfect guerrilla. PierNico Solinas in *Cinema* submits an opposing view:

> Franco Solinas' dialogue is so stimulating that it restores to words in film that value and importance some theorized was reserved to other means of expression. It becomes at times so strikingly provocative that more than once the audience is confronted with actual ideological debate; then the film's energy no longer seems to reside in the action, in the characters and in the objects, but rather in its dialogue that takes on both a creative and dialectic function.[36]

The dialogue is dense, rapid, and idealistic. Its richness invites and requires reflection.

Genre and Technique

State of Siege may be approached as a semidocumentary film, a type of historical fiction or fictionalized history in the sense that it is the closest approximation to a documentary that is possible for a work of fiction. The film can be regarded as journalistic because of its style of narration, its chronological day-by-day report of happenings from the day of Santore's kidnapping to the day of his death. Costa-Gavras and Solinas chose to be journalists in the accumulation of their data, accepting both positive and negative implications attached to this label. Vincent Canby in the *New York Times* calls *State of Siege* an "angry muckraker of a film," and comments on this type of approach:

> Journalism, most honorably, pursues truth through an inventory of avail-

able facts, while fiction seeks truth in essences. When journalism and fiction overlap, the result can be the utter foolishness we see in much of the New Journalism, including the New Television in which the personality of the reporter sits atop the story being covered like an elephant lounging on a toadstool. Or the result may be the more heady confusion of the fictional documentary.[37]

In the Fall 1973 *Film Quarterly,* Peter Biskind draws almost the same conclusions as Canby:

> Hesitating between the world of fiction and documentary, Costa-Gavras has given us neither. We have a documentary intent without internal documentation, which robs the film of conviction, no matter how true we may know it to be, and a fiction straightjacketed by fact, which deprives it of the imaginative depth we expect from art.[38]

Each detail of the documented aspect of the film was woven into the texture of a complicated narrative. A remark here or there—for example, concerning the absence of the archbishop at the funeral service—often had its origins in a newspaper report, interview, or conversation. On the other hand, the general style is dramatic and construed for popular appeal, even as it tries to stay faithful to the documents. It is more like Brecht than Hitchcock, admits Costa-Gavras. Brecht's principle of *distantiation* is employed in order to force the viewer to reflect ideologically on the situation in Latin America in the course of the narrative.

The result is this semidocumentary attitude toward historical events, a rational and reflective—some say cold and unromanticized—product. Only on occasion does a bit of humor slip into the narrative. The newsreel tone helps to stylize the historical milieu and adds to the veracity of the document.

Photography

With *State of Siege,* Costa-Gavras created a series of images that serve as a powerful vehicle of ideological thought. Pierre William Glenn replaced Raoul Coutard as the technician responsible for the photography. From the initial establishing shot of the patrols and barricades to the final close-up of the eyes of the Tupamaro porter at the airport, the compositions run the full range of cinematic expression. To be specific, the misty opening shot gives some spatial experience of the large Latin American city; the final close-up shot of the porter's face reveals the vigilance of the guerrillas who realize that with the death of Santore, "la guerre n'est pas finie." The struggle continues with his replacement. For the artistic framing of shots, one has but to look at the way Santore's coffin rises into the airplane at an angle with the honor guard cutting across the front of the shot. The image of the funeral mass, Santore's draped casket juxtaposed with the cross and candles, is equally as powerful. A frontal shot of the surprised Este as he faces the cordon of police is also well composed.

The very practical zoom shot is used and abused in the film. Normally it is used to focus the attention of the viewer upon a certain object, for instance, from the establishing shot at the opening to a close-up of the police at the barricades. When too frequently employed, it becomes manipulative. It forces itself on the spectator in order to make a point. Its effect could be sensationalistic at the same time, and this is where technical form mitigates against political content. Aesthetic contradiction ordinarily occurs when a serious ideological content is cast in a dramatized fictional form that glamorizes the message by its self-conscious technique. Vincent Canby recognizes that following this procedure could be the equivalent of printing sensational stories in tabloid newspapers.

But the process of going from long to short shot having elements subtly juxtaposed is a photographic and dramatic technique that can reward director and viewer alike. Hubert Hardt in the Belgian *Amis du Film et de la Télévision* observes that this way Costa-Gavras goes from the exterior to the interior, from effects to their causes, and from apparent motives to profound reasons. Glenn's and Costa-Gavras's photography becomes the medium of art and drama, and for the most part does not obscure the politics at hand.

Editing

No one can fault Franco Solinas, Costa-Gavras, and Françoise Bonnot for their construction and execution of a brilliantly designed narrative. The narrative may occasionally be convoluted and dialogue-heavy for the uninitiated, but its technical structure is a masterpiece. The editing in general is sober and meticulous. The rhythm is quick-paced and staccato in the beginning of the film as the drama of the kidnapping and of the government reaction unfolds. The pace is then slowed down for the interrogation, only to switch to a rapid tempo at the very end with a mesmerizing flow of images. When there is a repetition of events as in the requisitioning of cars, distribution of tracts, the arrival of Santore in each country, and the exaggerated entrance of the ministers into the high-level conference, the editing cleverly reflects an automatic and routine activity, without creating ennui.

In order to furnish a study of Santore's activities over the several years from his affiliation with the police in Brazil to his kidnapping, the scriptwriter, director, and editor had to make the film a vehicle of complex ideology, and also a vehicle of complex chronology. David Denby in *Dissent* comments on Costa-Gavras's editing style:

> He's perfected a style of cinematic exposition—short, explosive scene-fragments gathered together in rhythmic units—that allows him to pack more action and information into his films than almost anyone else.[39]

To recreate Santore's background nonsequentially, flashbacks are used, as noted earlier. They are clearly marked out, and the viewer is not unduly disoriented when Costa-Gavras changes registers or time zones with this technique. The sheer number of flashbacks may be overwhelming, but in the long run this technique may be more effective than a strict chronological exposition of the facts. Let us enter into some detail in our discussion of this technique.

The first two flashbacks during the nuncio's eulogy are predispositional insofar as they indicate the problem-free life of a diplomat's family, in contrast to the sorry lot of the local population. The third flashback also takes place during the eulogy by the papal nuncio. He bemoans the sudden burst of violence in the city that began last week. Cutting on the last words, the director and editor draw us into the main action of the narrative, starting with the moment of sequestration. We only return to the chronological exposition of the funeral mass after the vote of the guerrillas to execute Santore is taken and immediately before the transport of the body back to the U.S. In between there are constant graphic flashbacks to illustrate the interrogation—shots of Brazil, Dominican Republic, death-squad activities, torture sessions, bomb courses for the IPA in Texas. As in *The Sleeping Car Murder* and *The Confession*, there is also at least one equivalent to a flashforward. Two snipers on top of a roof fire upon a group of young demonstrators, wounding a young girl and killing a young man. The students carry a banner bearing the date 1971. The event actually did take place, but after Mitrione's death. The general effect of this use of both flashback and flashforward is fascinating, stimulating, and very pragmatic for the accumulation of data about Santore's unethical activities. The message, however, runs the risk of getting lost in the spectacular technique.

Sound and Music

Although *Z* is superior to *State of Siege* in its colorful display of sound and music, the latter contains its own wealth. The harsh visual torture sessions rival the dehumanizing aspects of *The Confession*, for example. A device that Costa-Gavras used once again is the trapped individual acutely listening to sounds for clues. In the People's Prison, Santore hears a rumbling noise. He makes it out to be a train and tries to get some idea of the location of the prison from it.

The music is once again provided by Costa-Gavras's compatriot, Mikis Theodorakis, now no longer in protective custody on a Greek island. Greek music (classical, modern, and folk) is his forte. For that reason, his recording for the sound track of *Z* succeeds remarkably. On another continent, he might be a bit out of his element when he uses foreign melodies, primarily Latin American. His critics chide him for being too folkloric in *State of Siege*, using music that diametrically opposes the serious content of the film. The theme of the Tupamaros, introduced early in the film and then developed later, is a slow, haunting melody on low pipes that changes midway to a quick-paced tune with a high-pitched flute. "A People in Struggle" is light and inspiring and has the same overall effect of the instrumental "America in Insurrection," which excites the viewer to sympathize with the revolutionaries.

The elaborate drum piece entitled "Liberators" is also most arousing. The theme used to illustrate Santore's arrival in each Latin American country is played nostalgically on a harmonica. This music, interpreted by the five-member group Los Calchakis, provides continuity during the exposition of Santore's career.[40] Daniel Sauvaget in *La Revue du Cinéma* claims that the sound track is almost exploitative in its resonance. As the pictures of the kidnap victims are distributed and as cars are requisitioned, the accompanying music makes the sequences appear more lyrical. In general, by providing music for this film, Theodorakis proves himself once again *musicien engagé*, but in light of the incompatability of folkloric sound and political content in his contribution, his reputation suffers slightly.

The Film's Epilogue

Z and *The Confession* both propose a type of afterthought to spark reflection, an epilogue to the film that leaves the audience with a poignant political statement. As Santore's body is placed on the plane, his replacement arrives on another flight. A guerrilla observes the new arrival. When asked why he decided to terminate the film with another "Santore," Costa-Gavras replied:

> First of all because that is how it was in reality and secondly because if we had not shown the new arrival it would have been like saying that the "villain" had arrived, had been killed, and everything was finished—the catharsis was ended. Instead Lee Echols, the new "adviser" would continue and did continue Mitrione's work. It is a fact that repression in Uruguay did not end with Mitrione's death; Fascist organizations and groups formed by Mitrione himself and headed by men of his choice continue the work he had begun.[41]

This epilogue, therefore, reinforces the notion of recurrent repression and adds to the conclusion a twist of irony.

Politics

It was the politics of the film that caused greatest dissension in the ranks of the reviewers. Precisely because the film contained highly polemical material, Costa-Gavras and Franco Solinas felt they were able to achieve their purpose—to oblige the public to consider the ethics of American involvement in Latin America, of torture, of repressive police forces, and of revolution. It is impossible then *not* to have an opinion on the political nature of the work. As Costa-Gavras said:

> But the cinema has never, or rarely, or insufficiently, tackled the reasons that are behind hunger or war. That's what the political film is trying to do today—define these causes and reasons. In my view, the cinema is a way of showing, exposing the political processes in our everyday life. In fact, a film is a political act as soon as one assumes a responsibility vis-à-vis a situation, a people, etc.[42]

How account for the politics of this film?

Costa-Gavras's primary intention was to raise controversial questions regarding North American involvement in Latin America, and thus to destroy the myth of the gallant American who plays the savior for a country currently undergoing development. Solinas hesitated earlier to go along with this intention, but later yielded. His presentation is Marxist and dialectical, that is to say that the political characters embody historical socioeconomic forces. Solinas shows each power exerting its own degree and variety of violence, legal or illegal, and shows certain individuals such as Santore trapped in the same type of uncontrollable political machinery that Gérard experienced in *The Confession*. Despite his favorable portrayal of the Tupamaros, Costa-Gavras intends mainly to present the Mitrione case as a true, documented cameo of American imperialism.

In *Midstream* Stanley Eskin addresses the challenge that Costa-Gavras and Franco Solinas faced when they decided to make *State of Siege*, and thereby touch a more sensitive spot in the American filmgoer because of the harshness and actuality of the theme:

> To keep a film—or a play or novel—"political" in a deliberate, sustained, and primary way is more difficult than it seems. Politics involve a measure of abstraction and generality. When political interaction is depicted in dramatic or narrative art, there is likely to develop an increasing specificity and concreteness that tend to make the depiction that much less political, because "politics" becomes atomized into more fundamental components—moral, social, economic, and especially psychological.[43]

The screenwriter and director accumulated reams of data for their case, but they eliminated almost every aspect that would make the authorities positive, favorable characters—except for the brief moment at the opening of the film when Mitrione is represented as the loving and caring father of a large family. Costa-Gavras and Solinas tried to provide a historical context; nonetheless, the various political strains in the film still exist in a historical vacuum. To a degree, this is deliberate on the part of Costa-Gavras, as he admits in an interview for *Cinéaste:* "So I try—this is, if you like, a very moral position—to condemn events by what they represent, in a sense to let events condemn themselves by what they are."[44] Let us look at the events that "condemn themselves."

AID and the American Government

The French critic Henry Chapier of *Combat* accuses Costa-Gavras of a visceral anti-Americanism throughout the film. American critic and public alike in America bristled under the accusations made by the director, though gradually both accepted in various degrees the strong, negative criticism of American foreign policy. As Theodore Sorensen pointed out in his critique of *State of Siege*, the allegations against the U.S. are to a large extent correct, but they form only one element of a complex picture. Costa-Gavras's negative presentation of the darkest forms of American participation in Latin America—blatant neocolonialism, imperialism, repression, torture, fascism, and murder—necessarily obliges the critic and filmgoer to want to discover the real truth. The director's purpose is to raise the consciousness of the public to the level of these horrors. Former CIA agent Philip Agee's *Inside the Company* and A. J. Langguth's *Hidden Terrors* indicate that there is certainly some truth to the allegations and that the Third World is a privileged locale for covert activity. Costa-Gavras, in his interview for *Télérama,* maintains that U.S. imperialism is built on the principle of making money—no holds barred. Hence an extensive empire is set up to provide the U.S. with resources.[45] In his criticism of American foreign policy, Costa-Gavras stresses that, although he is opposed to the unethical position of the American government, he is not against the American people.

One clear target in the film is AID (Agency for International Development), which was founded under the presidency of John F. Kennedy and put under the jurisdiction of the State Department. The United States Government Manual for 1978–79 (p. 417) sketches the purpose of the organization:

> The Agency for International Development (AID) carries out assistance programs designed to help the people of certain less developed countries develop their human and economic resources, increase productive capacities, and improve the quality of human life as well as to promote economic or political stability in friendly countries.

The aid through grants was designed to promote this economic and political stability in order to secure peace, or avert political or economic disaster, but it was not to be offered to countries violating internationally recognized rights. This was the rub when it came to Uruguay. To critics of American foreign policy, Costa-Gavras included, AID exists only to insure the reciprocal rapport and world harmony necessary to promote U.S. expansion. Ducas caustically tells the director of AID that as he sees it, it is the U.S. that needs "aid," more so than other countries. Solinas in the dossier interview uses the rhetorical device of synecdoche, presenting the part for the whole. He states that the International Police Academy *is* AID, and the Alliance for Progress depends upon AID.[46] It is accurate to say that at the time of the film's release, approximately 700 foreign police officials were being trained in the IPA every year. As Lauren Goin was replacing Byron Engle (Mitrione's supervisor) in April 1973, the Office of Public Safety was maintaining 115 police advisers like Mitrione in nineteen nations around the world. Costa-Gavras's concept of the program is thus accurate, though limited and partial, given the multiple facets of the program that are positively humanitarian.

Costa-Gavras also shows the U.S. abandoning one of its own officials. The U.S.-supported Uruguayan government did not want to give in to the demands of the guerrillas, according to the official statement in the film. The position of both the American and Uruguayan governments should be made clear. The exchange of correspondence between the American embassy at Montevideo and the State Department does indicate great concern for the health and safety of the wounded official. Yet the U.S. government did not press the Uruguayan government to meet the conditions of the guerrillas, especially with regard to releasing the 150 political prisoners demanded or to providing an exorbitant amount of money, lest this would encourage terrorists elsewhere to kidnap other American diplomats. President Nixon did not want to negotiate on these terms. The policy reached was that the U.S. government would ask the local government "to do everything practicable but not necessarily everything possible."[47]

The film implies that there were behind-the-scenes motives in the American government's assessment of the Mitrione predicament. The death of Santore/Mitrione would be more useful to the U.S. than his life. If he were considered only an innocent minor official, his death could possibly minimize the true role of the U.S. in Uruguay. If executed, he could also become an American martyr, as it turned out. The pure-innocence ploy was subverted, however, by the release of identification papers linking him to the police and FBI, and by the newspaper account of Mitrione's use of torture derived from the interview with Otero.

Tupamaros

State of Siege presents the urban guerrilla in an entirely different way from the authorities. On several occasions Costa-Gavras stated that if he had to choose between the Tupamaros and the regular authorities, he would not hesitate to opt for the guerrillas.[48] This bias has been looked at negatively by many of his critics. It weakens the principal message in the film concerning the global dimension of imperialism. Montand best expresses the film's weakness in the presentation of the Tupamaros:

> I do see one small vulnerable point in the film, but we knew that even before we started: we are shown the Tupamaros as irreproachable individuals. Their own contradictions—found in any revolutionary movement—are not explained. We would have liked to have presented them, but for reasons of unity of time, place, and action, we concentrated on the Mitrione-Santore case and its consequences.[49]

There are several perspectives one could take toward the terrorists and the image created of them in the film. One extreme would be to hold Moscow's view at the time of the release of the film—petit bourgeois playing at revolution as if it were a game. The opposite extreme would be to picture the guerrillas as the only systematic, organized, disciplined revolutionary force courageous enough to take on big business, American imperialism, and the Uruguayan government. The truth, at least in 1970 at the time of Mitrione's execution, lies somewhere between the two. It is best described by Abraham Guillén in *Philosophy of the Urban Guerrilla,* who assesses the pros and cons of this national liberation movement. Guillén does not hesitate to say, "The Tupamaros are perilously close to resembling a political Mafia."[50] If Costa-Gavras misses the mark, he misses by canonizing the movement.

For the police involved in the antiguerrilla campaign, this was a war. As the film shows, the end justified the means in the escalation of their dehumanizing interrogation procedures against terrorists. It justified the execution of Santore/Mitrione for the Tupamaros. Raúl Sendic admitted after his capture that Mitrione's death should not have been allowed, and that it was a technical error,

an accident due to an uncontrollable element in the movement. If the nucleus of
the organization (Sendic and others) had not been captured on 8 August, two
days before the execution, this would not have happened. George Stevens, Jr.,
will later say that the film rationalizes assassination, to which Costa-Gavras will
retort that it does no such thing. If anything, says the director, the film shows
both parties attempting to justify their own violent means by noble ends.

Another criticism offered about the film assessment of the Tupamaros is that
the guerrillas fall into a contradiction when they oppose torture, but support
killing Mitrione as politically expedient. The bus scene of the rank and file
voting, however, is meant to imply that, following the interrogation of San-
tore/Mitrione and the distribution of the report, the prisoner is fairly tried by a
tribunal and sentenced to death. For Costa-Gavras this is not an assassination but
a military type of execution in the style of the maquis during the resistance, for
example, in the case of Philippe Henriot.[51] Costa-Gavras's opponents, however,
challenge the legality of this style of kangaroo court.

From the interviews published in the *State of Siege* dossier and other sources,
we already know that the director is an admirer of the Tupamaros for their
political wisdom, the technical maturity of their actions, and for their military
efficiency. In the film, he and Franco Solinas depict them as genuinely concerned about Santore's health, as technicians with a wealth of data and resources,
as cultivated, educated professionals, and as young, handsome, and democratic
in their process. A side remark in the film about the Tupamaros drinking only
water in the People's Prison alludes to the strict discipline maintained in the
ranks, which, if ignored, could result in severe sanctions. Costa-Gavras comments further on his presentation of the guerrillas in the film:

> We have not tried to glamorize political struggle. In our film, the
> Tupamaros have certain attributes—a strong influence on public opinion, a
> parallel power structure, advanced technical knowledge, a diversified social
> structure, excellent organization and seriousness and passion without any
> revolutionary swagger. If that is how they appear in the film it is because that's
> how they are in reality.[52]

Unlike the more balanced and objective research by Labrousse, Weinstein,
and Nuñez, Costa-Gavras's picture of the Tupamaros shows only the positive
details of the movement, which he maintains is true. On 9 September 1971, the
British ambassador to Uruguay, Geoffrey Jackson, was released after eight
months of incarceration in the People's Prison. Omar Costa in *Los Tupamaros*
published an interview with Jackson by Leopoldo Madrugo which offered the
reactions of the ambassador to his captors. Jackson said that the youthful guerrillas appeared idealistic, intelligent, and dedicated to the cause. They treated him
respectfully, not sadistically, and allowed him to read such works as *Don Quixote*
and *War and Peace*. The ambassador was adequately fed and was more or less
comfortable during his imprisonment. He discussed classical music with his captors and listened to Beethoven and Brahms. In his eyes, therefore, they were
very humanistic, hardworking, serious people with a good sense of formation
and organization.[53]

The critics complain that the picture is, in fact, out of focus. It ignores the divisions among the urban guerrillas especially with respect to the tension created by their catering to the middle class. In their self-criticism of 1973, the Tupamaros acknowledged this fact. Their alienation as well as their widespread violence gradually brought about the indignation of the people. The conservative, Moscow-oriented element of the Communist party could not abide by their leftist, terrorist philosophy. Solinas himself originally hesitated to undertake the project for some of the same reasons. Viewing the many sides to the Tupamaros question, one can see that Costa-Gavras is accurate in his portrayal of the urban guerrillas, but only positive details are carefully selected to create an unflawed portrait of them.

Latin American (Uruguayan) Government

In *State of Siege* Costa-Gavras takes on an unnamed Latin American government. Although it is a democratically elected one, it is the target of a revolutionary movement. Only the repressive, antiterrorist side of the government's officials is witnessed in the film. Face to face with this crisis, the government is on the verge of collapse. It seems to exist to provide protection for the wealthy. The ministers themselves are all connected with big business. In the original form of the screenplay Costa-Gavras and Solinas first thought of including a scene of the denunciation of the ministers-industrialists, but did not have any proof of what they wanted to say. They hesitated. While they were on location, they received documentary evidence to support their hunches, so they inserted what could almost have been a clever satire of the group if it were not reduced to such a banal caricature. The question remains, and Costa-Gavras articulates it well— "Whom and what do these ministers *really* represent?"

While the ministers are meeting, Ducas at his newspaper prepared to depict the fall of the government by selecting a photo of the president as a boxer with the caption:

> He was a mediocre middleweight boxer. He became a mediocre newspaperman, then a mediocre politician. . . . Whoever would have expected him to make a mediocre President?[54]

The parliamentary side of the government appears as a healthy organism of expression for the people, but the Left seems the more forceful, articulate, and attractive, as in the case of Deputy Fabbri. The Left absents itself in protest from the session dealing with the vote for a day of mourning at the death of Santore. With serious, aggressive, shadowy faces, the Right votes for the day of tribute for Santore, raising their arms in agreement as if they were automatons.

The Catholic Church

The next target for Costa-Gavras is the Catholic Church. He attempts to show that the Church is divided on the issue of sympathy for the American government's aide. It all depends on the politics of the individual involved. The exotically dressed papal nuncio who offers the eulogy at the funeral mass is certainly of the Right. Ordinarily the Vatican representatives would be more conservative—Costa-Gavras says *reactionary*—than the local bishops. In the age of the radical, people-oriented Theology of Liberation in Latin America, the Church hierarchy in those countries has taken major steps to work more closely with the lower classes, turning away from its traditional ties with the ruling classes. The archbishop of Montevideo at the time of Mitrione's death was aware of the torture practices of the police. He protested against American involvement in the country. The Brazilian bishops challenged the regime for its dehumanizing methods of interrogation, as we see in the film.

During the high-powered government session on Saturday of that fateful week of Santore's interrogation, an ambassador from the Vatican arrives on the scene. He is the head of a group that controls eighty-five companies, nineteen of which are foreign. The information offered by Costa-Gavras and Solinas purports to underline the large *financial* investments the Vatican has in the country—dramatically contradicting its *spiritual* mission on earth—as well as the fact that 20 percent of the firms represented will take money out of the country.

Into the mouth of the Brazilian consul, Costa-Gavras and Solinas put statements concerning Pope Leo XIII's encyclical on social justice, *Rerum Novarum* (1891), and Pius IX's social justice orientation condemning materialism. The Tupamaro interrogator of the consul charges that these are only words, for he does not feel the prisoner lives at all by them. The argument is that justice is an ideal not achieved by this Catholic involved in this repressive government, linked as it is with torture.

The film points an accusing finger at the military and economic interests of the Church. The religious institution deviates from its ideals, and there is a gap between its official statements on social justice and its actual practice. Costa-Gavras had reasoned similarly in *The Confession*, in which he indicated Stalinist divergences from the pure socialist goals.

Criticism

The critics and the public have brought their own politics into the film. This is inevitable. The narrative—in many respects anti-American and pro-Tupamaro—had already laid the potential basis for controversy, but the critical reactions to the film took it one step further. Costa-Gavras, discussing the political nature of *State of Siege* with Grelier of *La Revue du Cinéma*, reflects:

> I prefer the term "reconstructed documentary." Is it a political film? I think that a film is or becomes political when it establishes a dialectical rapport with the viewer, and also when it can foster and develop action as a consequence of reflection.[55]

What patterns can be detected in the film criticism emerging after the premiere of the film? In France, the reviews were split. The documentary technique and acting were generally praised by the critics. Jean-Louis Bory of *Le Nouvel*

Observateur for 19 February 1973 praises the work highly, especially the remarkable acting style of Montand. Marcel Martin in *Ecran* for March 1973 feels that the film is more significant for its aesthetic and dramatic judgment than for its political one; nevertheless, it is a work that fulfills Costa-Gavras's intention of making a documented denunciation of American policy. Also addressing the artistic aspects of the film, Louis Chauvet in *Le Figaro* of 11 February 1973 concludes, "But it is a fact: art does not tolerate dogmas."[56] Costa-Gavras mentioned in an interview with the *Washington Post* that the extreme Right in France was against *State of Siege*. They did not claim, however, that the film rationalized political assassination, as did the American press, which echoed the accusation of George Stevens, Jr.

Jean Rochereau of the Catholic newspaper *La Croix* has reservations on the film, but considers it is worth viewing. That critic feels that Costa-Gavras here tackles a serious problem in the film's content and takes a most mature attitude toward it. In spring 1973, Pascal Bonitzer and Serge Toubiana of the Marxist-oriented *Cahiers du Cinéma* offered a pointed and positive analysis of the making of the film, but still referred to it as "*opium idéoloqigue.*" Guy Allombert of *La Revue du Cinéma* of April 1973 considers the film a didactic simplification of both camps.

American critics and officials spoke out more extensively and with greater passion, because *State of Siege* struck a nerve. One of the first to come down strongly on the film was the U.S. State Department, for it felt that in the film Costa-Gavras presented an unjust picture of American involvement in Latin America and calumniated the person of the AID official Dan Mitrione. In the *Washington Post* of 19 April 1973, Charles Bray, a spokesman of the department, reports that the film "quite unjustly besmirches and blackens" Mitrione's life. He added that no official of the State Department or of AID participated in torture or condoned police brutality of any kind. The State Department further stated that "the objective of the program in which Dan Mitrione served and for which he gave his life was quite properly to assist the country to develop effective and humane concepts of public safety administration." Lauren J. Goin, a criminologist in charge of the AID public safety, says of *State of Siege:* "It's as effective an anti-American propaganda film as we're likely to see for some time."

One of the most violent attacks on the film came from Ernest W. Lefever of the Brookings Institute in Washington, writing an article entitled "Hypnotic Lies about Terrorists" in the *Sunday Star and Daily News* of 1 July 1973. The Honorable Gene Taylor of Missouri included it in the House of Representative records. After giving the history behind the various scandals involved with the film, Lefever amasses a series of retorts to the filmmaker to prove the film was false— Dan Mitrione never set foot on Dominican Republic soil; there is no support for Mitrione's involvement with torture; the Tupamaros are not heroes but somewhere between the American Weathermen and the Black September militants; no martial law was imposed in Uruguay until 1972, two years after Mitrione's death; the filmmakers deliberately set out to make an anti-American statement, a staunchly biased one. In essence, Lefever accuses: "*State of Siege* is a Marxist diatribe that omits, fabricates or twists facts to serve its propaganda purpose."

Theodore Sorensen, cited earlier, referred to *State of Siege* in the *New York*

Times as "a provocative, disturbing film that will shake most viewers out of their slumbering indifference." He picks apart the various political arguments of the film, but encourages seeing it, despite its blatant oversimplification. This evoked a reply from José Yglesias in the *Times* mailbag of 15 July 1973. Yglesias criticizes the way liberals like Sorensen who worked for John Kennedy could not face what they caused in the political situation at the time. He makes an analogy between their blindness and the Germans' not facing the fact of the existence of concentration camps. We cannot bear to be told that we are imperialistic, is the point made by the author of *The Goodbye Land*.

For the most part, Costa-Gavras was pleased with the American critics' appreciation of the film. He felt that they were open to accepting criticism against their country and to allowing a provocative film such as this one to be produced and distributed with American funding. Costa-Gavras discussed the film criticism with Harold Kalishman and Gary Crowdus of *Cinéaste*. He stated that the critiques of Vincent Canby of the *New York Times* and Judith Crist of *New York* magazine caught the positive aspect of the film. Canby saw the film several times and wrote at least two reviews of it. Even though he criticizes it for its style of journalistic muckraking, he feels Costa-Gavras did a service by creating this work, for he asked the right questions:

> Among other things, the film asks if this must be the way of the world and, if not, what we are going to do about it. Most important to me, it wants to know whether we can be outraged by duplicity, corruption, violence and torture, even when they're presented as methods for maintaining not just law and order abroad, but the standard of living at home.[57]

Several of Canby's favorable comments on the film elicited a sharp reply from James L. Loeb, former ambassador to Peru and Guinea, in the *New York Times* of 6 May 1973.

> In my view, the film is in the revolting tradition of the late unlamented Sen. Joseph McCarthy. In line with that tradition, it uses the techniques of smear and innuendo. I am certain that Mr. Canby was as opposed to McCarthyism as I was. But why does he now condone it when it is used by the so-called left?

The former ambassador especially finds it difficult to accept, on one hand, the positive treatment of the terrorists as heroes and, on the other hand, the insult to the memory of John Kennedy, who established the Alliance for Progress, a most progressive and innovative program that is referred to negatively in the film.

Besides her positive critique of the film in *New York* magazine, Judith Crist also spoke on the NBC Today show on 20 April 1973. Despite all the anti-American invectives in the film, Crist still can call the film "pro-American." Her reasoning is similar to Canby's in that she feels the subject involves all of us today and it obliges us to examine our personal conscience and that of our country.

Time and *Newsweek* were especially fascinating to Costa-Gavras, for he considered them to be a bit like *Pravda*, offering a political view that would be acceptable to the American public, perhaps middle America. Be that as it may, Costa-Gavras felt that the *Time* article of 23 April 1973 was favorable. Jay Cocks's critique appears honest and perceptive. He came out strongly against the technique of the film more than against the politics; another segment of the press took the same stance. Cocks says that Costa-Gavras

> is angry all right, and with cause, but it [*State of Siege*] is also unnecessarily emphatic, too easy and simplistic, and stylistically jazzy past the point of stridency. His movies are like glossy international versions of *Dragnet,* with a rather different political bias.

The critic who provoked the most hostile response from Costa-Gavras was Paul D. Zimmerman of *Newsweek* of 23 April 1973. The director considered this critic "reactionary." Zimmerman's critique reads: "From the outset, even the smallest details are so slanted as to embarrass even those sympathetic to Costa-Gavras's vision of an imperialist America supporting oppressive Latin governments." He then refers to the film as an "arid exercise in ideological complacency" and a "diatribe cum melodrama."

The critical tone grew sharper once beyond the circle of leading American newspapers and journals and of intellectual leftist critics in Washington and New York. In the majority of cases, one can ordinarily discern a positive appreciation of the brilliant film technique, but then, a harsh criticism of the film's biases and its one-dimensional representation of the characters and situations. William Collins of the *Philadelphia Inquirer* of 7 October 1973 writes: "Esthetically it is a virtuoso piece of film-making. Politically it is arrogant propaganda on behalf of the violent revolutionary Left, an anti-American statement of considerable effectiveness." Kevin Kelly of the *Boston Globe* of 4 May 1973 describes the film as frightening, impassioned, and powerful, despite its biases.

Of the American critiques, *Cinéaste* offers the best analytical and perceptive study of *State of Siege*. It picks holes in the intentions of the filmmakers but also discusses the film as most significant and as worthy of consideration both as a work of art and as a political weapon.

Hugh Bernard in *Films in Review* of June/July 1973 refers to the film as a "2nd rate *roman policier*," which lacks balance and is overly preoccupied with polemics. Stephen Rosenfeld in the 20 April 1973 issue of the *Washington Post* considers it art, but also a pale imitation of life.

For Peter Biskind, in the fall 1973 issue of *Film Quarterly*, the sins of *State of Siege* are sins of omission more than anything else. The director fails to go beyond a superficial view of the politics of both the guerrillas and the U.S. government. In a very impartial fashion, Biskind states that the politics behind such a film ought to have been extremely important, but the work takes on fictional status right from the introduction, even as we read on the screen that the events in the film are true.

In a perusal of the headlines of some twenty newspapers from all sections of the U.S., one can discover several patterns: *State of Siege* is biased, leftist-oriented, a big lie, a scathing attack on America. The film is timely, hypnotic, provocative, politically significant. It is further considered a political pamphlet, powder keg, a clever thriller. Much of this criticism underlines the political nature of the film and scarcely attends to the technical mastery of the work. In general, to those critics who charge that this film is a classic example of propaganda, there is the refutation that states that the film is historically accurate in light of the thoroughly accumulated documentation. The question still must be asked, "Can a true artist in conscience blind himself or herself to the other side of a problem?" *State of Siege* perhaps can be considered true in the same fashion that Shakespeare's *Richard III* and Rolf Hochhuth's *The Deputy* are considered true.

When asked by interviewers for *Cinéaste* if film criticism influences him at all, Costa-Gavras replied:

> This is a big problem for the director. Generally, we say no, criticism doesn't influence us—this isn't so, but the complete opposite isn't true either. Nobody makes a movie because of a review or something a critic says. But, speaking for myself, favorable reviews—that is, not just from any reviewer who makes compliments, but from critics who are respected and who analyze the film in depth—these are an influence on me. That is, first I try to see if certain things they have written are true, are really there, because people sometimes see things you never thought about before. So that's a certain influence.[58]

In the long run, however, Costa-Gavras feels it is more a cumulative impact that film criticism has on him, rather than something precise and definite as communicated by one particular critic at one specific moment.

Double Vision

It is very difficult to take a clear-cut and absolutely objective stance on Daniel A. Mitrione's responsibility for torture. That responsibility is the critical thesis of the film. Is he guilty or not of the accusations made by Costa-Gavras and Franco Solinas? To put it very simply, there are at least two basic views of Mitrione, which are at times impossible to reconcile: the one of the State Department, AID colleagues, family, friends, and patriotic individuals, basically of the Right. Their perspective is colored by friendships, family ties, and political relationships. Then there is the one of the Left—the Tupamaros, Costa-Gavras, Franco Solinas, the former police agents from Uruguay, Amnesty International, and political liberals in the Uruguayan Parliament. Their image of Mitrione arises out of enmity for authority, frustration with a repressive system, and concrete documentation linking Mitrione and AID with dehumanizing torture tactics.

When the White House learned of Mitrione's death, a statement was read by Press Secretary Ronald Ziegler on 10 August 1970: "Mr. Mitrione's devoted service to the cause of peaceful progress in an orderly world will remain as an example for free men everywhere." Secretary of State Rogers viewed him in this way: "We earnestly hope that they [wife and children] may be fortified by the knowledge that his outstanding personal and professional qualities had won him the respect and admiration of his fellows." AID Director John Hannah lamented his execution: "The agency has lost a fine and dedicated man who served his country well."

U.S. officials of AID in Rio de Janeiro vigorously denied that Mitrione was involved in torture as the *Jornal do Brasil* alleged in Alejandro Otero's exposé. Other colleagues said that he was definitely not a spy for the police department. Laurin J. Goin, the director of the public safety sector of AID in Washington, also denied the torture charge and stated that he knew Mitrione well, having served with him in Brazil. Mitrione was known above all for his efforts to bring the police closer to the community, testified Goin.

The *Congressional Record* of the House of Representatives for 3 August 1971, at the time of the first anniversary of Mitrione's death, includes Peter T. Chew's article "Dan Mitrione's Legacy," taken from the *National Observer* of the previous day.

> He was a quiet, gentle man, the son of Italian immigrant parents, a staunch Catholic, and the father of nine children. Before joining AID, he served as the popular police chief of Richmond, Ind., where he was noted for his work with youth.

The Reverend Robert Minton, pastor of the Holy Family Church in Richmond, Indiana, preached at the funeral: "God was no stranger to him. He illustrated ideals to be a full Christian man, and when the time came for him to die, he would be unafraid. For death is not an ending, it is a beginning."[59]

President Richard Nixon and Pope Paul VI both considered Mitrione a tragic victim of terrorism. They added their condolences to those of governments, family, and friends. Frank Sinatra and Jerry Lewis paid their tribute by giving a benefit performance for the family in Richmond.

The family felt defensive about the image of Mitrione established by the Left, which made of him an undercover agent and inhuman torturer. Dan A. Mitrione, Jr., wrote a response to a published letter by the Reverend Philip E. Wheaton in the *Washington Post* of 24 September 1970. Wheaton, director of the Ecumenical Program of Interamerican Communication and Action, had referred to Mitrione as a "listed CIA agent." Mitrione's son expressed his shock that a clergyman would accuse his father of working for the CIA and called this slur McCarthyism. His father's name was listed on page 364 in the East German publication of Julius Mader, *Who's Who in the CIA* (1968), but, the son observes, the names of Dean Rusk, Hubert Humphrey, and Eugene McCarthy were also included. Elsewhere the children would say that he was indeed a committed man, and that he dedicated his professional life to police work.

Others believed him to be a patriot, a humanitarian, a martyr who struggled in the crusade against communism, attempting to make the world safe for democracy. They saw him as coming from a hardworking immigrant tradition and being a model American citizen. As the father of nine children, he immediately drew great sympathy from the people. The press showed heartrending pictures of the family in Montevideo. It used strong language detrimental to the image of the guerrillas, saying that this good American official was slain (murdered, killed, or executed) by criminals (seditious individuals or conspirators). The word "Tupamaros" was never used because it had been outlawed since 1 December 1969. *El País* of 10 August 1970 called his execution "*el bárbaro asesinato*" and "*absurda violencia.*" *El Diario* of the same day published recent photos of the family with the headline: "En la Mañana del 31 Julio su Esposa e Hijos le Vieron por Ultima Vez" (On the morning of 31 July his wife and children saw him for the last time). In this way Mitrione was canonized by one sector of society.

For the other side of the picture we must take the perspective of the filmmakers, the liberal press, and the Tupamaros. To these individuals Mitrione was an agent of imperialism, a type of "our man in Montevideo," working under the cover of the AID organization. In "CIA-ese" or "spookspeak," the language of the intelligence community, Mitrione would be part of a "sheep dipping" operation. *Safire's Political Dictionary* refers to this technique as the utilization of an officer in a clandestine operation under civilian cover.[60] The Left linked him with the FBI since he had gone to the FBI Academy and carried an FBI card when he was captured. These same critics accused him of being a member of the CIA, as noted earlier. The 7 August 1970 communiqué from the Tupamaros read: "This man is an American spy placed by the government within the security services of the Uruguayan state. He himself has admitted that he was a technical adviser to the metropolitan police."[61]

In the eyes of the Left, Mitrione was not simply an American official or diplomat, as the first press releases in the newspaper indicated. He was something more. For them he was a policeman and would always be one, from his work as chief of police in Indiana to the moment he was executed. His mission was to teach new techniques for security; this would later earn for him the label torture specialist. The dossier on *State of Siege* included the list of police activities for which Mitrione was responsible—the creation of a spy network in universities and high schools in Uruguay; the enlarging of police weaponry; the giving of orders to photograph all people flying to and from socialist countries and keeping files on their correspondence; the choosing of men to train at the International Police Academy in Washington, where he himself taught for two years.

On this anticommunist crusade, according to Alejandro Otero, Mitrione had systematized torture in Brazil and especially in Uruguay to such an extent that the guerrillas were forced to escalate their warfare against the state. Through diplomatic pouch Mitrione was said to have imported sophisticated torture equipment to combat these insurgents.

He was a man of principle. The wrong ones, according to his critics—pro-state and antihuman. His allegiance was to the status quo. With peaceful conscience he went about institutionalizing new, swift ways of interrogation. Occasionally, it was claimed, he was present during interrogations by torture. This was the report given by the Cuban double agent Manuel Hevia Cosculluela, alluded to earlier. Costa-Gavras feels that Mitrione is very much like a judge in good faith during the Inquisition, thinking that the end always justifies the means. He elaborates on this:

> He is like a man of the Inquisition, a man who believes he is defending the free world and keeping it "clean" and he would do anything to keep it "clean." He believes that Communism as well as liberalism will bring society to the brink of destruction and down in his very guts he is convinced that the only way to prevent this from happening is by physically eliminating the Communists.[62]

In the film, Mitrione is the one ultimately responsible, given the trend of all the evidence. Costa-Gavras's reply to the question raised by the Tupamaros in their interrogation of Mitrione is that the American aide is without doubt guilty. The film thus implies that he should have been executed.

Epilogue

On 1 April 1973, the *New York Times* published a statement by George Stevens, Jr., director of the American Film Institute, with respect to the AFI's programming for a forthcoming festival at the new Kennedy Center: "We believe in our responsibility to present the best films we can, both American and foreign, to our patrons and the public. The fact that a film or subject is controversial doesn't eliminate it from our list." Stevens would have to swallow these words, and he had already begun to do so. He had made the statement several days earlier in light of a *New York Times* deadline. Then, a short time later, on 29 March, he dramatically canceled the showing of *State of Siege* at the festival marking the opening of the AFI theater in the Kennedy center. The film was to be the third in a series, scheduled for 5 April, with D. W. Griffith's *Broken Blossoms*, billed for the opening 3 April presentation.

The reasons for the cancelation were *moral*, for Stevens stated that the film "rationalized assassination," and an American ambassador and a chargé d'affaires had recently been assassinated by Arab terrorists; *personal*, for the Kennedy family would be present at the festival, and it would be in poor taste to show an assassination film to a family twice marked by such tragedy; *political*, for the AFI received funding from the Nixon administration and Stevens would shortly be entertaining Nixon at the AFI dinner in Los Angeles. Stevens replies to his critics:

> I cancelled the showings entirely on my own judgment. Nothing to do with losing Nixon's money for the Institute. Though there were a lot of congressmen getting ready to support me on the cancellation. It was a question of taste, not of censorship; this picture rationalizes political assassinations. I'm not against pictures people might call anti-American.[63]

Stevens felt that this was not censorship since the film was not banned and could be seen in local theaters in Washington. The American public would thus have every opportunity to see it, he observed. Yet there was political pressure all around. The Fort Wayne, Indiana, *New Sentinel* of 25 April 1973 stated that it was through the efforts of the Veterans of Foreign Wars and the ambassador from Uruguay that the film was canceled. Stevens's final decision was supported by the executive committee of the AFI, so the burden of responsibility could be shared with several other individuals.

When Stevens was planning the festival, he did not have the opportunity to see the film. Only when he heard Max Palevsky, the co-producer, express surprise that *State of Siege* was chosen for the festival did he realize that he had a tough decision ahead of him. Stevens's assistant, Richard Kline, had grasped somewhat the political import of the film, for he had read the reviews of the film in the

European edition of *Newsweek*. Once Stevens saw the film, it was obvious to him the direction he had to take.

The subsequent repercussions were loud and multiple. Jack Warner, the film mogul whose $250,000 gift helped construct the Kennedy Center, was to be feted at the time of the festival with an award and a montage film, *Jack L. Warner: 50 years in Hollywood.* He sent his regrets. The New York Film Critics charged Stevens with censorship and said this undermined his credibility, for he had shirked his responsibility to show controversial films. Other critics called him naïve. In protest, approximately a dozen film directors pulled their films out of the festival. They did this through the organizational efforts of Julia Reichert of New Day Films. The films of François Truffaut, Lindsay Anderson, and Jacques Rivette were not projected, while those of other directors including Jonas Mekas were allowed to be shown, but these latter filmmakers decided to make a public statement before their work was screened. When Stevens was about to go through with the cancelation in Washington, Donald Rugoff, the co-producer and American distributor, told Stevens from Paris that he was shocked and appalled, but admitted, "If you do what you are going to do and take the film out of the festival, you'll make a fortune for me."[64]

Costa-Gavras's tranquil reaction to this tempest in a teapot was:

> The problem of the Kennedy Center is, for us, an American problem. All we can do is thank them for inviting us in the first place. We did not ask to be part of the festival. We are not happy to see the film withdrawn.[65]

This was a gentle, balanced statement. Later on he would call the whole affair *"une bêtise,"* a blunder on the part of Stevens. Stevens showed himself doubly inept with this controversial stance, according to certain critics, such as Hugh Bernard in *Films in Review,* for "he betrayed himself into censorship and he caused what is essentially a 2nd rate *roman policier* to be assured of a success before it had even been shown."[66] This reaction may be a bit exaggerated, but, generally speaking, the scandal did draw an audience, distracting the spectator from the film's true merits—or demerits.

To conclude *"l'affaire* Stevens," the *Washington Post* printed an editorial on 13 April 1973 with a realistic *point de départ:* "We believe we take a back seat to no one in our opposition to censorship." The *Post* had shown its courage in publishing the Watergate drama as it was being acted out. The editorial, accepting Stevens's reasoning, goes on to say that what happened was a far cry from censorship, and that the press and filmmakers overreacted. The film was not censored, for it could be seen at three different Washington theaters. The *Post* believed that in the withdrawal of the film taste and not ideology was at work. The editorial laments the withdrawal of the other films in protest and concludes, "There is, to be sure, cause to be sensitive about government censorship these days, even in America. But vigilance on this score should not be confused with vigilanteeism."

7

Special Section: Vichy and the Reason of State

> What I have been constantly expounding since *Z* (and even before) is the relationship between an individual and a government. This rapport can also be called political. What holds my attention and interest is the elaborate machinery constructed by Man. It escapes his control and he eventually becomes controlled by it.
>
> —COSTA-GAVRAS

In the late 1960s and early 1970s, the accent in World War II films shifted from action-packed epics in which the Nazis always lose to the heroic Allies, to psychological dramas in which we see a very human side of both combatants. From the end of the war up to the present there have been more than 130 major French films on this subject treated from multiple perspectives. Jean-Pierre Jeancolas in *Positif* of June 1975 begins his classification of these films with a documentary film, *La Libération de Paris* (1944), and concludes it with Costa-Gavras's *Section Spéciale* (1975).[1] If we consider various fictional and documentary films on World War II, for example, Louis Malle's *Lacombe, Lucien,* Marcel Ophüls's *The Sorrow and the Pity,* and Michel Drach's *Violins at the Ball,* we see that the medium of film can be thought of as a sociological witness to the values, politics, and collective mentality of each decade following this apocalyptic moment in history. Yet film, especially historical film, rarely if ever remains a neutral witness.

With a film on the Vichy government of 1941, Costa-Gavras entered the mainstream of public interest. He was following on the trail of his documented but fictionalized treatment of the assassination of the Greek pacifist deputy Z (Lambrakis), the show trial of the innocent Artur London in Prague, and the execution of AID official Dan Mitrione by the Tupamaros. Like his other films, *Special Section* is controversial since it touches upon a taboo topic, French collaboration with the Nazis, while some of the actual performers in this tragic drama were still alive.

In *Interview* for March 1971, Costa-Gavras said: "I want you to know that it isn't easy to make political films in France. It's not by chance that we haven't done until now a film which covers the political situation in France. In fact what we are doing is a strategic detour."[2] In *Special Section,* the filmmakers followed the assassination of a German noncommissioned officer by young communists and the setting up of a retroactive antiterrorist law by the French government that would result in the guillotining of three innocent men. The film implicates many French government officials in the web of a legal conspiracy and attempts to raise the consciousness about the use and abuse of power.

History

Four days after the entry of German troops into Paris, the French poet Paul Valéry on 18 June 1940 lamented: "In the space of several days, we have lost all certainty. We are on a terrifying and irresistible slope. Nothing that we could fear is impossible; we can fear and imagine absolutely anything." The worst that could be feared and imagined would be the French turning on their own in this hour of crisis. This did occur; France established "Special Sections," the kind graphically illustrated in Costa-Gavras's film. Costa-Gavras refers to this epoch as "the darkest period that France has known." For one of the more in-depth analyses of this period we can turn to Robert Paxton's *Vichy France: Old Guard and New Order, 1940–1944.*[3] His scholarly work is based on captured German archives and contemporary materials, more so than on self-serving postwar memoirs or war-trial testimony. Paxton's research provides a fine parallel to Hervé Villeré's text *L'Affaire de la Section Spéciale,* which is the source of the Costa-Gavras film.[4] Both are limited, however, insofar as they do not adequately present the position of Marshal Henri Philippe Pétain and Pierre Laval of the Vichy government.

For an embarrassing number of French citizens, the Vichy government was a peaceful and pragmatic means of handling the German Occupation. In essence, Paxton asserts that collaborationist Vichy, contrary to the comforting myth, obtained for the French (especially communists and Jews), no better treatment than that accorded to the fully occupied nations, such as Poland and Czechoslovakia. The historian shows mass French agreement with Vichy policies at the outset of the Occupation. The people feared social disorder as the worst imaginable evil. They rallied to the support of the state, and, in Paxton's eyes, thereby brought about the betrayal of the nation as a whole. With Marshal Henri Philippe Pétain as its head, the French government moved to the Vichy spa— approximately 100 miles northwest of Lyons—on 2 July 1940, just a few weeks after Charles De Gaulle's rousing appeal from London to resist the fascist onslaught.

In terms of the armistice with Germany, the French people were split, not unlike at the time of the Dreyfus controversy. One simple indicator of this is the wide range of images of Pétain held by the French. Some saw him as a heartless collaborator and traitor who sold France to the Nazis. Paxton and Villeré at times more than imply Pétain's culpability. Others considered the marshal a concerned patriot who wanted to avoid war with Great Britain and also to prevent France from experiencing the same brutal suffering it did in World War I. For a laudatory view of Pétain it would be sufficient to glance at *Le Maréchal et son peuple*, published in 1941 by René Benjamin of the Académie Goncourt. Pétain here becomes a *démi-dieu*.

One event after another and one law after another—often with political and racial overtones—tightened the occupation noose around the neck of the free French citizen. On 27 August 1940, censorship against political opinions and groups was introduced. The communists were among the first to be threatened by the government. The Jews were next on the lists. According to the film, communists and Jews were considered and treated as "scum of the earth." On 3 October 1940, a French law was adopted to exclude all Jews from public office and from all functions influencing the cultural life and opinion of the country, from teaching, journalism, film directing, and so on. Paxton holds that this Jewish persecution emanated less from any compulsion on the German side than from long-festering internal conflicts in France:

> It is vital to expose the French roots of early Vichy anti-Jewish measures, for nowhere else has the claim of German pressure and French passivity been more insistent. It is true that, from 1942 on, the German project of deportation was imposed on France by fiat and despite a certain amount of Vichy foot-dragging. At the beginning, however, the Germans cared so little for French internal matters that France was used as a dumping area for German Jews. On 23–24 October 1940, over intense French government objections, six thousand German Jews were sent into France from Western Germany. Just as France was not included in the "Middle European Great Economic Region" German peace plans, so it was not considered part of the area to be "purified" of Jews. In 1940, therefore, an indigenous French anti-Semitism was free to express its own venom.[5]

General xenophobia, explains Paxton, was heightened after the Spanish civil war when France was used as a political refuge for exiles from Spain. Vichy xenophobia, however, was more cultural and national than racial. It differed from German anti-Semitism. By issuing the laws of 3 and 4 October 1940 that prevented French Jews from participating in civic life, on one hand, and by calling for the deportation of foreign Jews to internment camps, on the other, Vichy laid the groundwork for the more intensive and extensive work of the Nazis.

> The fact remains that the Vichy government had tried to single out a group for special contempt for measures of discrimination. Those measures were a great help for the Germans when the more bestial program of the Final Solution began.[6]

The communists did not fare any better in the Vichy regime. Let us look at the background of this political battle against the Left to understand better Costa-Gavras's perspective in the film. On 22 June 1941, the Werhmacht invaded the U.S.S.R. A week later there was a rupture in diplomatic relations between Vichy and the U.S.S.R. Like the official crusaders against communism in *State of Siege*, there would be many in the Vichy Unoccupied Zone prepared to fight against the communist evil. A large subsidy was offered to the Legion of French Volunteers to battle Bolshevism on 18 July 1941, the same day that the communist organization Francs Tireurs et Partisans entered the clandestine battle. A month later, as we see in the opening of the film, Henri Gautherot and Samuel Tyszelman were shot by a firing squad. The Communist party responded with a demand for the death of twenty German officers in retaliation.

Subsequent to the invasion of Russia by the Nazis, terrorist acts in France escalated, with the communists most often accused of them. Colonal Hans Speidel, chief of staff of the German military command in Paris, reported fifty-four acts of sabotage in July 1941, seventy-three in August (the month in which the action of the film takes place), 134 in September, and 162 in October. Paxton indicates that the reaction of the Germans to these terrorist activities was ferocious and random as they gathered and shot in batches common-law prisoners and jailed communists. The Vichy government labeled all this terrorist activity "communist," and Pétain, Admiral Jean Darlan, and Joseph Goebbels tacitly agreed, for propaganda purposes, to blame all active resistance on Bolshevism.[7] In the forum of the law, explains Paxton, the Vichy government moved into full swing against the red menace:

> The Darlan government had already begun to react in August to the rise in Resistance terrorism with the busiest burst of legislation since the first days. This time, however, the theme was order and not the National Revolution: a sign of evolving priorities. "Special Sections" of the departmental courts-martial were set up under a new law empowering the government to act with exceptional rigor against "Communists and anarchists." Justice Minister Barthélemy asked the Cours d'Appel to choose judges "known for the firmness of their character and for their total devotion to the state" for the civilian component of these courts, applied the new procedures retroactively to current cases, and singled out the Third International as the "first-ranking target."[8]

Paxton discusses very briefly the Special Section that is at the heart of the Costa-Gavras film, while Villeré consecrates his entire text to it. In the context of this Special Section, Paxton writes about the harassment of communists and Jews alike while Pierre Pucheu was Minister of the Interior:

> The Paris "Special Section" was hurried into existence on August 23 in time to sentence three Communists to death for infraction of the decree of 26 September 1939 dissolving the party (Bréchet, Trzebrucki, and René Bastard). But the German taste for vengeance was not slaked by such paltry numbers. In November Pucheu also produced a Communist terror group headed by an Alsatian Jew who he said had carried out the Nantes asassination, but one never knows how accurate the police are when they need an accused so badly. In the end, the Germans went on choosing their hostages, to Pucheu's great regret. It is ironic that Pucheu was shot in 1944 largely for something he tried to do but failed.[9]

Thirty years after the establishment of the Special Section in August 1941, Thierry Levy pointed out in the publicity notes for the film that the same legal process operative in the Vichy regime could get underway again through officials like Pierre Pucheu, because nothing new or radical had been introduced into contemporary texts or juridical practices that would permit judges to oppose the dictates of power without risk of personal danger. He speaks in this manner about the abuse of power by means of the legislation of a retroactive law:

> This judiciary monster is the result of negotiation between the German occupation forces and Pétain's Government. The Germans are willing to defer reprisals accepting instead the French proposal to immediately try six militant communists before a special court, sentence them to death and execute them. It matters little if it were the Germans who pressured the French into action or if it were the collaborators themselves who took the initiative. The controversy over political justifications can never be resolved. It is another matter to have dragged justice into the deal. These men who condemned to death Trzebrucki, Bréchet and Bastard were judges in the Justice Department. Nothing went by them unnoticed. They knew that the sentences had been dictated in advance, that they were basing their judgments on a text that went against the basic principles of the penal code, and that it would strike men who had already been tried and sentenced for the same crimes. This task, which would forevermore disqualify them as judges, could always be refused without serious risk. One of them, only one, did refuse and he was left in peace. Nonetheless, and despite the fact that they were not forced to do so, all the others accepted.[10]

Levy confirms that there was no physical external pressure on the judges to accept the role of executioner and that they could have refused in conscience. Some of the judges, however, were ambitious. Others were just following orders, and this is most peculiar. When Doctor Stanley Millgram did his studies on authority at Yale University in the early 1960s, he discovered that in his experiments, many individuals could consciously and deliberately apply electrical shocks to push the "experimentee" over the threshold of death as long as someone else claimed or implied that he would accept all responsibility for the consequences. This was certainly the case in the concentration camps, and it becomes obvious that a similar mechanism was at work here in the setting up of the lethal apparatus by means of a retroactive law. The agreement here was that the judges would sit in judgment on prisoners already tried, and that they would sentence innocent men to death before the trial. *Special Section* clearly shows that Pétain agreed to the process of establishing the retroactive law and signed it, thus obliging the ministers and judges to follow suit. Nonetheless, they all invoked the national interest whereby the collective state was of greater importance than private human life; national interest appeared to be a mask for fanaticism, ambition, and blindness. Thierry Levy implies that this prostitution of the law might happen again if people are not vigilant. That is Alain Resnais's comment about the concentration camps at the conclusion of *Night and Fog*. In the publicity notes for *Special Section* Georges Conchon echoes something of the same, stating that, in fulfilling unethical tasks, "someone can always be found." It is only later, with hindsight, that one realizes what has unfortunately happened in the process. Conchon observes:

The film borrows the detour of History in order to discover, from a distance, from a greater height, exactly where the threat originates, and to involve us in a process that began long ago, but whose ravaging effects we are only now beginning to understand.[11]

Literary Document—Hervé Villeré's *L'Affaire de la Section Spéciale*

An old Latin adage reads *"Nulla poena sine lege,"* or "No sentence without the law." Hervé Villeré gets at the essence of this phrase in his study of the travesty of justice with regard to the execution of the three innocent men. Villeré is a graduate of the Institute of Political Science in Paris and postdoctorate scholar in Civil Law and Economics. He does not let us forget article two of the French Civil Code—"La loi ne dispose que pour l'avenir; elle n'a point d'effet rétroactif," or "The law only prescribes for the future; it has no retroactive effect." A year after Paxton's book on the Vichy government was published in the United States, Villeré's book made a bloody entrance into the French politico-literary scene. Within a short period, Editions Arthème Fayard sold more than 300,000 copies—according to the Universal publicity notes—surely because of the explosive material in the book. The names involved in this scandal were not changed, much to the chagrin of the few participating officials still living and of the families of the deceased authorities.

Hervé Villeré begins to relate the difficulties he encountered with the publication of his book on the Special Section by quoting Sophocles—"Night is the only time to judge the day." When Editions Arthème Fayard decided to publish Villeré's document, the president and director of the publishing firm, Charles Orengo, wrote to the Minister of Justice (Garde des Sceaux) René Pleven on 3 January 1972, requesting permission for the author to have access to dossiers dealing with the Special Section of August 1941. Two days later Villeré personally wrote to the Minister of Justice. Pleven's reply in early February stated that consultation of these documents was restricted, and they could only be examined 100 years later, decreed by laws of 1970 and 1971. Only the director of the French Archives, with the permission of the Minister of Justice, could allow consultation of these documents. Pleven replies to Villeré:

> The reasons for these arrangements are to reconcile the obligation of secrecy to which the administration is committed and the public's right to know, when research in these archives is done for historical purposes.
> But you will admit that the greatest discretion must be exercised in this domain.
> It is a matter of concern, indeed, to the utmost degree, that one avoid anything that could be prejudicial to private interests and that could arouse strong reactions in public opinion.[12]

Thus, after careful consideration, the Minister of Justice declined to give permission to consult the texts that would have greatly clarified the nebulous situation of the Special Section.

To document his thesis, Villeré, like Paxton, scrutinized sources that were for the most part unpublished. Among them were the German documents of General Otto von Stulpnagel and Chief of Staff Colonel Speidel, various types of materials from the German administration in occupied France, for example, the daily reports from the office of Major Beumelburg, General von Stulpnagel's liaison officer with the French government. Such documents allowed Villeré to represent the German perspective on establishing of the Special Section. The most detailed account emanated from the "Dossier Moser" on Alfons Moser, the assassinated noncommissioned officer. This document was seized by the Americans in 1945, microfilmed, and preserved in the military archives in Fribourg-am-Breisgau.

To get an actual perspective from the French side, Villeré interviewed successively the wartime procurator of the Republic, the three *avocats généraux* (Deputy Directors of Public Prosecution) who received the orders from the *Parquet Général* (Well of the Court), the last survivor of the five judges, and finally the two lawyers of the condemned. He then systematically gathered the recollections and notes about the events from 110 witnesses, then other significant details from the families and comrades of the three executed men, including the prison diary of André Bréchet. This style of documentation in 1972 and 1973 recalls the process of verification followed by Costa-Gavras and Franco Solinas in preparing the scenario of *State of Siege* at exactly the same time. Villeré proceeds with caution in establishing the several perspectives of "the truth." His is a very readable synthesis of many little-known documents that have major consequences with respect to the culpability of the French officials in the Vichy government.

The resultant book, which would later be faithfully transposed by Costa-Gavras and Jorge Semprun, has three major parts, then an epilogue, and is supplemented by illustrations, documents, and a list of sources. Part One—"The Roads of Honor"—introduces the characters, victims and executioners alike by devoting a chapter to each individual. Villeré describes, for example, (1) "A Jew," Abraham Trzebrucki, a Polish Jew in France imprisoned for possessing false papers and for helping the International; (2) "A Minister," Pierre Pucheu, Minister of the Interior, who fought in the Spanish civil war on the Franco side and later was involved in big business before entering the government; and (3) "Frédo the Magnificent," in reality Pierre Georges, a lieutenant in the International Brigade in Spain who, in 1941, headed a group of twenty communist youth and gave them an order to avenge the communist executions by killing German officers—he is the individual responsible for the death of Alfons Moser.

Part Two—"The Settling of Accounts"—records the spirit of vengeance on both sides of the fierce struggle. To avenge the death of two communists, Frédo and Gilbert Brustlein assassinate Moser. Villeré announces the date of each major event from 21 to 24 August at the beginning of the chapter. In Part Three—"The Lives of Men"—the author narrates the events from 25 August and the deliberations of the ministers in Paris, to the execution of the three men at dawn on 28 August.

Villeré's epilogue is very much like the epilogues of Costa-Gavras's earlier films, a sobering message that the author places at the end of a work to show that the tragic situation did not really end there but unfortunately drags on. The Vichy government is shown to be more severe than the German occupiers, for it handed over other victims to the Nazis to avoid any further problems for itself. Villeré concludes by narrating the subsequent lives and deaths of the magistrates.

Scenario

Costa-Gavras mentioned in the April 1975 *Film Français* that in 1974 he no longer had the courage to write his own scripts as he had earlier in his career, so he turned again to Jorge Semprun, whom Paul Deglin calls the "intellectual twin" of the Greek-born cineaste.[13] Semprun had just completed a screen adaptation of a Drieu La Rochelle novel for Pierre Granier-Deferre's *Une Femme à sa fenêtre*. To lay the groundwork for their project, Semprun and Costa-Gavras relied upon the Villeré text. They attempted to recreate the tone, documentation, and chronology leading up to the execution of the three men. They also did their own research. Before Counsellor Linais (Jean Bouise in the film) died in May 1972, he made a tape of the affair which Hervé Villeré allowed the filmmakers to use. In our 9 March 1981 interview, Semprun emphasized that this tape and others clandestinely made by Villeré in the course of the interviews were invaluable in the scriptwriting. The Linais tape gave the cineastes some bearing on this counsellor's refusal to go along with Vichy's death-sentence policy.

Obtaining further verification from participants in the events was a bit more complicated for them. When asked by Betty Jeffries Demby in *Filmmakers Newsletter* about their method of procuring the necessary controversial data from the participants of the events, Costa-Gavras replied:

> In talking with them, I talked about many things—not just the one or two things I really wanted to find out about. I talked around things, around the subject. Eventually, when they were comfortable and relaxed, I asked them the things I was really concerned about—and often by then they would answer. But if I had gone straight to the point at the beginning, they might not have.[14]

In the same interview Costa-Gavras stated that there was quite a bit of archival material in England, France, and Germany, but he felt that England had the best documentation.

Prior to working with Costa-Gavras on *Special Section*, Semprun also worked with Resnais on a screenplay dealing with the controversial figure Stavisky. From his research for the film *Stavisky* he was able to use some material for *Special Section*. In the film, for example, there is an allusion to the file cabinet that contained the Stavisky dossier.

Costa-Gavras believed that from their extensive collaboration a tightly knit script resulted, each element being dramatically and psychologically linked to the preceding one. For the director the script was a type of architectural construction that would serve as the foundation for the film. It was not an inviolable element in the creation of the film, but a key supportive one. The result was a *récit classique,* a traditional or classical narrative, although the flashbacks in the second half of *Special Section* would make it less conventional than a normal chronological narrative. In Universal's press release, Semprun discussed the essence of their project:

> In *Section Spéciale* there is not, strictly speaking, what we would call a plot in the traditional dramatical sense of the word. Nor are there characters, heroes—negative or positive—bearing the psychological attributes necessary to an action structured by a denouement according to the usual precepts of the genre.
> In short, there is no story.
> But there is History. And very precisely, that of—in part at least—France during the Vichy period, August 1941. There are the forces, the men who made this History in the apparent incoherence of their personal interests and of their contradictory ideologies.
> This deliberate obliteration of traditional plots and heroes allows Costa-Gavras to trace, with the precision of an etching needle, the portrait of one of the most terrifying characters known to the 20th Century: the totalitarian State. *Section Spéciale* seems to me to be an analysis of the State, of its irrationality, of its large-scale display, of its repressive machinery.[15]

Production and Filming

In the making of *Z* a few years earlier, Costa-Gavras found it nearly impossible to find financial backing. No producer dared to take the risk. A political film at that time was supposedly taboo, an assured money-loser at the box office. In the case of *Special Section* in 1974, the situation had changed radically. Costa-Gavras mentions that there was a group of private investors who were more than willing to back his work. The new film project thus drew the support of production companies from Italy (Goriz), Germany (Janus), and France (Reggane/United Artists). Giorgio Silvagni and Jacques Perrin would be the co-producers. Costa-Gavras himself accounted for 30 percent of the investment, while Perrin of Reggane Films and the others provided the other 70 percent. The filming was a serious financial undertaking. There had been a 25-percent escalation in costs from the time of filming *State of Siege* to this project, a large part of the costs, as usual, going for actors' contracts, film equipment, and shooting on location. It was necessary to reconstruct the Vichy of 1941 in order to have realistic-looking costumes, vehicles, and sets.

Three locales were finally required for the filming—Vichy itself, and the Palais de Justice and rue St. Denis, both in Paris. The subject matter was controversial, and as Costa-Gavras and his crew were about to begin shooting, it seemed likely that the director might not obtain permission to shoot in the spots he chose. He discusses permissions for specific locations in this way:

> I went personally to the Prime Minister's secretary and told him the kind of movie I was making and the story and asked him to give us the authorization

to shoot in some tricky places like the Palais de Justice. I explained to him that
I would have to shoot there, and if he refused me permission, I would simply
have to shoot in another place—and then have to explain to the press why I
had to shoot in another place. In other words, it would be like censorship if
they refused. So finally they were very clever and gave me permission to shoot
there.[16]

Narrative

August 1941, Vichy—a spa in central France.

With the tapping of the baton, the musical performance begins. Mussorgsky's
opera *Boris Godunov* is being staged at the Grand Casino of Vichy, a locale known
for its curative waters. The singer prophetically laments, "Weep, my country,
weep for yourself. Doom is about to fall." When the curtain closes, Marshal
Philippe Pétain, in charge of the French government located presently in Vichy,
is heard droning out his message about the cordial relations now existing between France and Germany. He gives unrestricted power and freedom to the
Minister of the Interior, Pierre Pucheu (Michel Lonsdale), passing over the
Minister of Justice, Joseph Barthélemy (Louis Seigner).

The scene then shifts to a demonstration of a group of young Parisians singing
the "Marseillaise" and brandishing a tricolor. They want to sing the communist
"Internationale" but hesitate. A Nazi force quickly breaks up the rally, wounding
some of the participants. When some of the demonstrators gather again, they
feel they should do something more in the spirit of resistance. The tale of Old
Man Milon is told—he did his share for his country during the Franco-Prussian
War (1870) by systematically slaying Germans with his scythe.

Next, the Nazis take reprisals for the flagrant demonstration against the occupiers. They execute Samuel Tyszelman, a twenty-year-old Jew living in Paris,
and Henri Gautherot, a twenty-one-year-old communist. Their comrades seek
vengeance for this brutal act of the Nazis. They decide to take into their hands
what little of justice is left and pledge to kill some Germans themselves.

After several failures, the moment arrives. Frédo (Jacques Spiesser) and his
assistant spot a young naval officer at the Barbès metro station in Paris and shoot
him in the back. They escape.

The Minister of the Interior in Vichy calls for a meeting of officials, so that
they can take swift and drastic measures concerning the assassination before the
Germans react. He reasons that the act could be the work of Gaullists—though
not their style—the Jews, or the communists. Recently the communist newspaper
L'Humanité had called for someone to revenge the two youths executed by a
firing squad. The officials speak of either executing a few terrorist leaders in jail
to set an example, or setting up a retroactive law to judge them. The latter
alternative is accepted. As a result of this session, a statement is drafted by the
Vichy government urging that the occupying forces should not hold Parisians
responsible for the terrorist act. Instead, the French themselves would set up a
special tribunal and then bring six terrorists before it. The sentences would be
carried out immediately with execution by guillotine in the Place de la Concorde.

Special Section: Frédo (Jacques Spiesser) assassinates the German officer, Alfons Moser. *(Permission of Universal City Studios, Inc.)*

Even the German major (Heinz Bennent) is surprised that in the land of Montesquieu—grand patron of law—a particular law could work retroactively to judge prisoners already in jail, that the sentences are determined in advance, and that the execution by guillotine would be in public. In the eyes of the Germans this whole situation is considered immoral and in poor taste.

Once the Germans accepted the French decision about restitution—though not about the public execution—the machinery gets into operation. On 23 August, the ministers decide to backdate the antiterrorist law to 14 August. The officials reluctantly put their signature to the document, but when told by the aide that Marshal Pétain had already signed it, their consciences are somewhat appeased. The Minister of Justice opposes the law but is forced by political pressure to go along with it. He is told that as an alternative the Germans will execute fifty hostages. Unfounded rumors state 100 hostages, including the Archbishop of Paris. The task of the Minister of Justice is now to choose the members of the court to sit in on the Special Section. He is told to look into the ranks of decorated war veterans, for, as good soldiers, they will follow the orders of their marshal.

When the Minister of Justice returns from Paris to Vichy to establish the members of the court, he first calls in Judge Cournet (Michel Galabru), who is insulted, outraged that his colleagues suggested him for the dirty work of presiding judge. He courageously and adamantly refuses. Finally the authorities arrive at the name of Benon (Claude Pieplu), wounded in war, and he is "mobilized" by the Minister of Justice. The group next drafts four other judges—a soldier wounded at Verdun, a recipient of the Military Cross, a member of the Action Française, and another willing candidate.

It is a challenging and disheartening chore to choose six men to execute, even if they are terrorists. The newly formed judicial body pores over the files of all the communists and Jews—only minor cases. On 25 August 1941, the elaborate ceremony of the installation of the court, with the judges finely dressed, ritually takes place. Following the ceremony, the final dossiers are chosen—a casual, insensitive process.

When the machinery of selection eventually grinds to a halt and the victims are at hand, the scene shifts to the prison where the defendants are being detained. They are led to the trial. One by one the men are called into the closed court room to offer their testimony.

—Redonneau (Guy Mairesse) called police *"une bande de cons"* (a bunch of idiots) and gets a ten-year prison term.

—Bernard Friedmann, caught putting up communist posters, draws a one-year sentence.

—Abraham Trzebrucki (Jacques Rispal), Jewish, arrested for possessing false papers and stamps for Jewish solidarity, receives the death sentence. Counsellor René Linais (Jean Bouise) violently opposes this, but the vote is four to one for capital punishment. The young attorney, Maître Lafarge (Jacques Perrin), returns home to relate with disgust the situation of the condemned victim.

—André Bréchet (Guy Retore), tried and found guilty of subversion nine days earlier, was sentenced to fifteen months in prison. At this trial of the Special Section, he is again brought before the court and condemned to death by guillotine.

—Emile Bastard (Yves Robert) has had a penchant for women and for taking things that were not his, as we learn through flashbacks. He was framed by police because he liked Rita. Bastard eventually had eight convictions, but has settled down over the past ten years. Like Trzebrucki and Bréchet, he gets the death penalty. Only three more to go.

—Lucien Sampaix (Bruno Cremer), the sixth person to go before the tribunal, is the outspoken journalist of *L'Humanité*. He launches a verbal attack at the court, saying that the death sentences were already prepared in advance. Sampaix prophetically declares that the Nazis would be defeated and that France would be liberated. The judge calls a recess. During the course of deliberations it is difficult to decide Sampaix's case. He gets hard labor instead of the death sentence.

There is a flashback to the previous Saturday. Ironically a poem is read—"To the Maréchal."

The film concludes with preparations for the guillotine and an epilogue that describes the fate of those brought to trial. The three men—Bastard, Trzebrucki, and Bréchet—were executed according to plan. Four others, including Sampaix, were put to death by the Nazis. Five died in concentration camps. As for this style of justice—"Special Sections functioned throughout the Occupation. Most judges sat on them." And then the prophecy is fulfilled: "Sampaix was

Special Section: A final plea before the Special Section.
(Permission of Universal City Studios, Inc.)

right. The Nazis were defeated. France was liberated. After the Liberation, no serious action was taken against the judges of the other Special Sections. Again, the Reason of State prevails." The music of the opera *Boris Godunov* returns to conclude the film.

Book Versus Film

There is a definite evolution from the book to the film. One of the first tasks of Semprun and Costa-Gavras was to get to the essence of the Villeré historical text. Above all, they wished to zero in on the state as the mechanism in the destruction of the three victims.

Generally speaking, Semprun and Costa-Gavras remain faithful to Villeré's controversial thesis that the French took harsher and more insensitive measures against the detainees than the Germans. The film characterizes the Germans as cultivated and sensitive individuals, not unlike the German officer in Vercors's literary cameo *Le Silence de la mer,* adapted for the screen by Jean-Pierre Melville in 1947. Costa-Gavras and Jorge Semprun use the same basic chronology of 21 to 28 August 1941 as Villeré does, and it is projected on the screen in a journalistic fashion in order to facilitate the spectator's grasp of the intricate sequence of events. The director and screenwriter render accurately even some of the fine detail of the literary piece. They include symbolically, for example, the performance of the opera *Boris Godunov* in Vichy on 12 August; they utilize it at the opening and closing of the film. The rally of young communists, the Old Man Milon story, and the execution of Gautherot and Tyszelman with the subsequent *L'Humanité* cry for revenge—all are retained in the passage from text to film. The actual assassination of the officer is inserted as well into the body of the film and then more graphically developed. It is enacted in slow motion to underline its political and psychological importance. Also kept are the meeting of the ministers to make the anti-terrorist law retroactive and the sheer surprise of the Germans at this. Very significantly, most of the deliberations of the judges are retained to illustrate the gradual corruption of power, but they are telescoped. Minister of Justice Barthélemy is at first opposed to the whole affair of the retroactive law, as Villeré demonstrates, for Barthélemy had written his doctoral dissertation on retroactive law. Little by little he is shown in both works as succumbing to and then drawing others into the juridical travesty. Among the other various scenes kept are those dealing with the selection of dossiers, especially from the Stavisky file cabinet, and the deliberation of Judge Drion with the other four judges. Drion tells them that this retroactive law is created for a *Raison d'Etat*.

Then there is the process of selection. It would be impossible to film the real history that was Vichy of August 1941, or even the slice of it seen in Villeré's work. So Costa-Gavras and Jorge Semprun streamlined the narrative. The prison life of the three victims is drastically reduced and almost eliminated. Instead, Costa-Gavras and Semprun took the material of the introductory chapters of the book on the three men and successfully created flashbacks interspliced with the courtroom testimony. They telescoped the biographies, the private lives especially, of the remainder of the characters, for instance, Alfons Moser and Pierre Pucheu. The director and screenwriter included just enough material—a fraction of the original facts available in Villeré's work—to give the audience an idea of the politics of the individual and his role in the grandiose parody of justice. They deliberately chose to strip the literary work of any emotion; witness the touching exchange of letters between Marie and André Bréchet, Pauline Bastard's late discovery of her husband's execution by way of a pneumatic express letter, or Marie Bréchet's learning of the tragic news through the press. The double epilogue of the book is transformed into a final brief picture of the destiny of the major characters.

Much more emphasis is given in the film to Lucien Sampaix in his testimony before the court and to Maître Lafarge in his concern for the fate of his charge. Both become heroic and altruistic in their gestures and dialogue. They can be singled out despite the fact that the fresco is so vast that noble and villainous characters alike can get lost. The problem was to simplify the personalities of the characters so as to make them recognizable and also have them correspond to the historical moment. The results are alternately considered by the critics as realistic portraits or caricatures of these Vichyites. Yet it is through these portraits that Costa-Gavras and Semprun capture the blend of the actual operetta and tragedy in the Vichy regime.

Actors and Characterization

Commenting on the manner in which he collaborates with his actors, Costa-Gavras remarked:

> Every actor has a different character, a different figure—they are like musical instruments, and you don't play every instrument the same way. You need a different technique, a different passion and sentiment for each one. It's the same with actors.[17]

Since this adaptation was a vast panorama of history peopled by all types of characters on both sides of the issue, a large cast of actors was mobilized. The director and screenwriter eliminated certain characters from the book, and they reduced others in order to bring the narrative into sharper focus, but they did not dilute the essence of the work. In restricting themselves to specific characters without changing their names or function, they produced results that are less universal than those of *Z* or *State of Siege*.

Unlike his other films in which Yves Montand played the protagonist, *Special Section* boasts of no central actor or character with whom the filmgoer can identify. Costa-Gavras recognized a problem here and tried to compensate for it in many ways. There may be a dramatic and psychological flaw to the decision, for a filmgoer ordinarily requires a focal point of attention and sympathy. The closest we come to an earlier image of a protagonist is Lucien Sampaix and young Lafarge, but both only appear in the last several sequences of the film. Through the idealized flashbacks of the three victims receiving unjust and immoral treatment from justice, Costa-Gavras tugs at our feelings despite his intention to remain unemotional in the presentation. The biographies of these men are restricted primarily to the trial scene. These little people are the quasi-heroes of the day although Jack Kroll of *Newsweek* feels that Semprun and Costa-Gavras have sentimentalized the defendants with "nostalgic flashbacks that turn them into corny travesties of Sacco and Vanzetti."[18]

Costa-Gavras sketches his philosophy of character as spokesman: "The character is only a vehicle which helps you tell the story. What is important in each character is the personal position which he or she holds."[19] In the enormous flow of dramatis personnae, our vision wanders from one to another, never alighting for any extent of time on a particular character. We never sufficiently focus on an individual to penetrate the person's true beliefs, values, and ideals. It would be impossible to do so at length in a film of two hours. The result consequently was a superficial understanding of the characters and their motivation. As Vincent Canby observes, they are only "on the screen long enough to register a political position."[20]

The results of this approach to a large cast are twofold, stereotyping and facilitating the comprehension of the historical narrative by immediately labeling certain individuals. Jay Cocks of *Time* is hardly positive vis-à-vis the black-and-white interpretation of the characters:

> There are no real characters, only cameos enacted by a large cast of mostly unfamiliar actors [that is, to Americans]. The judges are straw men in scarlet robes, passing out death sentences like souvenir fountain pens. Their victims are a ragtag gallery of the common man meant to embody some evergreen liberal shibboleths: the fiery left-wing journalist; the good-humored, faintly ironic petty crook; the humble shopkeeper.[21]

Nancy Schwartz in the *Soho Weekly News* is no less severe, for she says that Costa-Gavras and Jorge Semprun "created a world of stooges, victims, and political baddies," and rendered them "like an editorial comic strip."[22] Pauline Kael in the *New Yorker* also underlines the stereotyping and bias:

> The prisoners brought to trial are touching and heroic figures—they shine with humanity—while the judges who condemn them are vain, ambitious, militaristic weaklings, easily soft-soaped. The collaborators are smaller than life, and we feel contemptuous of them from the first glance. The casting and the writing are so prejudicial that the film's purpose is undercut.[23]

One example of stereotyping similar to that of *State of Siege* appears in *Special Section*. All that is dynamic, youthful, and vigorous is painted idealistically, while all that is older, bourgeois, established is drably presented. The authorities wallow in their ignominy, baseness, and senility. Although Sampaix and the defendants do not fall into the young-old categories, they still wear halos—saintly victims in opposition to a satanic power machine. Nancy Schwartz catches this symbol of youth in the film: "The lawyers for the defense are fresh-faced fellows with self-imposed muzzles, except for an enthusiastic moralist [Lafarge] who goes to Vichy to appeal."[24] Jack Kroll uses the same terminology to describe the assassins as "fresh-faced Communist kids who can hardly hold a gun in their nonviolent hands."[25] They appear on screen as young rebels with an ambiguous cause.

Prescinding from this general simplification of characters for both political sides, there are, nevertheless, fine performances among certain actors who are cast in the principal roles. To play Joseph Barthélemy, Minister of Justice, Costa-Gavras persuaded Louis Seigner to come out of retirement. He could very well pass for an old twin brother of O. E. Hasse, the outspoken journalist Ducas in *State of Siege*. Seigner is known for his superb work in the Comédie Française. Jack Kroll pictures him representing symbolically the bowed spirit of France with his white hair and stoop. The bilingual actor Michel Lonsdale, who headed the hunt for the would-be assassin of De Gaulle in *Day of the Jackal*, and who also performed in *Murmur of the Heart*, *The Bride Wore Black*, and *Destroy, She Said*, plays the cunning and ambitious Minister of the Interior, Pierre Pucheu. Costa-Gavras calls Pucheu "*un jeune loup*" (a young wolf) and is fascinated by this individual who was executed under De Gaulle—also for a *raison d'Etat*. As the Attorney General, Pierre Dux, often cast as an evil person—the general in *Z*, for instance—is convincing. In his professional acting work he alternated between the cinema and the theater. He has been in theater administration as well since 1970, working with the Comédie Française and the Théâtre National at Odéon.

Among the more sympathetic characters in the film is Counsellor René Linais, played by Jean Bouise. Once again Bouise plays a courageous hero pitted against impossible odds, as in *Z* and *The Confession*. In *Special Section*, as Linais, he is in the vocal minority, fighting against the death sentence for the defendants demanded by his judicial colleagues. Jacques Perrin—producer, director, and actor—helped finance and starred in several of Costa-Gavras's earlier films. Here he becomes the young attorney, Lafarge, who opposes the manner in which the defendants are judged. He, too, speaks out vehemently against this obstruction of justice. Costa-Gavras used Bruno Cremer for the role of the resistance leader Cazal in *Shock Troops* and now for that of Lucien Sampaix, editor of *L'Humanité*. Cremer, often typecast in war films, even in Raoul Coutard's *La Légion saute sur Kolwezi* (1980), in which he also defies the authorities, comes from a solid background in theater and performed in such plays as Anouilh's *Becket*. He has worked considerably in cinema, in *Octypus*, *L'Attentat*, and recently in *Une Histoire simple*. The young communist Frédo is played seriously by Jacques Spiesser, another actor whose origins are in the theater. He has gradually come to the attention of the filmgoer, working with Jeanne Moreau in *Lumière*, Yves Boisset in *R.A.S.*, and Resnais in *Stavisky*. Jacques Rispal as the humble, simple-minded Abraham Trzebrucki makes us sympathetic to the character, another victim of the political apparatus like the pants-dropping Otto Sling in *The Confession*. The actor-director Yves Robert (*Courage, Fuyons*, and *The Tall Blond Man with One Black Shoe*) humorously portrays the lovable creature Emile Bastard, who made a few wrong turns while growing up, but has lately followed the straight and narrow path.

What would a Costa-Gavras film be without Yves Montand? Montand is not in the starting lineup, but the director has him make a brief appearance in the film. He is seen in the role of a *milicien* on the terrace of a restaurant.

From the point of view of characterization, it is the actors who save the day for Costa-Gavras, for this type of epic drama splits at the seams with the large cast not unlike Clement's *Is Paris Burning?*. Despite the unfortunate lack of a focal point, Costa-Gavras does justice to the talents of the actors.

Technique and Tone

In general, the tone is more subdued and less spectacular than *Z*. It was as political and controversial in France as *The Confession*, and less complicated in structure than *State of Siege*. Costa-Gavras's aesthetic technique is responsible on the whole for this successful evolution from the scriptwriting through the filming to the final editing. As with all of his works, Costa-Gavras can play on several registers at the same time, amplifying the image on the screen several degrees by simultaneous action and clever juxtapositions. During the meeting of the ministers there is a discussion about the assassins of the German officer and the possibility of taking a few terrorist leaders from jail and executing them as an example. In the meantime, a woman chases a chicken around the hotel; children playfully jump about in oversized boots ignorant of the political execution squad nearby; and a group of people outdoors create a folkloric and traditional atmosphere by singing "Au Clair de la Lune." The effects are almost surrealistic.

Excerpts from the life story of Emile Bastard are lyrically presented through the flashback recreating the good old days. Music reinforces the image. Bastard steals a bicycle and gets caught. He loves Pauline and Rita. The police frame him because of his love for Rita. The flashback creates an aura of innocence around and endearment for this gentle, mischievous lad who grew up too late—he already had eight convictions by that time.

Photography

Costa-Gavras no doubt worked differently with Raoul Coutard (Z, *The Confession*) than he did with Andreas Winding in *Special Section*. When asked how closely he worked with his cameraman, he replied:

> I am always surprised at how you Americans seem to think the cinematographer plays an important part in a movie. In France the cinematographer plays a very, very small part. I personally supervise the lighting, the camera positions, all of that. I do them, and he just has to execute them.[26]

Speaking of his camera technique in general, Costa-Gavras went on to say:

> I think camera movements play an important dramatic part. But one should not make a camera movement just to use the camera. I frankly feel it is fine to use the camera without any movement—sometimes for very, very long periods. Sometimes it is important just to take the actors and what they are playing. I think the story should dictate the movement. However, I usually prefer a camera that just sees.[27]

For *Special Section,* the narrative does determine the movement, but Costa-Gavras in turn imposes a style and order upon the film, and carefully decides upon a specific tone in advance. With respect to visual imagery, *Special Section* is not so brilliant as his preceding films, or it may be that the viewer is too accustomed to what the director says by way of his camera statements. For Marshal Philippe Pétain (1856–1951) Costa-Gavras uses the same allusive technique as he did with the almost invisible Slansky in the trial scene from *The Confession.* We see Pétain's hand signing the documents, earlier in the film we heard his raspy voice announce, following the *Boris Godunov* performance: "My fellow Frenchmen, I have some serious things to tell you." It recalls the old Hollywood biblical film in which we see only the brilliant light around Yahweh and hear his voice, or perceive the silhouette of Jesus without a frontal view in order to present a certain distance and create a holy, transcendental aura.

An ironic commentary on the legal situation is made by the camera prior to the trial. There is a cut from the detainees being transported from the prison to a lawyer going into the court. The eye of the camera fixes self-consciously on the floor inscription in large letters—"JUSTICIA." The lawyers are then gathered together and briefed on the retroactive law. The statement is made.

For the most part, there are no glamorous or exotic shots that distract the viewer from the political kernel of the film. In one case, however, Costa-Gavras utilizes slow motion to dramatize Frédo's assassination of Alfons Moser. In the subway station, the zealous communist fires two shots into the back of the German officer, who slowly and agonizingly crumples to the ground. The onlookers in the first-class car react somnambulistically to the horror, while Frédo and his accomplice escape in laborious slow motion through the tunnel. By using this technique, the director expands the climactic moment of the assassination.

The Eastmancolor process chosen by the director provides the images with a rich, lustrous dimension that makes the general effect most attractive. Conversely, the viewer has the uncomfortable sensation that there is something anachronistic about the images because of their rich effects. It is ordinarily difficult to recreate historical events of the recent past with realism and conviction. It is less difficult with events of several hundred years ago. Sometimes the best solution is to choose the type of washed-out image used by Ettore Scola in *A Particular Day,* in which he was able to present realistically Hitler's 1938 visit to Rome. To conclude his analysis of *Special Section,* Jean-Pierre Jeancolas discusses the challenges of reconstructing an historical epoch:

> More important . . . is the gap that exists between the reconstruction of the recent past and the present notion we have of it. Here we must establish a criterion of *credibility.* The most careful, minute, and precise reconstitution, even on the level of a tiny button on a pair of gaiters, is perceived through a camera lens. The camera imposes a very strong coefficient of reality on the texture of cloth, the stones of a building, the faces of human beings, and we know that this reality is contemporary.[28]

Only the *Sleeping Car Murder* was shot in black and white. All of the other works of Costa-Gavras were filmed in color. Each of the latter films has its own nuanced colors. Somehow the color process and technique used in *The Confession* to reconstruct Prague of the early 1950s is more convincing than that used in *Special Section* to recreate Vichy of the early 1940s. The director chooses to use color over black and white for the film and defends it in this way:

> So why does black and white seem to be more real? There are just historical reasons: the first photos we saw were black and white. Frankly, I think black and white is *less* real than color because it's totally out of life—nothing is black and white. Color is more real—and more poignant sometimes.[29]

Costa-Gavras also felt that for commercial reasons color was necessary since the distributor depends on the public's preference for color over black and white.

Color dominates the ceremony of the inauguration of the *Special Section.* The court officials sport their majestic ermines—brilliant contrasts of reds and whites—parading into the courtroom. Some critics call this a scene from Honoré Daumier's nineteenth-century engravings. In the background organ music amplifies the judicial pomp and circumstance. Tradition and fossilized elite forms of society are all emphasized, in contrast to the humble aura surrounding the political prisoners who are soon brought before the court. This resplendent procession borders on caricature, just as the entrance of the wealthy ministers does in *State of Siege,* or the exit of the military officials in *Z* with their chests laden with polished medals. In the courtroom scene, Costa-Gavras translates perfectly the impression that one gets reading Villeré's description of the ceremony:

> The members of the court enter at the back of the hall. The magistrates who are to be installed, rise, with their four Legion of Honor ribbons, their six Military Crosses, and their three war medals. President Villette, first president of the Court of Appeals, advances, followed by the procurator, General Gavarroc. Both are in full dress and, as heads of the court, they wear four stripes on their magistrate's cap.[30]

The lush color and the tongue-in-cheek style of the director here make of these men judicial marionettes in a tragic show.

Editing

In the last four films of Costa-Gavras, Françoise Bonnot was his most faithful technician. From the raw materials of the filming, Costa-Gavras and Bonnot cocreated the final version of the film. The director discusses his own evolution with respect to editing:

> There, too, I work very closely. When I made my first movie, I did the editing and saw that it was virtually a re-write for the movie—you have your script, you have your shooting, and you write your movie in the editing. So I think it's quite important just to have a technician editor come in from the outside to do that work.[31]

Costa-Gavras further specifies:

> In order to make the editing work, you must have the material. So you have to carefully think through the effects during the shooting—even though, during the editing, things will change for hundreds of reasons.[32]

When discussing Costa-Gavras's tone and the editing style, critics ordinarily point out that his material is often presented in dossier fashion. This was especially evident in the documentary approach to *State of Siege.* His less flattering critics say this borders on a cold, academic style.

Françoise Bonnot, in our 7 January 1980 interview in Paris at the Billancourt film studio, stated that through cutting, which determines the pace of the film, Costa-Gavras established a triple rhythm throughout the work. In the first part of the film he concentrates on presenting the milieu of Vichy, and in the second, the inner workings of the judicial system. Then suddenly, during the trial, he shifts to the private lives of the three men who are being judged. Initially, the spectator may have the sense of being bogged down in the heaviness of the content and perspective, but the tone heightens during the court proceedings. Normally a trial can be long, dull, and slow-paced for the lay observer, a drawn-out exchange of opinions and/or facts. In the hands of Costa-Gavras the trial of *Special Section*—like the interrogation in *Z*, the Slansky show trial of *The Confession*, and the questioning of Santore in *State of Siege*—takes on a lively, dramatic spirit by means of an alternation of camera angles and quick cutting. Sampaix's testimony serves as the focal point of the scene and immediately renders the spectator sympathetic to his cause.

The flashbacks are not so frequent as in Costa-Gavras's earlier films. They are inserted naturally during the testimony of the witnesses. Their insertion is less self-conscious than the insertions in *State of Siege*. Since each personal background is being presented subjectively by the individual on trial and challenged by the judge, Costa-Gavras tries to change the coloring of the narrative as presented by both parties. He modifies lighting, staging, and tone to capture this personalization. The biographies are romanticized in the telling, blending lyricism and comedy. Nancy Schwartz in the *Soho Weekly News* refers to these flashbacks as "affectionate bursts of impish tableaux (impish Polish immigrant and family posing outside their store, impish petty criminal stealing a bicycle)."[33] Because of these pleasant, lyrical flashbacks, it is difficult for a viewer not to sympathize with the pathetic figures who are caught in the machinery of *Justicia*. They are contrasted with the pompous bourgeois magistrates who connive to attach a death sentence to six communists and Jews before the trial gets underway. There is, however, no lyrical flashback to the lives of the judges or to scenes from their happy family lives. In this manner the technique is manipulative and one-sided.

Sound and Music:

Costa-Gavras is highly sensitive to sound effects in his works as can be especially verified in *The Confession*. There the imprisoned Gérard listens intensely to every sound. Solitary confinement sharpens his awareness to prison noises. The same is true in *Special Section*, but to a lesser degree. In prison, the men are being assembled for transport to the courtroom. There is the strident clanging of prison doors and the barking of names to punctuate this travesty of justice. Our ears and our sensitivities are irritated and disturbed. The most obvious accentuation of sound occurs during the assassination of Alfons Moser. As Frédo and Gilbert escape from the metro platform, a thumping heartbeat—as in *Z*—dominates the sound track. When they arrive at street level, they spot a policeman; tension mounts. The heartbeat has stopped and there is absolute silence as if their action is suspended in time and space. The contrasting effects turn what could be a cinematic cliché into a powerful aural sensation.

The musical background differs in each Costa-Gavras film, depending upon the composer and the historical situation. Sometimes Costa-Gavras knows ahead of time what type of music he would like and what effect he wishes to produce.

With *State of Siege* he knew from the beginning how he wanted it, while at other times he chose it during the filming or editing process, for example, the simple melody for *The Confession.* Ordinarily Costa-Gavras trusts his instincts in deciding what scene needs musical support. He tries not to succumb to the temptation to insert music throughout *Special Section,* saying that if musicians had their choice, they would have put music into the film from beginning to end.[34]

Eric Demarsan was responsible for the musical sound track of *Special Section.* Demarsan had his formation in classical music. He also had experience in publicity films as well as in industrial shorts. Prior to his work with Costa-Gavras he furnished the sound track for *L'Armée des ombres* (1969) and *Le Cercle rouge* (1970) of Jean-Pierre Melville.

During the escape of Frédo and Gilbert following the assassination, "magnetic music" (electronic music) is blended with the heartbeat. This music is the work of Takis. Music from the opera *Boris Godunov* opens and closes the film. Its insertion, based on a literary fact, produces a symbolic effect. Tsar Boris Godunov (1551–1605) encouraged informers and persecuted suspects on their unsupported statements. In the closing scenes of the opera Boris prays to heaven to forgive him his heinous crimes before his death. The opening excerpt for the film—"Weep, my country, weep for yourself. Doom is about to fall!" is ominously sung by the simpleton in scene 2 of act 3.[35] It is easy to read this prediction of the enemy's arrival and of the coming of terrible, impenetrable darkness in light of Paul Valéry and Costa-Gavras's references to the dark period of the Occupation, at this time of *"une guerre franco-française,"* as Stanley Hoffmann aptly describes it.

The uses of music are thus varied and readily support the action. Although the music has not been as memorable as the theme of *Z*, it is used creatively by the composer and director.

Politics

As Costa-Gavras mentioned in interviews for his preceding films, it is often the public and critics—and those directly touched by the film's content—who politicize the work. Ann Powell in the *Soho Weekly News* quotes the director:

> I'd like to think . . . that my audience politicizes my movies more than I do. You see, I shoot these stories the way I feel I have to. For me, it's a passion. At the same time, if the public after leaving the theater learns from my films or even just thinks about them, they are making my films political.[36]

Costa-Gavras feels that this requires the audience to participate and reflect along with him and not remain passive. In *Special Section* he makes a valiant effort to reexamine contemporary history and to include the spectator in the process.

With *Special Section,* Costa-Gavras, along with Jorge Semprun, remains the spokesman for the Left. Although the historical facts presented here by the director have been thoroughly documented, first by Villeré and then by the screenwirter and himself, they are only one side of an intricate political picture. The anti-Establishment element appears very attractive. No vision of history is absolutely objective, and one would expect too much of the director to take a purely academic, objective, and abstract view of these events. Costa-Gavras does slant his historical presentation by a one-sided glorification of the Left and of the forces in opposition to the authorities. We noted this earlier in our discussion of characterization. He also gives a revisionist or reformist view of the events of 1941. The filmgoer may have the uneasy feeling at times that the film reads back into well-documented historical events, highlighting problems and situations that leap to the eye today, but in 1941 would have had another political, economic, and psychological bearing. On the other hand, we should perhaps admit that unethical procedures of law should have posed a problem then, but participants and authorities were blind to the situation. Today with our "20/20 hindsight" we can see more clearly the agonizing problems.

The significance of Costa-Gavras's political thesis still stands. He touches the untouchable subject of the corruption of justice and judge. Costa-Gavras deliberately sets out to show the Machiavellian abuse of power by officials of the Pétain government. It is important to note that Costa-Gavras does not condemn French justice, but the perversion of the system, just as he did not damn socialism in *The Confession*, but the Stalinist aberration from the pure doctrine. In this miscarriage of justice, the director shows that the judges felt trapped but, nonetheless, acted out of a misguided sense of duty.

Costa-Gavras illustrated the driving force from above that pushed the political puppets of the Pétain regime to act illegally and lethally, to destroy the dignity and life of fellow human beings but always under the guise of Justice. Institutions became more important than the humans who made them, Costa-Gavras indicates. The government thus sends these political scapegoats to their death in the name of the law, but behind the law is a melange of blindness, fanaticism, racism, nationalism, and patriotism, or, as Paxton proposes, a basic fear of social disorder. The blood of the innocent victims, according to Villeré and Costa-Gavras, is not on the hands of the occupying force, but on the hands of the French legal agents. The final words of the film say it all in a sardonic tone— "The Reason of State prevails." The victor at Vichy is the questionable consideration of higher interest that one invokes as a state when an illegal or unjust act is taken.

To promulgate the retroactive law, Vichy government authorities follow the pyramid or chain-of-command approach. The Minister of the Interior puts pressure on the Minister of Justice to go through with this illegal law for reason of State. The officials assert that if Pétain signed the retroactive law, it must be legitimate. Then they select the judges and one in particular who would be willing to be the presiding judge. Finally the legal authorities oblige the young lawyers to carry out their orders, though only allowing them to prepare their defendants very briefly. One mockery of justice after another follows the line of action from the top of the pyramid to its base. Costa-Gavras carefully focuses on the process of this "white-collar crime" of the government in its manipulation, pettiness, intrigue, and destructive power. Many individuals can simply destroy others by bowing to authorities who accept the full responsibility of the action, as suggested by the Millgram studies at Yale.

The director does present the issue of aborted justice, dramatically showing that it was a class problem certainly tinted with racism. The eternal sacrificial victims of corrupt power in Costa-Gavras's four major political fiction films remain the Jews and the communists. The prejudice described in *Special Section* not only existed in 1941, as Paxton documents in his research, but was most widespread among the occupying force as well as among French collaborators. Costa-Gavras's development of the issue follows closely the arguments proposed by Villeré, which are also shared by Paxton. During the process of selecting which terrorists will be among the six scheduled victims, one of the authorities carries a stack of dossiers from the Stavisky file cabinet and crassly says, "Here are the Jews!" The opening of the film notes that of the two demonstrators to be executed, one is Jewish and the other communist. Political and racial prejudice is obvious during the trial; one can readily detect major class differences here. A wide gap separates all the defendants, poor, struggling members of the working class, from the bourgeois men who sit in pompous judgment upon them.

Special Section, through Costa-Gavras's leftist reflections on the travesty of justice, unethical use of the law, corruption of government, and class differences, jolts the viewer to rethink his or her position on judicial systems because of their fallibility, their weak judges. The filmgoer may react pro or con, but either way Costa-Gavras has achieved his purpose of making the public reevaluate these systems.

Epilogue of the Film

In the epilogue, a picture of each of the participants in the trial is flashed before the audience. There is an updating of their sketchy biographies. The Special Section gave the Nazis satisfaction for the Moser assassination with only three heads instead of six. Four other prisoners, however, were handed over to them, including the valiant Lucien Sampaix and Bernard Friedmann. Five men were sent to the concentration camps, where they met untimely deaths.

The final statement of Costa-Gavras and Jorge Semprun is most powerful and incriminating. This is only one isolated case of Special Sections, but there were many others, and most judges sat on them. At this point in the epilogue there is an ironic shot of a judge in red robes passing over the emblem on the courthouse floor that reads "JUSTICIA." Then Costa-Gavras underlines the pathos behind all of this grim story—these judges who deliberated and judged illegally were never tried after the Liberation. The status quo was maintained. In the book the letter of Minister of Justice René Pleven denying permission to Hervé Villeré to delve into this tragic history reconfirms the maintenance of the status quo.

Villeré's extensive double epilogue of thirteen pages is reduced to a few precise film details, but the brevity does not obscure the fact that there was indeed something askew in Vichy, France!

Criticism

The production notes from Universal Studios for the American distribution of *Special Section* stated that in France the film "opened to generally rave reviews from the usually blasé Paris press, who called it Costa-Gavras's most beautiful film, the most moving and without doubt the most objective." This reading of the French critical scene may be rather selective and slightly exaggerated. To appreciate fully the French and then the American film criticism of *Special Section*, it would first be to our advantage to discern the various levels of evaluation—the aesthetic and the political—on both continents in their respective milieus.

The first series of French reviews situates *Special Section* in its historical film context. These critics compare and contrast it with World War II films of the same vintage, such as *The Sorrow and the Pity* and *Lacombe, Lucien*, stating, however, that Costa-Gavras would have done better to take the same basic material and make of it a documentary in the style of *The Sorrow and the Pity*. If the opportunity offers itself, Costa-Gavras maintains he would like to develop a documentary-type narrative around the character of Pierre Pucheu, the Minister of the Interior. It may be unfair to judge Costa-Gavras severely for not making a documentary. This was not his intention. Instead, he wanted a political fiction film thoroughly documented and directed at a large commercial audience. The director should be judged in the light of his original purpose.

Secondly, one can detect that French critics and public alike are more sensitive than Americans to the accusatory perspective that Costa-Gavras and Jorge Semprun took in creating this film. Both scriptwriter and director are not native French, and when they take up arms against the French, albeit the Vichy French of 1941, certain established forces vehemently react.

Jean de Baroncelli in *Le Monde* of 25 April 1975 is for the most part very positive in his critique, although he does feel that there is evidence of caricature and anecdote in the film. He also notes that the material appears to be too close to the contemporary French spectator for him or her to be objective about it. The real forte of Baroncelli's critique is his sense of the film as operating on three simultaneous levels: the historical, with a discussion of an odious act of Vichy in 1941; the political and reflective, with an illustration of the rapport of Man to the forces of power; and finally social and psychological, with a glimpse of the magistrates' disguising their cowardice and ambition behind a questionable sense of duty.

Claude Benoît in *Jeune Cinéma* of May–June 1975 situates the French criticism of *Special Section* in the larger context of Costa-Gavras's preceding works:

> *Section Spécial* has, in my opinion, all the effectiveness of *Z*, the precision of *The Confession*, and the political clarity of *State of Siege*. It is his best film and one of the most important films produced in these last few years. Costa-Gavras's cinema, however, stirs up strange reactions. Some denounce *The Confession* in the light of *Z*, others praise *State of Siege* after having denounced *Z*. Still others haggle over *State of Siege* after having praised *Z* and *The Confession*. And there will be some who find fault with *Special Section* after having extolled *Z*, *The Confession*, and *State of Siege*. It is bewildering, because the four films very

closely resemble each other. The author's political views are the same in each and the method used identical for all. Costa-Gavras's cinema is flawlessly coherent. And ironically, if on a higher level, he condemns the injustice, oppression, and violence in government—in whatever shape it may take—on a lower level he evokes the fickleness of the critic—in whatever form it may take.[37]

In evaluating the political fiction of Yves Boisset and Costa-Gavras, Guy Hennebelle in *Ecran '75* of July–August 1975 stresses the national and popular trends that their cinema has taken and upholds the positive aspects of *Special Section*. He is especially moved by the film and most in particular by Sampaix and the young communists rallying against fascism. Hennebelle reacts strongly to the negative criticism of Marcel Martin in an earlier issue of *Ecran '75*. Martin, according to Hennebelle, assassinates the film when he writes:

> Disgust, not only astonishment and anger, but disgust is what *Special Section* inspires in me. When a film director and scriptwriter, in all other respects most esteemed, arrive at this degree of blindness and insensitivity about their own work, then it is time to cry out a warning.[38]

Martin further condemned *Special Section* for its exotic color as well as for its anecdotal style.

Writing in *Télérama* on 23 April 1975, Alain Rémond criticizes the director for casting "a gallery of portraits, each one more stereotyped than the next." He also says, "The picturesque, the anecdote, the caricature, and the obvious polarities have killed the essential."[39] In general, the film comes across for him as "too easy"; he may really mean "too slick."

Henry Chapier in *Quotidien de Paris* of 24 April 1975 calls the film "*un vaudeville politique*" with a parade of characters such as Bruno Cremer in the role of Sampaix. The same theatrical analogy is also used by Michel Marmin in *Valeurs Actuelles*. He calls the film a "melodrama," "boulevard comedy," and "very bad Sacha Guitry."[40]

In *Jeune Cinéma*, in its *critique ouverte*, Maurice Peling, director of the Ciné-Club de Jeunes d'Aix-en-Provence, describes the viewer's lack of psychological engagement in the work:

> At the end we have the impression of having attended a very ingenious, historically reconstructed drama, at times very moving, at other times, amusing. We always remain, however, *on the outside*. We saw a film but we did not participate in any action. The political message which is the principal aim of the film is hinted at but never fully communicated.[41]

In the first few months of screenings, about the time that the film went to Cannes in May 1975, Costa-Gavras discussed the work with viewers in Evry, Toulouse, Bordeaux, and Lyons in order to represent his case to those who might reject the film. Thérèse Fournier's article for *France Soir* of 13 May 1975 sketches some general patterns of criticism Costa-Gavras encountered: The young, the Left, and the liberals say, "C'est Vichy!" while the Right and the older generation say it is opportunistic! Justice really is not the same for everybody! It is an incorrect picture of the magistrates![42]

Negative reviews by the French press are numerous. That tones down the elegaic words of Universal Studio's publicity. In-depth research into French criticism reveals an attack against the theatricality of the film from beginning to end, and yet an agreement with Costa-Gavras's perception of the Vichy government as having actually been a comic operetta. Some critics label it a "thesis film," others feel it lacks any true lyricism or political impact.

In the U.S., several complications affect the reviews and distinguish them from the French. Firstly, Americans watching the film were obliged to read the English subtitles if they did not know French. These were faithful to the original dialogue, but hardly captured the denseness of the real political situation in the film. Secondly, tr e judicial scene is not easily comprehended, although Costa-Gavras tries his best to simplify the actual complexity of the system with his scenario and characterization. Lastly, Americans were thirty years and more than 3,000 miles away from historical events of 1941, which were not clear in their minds. Even then something was lost in the crossing of the Atlantic.

One of the first impressions that came to critics' minds in the American screenings of *Special Section* was its similarity to Watergate and the government cover-up. Frank Rich in the *New York Post* of 13 December 1975 draws the analogy with the American situation and the perversion of power by the Nixon regime. He assesses the public attitude toward the former president:

> Even now, there are probably a frightening number of Americans who believe Nixon's sin was to break a few technical-sounding laws, when his real crime was that he attempted to subvert the entire legal framework of the nation.[43]

This view is not unlike Jack Kroll's in *Newsweek* about Watergate and Vichy. He calls both a problem of law and conscience. The value of Rich's article, however, is to have underscored the parallel, even though his reaction to the film is negative. He feels that the filmmakers distort history and are far from instructive. Instead, he claims, they squander the Vichy lesson and use a lackadaisical cast of French villains who are really interchangeable with the German high command. Rich is decidedly hostile to the film when he says that *Special Section* is "a particularly useless, counter-productive piece of work," and "significant step backward for its director."[44] His would not be the only negative view of the film.

Jay Cocks in *Time* of 8 December 1975 does not flatter the filmmaker when he says, "*Special Section* lacks the narrative drive that can make a good melodrama with political meaning. Instead, the film is a puppet show of moral indignation."[45] Cocks concludes his critique by saying, "But Costa-Gavras and Semprun only make the outrageous seem petty, and tragedy a thing of not greater consequences than another bad movie."[46] Vincent Canby of the *New York Times* does not find the film engaging on any level, referring to it as "cool and unmoving."[47] He laments the poor acting and the characters' extensive dialogue, and then admits, "Perhaps Brecht could have pulled it off."[48]

Nancy Schwartz in the *Soho Weekly News* is critical of the stereotyping of characters and of the lack of a climactic conclusion, which leaves the film "oddly truncated." She addresses the various complicated perspectives of the film:

These abrupt shifts in point of view are confusing. In conjunction with the grotesque leaning towards parody displayed in the earlier part of the film, you get the feeling that what Costa-Gavras really wanted to make was a Keystone Kops slapstick in which the plump, evil banker is the Vichy regime.[49]

Pauline Kael in the *New Yorker* of 15 December 1975 is very succinct in her description of the technique of Costa-Gavras, referring to him as "a cross between an investigative journalist and melodramatist."[50] She criticizes the acting and characterization, scenario and tone, and then calls the work "prosaic," stating that Costa-Gavras lacks the imagination to make the great themes come alive.

In the *New York* magazine of 8 December 1975, John Simon picks holes in the ensemble of the production, claiming above all that the cast of characters is too vast and that Costa-Gavras plays key scenes melodramatically. Simon then assesses the filmmaker's work, "With *Special Section,* Costa-Gavras and Semprun return to their Z mode, trying to graft suspense and black humor onto a record of true and appalling political machinations."[51] He further criticizes the film, "Slickly and scurrilously, the movie holds our interest; yet in the end we wonder whom to resent more: the filmmakers, for turning tragedy into a *divertissement,* or ourselves, for falling for it."[52]

Jack Kroll, writing for *Newsweek* of 15 December 1975, presents one of the few balanced and even positive reviews in the American press. He observes, "Costa-Gavras's talent is to convert this simplicity [of the presentation of the issue of law and conscience] into a gripping calculus of image and rhythm."[53] His final remarks are most poignant: "Costa-Gavras has created a new species—creatures struggling to find their humanity amid the conditioned reflexes of history."[54]

Epilogue

In the production notes of Universal Studios we read:

> The French Institute of Public Opinion conducted a poll on Justice and politics prior to the Paris premiere of *Special Section.* Some 53 percent of those questioned allowed that they preferred crimes committed for political reasons to be judged by special tribunes, but one out of every two admitted that they did not know that such a court exists and three-quarters answered that there was no special tribunal at all. Twenty percent had heard of the Special Sections instituted by Vichy, but only two percent knew that these were Courts of Special Sections Sessions.

Costa-Gavras privately screened *Special Section* for members of the French judicial system, just as he did with members of the French Communist party prior to the premiere of *The Confession.* The president of the lawyers' union, the Syndicat de la Magistrature, M. Hubert Dalle, called the film "simplistic" but remarked that it does raise the very important question, "Is this still possible or not?"

From *Clair de Femme* to *Missing:* Back on the Political Track

> . . . To kill an American quite officially, as in Horman's case,
> marked the beginning of a new period. It all supports my
> feeling that there are not any more geographic frontiers.
> They're ideological frontiers—that even if you are Ameri-
> can, if you don't think and feel like us, we'll exterminate
> you. It's important, I feel, to understand these ideological
> frontiers.
>
> COSTA-GAVRAS, 1982

In *Film Français* of 4 April 1975, Costa-Gavras was asked if he felt trapped in the political fiction genre. He replied "yes" and "no," and then more specifically: "To answer your question, let us say at the moment that I would like to vacation a bit in another genre, and then afterwards I'll surely return to the political film." This was very perspicacious of him. He had no immediate, specific film in progress, although he was musing over several projects. Yet he would soon go on to make a nonpolitical film, *Clair de Femme* (1979) and a political adventure *Missing*, with plans for Malraux's *La Condition humaine* still in abeyance.

The screen adaptation of Romain Gary's novel *Clair de Femme* (A Woman's Glow) is a significant departure from Costa-Gavras's political fiction work. It is what Robert Hatch of *The Nation* aptly calls "a love story, a lugubrious one." Michel Folain (Yves Montand), an airline pilot, literally bumps into Lydia To-warski (Romy Schneider) in Paris, thus initiating a mutual therapeutic relationship. The isolated fragments of their separately desolate lives gradually fall into place because of their sensitivity to and dialogue with each other. Michel has just left his wife, Yannik, in a deteriorating physical condition to allow her to choose death. Lydia's husband, Alain (François Perrot), has lost his ability to speak coherently following an automobile accident. Guilt-ridden, he claims full responsibility for his daughter's death in the accident. Michel and Lydia sensitively offer each other badly needed support in their loneliness, a comforting balm to their emotional wounds. Despite their desperate need for each other at the

Clair de Femme: Costa-Gavras directs Romy Schneider at Paris café.
(Permission of Atlantic Releasing Corp.)

moment, they understand that a full, rich love relationship between them is virtually impossible.

In this adaptation dealing with what he refers to as the smallest political cell—the couple—Costa-Gavras returns to his earlier penchant for clever cutting, humor and surprise, gradual assembling of separate facts, and rich visual images. However, he has not abandoned the heavy, almost literary tone, nor has he lost the convoluted style and hermetic atmosphere evident in *The Confession.*

Critics try to attack Costa-Gavras for not making *Clair de Femme* a political film. Costa-Gavras responds outright that he is not trying to politicize this film, for it is not a political film as such. He is much more interested in showing the relationship of a couple to society, stressing the symbolism that the way a couple goes, a society goes.

Costa-Gavras's vacation in a nonpolitical genre was most brief. While the faint praises of *Clair de Femme* were still echoing in Paris and the United States, Costa-Gavras was already contemplating his next production. He mentioned in 1982 that over the past ten years he had received approximately 150 scripts. He would normally have to discover something within a script in either an event or the characters that would warrant his spending the next year and a half or so wedded to the production. Hence he must practice great selectivity. He chose this story of a missing person because of its political timeliness and its human tragedy. He also had very personal reasons for doing so.

The spark that caused a small flame and then later the political bonfire known as *Missing* (1982) began as a news item. Costa-Gavras read of the plight of the American free-lance journalist Charles Horman who mysteriously disappeared in the bloody 1973 coup in Chile which replaced the socialist Allende government with the military junta of the Pinochet regime. Costa-Gavras was struck by this news report and reflected on the similar fate of the approximately 20,000 Chileans missing during and following the bloody military coup. Their disappearance brought tragedy into the lives of their families and friends.

Like Edmund and Joyce (Beth in the film) Horman, Costa-Gavras himself experienced the same personal frustration and bitterness over the bureaucratic runaround he received when Michèle Ray disappeared a year before their marriage. The director recounts his experience:

> . . . . she went over to Vietnam as a journalist in 1967 and was captured by the Viet Cong, and I spent my time phoning the French embassy in Saigon and the Hanoi representatives in Paris. I tried to see them, but I couldn't. All I could do was wait. And I heard every possible version of what might have happened to her. Some right-wing people said she'd been killed or raped. The other side said the Viet Cong were good people; nothing would happen to her. You know, I was living day to day for five weeks. It was an experience. To have her family call all day asking, do you have any news. And I didn't.[1]

Clair de Femme: Lydia Towarski (Romy Schneider), a wounded soul.
(Permission of Atlantic Releasing Corp.)

Clair de Femme: Two desolate individuals, Michel (Yves Montand) and Lydia (Romy Schneider), initiate a relationship.
(Permission of Atlantic Releasing Corp.)

The disappearance of a person, Costa-Gavras believes, is something new in the politics of contemporary society. It results in feelings of insecurity, hope, and anguish on the part of families and friends. Costa-Gavras observes:

> The horror is of a family which hopes the missing person is alive, but does not know. It is a kind of game between hope and death. You go on with hope which every day becomes bigger—and thinner. It's a permanent torture, and some governments use this as a message of repression. When one man disappears, 10 people around him are scared. And the man who is gone cannot become a hero for people to rally around, because no one knows if he is in prison or dead. He is just gone.[2]

Mildred and Edward Lewis (producer of John Frankenheimer's *Seven Days in May, Seconds,* and *Harold and Maude*) gave Costa-Gavras a copy of a recently published book by Thomas Hauser, *The Execution of Charles Horman* (1978).[3] Costa-Gavras read it on a New York–Paris flight and was profoundly moved by it. Edward Lewis also offered the director a script based on the book. Costa-Gavras seriously considered the book and the screenplay, then accepted Lewis's offer to direct a film on the subject. His only major stipulation was that he write his own screenplay. "The script they sent me was oriented toward the Allende regime, too much in favor of it. I'm not against it, but I don't think it's time yet to do that kind of film."[4] Costa-Gavras later stated that Patricio Guzman's *Battle of Chile* already studied the political situation. Costa-Gavras primarily wanted a human story in which flesh and blood characters could be seen in tragic conflict.

In *Film Comment,* the director further explains the origins of the film:

> My first instinct was not to offer it [a film based on Hauser's book] to an American studio because the subject was too inflammatory, too violently political. But Universal has been asking me for several years to make my kind of film for them, so when Edward Lewis, the producer, approached me, I decided to go with it. I felt that the problem of disappearing people was very important as an unveiling of the increasingly vicious methods that so many governments practice.[5]

The American producers and Costa-Gavras reached an agreement. They accepted his sixty-page treatment and had him eventually collaborate with Donald Stewart on a fresh script. He worked on it further, according to *Film Comment,* with novelist John Nichols, author of *Nirvana Blues.* As with most of his other films, except *State of Siege,* Costa-Gavras thus used a published text as a basis for the film. The book, however, would only serve as a *basis* for his film, since he prefers to supplement its contents with his personal political and aesthetic vision. He would also go about his independent investigation that in the past always brought him similar but further nuanced results.

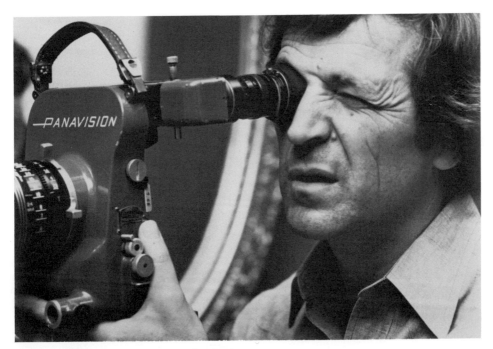

Missing: Costa-Gavras on location in Mexico.
(Permission of Universal City Studios, Inc.)

What did Costa-Gavras first discover in the text of Thomas Hauser, the attorney for the Horman case? He found that Charles Horman was a young man who was idealistic, artistic, and questioning. Charles had gone to all the "right" schools; after his years at the Allen Stevenson Grammar School in Manhattan, he attended Philips Exeter Academy in New Hampshire and Harvard in Cambridge. Being a witty honors student, and interested in writing, put him on the par with the traditional best and the brightest. Yet he retained his individuality. Given the inflammatory situation in Vietnam, he enlisted in the Air Force National Guard following his graduation from Harvard in 1964. After six years of reserve duty, Charles became more and more fascinated with communications, making films that dealt with social issues. He also began writing for television and journals.

Costa-Gavras further learned that Charles and his wife of two years, Joyce, moved to Chile. There he continued to write, involve himself with the weekly political newsletter FIN (acronym in Spanish for Source of North American Information), and prepare an animated children's film, *The Sunshine Grabber*. The Chile Charles and Joyce found was fraught with political unrest.[6] Since September 1970, the Socialist physician Salvador Allende Gossens had been the elected president, much to the dismay of the American government. Chile had once been a favored daughter of the American government, receiving millions of dollars annually through AID. During the Frei government from 1964 to 1970, the United States channelled $397.7 millions into the country's economy. From 1971 to 1973, following Allende's election, it was reduced to $3.3 millions.[7] The dramatic shift in assistance indicates America's unfavorable attitude toward Allende's socialist regime. In Senator Frank Church's Committee Report on U.S. involvement in Chile, Hauser notes, it was reported that the U.S. poured millions of dollars into a campaign to prevent Allende from being elected and then from being sworn into office. Following the elections all types of pressure tactics were organized by the American government to create economic destabilization and eventual collapse of the Allende regime.[8]

Charles Horman was intellectually—and at times politically—curious. In December 1972, Charles did an investigative study of the assassination of General Rene Schneider which allegedly involved American assistance. Charles wrote to his family:

> About two years ago, when Allende was to take office, a fairly extraordinary attempted coup occurred in which a retired general tried to get the army to rise and keep Allende from taking office. He organized a plot involving army generals, the head of the national police, some very rich growers in the South, remnants of the Chilean Nazi Party, and some armed groups associated with the right wing.
>
> The groups killed Rene Schneider, head of the Chilean Army and the man most opposed to political intervention by the armed forces. An interesting thing is the enormous number of people who knew about it ahead of time, including Frei, his Ministers, the CIA, the American Ambassador, and several Senators. I got interested and started reading court records and police statements and talking to people. The whole thing is like a novel; like *Z*.[9]

While Charles and Joyce Horman were in Chile, Allende was reelected in March 1973. Several months later, in August, Charles visited with his parents in Manhattan for the last time. On 17 September 1973, Charles was allegedly picked up by fifteen soldiers in a military truck as part of "Operation Cleanup." He became one of the thousands of victims of the coup that toppled the Socialist regime.[10] The remainder of the Hauser book—Parts Two and Three—would become the focal point of Costa-Gavras's work. The film would concentrate on Charles's father Edmund and his wife Joyce/Beth in their search for information concerning the mysterious disappearance, through the labyrinth of red tape, half-truths, lies, and wild-goose chases.

Although relying heavily on the original notes of Hauser, Costa-Gavras began his own fact-finding study. He observed:

> I traced everything from the beginning to see how the whole thing happened and each one's reason for doing what he did. I spoke with all of the characters involved in the case, including the American ambassador. I met with the Hormans and spent four weeks with them to see if they agreed and what their thoughts were about the movie.[11]

As usual, Costa-Gavras amplified, sculpted, and reinterpreted the raw material of the original text. He restructured events according to his personal feeling that the U.S. government officials in Chile were well aware of Charles's disappearance at least several days before Ed Horman arrived in Chile on 5 October 1973, and concealed this from the father. The more incriminating part of Costa-Gavras's thesis implicates the United States for its involvement in the coup and its elimination of Charles because of his knowledge of it.

As the production got underway the director considered the possible cast to convey the personal and political drama of the Hormans. He first searched for an actor who could play, and physically and psychologically *become*, Ed Horman. A short time prior to the production he had seen Jack Lemmon in the play *Tribute*. The director sensed that despite a long repertoire of comic roles, Lemmon was able to bring great life to a more serious role. Sidney Lumet's casting of him in *The China Syndrome* also proved that. Costa-Gavras further felt that he could still succeed by counter-casting the comedian Lemmon as an emotionally distraught middle-American Everyman Ed Horman, a Republican businessman who had in good conscience voted for Nixon. To the director, Ed Horman was "typically American . . . liberal, humanist, and very much attached to American democratic ideas."[12] Horman had a "conservative wisdom," which is for him a type of biological defense mechanism, believes Costa-Gavras.[13] Costa-Gavras gave Lemmon the script on a Thursday and on Saturday morning the actor called the director to say that he was eager to do it.

> I read it through and thought it was highly literate, highly intelligent and also terribly dramatic. It appealed to me, as did "The China Syndrome," because whatever political elements were there were secondary to a very strong story. So I, the actor, didn't feel like I was delivering a message. In-

stead, I'm playing a hell of a part. And it is one of the greatest parts I've ever had . . . in my opinion.[14]

Lemmon would soon resemble a surgical instrument in the deft hands of a surgeon.

For Beth Horman, Costa-Gavras proposed Sissy Spacek, for "she has a fragile appearance and yet is so strong inside. You can find a Sissy in any supermarket. She's not a star in appearance, but she's got it all inside."[15] After signing up Spacek, Costa-Gavras advised her not to meet with her real-life counterpart until near completion of the film, for Joyce had radically changed over eight years, matured significantly during her extensive and painful quest for the truth. Instead the actress prepared for her role by learning Spanish, poring over books about the Chilean coup, and viewing documentary footage about these events. When asked at a screening and conference on *Missing* at MIT on 14 February 1982 why he chose the particular actors Spacek and Lemmon, he replied, "There is an element of them in all of you, middle class . . . I saw Spacek in *Three Women,* and they are good actors. . . ."

Although Charles disappears early on in the film, like the doctor-deputy "Z," he returns through flashbacks. To portray the impetuous, intelligent Charles Horman, Costa-Gavras cast John Shea, prompted by Shea's first film performance in the recent British film *Hussy.* Up to that moment he had performed on Broadway *(Yentl, American Days),* in the Shakespeare Festival *(Romeo and Juliet),* and television productions *(Family Reunion, The Nativity).* Shea studied Hauser's book, government files and documents, and Charles's diary to better grasp this part. Spacek and Shea were then instructed by Costa-Gavras to live in their house used in the film in order to acclimate themselves totally to the husband-wife roles and the milieu.

The other actors and actresses gradually fell into place through the casting efforts of Wally Nicita. For Terry Simon, Charles's charming old friend who comes to visit in Chile, Melanie Mayron was chosen. She played in *Harry and Tonto* and *Car Wash,* and also had a principal role in *Girl Friends.* Janice Rule, like Sissy Spacek, played in Altman's *Three Women.* She was selected for the New York newspaper woman Kate Newman who covers the coup in Chile and then heads off to La Paz, Bolivia. She is a composite of three journalists, much like the aggressive journalist in *Z.*

The government officials in Chile linked with deceiving Ed about his son's disappearance were well played, though at times they come across as the traditional Costa-Gavras "cardboard villains": Charles Cioffi (Capt. Ray Tower), David Clennon (Consul Phil Putnam), and Richard Venture (U.S. ambassador).

As director of photography Costa-Gavras chose the Argentine Ricardo Arnovich, responsible for the camerawork of *Clair de Femme,* as well as Tony Laruschi's *The Outsider.* In the collaborative visual work of Arnovich and Costa-Gavras, the rich colors, wispy mists, art nouveau stained glass, haunting night scenes, and eerie morgues take on a striking aesthetic beauty. Once again, Costa-Gavras drew upon the experience of Françoise Bonnot along with several other assistant film editors. The fine blend of narrative and dramatic tension comes

Missing: Terry Simon (Melanie Mayron) is on a trip to Viña del Mar with her friend Charles when the coup breaks out.
(Permission of Universal City Studios, Inc.)

about with Bonnot's technical and sensitive handling of filmed footage since the days of *Z*, as well as her facility to grasp intuitively what Costa-Gavras envisions.

When Costa-Gavras searched for a site to portray the dramatic events of the Mitrione-Tupamaros confrontation in *State of Siege*, he chose Chile to represent Uruguay. With *Missing*, he was unable to film the tragedy of Charles Horman *in situ*, in Chile, given the current government's hostile reaction to leftist activities. Costa-Gavras considered Venezuela, and then finally decided upon Mexico. The studios, film equipment, experienced technicians, and laboratories in Mexico were much more advanced technologically than those in Venezuela. Although he did not get the cooperation of the Mexican government, at least he felt the film company was not harassed. Tolerance would best describe the relationship he had with the government. To create the military image of the coup, he needed tanks, army personnel, and weapons. The Mexican Army did not cooperate here. The tanks stationed in the streets of Santiago/Mexico City and at the airport were made of cardboard, but still appear most convincing and threatening. For government soldiers Costa-Gavras resorted to countless extras from the police force, for they knew how to handle weapons. The elite police force also provided military vehicles.

Approximately thirty different locations in and around Mexico City were selected and slightly modified to re-create Santiago of September 1973. The Latin American country will not be formally identified as Chile in the film, but

Missing: Charles Horman (John Shea) has decided to try to leave his South American
home following the coup.
(Permission of Universal City Studios, Inc.)

sufficient clues reveal this. The American consulate and embassy were wealthy
private mansions and provided a sharp contrast to the working class homes and
the poorer *barrios*. The Gran Hotel de la Ciudad in Mexico City became the
Hotel Carrera with its exotic art nouveau decor. When the earthquake hits the
hotel, it offers Ed and Beth the critical opportunity to dissolve their differences
in the lounge. The Central Post Office was transformed into the Ford Foundation of Santiago where Ed is told of his son's death. The sports stadium adjacent
to the Plaza del Toros was turned into the nightmarish National Stadium in
Santiago. The Santo Domingo Plaza was the focal point for mass arrests. For the
resort area of Viña del Mar, Costa-Gavras used Acapulco.

The filming took place during the Easter holidays of 1981 to allow for more
tranquil shooting. The Spanish shops and signs were juxtaposed with American
ones offering a convincing backdrop. The six or seven cinematic references to
the book-burnings reproduced the actual book-burnings in Chile and recalled
the similar anti-intellectual act in Nazi Germany in the destruction of the works
of Bertolt Brecht, Karl Marx, Sigmund Freud, Henrich and Thomas Mann, and
others. The interiors were shot in the Cherebusco studios in Mexico City. The
result of the shooting was a most lifelike—or deathlike—equivalent to a city
under siege. The special effects of the earthquake and the pursuit of a white
horse by the trigger-happy soldiers in their jeep add surrealistic color to the
visual image.[16]

Costa-Gavras moved painstakingly from the original experiences of the Hor- mans to Hauser's well-documented testimony to the case, through the filming, to the final edited copy. In this process he attempted to fuse realism and lyricism with his sensitive humanism. The plot of the completed film reads like a complex quasi-detective novel wherein the reader at times discovers the clues at the same moment as the protagonists, as in the case of identifying the body of Charles's friend. Through flashbacks, with the complicity of characters and viewers alike, Costa-Gavras reconstructs the events that led up to the disappearance of and search for Charles Horman.

Synopsis

Charles Horman (John Shea), a young American journalist and filmmaker, along with an old friend Terry Simon (Melanie Mayron), happen to be in the resort area of Viña del Mar, when a military coup topples the legitimately elected Allende government in September 1973. Charles discovers that, coincidentally, a multitude of American military personnel and a naval fleet are in the area. Suspecting some type of political connection between American presence and the coup, Charles keeps a diary of discoveries and observations. Through the assistance of Capt. Ray Tower (Charles Cioffi), Charles and Terry return to Santiago to find it an apocalyptic police state—streets filled with sniper fire, book-burning, military harassment, and unclaimed corpses. Their American friend Frank Teruggi (Joe Regalbuto) feels the city has become a Vietnamese "free fire zone." Terry, Charles, and Beth (Sissy Spacek) are caught in the bloody coup and forced to remain in Santiago.

Beth spends a terror-filled night in the streets of the city. The next morning she returns to their apartment house to find it ransacked and Charles missing. She pursues all possible leads in order to locate him. In the meantime, busi- nessman Edmund Horman, Charles's father (Jack Lemmon), goes through all New York state and then federal channels. Bureaucratic red-tape confronts him at every turn. He arrives in Santiago to continue his search with Beth, who cooperates very little with the authorities. Her anti-Establishment attitude is not well appreciated by U.S. Consul Phil Putnam (David Clennon) and the American ambassador to Chile (Richard Venture). Yet, the American mission in Chile says it is doing everything possible to locate Charles. Not too convincingly, the officials opine that he may be in hiding, or been kidnapped by leftist guerrillas disguised as soldiers, or have clandestinely escaped to the North.[17]

New York journalist Kate Newman (Janice Rule) arranges a talk with the former secret service policeman Paris/Perez (Martin Lasalle). Paris recounts the torture of the American under the supervision of the director of Chilean Intelli- gence.

From one body-strewn hospital and morgue to another, Ed and Beth system- atically try to track down Charles, dead or alive. They come upon the body of Charles's friend Frank Teruggi, co-writer for the leftist newsletter FIN. Accord- ing to the American government officials, Teruggi had left Chile. Still no Charles.

Missing: David (Keith Szarabajka) and Frank (Joe Regalbuto) wait for processing with the other prisoners in the National Stadium.
(Permission of Universal City Studios, Inc.)

It is only through the clandestine assistance of Peter Chernin (Robert Hitt) of the Ford Foundation that Ed Horman learns that Charles was executed in the National Stadium on 19 September, a few days after the military coup. Consequently Ed lashes out at the ambassador, consul, and naval military commander, Ray Tower, for having known about the death of his son and lying to him. Tower cavalierly responds, calling into question Charles's inquisitiveness, "You play with fire . . . you get burned."

Epilogue

The body is flown back to the States after seven months of delay, making an autopsy impossible. The family is required to pay $931.14 for shipping costs. Ed Horman subsequently sued eleven American officials including Secretary of State Henry Kissinger for complicity and negligence in the death of his son. After years of litigation, the case was finally dismissed.

When challenged for the pessimism and hopelessness of this conclusion, Costa-Gavras replied that it is very positive and realistic. The father decides to change. His eyes are opened to the beauty and integrity of his daughter-in-law and to the genuineness of his son whom he had originally considered a restless "hippie." He reaches another level of understanding of the constructive and destructive nature of the American government. It is this crucial awakening that Costa-Gavras offers the public as the most valuable lesson of *Missing*.

Politics

Ten years prior to making *Missing*, Costa-Gavras met with Salvador Allende in Chile several times to discuss the production of *State of Siege* and to obtain his approval if not his political blessing.[18] Costa-Gavras was preparing a print of *State of Siege* for Allende when the president was killed during the 1973 coup. The socialist reforms that he had brought about in three years' time immediately evaporated.[19] In *Missing*, Costa-Gavras unravels the facts surrounding the disappearance of Charles Horman against the backdrop of the Pinochet coup. He continues the polemical discussion begun in *State of Siege*, which can be readily seen in a comparison of the two films. The image of the American government in both films is anything but positive. Americans here are depicted as the privileged race in Latin America, deeply involved with these countries' culture, economy, and government. In both films, the situations are universalized, so that Uruguay and Chile represent any country where American colonialism/oppres-

Missing: Ed (Jack Lemmon) comforts Beth (Sissy Spacek) after she discovers the dead body of Frank Teruggi in a morgue.
(Permission of Universal City Studios, Inc.)

sion may interfere. The two works engendered controversies stirred up in Washington. *Missing* takes up where *State of Siege* left off, evoking an even stronger reaction from the State Department.

The double indictment by Hauser and Costa-Gavras as noted earlier is most controversial: the U.S. government in Chile is accused of negligence in handling the Horman case of disappearance and of perhaps having cosigned the execution release.[20] Costa-Gavras pits the underdog Ed Horman and his daughter-in-law Beth against the bureaucratic machinery of the American mission in Chile, which he feels is fascist. Using Ed Horman as focal point, Costa-Gavras vividly can trace the gradual political enlightenment, the growth of consciousness, of the protagonist. As an average American citizen involved in business, Ed is most convincing, for he first appears to have great faith in the American government, democracy, and efficiency.

The director portrays Charles as a "political neophyte," to use his friend's words. He is certainly not a political extremist, not a threat to American presence in Latin America. His affiliation with FIN is downplayed, as the paper is not considered to be a stab at America, but a medium of American-oriented news. Beth denies it is a leftist paper. In light of the above, Charles eventually emerges as the innocent victim, eliminated because he knew too much about the preparation of the military coup in Viña del Mar with American assistance.

The film implies that the U.S. engineered the coup: Babcock's remark to Charles and Terry, "I had a job to do, and now it's done." Ryan's strategic presence in the Bay of Pigs and here; Tower's ability to move about freely despite curfews and roadblocks; their frequent and easy liaison relations with the military junta and Chilean Intelligence. This would certainly oppose the American government's position on this:

> "I can say quite flatly that we did not (finance the activities that brought down the Allende government) . . . we had nothing to do with the political destabilization of Chile, the U.S. government had nothing to do with it."
> —Harry Shlaudeman,
> Deputy Chief of Mission,
> U.S. Embassy in Chile, 1969–1973.
> (June 1974)

> "Let me take the opportunity at the outset to restate that the United States government, the Central Intelligence Agency, had no role in the overthrow of the regime in Chile."
> —James Schlesinger,
> Secretary of Defense
> (June 1974)

> ". . . there's no doubt in my mind, our government had no involvement in any way whatsoever in the coup itself."
> —President Gerald Ford
> (September 1974)[21]

In light of what the U.S. public presently knows through Senate hearings and the Freedom of Information Act, these statements now appear as bold-faced lies.

Throughout *Missing* the viewer can witness the American "Dream" and "Myth" gradually disintegrating as Ed and Beth chance upon one piece of controversial information or another about the American government's role in Latin America. The typical American in Latin America leads "the good life." Armed with credit card, a supposed superior nationality to hide behind, and a vast power structure as support, the American has a remarkable edge even over the wealthy Chileans, but above all, over the disadvantaged. American presence in Chile is all too obvious. One can simply read the litany of American corporations and products represented on signs: Avis, Kent, Marlboro, Ford, Texaco, Wildroot, Kellogg's, Coke, and Pepsi. There are supposedly 3000 American businesses represented here, although former Ambassador to Chile Nathaniel Davis claims this is an exaggeration. As in *State of Siege,* these multinationals have almost become parasitic, despite their supposed contributions to the economy of the country.[22] Costa-Gavras ironically situates the Gestapo-like treatment of the detainees at the National Stadium within range of the colorful Pepsi vending machine, and juxtaposes corpses with the familiar Coke machine. His political point in cinematic language is well articulated.

In the film the American ambassador assures Ed that the American government representatives are here (in Chile) to protect American interests, primarily economic. Allende's nationalization program, as exemplified in the copper mines, was certainly a threat to this. A short time later in the film the ambassador tells Ed, "If you hadn't been personally involved in this unfortunate incident, you'd be sitting at home, complacent and more or less oblivious to all of this."

The image of American officials is not flattering. On the surface, the ambassador (Nathaniel Davis in reality) appears friendly, cooperative, eager to solve the disappearance problem. Bureaucratic red tape, cover-up, deceptive tactics, and transparent duplicity, however, all seem to be orchestrated through his office. Ed Horman, according to Hauser, observed, "Nathaniel Davis is a very polished liar."[23] Consul Phil Putnam (Fred Purdy) is characterized as insensitive, boorish, and deceitful, covering up either the errors or the guilt of American officials in this embarrassing situation. Capt. Ray Tower (Ray Davis, commander of U.S. Military Group) is a lecherous man, equally deceptive, perhaps involved with arranging some aspects of the military coup. Colonel Sean Patrick (Patrick Ryan) is a sympathetic military man, generous with his assistance to Charles and Terry in time of need. Nonetheless he has misguided ideals.

Costa-Gavras analyzes the characters in the film, as he did with Dan Mitrione for *State of Siege:*

> The government officials are not basically cruel men . . . They have their duty—a duty dictated by their government—to keep their involvement in the coup a secret. If they explain what happened to the young man, they would be revealing "classified" information. If they have any sin, it's the sin of ignoring the human, emotional turmoil of a wife and father searching for someone they love. That's the tragedy.[24]

That sin is a mild one compared to the others that are *implied* in the film—aiding and abetting the military coup, and being jointly responsible for the torture and death of Charles Horman. Costa-Gavras further suggests that these individuals are acting under guidance from above. One could recall *Z*, where the culpability for the assassination of the deputy could be traced even as high up as the palace. Nixon and Kissinger's presence through all of this is obvious, as indicated by Costa-Gavras's iconography. Their photos overlook the various conversations at the embassy and consulate, especially those that suggest duplicity. The ambassador replies to Ed's suspicions of the existence of a police network directed by Americans: "No such thing exists." A photo of Richard Nixon ironically looks on.

One of Costa-Gavras's primary purposes in filming *Missing* is to reveal the social ills that come about through American intervention in another country's economics, culture, and politics. He delineates class differences: the wealthy support the coup, cheering the barbaric soldiers while corpses of the working class line streets. The director reveals in graphic form the censorship, book-burning, raids, detentions, and torture brought on by the military junta. Human rights have ceased to exist in this regime, Costa-Gavras testifies on film. At the conclusion of *Missing*, the enlightened and now embittered Ed Horman tells American officials at the airport that he is grateful he comes from a country where they put people like them behind bars. The subtle reference to Watergate is no doubt intended by the director.

Since Costa-Gavras guides the viewer to grasping the events of the cover-up through Ed's eyes, there is little possibility of forming a favorable opinion of the American officials. At the end of the film the audience normally feels outraged at the conduct of the American officials, and disillusioned about the role of American presence in Latin America. The evidence presented by the director is very damning. America, the supposed protector of human rights, has become the politico-economic octopus with its tentacles firmly wrapped around the neck of a less fortunate Third World country. This very critical view of U.S. intervention in the politics of Latin American countries was most timely and struck a raw nerve in the American filmgoer. The director recounted to Andrew Kopkind of the *Nation* in spring 1982:

> Six months ago—even six weeks ago—the reaction would have been very different . . . There is this sudden parallel with El Salvador, where people are being killed every day. We see the use of (U.S.) military strength in the background, behind the scenes, while we say that "those Latin Americans are killing each other, they are like that, they enjoy fighting one another." In Poland, the Russians do not directly use their own forces; they are in the background behind the coup. That is one of the lessons the Russians took from America in Latin America: they learned it is politically very negative to use their own troops.[25]

Such statements about this type of recurrent political nightmare have usually earned for Costa-Gavras the label "anti-American." He qualifies this again by insisting he is "anti-American *government*," and not simply "anti-American [people]." On National Public Radio, morning edition, on 27 May 1982, the director told his interviewer, "*Missing* is not an anti-American polemic but a portrait of global oppression."

Refutation

As with the Kennedy Center controversy surrounding the projection of *State of Siege* in 1973, another political uproar was sparked by the implications of Costa-Gavras's work. On 9 February 1982, the State Department took unprecedented measures to deny the insinuations made by the film. In a three-page statement the department established that over a period of eight years it made "extensive efforts to locate Charles Horman and, later to obtain a full explanation of the circumstances surrounding his death." The officials also designated that the State Department and other government agencies provided numerous documents to the Hormans to elucidate the work of the State Department on their behalf. It did, however, withhold sixty-seven entire documents and portions of forty-six others for reasons of security. Secretary of State Muskie, the statement read, testified at that time that no U.S. personnel were involved in the disappearance and death of Charles Horman. The CIA (represented in the film by such types as Babcock and Tower) through its director Stanfield Turner, also denied advance knowledge of the abduction and subsequent death of Horman. The statement concludes: "The Department regrets the sad death of Charles Horman as well as the efforts by some to read into it possible involvement by the United States Government and its officials, which the record indicates is wholly unwarranted."

Former embassy aide and counsel to the State Department attorney Judd Kessler, said in the 11 February 1982 edition of the *Washington Post* that the film was "one big fat lie." The ambassador to Chile, Nathaniel Davis (1971–73) wrote a special letter to the *Boston Herald American* (23 April 1982) to comment on the film. He asserts that the stacks of documents obtained from the various agencies by the Freedom of Information Act prove that the American officials did not authorize Charles's execution. This insinuation comes in the film through the character of Perez/Paris (Rafael Gonzalez, former member of the Chilean secret police) who took refuge in the Italian Embassy. Davis points out that the Hormans did not meet with the police official as the film portrays. Paris's evidence of seeing an American present at the torture of Charles is based on his wearing of American shoes; it is shaky. Charles and Terry's encounter with Babcock (Arthur Creter) implies that he was a type of CIA agent with a covert action to complete. Creter, clarifies Davis, was only an engineering technician who had just finished his job of servicing Chilean Navy fire extinguishers. Lastly, the former ambassador asks why Terry Simon was not eliminated if she also carried such an explosive secret about the U.S. role in the coup.[26] In an earlier article in the *Washington Post* for 7 March 1982, Davis challenged the scene of the film concerning the confrontation of Ed and the ambassador. In *Missing* the ambassador says there are no special police assistance programs in Chile whereby American officials can participate in local security matters.[27] The former ambassador said that he never lied to Ed Horman, never told him a CIA station did not exist in Chile. Moreover, he stated, he himself does not understand what program is alluded to in the film. A bit on the defensive, Davis continued in the *Post* article:

> Nobody is accusing the United States government of having been complicit, of having fingered the three nuns who were murdered in El Salvador. Why are we being accused of complicity here? It doesn't hold water. When a coup is going on and all the lot is unstuck, things happen. I don't see the rationale that says if he died we had to know about it. There were a lot of things going on they didn't consult us about.[28]

Flora Lewis, foreign affairs columnist of the *New York Times*, challenged Costa-Gavras for the technique he uses in misrepresenting the Horman case. "It is a technique which raises serious ethical, moral and political as well as artistic questions."[29] Lewis argued that Costa-Gavras did not make any efforts to speak with American officials involved, or to consult the records of Sen. Frank Church's Committee hearings on "Covert Action in Chile: 1963–1973." She argued that, with respect to the CIA's collaborating in the coup, William Colby testified that when there were rumors of a coup he sent a message to American officials. He basically told them to stay away from the Chilean military and their activities. *New York Times* columnist Seymour Hersh had done extensive investigating and reporting on the CIA's intervention in Chilean politics, she observed, but did not find any complicity in the disappearance of Charles Horman. Lewis, like Davis, also suggests that the evidence of Gonzalez (Paris) is not substantial. She concludes that in light of the above, Costa-Gavras distorts the facts without even noticing it.

Flora Lewis's reasoning may appear convincing on the surface. Alan Berger, columnist and film critic, writing in the *Boston Globe,* however, called into question her argument. Following upon his own investigative research, Berger noted that the American embassy was in fact notified by Chilean Intelligence that Horman was arrested as an extremist. Secondly, U.S. Consul Fred Purdy knew about the death of Horman but acted as if he were unaware of his execution. Lastly, the Foreign Ministry of the junta acknowledged in a note to Kissinger on 3 October 1973 that Charles was being detained for curfew violations.[30] Berger supports the statement of Gonzalez/Paris that there was complicity of the CIA and local authorities on the death of Charles, for "he knew too much." The critic admits that the material in the film is elliptical and that Costa-Gavras omits the actual chain of events. He concludes, however, that

> Flora Lewis of the *New York Times* was no doubt right to suggest that the film, 'Missing' is not an exact replica of reality. But if she had consulted the facts she accused Costa-Gavras of distorting, she would have found a reality far more disquieting than any cinematic recreation.[31]

Alan Berger's personal communique of 20 June 1982 offers a critical footnote to the approach taken by Flora Lewis:

The Flora Lewis article is a disgraceful performance: journalistically shabby, politically devious, and utterly at odds with the historical record. It is the work of a writer who is either too lazy to check her facts, too indebted to government officials to seek the ugly truth, or too ideologically committed to an *a priori* position to do justice to the film.

Andrew Kopkind of *Nation*, like Berger, challenged Flora Lewis's analysis of the political defects of the film. Kopkind stated that Richard Helms and William Colby (former directors of the CIA), and former Ambassador to Chile Nathaniel Davis, would hardly be the fair witnesses to American nonintervention in Chile that Lewis makes them to be. Helms is a "renowned perjurer," Colby professes a disputable code of ethics with regard to intervention in Latin American politics, and "meticulous" Davis may have a tainted service record given the controversial areas (Guatemala, Chile, Angola) where he was stationed. Kopkind also updated Lewis's use of Seymour Hersh, veteran of the *New York Times*, in support of her position. He maintained, "Hersh has protested to Lewis and *The Times* that his failure to get that big story in Chile proves nothing except the limitations of his reportage."[32]

Fact versus Fiction

Dave McGeary, the American aide who assists Ed Horman in the search through hospitals and morgues for his son, asks the religious father of Charles what Christian Science is all about. Ed answers, "Faith in truth." In *Missing*, "truth" is the pivotal word: Ed is in dire need of it; the government denies that it exists in any form throughout the film; Hauser and Horman testify that the film offers it in close to absolute form; a large sector of an uncritical public believes that this exposé reveals it in a pure and unadulterated form. We must therefore raise here the critical question on the veracity of the film's contents and the director's perspective.

The film credits open with a preface not too unlike that of the classic television series *Dragnet*: "This film is based on a true story. The incidents and facts are documented. Some of the names have been changed to protect the innocent and also to protect the film." Costa-Gavras is correct in maintaining that the film is *based* on a true story. He does not say that his film is an *absolutely* true account of the events that transpired during the search for Charles Horman. Hauser states that the film is an excellent *dramatization* of his book. He admits, "It is true in spirit, but not precisely accurate in each and every detail."[33] Horman himself swears that for the most part this is absolute fact. He wept at the screening of the film, appreciating how close it came to revealing his quest for Charles.

Although Costa-Gavras has followed Hauser's line of reasoning in the book he alters certain elements and highlights others for dramatic purposes. In the film Beth and Ed discover Frank Teruggi's body in the morgue, revealing that the American government had lied about his having left Chile. It was actually found by a friend, Steve Volk, and the American official Donald McNally (whose role resembles that of Dave McGeary in the search for Charles), according to Hauser.[34] They came upon the body shortly prior to Ed's arrival in Chile. In the film Ed and Beth visit with Paris (Perez) at the Italian embassy through the assistance of journalist Kate Newman. Actually, Rafael Gonzalez only reported what he knew about the arrest, torture, and possible execution of Charles Horman in 1976 after he had taken refuge in the Italian embassy. Ed and Joyce never met with Gonzalez. Other events which are not placed in chronological order create excellent dramatic narrative and yet to some critics appear to stray from the path of historical, documented evidence. In this respect, the director attempts to balance the conflicting values of drama and ideology. One may also perceive here a slight willingness on the part of Costa-Gavras to sacrifice a political thesis which is even more damning or disquieting (in Berger's words) than witnessed in the film, for a heightened dramatic form, melodramatic suspense, and sheer plausibility.

In principle, Costa-Gavras follows the truth. It may be only one side of the truth, but it is a significant part of it. The other side would have to be represented by the government officials who appear as very shallow, self-serving individuals in the film. Costa-Gavras has repeated that he in no way attempts to make the film a court case where both sides are meticulously represented. *Missing* is in fact an aesthetic work, a means of entertainment, and a dramatization of actual events. There is room here for poetic license. The director insists on the difference between a journalist and an artist, claiming only to be the latter. The result of his cinematic production is a highly researched semidocumentary work, but in light of the editing technique (telescoping events), characterization (one-dimensional government officials), and enigmatic and elliptical statements (from Babcock and Paris), *Missing* remains a creative act and not an historical, accurate testimony to the situation of September–October 1973. As a dramatic work it succeeds, nonetheless, in provoking the public and critic to search further for the truth.

Epilogue

The tragic case lived on well after the coup and the search for Charles Horman. The film critics joined in on this controversy over the historical and dramatic value of the film, fanning the flames of argument in some instances. Pauline Kael in the *New Yorker* for 8 March 1982 called it a "catechism," a "didactic melodrama." In the *Village Voice* for 23 February 1982, Andrew Sarris referred to the characters, especially those representing government officials, as schematic, programmed, and too predictable. Vincent Canby of the *New York Times* for 14 February 1982 praised the film, with the reservation that Costa-Gavras should have said that the film was *suggested* by documented events, but that the conclusions reached are his own. Stanley Kauffmann in the *New Republic* of 10 March 1982 disagreed about the power and conviction of the film and thought "it's the weakest of Costa-Gavras's political films, a very Hollywood work of daring, and that the outcry about it, to different ends from different sources, says more about the sources than about the film." Most critics, even though they did not agree with Costa-Gavras's political thesis, believed that it was a powerful, human drama, a bitter insight into a personal tragedy.

• Following much publicity in the French press in early May 1982, as "the film which divided America," *Missing* went to the Cannes Film Festival as the official American entry. It won the Golden Palm (exaequo with the Turkish film *Yol*) and Jack Lemmon took the prize for best actor.

• On the political level, two reporters managed to interview Rafael Gonzalez on 7 June 1976. Gonzalez declared to them: "I knew that Charles Horman was killed because he knew too much. And this was done between the CIA and the local authorities."[35]

• Ed Horman blatantly accused the American mission in Chile for a cover-up of the actual events: "I have spent over four years of my life investigating the death of my son. Reluctantly, I have reached the conclusion that the government of Chile is being shielded from blame for a very simple reason. If the finger of guilt is pointed at them, they will point it right back at Washington. Our own Embassy was responsible for Charles's death. His life was sacrificed to cover up American actions in Chile."[36]

• From this harrowing experience derived Mrs. Elisabeth Horman's personal and political enlightenment: "Charles's death taught me the lesson of political responsibility. I used to think that I could till the soil on my own little plot of land and let the rest of the world care for its own problems. What our country did in Vietnam, what happened to people overseas, was no concern of mine. I was wrong. I know now that each of us is obligated to fight for what is right and take responsibility for what our government does. If we don't, sooner or later it will affect us all."[37]

• Though non-American, Costa-Gavras, with his film *Missing*, could almost echo Thomas Hauser's purpose in writing his book: "I grew up with an abiding faith in America. It is, in my estimation, the greatest country in the world—not for its wealth or military might, but because its people have achieved a balance of security, freedom, and human rights unmatched in history. The preceding pages have been written, not to cast doubt on this country or the men and women who serve so well in our military and diplomatic corps, but rather in the belief that only by self-analysis of this kind can we purify our government and make it better."[38] Costa-Gavras praises America for its dedication to freedom of expression. It is one of the few countries, he maintains, in which a film such as *Missing* could be produced.

Conclusions and Epilogue

> What I am trying to do in my films . . . is to inspire an awareness of what is happening in this politicized world of ours, to present the problems, reveal the circumstances. I leave the spectator to find his own solution. Ideally he bathes in a series of images that surround him completely; only afterward should he start thinking about what he has seen.
>
> —COSTA-GAVRAS

Approximately twenty-five years have elapsed since Costa-Gavras's technical training at the film school of IDHEC, and more than ten since *Z* made a leading figure of him in the international cinema world. The other four major political films at the heart of his professional career have reinforced the image of Costa-Gavras both as a brilliant political fiction filmmaker and as an especially controversial one.

How has Costa-Gavras fared in his political fiction film venture? With the completion of *Missing* (1982) we have sufficient data to assess his impact upon the cinematic world. Both critical sides must be fairly reflected to bring his work into sharper focus. To flatter the director with naïve praise or damn him with superficial judgment would do him an injustice either way. Though written from "within the pale," in the spirit of Artur London's *Confession,* our reflections will be an attempt at furnishing a much-needed balance.

Costa-Gavras has been a revolutionary in the genre of the political thriller or political fiction film, accepting the same serious risks as had the earlier Francesco Rosi and Gillo Pontecorvo in Italy. He has helped shape the form that the political fiction film eventually took. He has sparked an interest in this medium among producers, directors, and public alike. *Z* has become the prime model for this genre of film.

Historically speaking, without being overly critical of Costa-Gavras's work, we can say that after ten years the political fiction film in general may need some immediate vitalization. It can limp, as was already the case with *Special Section* in 1975. The political mood in Europe and America has changed, and along with this the interests, tastes, and values of both societies have changed. What may have been revolutionary and visionary in 1969 could tend to become stagnant or fossilized in the late 1970s or early 1980s. Furthermore, by staying faithful to the political thriller genre, Costa-Gavras faces another risk. Jean-Pierre Jeancolas reflects on the evolution of Costa-Gavras from *Z* to *Special Section*, but more so on the role of the public and critics in their view of this evolution:

> For it is true that his style is no longer acceptable. I do not believe it is simply the swing of the pendulum found in critics whom everyone knows are fickle—critics who today burn in effigy what they worshipped yesterday. It is true that Costa-Gavras's work here is no different than what it was in *Z*. Our perspective, however, has changed.[1]

Jeancolas puts this more succinctly when he observes:

> Cinema integrates two partners—the film and the public. The public changes, hence the function of cinema changes. A filmmaker runs the risk of becoming old-fashioned simply by standing still.[2]

What Jeancolas obliges us to do implicitly in the evaluation of Costa-Gavras's contribution to cinema is to question whether the director has been able to remain original and vital after his initial successes.

Costa-Gavras has made his mark on the genre of political film despite the gradual stagnation recently in its evolution. His impact on society does not go unnoticed. Using his films as a vehicle for his sociopolitical ideas, he has helped raise key questions about various forms that oppression assumes in our contemporary society. With great insight he shows the connection of an event in the past with a current problem, alerting us to what happens when power runs beserk. As the filmgoer leaves the theater, he or she has the possibility of weighing the film's political content or forgetting it completely. This is a possibility rarely offered by commercial cinema. There is a certain level of consciousness raising throughout his films, whether produced through subtlety or not. These films begin to raise compassion for a specific segment of humanity that is abused. Yet, Costa-Gavras only lightly prods the conscience of the filmgoer. He or she is not ordinarily disturbed to the roots of conscience. This scratching at the surface of a political problem is, nonetheless, important. It resembles Alfred Whitehead's thesis in the *Aims of Education* that in any knowledge there is a state of "romance" and another of "precision." The first level, if properly presented, will prepare for and lead to the second, more profound level. The films of Costa-Gavras help the public to make the romantic step toward understanding a precise political abuse in society.

In the presentation of these sociopolitical concerns, Costa-Gavras's ideology is consistent—liberal, left, and above all, humanitarian. The political scene he depicts is carefully documented. The resulting film thus goes beyond being fiction while still remaining commercial entertainment. His long-term research in conjunction with his screenwriters testifies to each fact that is presented. These accumulated facts, however, are colored, made more appealing and digestible for a mass public, not for a small, sectarian group of filmviewers. Hollywood shows up sometimes in the form of spectacular effects, rich color, attractive action, and in general, a slick appearance that endangers his message. It shows his ongoing love-hate relationship with American cinema. He blatantly imitates its enticing fast-paced style. He wins the major studios as producers. Yet he rejects the general tone of the American cinema as well as its particular defects of happy endings, romanticized characters, and pure entertainment. At times his political message—necessarily diluted—gets lost in the other appealing elements of the film, especially in technique.

Since *The Sleeping Car Murder,* in which the director already showed great promise with his clever technique, Costa-Gavras has matured with respect to this element of his production. His creative mind is constantly at work; no two films completely resemble each other in technique. A film such as *State of Siege* may be considered recherché and journalistic. Yet it has a power all of its own, a power that encourages the public to stay with the director in his presentation of highly developed ideological content. In the hands of Costa-Gavras and his technicians—especially Jorge Semprun, Françoise Bonnot, and Raoul Coutard— technique becomes a lavish, creative vehicle for the political doctrine. To certain critics who do not feel at home in this style of self-conscious technique, the form does not complement the ideological content, but opposes it. It destroys the value and purpose of filming such a controversial subject as the cover-up of an assassination.

Throughout his filming career, Costa-Gavras has been haunted by the criticism of his way of presenting characters from the general of *Z* to the Establishment judges of *Special Section.* It is rare that they escape being labeled stereotypes. Costa-Gavras is thus accused of blatant Manicheism, thoroughly whitewashing the heroes, and carefully discoloring the villains. Only on occasion does he include an ambiguous character (the thirteenth man in *Shock Troops*) or a middle-of-the-road personality (the judge in *Z*). His characters are clearly drawn to be easily recognizable to a public unfamiliar perhaps with the polititcal nuances of the situation, such as the American spectator watching *The Confession.* This is a weakness of the director that has not disappeared during his evolution.

The actors who embody the living political forces in Costa-Gavras's five political films fare better than the characters they represent. They do justice to the content, for they vivify the scenarios with exciting action *(Z),* profound emotion *(The Confession),* subtle acting *(State of Siege* and *Missing),* and crisp ideological dialogue *(Special Section).* The closely knit troupe of actors—especially Montand, Signoret, Bouise, and Dux—responds to the wishes of the director to create a powerful ensemble in addition to the individual cameo roles.

Besides the criticism launched at Costa-Gavras for his political stance and for his characterizations, the most basic challenge he encounters is from the criticism dealing with the aesthetic treatment of a political problem. The area of tension is the one resulting from an artistic rendering of an actual historical event. He has walked on the same dangerous ground that Brecht walked on with *Galileo* and *Mother Courage,* but Costa-Gavras's steps have been more perilous. He has examined easily recognizable, recent historical events. His precarious optic could possibly have distorted the reality as he sought to prove his thesis about perverted Stalinism or destructive justice. His aesthetic vision in such cases may have become myopic.

Costa-Gavras renders dramatic a static, historical moment situated concretely in time and space. This dramatization could be of the ten-day hostage ordeal in Latin America or of an extensive cover-up in a Mediterranean government. To make such content viable on the screen, the director had to dramatize it significantly for it not to remain a mere isolated fragment of historical data. In such cases, popularization through the film medium could interfere with the ideological content, as noted earlier. With *The Confession* he dared to play down the drama; with *Special Section* he attempted the contrary and thereby destroyed the aesthetic viability of his production.

Costa-Garvas claims that, despite his dramatization of the material, what he says is absolutely true. He is correct in this statement. His presentation of any particular situation, however, does not encompass *all* of the truth. His evidence is most often limited to facts that support a specific thesis. His works manifest a reduction of a complex truth to a single element, no less true, but also highly selected. Is it that Costa-Gavras grasps the whole truth but for the sake of unity and of a heightened drama and conflict he only wishes to isolate the obvious injustice? Or is his aesthetic and political vision restricted to one aspect of a cause? Try as he may to present convincingly both sides of an issue in a dramatic, artistic fashion, he falls short of the goal of objectivity. He crosses over onto the terrain of the partisan filmmaker.

The question of artistic *form* must also be raised in evaluating Costa-Gavras's works. He deliberately chooses and develops a specific form that is geared more toward entertaining than educating (or inciting) an audience. To move more in the direction of revolutionizing the masses would militate against his purpose of reaching a large audience with his political philosophy. He realizes and accepts the consequences of the chosen form.

In our reflections on the films of Costa-Gavras we have seen the curious blend of fiction and politics. Is this symbiotic relationship successful in his works? With *Z* and *Special Section* there appears to be more fiction than politics, and with *The Confession* and *State of Siege* more politics than fiction. *Missing* may provide the balance. The two modes of expression, nonetheless, are intertwined in the five major films of Costa-Gavras. Where the accent lies in a given production depends on Costa-Gavras's specific political leaning at the time of filming, his collaboration with the screenwriter, and his aesthetic vision. This does not discount the role of the filmviewer in the process. For Costa-Gavras, it is the public that eventually politicizes the film.

Throughout his film, Costa-Gavras claims that he does not wish to impose lessons or morals on his audience. When Ann Powell asked if solutions are necessary, the director answered:

> Solutions, always a problem. There are many people around giving dogmatic solutions to problems, most of them are our political leaders. I don't want to give any solutions in my films. The only responsibility I have is to try to tell the truth.[3]

Our critical text, created as dialogue of critic and reader has the same essential goal. It is not a definitive study of Costa-Gavras's sociopolitical opus, for this can only be done at the close of a director's cinematic career, not at its midpoint. The present analysis serves as a first—although indeed major—step in appreciating an artist who has made a recognizable impact on the world of political fiction film.

Notes

Introduction

1. The titles of Costa-Gavras's films and all foreign films distributed with an American or English title will be given in English in the text. The others will be kept in their original language.

2. Jean-Patrick Lebel, *Cinéma et idéologie* (Paris: Editions Sociales, 1971), p. 84.

Chapter 1

1. Christian Zimmer, *Cinéma et politique* (Paris: Seghers, 1974), p. 8.

2. For a similar breakdown into *cine de lucha,* a clandestine and tolerated film of struggle, and *cine cívico,* a commercial and less controversial form of cinema, see Luis Urbez, "El cine político de Costa-Gavras," *Razón y Fe* 973 (February 1979): 208–13.

3. Guy Hennebelle and Daniel Serceau, "L'Irrésistible ascension du cinéma militant," *L'Ecran* 74 (December 1974): 49–50. This article is translated and reconstructed in English: Guy Hennebelle, "Z Movies, or What Hath Costa-Gavras Wrought," *Cinéaste* 2 (1974): 28–31.

4. See the special issue on *cinéma militant* in *Cinéma d'aujourd'hui* 5/6 (March–April 1976). The issue has a detailed bibliography and filmography.

5. Guylaine Guidez, "L'Aurore d'un cinéma ouvrier," *Cinémonde* 1840 (16 June 1970): 8–10.

6. These diverse functions of the documentarist are developed in Erik Barnouw, *Documentary: A History of the Non-Fiction Film* (New York: Oxford University Press, 1974).

7. PierNico Solinas, ed., *Gillo Pontecorvo's "The Battle of Algiers"* (New York: Charles Scribner's Sons, 1973). For an interview with the director, see "Rencontre avec Gillo Pontecorvo," *Cinémonde* 1840 (16 June 1970): 20–25.

8. For a detailed analysis of this antinuclear film, read Alan Rosenthal, "*The War Game:* Peter Watkins, Writer-Director," *The New Documentary in Action* (Berkeley: University of California Press, 1971), pp. 151–63.

9. Joan Mellen, "Hollywood's 'Political Cinema,'" *Cinéaste* 2 (Spring 1972): 26.

10. Ibid.

11. Amos Vogel, *Film as a Subversive Art* (New York: Random House, 1974), p. 120.

12. Guy Braucourt, "Entretien avec Costa-Gavras et Jorge Semprun," *Cinéma '70* 151 (December 1970): 40.

13. Louis Seguin, "Le Cinéma dans la politique," *Positif* 113 (February 1970): 11–27. This panel, with Robert Benayoun, Albert Bolduc, Michel Ciment, and Louis Seguin, offers diverse opinions on the political cinema.

14. The bibliography reveals this series of works that document the history and evolution of political film.

15. Braucourt, "Entretien avec Costa-Gavras," p. 48.

16. Franca Rovelli, "A Colloquio con Costa-Gavras, un regista scomodo: 'Sono contro il potere perché il poetere è contro la dignitá,'" *Epoca,* 3 May 1978, p. 71. One should note the evolution of this attitude when he makes an American film three years after.

17. For a rich political analysis of Godard's revolutionary films see James Roy MacBean, *Film and Revolution* (Bloomington, Ind.: Indiana University Press, 1975), pp. 13–180.

18. Vogel, *Film as a Subversive Art*, p. 27.

19. "Le cinéma politique français," *Le Cinéma Français* 12 (1977): 19.

20. Other politically oriented filmmakers discussed in the above issue of *Le Cinéma Français* include Joris Ivens, Jean Rouche, Louis Malle, Agnès Varda, Marin Karmitz, René Vauthier, René Gilson, Bernard Paul, Chris Marker, René Gillio, Jean-Louis Comolli, Pascal Aubier, and Michèle Rozier. Some cineastes, such as Marguerite Duras, a former Communist party member, manifest a peculiar but justifiable political thrust in their works; Duras's esoteric touch, however, makes for a noncommercial film, for example, *Le Camion* (The Truck).

21. From the publicity materials for *Eboli* from Scanlon Shaw Associates, New York. I am grateful to Francesco Rosi for the invaluable information he provided me on political film in an interview in Rome on 11 May 1981.

22. Joan Mellen, "*Executive Action:* The Politics of Distortion," *Cinéaste* 2 (1974): 10.

23. Ibid., p. 12.

24. Jean Collet, "*Blue Collar,*" *Etudes*, January 1979, pp. 51–53.

25. For a succinct but excellent treatment of the Latin American political film in bibliographical form, see Julianne Burton, *The New Latin American Cinema* (New York: Cinéaste, Inc., 1976). More specifically on the Chilean political film, consult Michael Chanan, ed., *Chilean Cinema* (London: British Film Institute, 1976).

26. Frantz Gevaudan, "Le cinéma politique face à son public," *Cinéma '73* 173 (January 1973): 92.

27. Guy Hennebelle, "Z Movies, or What Hath Costa-Gavras Wrought," p. 31.

Chapter 2

1. André Malraux, *Man's Hope*, trans. Stuart Gilbert and Alastair Macdonald (New York: Bantam Books, 1968), p. 423.

2. *Unifrance: Dossiers-Portraits: Costa-Gavras* 453 (December 1972).

3. Franca Rovelli, "A Colloquio con Costa-Gavras un regista scomodo: 'Sono contro il potere perché il potere è contro la dignità'," *Epoca*, 3 May 1978, p. 68.

4. For an excellent recreation of this passion for cinema among the New Wave filmmakers, read James Monaco, *The New Wave* (New York: Oxford University Press, 1976), pp. 3–4. Costa-Gavras refers to Monaco's study as "the most complete book I know on the five most important directors of the New Wave."

5. For the academic and technical program that was offered when Costa-Gavras studied at the school, consult Rémy Tessoneau, *L'Enseignement de l'IDHEC* (Paris: IDHEC, 1958).

6. His cinematic formation is sketched out in *IDHEC: Annuaire des Anciens Elèves* (1965), p. 199.

7. Peter Cowie in his *Eighty Years of Cinema* refers to Blue's film as "the most disquieting and elegiac film to emerge from the French-Algerian conflict. A highly personal, almost Bressonian portrait of a young man's return to his native country."

8. See Annette Insdorf, "Costa-Gavras Explores the Politics of the Heart," *New York Times*, Arts and Leisure, 27 May 1980, p. 19.

9. David Austen, "Pointing Out the Problems," *Films and Filming*, June 1972, p. 33.

10. In a short time scripts would pour in: an offer to make a film on François Mitterand's 1974 presidential election in France, on the race problem in the United States with James Baldwin, another on multinationals, *(Cormoran)*, an adaptation of Robert Kennedy's *The Enemy Within*, and one on the Vietnam War, among others.

11. Melton S. Davis, "Agent Provocateur of Films," *New York Times Magazine*, 21 March 1971, p. 32.

12. Rovelli, "A Colloquio Con Costa-Gavras," p. 71.

13. Bruce Berman, "A Conversation with Costa-Gavras," *Take One* 12 (December 1973): 26.

14. "A German Cinema for a German People: An Interview with Heinz-Dieter Rauchendorf," *Cinéaste* 2 (1974): 42.

15. Ibid.

16. PierNico Solinas, "Costa-Gavras: Article/Interview/Filmography—*State of Siege*," *Cinema* (U.S.A.): 34 (1974):36.

17. Jean-Pierre Bouteiller and Denis Offroy, "*Section Spéciale*," *Cinématographe* 13 (May–June 1975):35.

18. Ed Rampell, "The Politicization of Film Noir," *1000 Eyes*, December 1975, p. 8. For a succinct discussion of this genre, see Steven C. Earley, "Film Noir, or Black Cinema," *An Introduction to American Movies* (New York: New American Library, 1979), pp. 138–42.

19. Thérèse Fournier, "Costa-Gavras: Un cinéaste qui croît en l'homme," *France Soir*, 6 February 1973.

20. Guy Braucourt, "Entretien avec Costa-Gavras et Jorge Semprun," *Cinéma '70* 151 (December 1970):38.

21. Insdorf, "Costa-Gavras Explores the Politics of the Heart," p. 13.

22. Geoffrey Stokes, "Costa-Gavras: It's Art, But Is It Politics?" *The Village Voice*, 8 December 1975, p. 103.

23. Davis, "Agent Provocateur of Films," p. 46.

24. From the press materials issued by Cinema V in 1973 at the American release of *State of Siege*. See Costa-Gavras and Franco Solinas, *State of Siege* (New York: Ballantine Books, 1973), p. 41.

25. For his defense, see Hervé Villeré, *L'Affaire de la Section Spéciale* (Paris: Arthème Fayard, 1973), pp. 326–27.

26. See this author's essay "Alain Resnais: Literary Origins from *Hiroshima* to *Providence*," *Literature/Film Quarterly* 1 (1979):16–25.

27. Costa-Gavras and Franco Solinas, *State of Siege*, p. 94. The actual photos in the possession of the guerrillas appear in the dossier between pp. 104 and 105.

28. Judy Klemesrud, "Costa-Gavras: 'I'm Not Anti-American,'" *New York Times*, Arts and Leisure, 22 April 1973, p. 9.

29. Alain Rémond, *Montand* (Paris: Editions Henri Veyrier, 1977), p. 9.

30. Ibid., p. 96

31. Simone Signoret, *Nostalgia Isn't What It Used To Be* (London: Granada Publishing, 1979), pp. 109–10.

32. "Des intellectuels communistes s'interrogent sur leur fonction dans le parti," *Le Monde*, 9 June 1978, p. 10. A more extensive coverage of this debate can be found in *Les Nouvelles Littéraires* 2639 (8–15 June 1978):15–23, especially p. 18 on Semprun.

33. Louise Sweeney, "An Interview with Costa-Gavras, Director of *The Confession*," *Christian Science Monitor*, 26 January 1971, p. 9. I am indebted to Jorge Semprun for our 9 March 1981 interview which furnished innumerable details on his collaboration with Costa-Gavras.

34. Yan Auric, "Françoise Bonnot: Monteuse," *Cinémonde* 1840 (16 June 1970): 30.

35. Sweeney, "An Interview with Costa-Gavras," p. 9.

36. Insdorf, "Costa-Gavras Explores the Politics of the Heart," p. 13.

37. Paul Vecchiali, "Saison cinématographique, '73," *La Revue du Cinéma: Image et Son* 323 (December 1977):36.

38. Mikis Theodorakis, *Journal of Resistance* (New York: Coward, McCann, and Geoghegan, 1973).

39. Consult George Giannaris, *Music and Social Change* (New York: Praeger, 1972). For an extended discussion of film music, see Roy M. Prendergast, *Film Music: A Neglected Art* (New York: W. W. Norton, 1977).

40. Charles Moritz, ed., "Mikis Theodorakis," *Current Bibliography* (New York: H. W. Wilson Co., 1973), p. 411.

41. "Great Cameramen" (Special Issue), *Focus on Film* 13 (1973). See 21 on Raoul Coutard.

42. Davis, "Agent Provocateur of Films," p. 38.

43. Pauline Kael, "Politics and Thrills," *New Yorker*, 19 November 1973, p. 236.

Chapter 3

1. "Bonne Chance à Costa-Gavras," *Cinéma '65* 94 (1965):17.

2. Andrée Tournès, "Entretien avec Costa-Gavras," *Jeune Cinéma* 38 (April 1969):25.

3. For studies in this genre, consult Jon Tuska, *The Detective in Hollywood* (Garden City, N.Y.: Doubleday, 1978); William K. Everson, *The Detective in Film* (Secaucus, N.J.: Citadel Press, 1972); and Carlos Clarens, *Crime Movies: From Griffith to the Godfather . . . and Beyond* (New York: W. W. Norton, 1980).

4. See François Guérif, *Le Film Noir* (Paris: Editions Henry Veyrier, 1979) as well as Steven C. Earley, "Film Noir, or Black Cinema," *An Introduction to American Movies* (New York: New American Library, 1979), pp. 138–45.

5. Sébastien Japrisot, *The Sleeping Car Murders* (New York: Pocket Books, 1963), p. 6. Among American and British critics the title of the film alternates between the singular and the plural.

6. Ibid., p. 14.

7. Bosley Crowther, "*Sleeping Car Murder,*" *New York Times,* 8 March 1966, p. 45.

8. Alain Rémond, *Montand* (Paris: Editions Henri Veyrier, 1977), p. 96.

9. Japrisot, *The Sleeping Car Murders,* p. 165.

10. John Simon, "Overblown, But Not Blown Over," *New York,* 8 December 1975, p. 107.

11. Richard Davis, "*The Sleeping Car Murders,*" *Films and Filming,* December 1966, p. 52.

12. Aimé Vielzeuf, *On les appellait "les bandits,"* in *Histoire vécue de la Résistance* (Geneva: Famot, 1977), pp. 105–28. For a thorough investigation of the resistance see the four-volume work by Henri Noguères in collaboration with Marcel Degliame-Fouche, *Histoire de la Résistance en France* (Laffont), but especially volume 4, pp. 361–413 on the events of February 1944. See also Kenneth Macksey, *The Partisans of Europe in World War II* (London: Hart-Davis, MacGibbon, 1975).

13. Jean-Pierre Chabrol, 26 November 1979: personal communication.

14. René Bibault, 9 December 1979: personal communication.

15. Richard Jameson, "*Shock Troops,*" *Film Quarterly* 1 (Fall 1969): 55.

16. David Austen, "Pointing out the Problems" *Films and Filming,* June 1970, p. 34.

17. Chabrol, personal communication.

18. Bibault, personal communication.

19. Jean-Paul Sartre, *Existentialism and Human Emotions* (New York: Philosophical Library, 1957), pp. 24–28.

20. Aimé Vielzeuf, 4 December 1979, personal communication. M. Vielzeuf generously furnished many details that were excellent leads in this research on *Shock Troops.*

21. Penny Yates, "Costa-Gavras," *1000 Eyes* 5 (December 1975): 8.

Chapter 4

1. From the statistics of the U.S. Department of State, Bureau of Intelligence and Research, "World Strength of the Communist Party Organizations": At the time of Lambrakis's death in 1963, the estimated number of Communists in Greece was 20,000 and near the end of the colonels' regime in 1973, 28,000.

2. Statistics found in the AID report for the Bureau for Program and Policy Coordination, Office of Statistics and Reports: U.S. Overseas Loans and Grants and Assistance from International Organizations, 14 May 1971, p. 14.

3. Pauline A. Mian, "Greece Since the Coup d'Etat," Foreign Affairs Division (U.S. Government), 26 July 1972, pp. 34–35.

4. For a succinct study of the assassination written by a Greek-American in Greece during the actual events, read Dan Georgakas, "*Z,*" *Film Society Review,* December 1969, pp. 28–35. For other descriptions of the Lambrakis case, consult Jacques Lacarrière, "L'Affaire Gregorios Lambrakis Qui a Inspiré le Film *Z,*" *Journal du Show Business,* Cannes (May) 1969, no pagination; and the publicity notes prepared by the American distributor, Cinema V.

5. Vassilis Vassilikos, *Z* (New York: Ballantine Books, 1966).

6. In Paris, in 1971, Vassilikos also published *Journal de Z,* written from October 1965 to April 1966.

7. Vallilikos would soon become another Solzhenitzyn, banned from his country's bookshelves. For diverse literary criticism of this novel, consult Janice Elliott, *New Statesman* 77 (28 February 1969): 302. See other reviews in *Book Review Digest* for 1969, p. 1342.

8. Pierre Acot-Mirande et al. "*Z*," *Téléciné* 151–52 (March–April 1969):8.

9. The script was eventually published in French by *L'Avant-Scène du Cinéma* 96 (October 1969).

10. Jorge Semprun, Cinema V publicity materials.

11. Gérard Langlois, "Costa-Gavras et Jacques Perrin parlent de *Z*," *Les Lettres Françaises*, 26 February 1969 p. 19.

12. Dan Georgakas and Gary Crowdus, "Costa-Gavras Talks about *Z*," *Cinéaste* 3 (Winter 1969–1970):12.

13. The list of the interdictions in the film differs slightly from a more extensive one published in the *L'Avant-Scène* script.

14. Georgakas and Crowdus, "Costa-Gavras Talks about *Z*," p. 15. Costa-Gavras said the Algerians picked up the cost of hotels and transportation, almost 40% of the budget.

15. Langlois, "Costa-Gavras and Jacques Perrin," p. 20.

16. Guy Flatley, "Movies Are Passions and My Great Passion Is Politics," *New York Times*, 11 January 1970, Arts and Leisure, p. 15.

17. Ibid.

18. Robert Grelier, "Entretien avec Costa-Gavras," *La Revue du Cinéma: Image et Son* 228 (May 1969):61.

19. For a better understanding of the phenomenon of "apotheosis" in film, see Folke Isaksson and Leif Furhammar, "From Personality Cult to Apotheosis," *Politics and Film* (New York: Praeger, 1971), pp. 168–86.

20. Gordon Gow, "*Z*," *Films and Filming*, December 1969, p. 38.

21. Andrée Tournès, "*Z*: un film de notre temps," *Jeune Cinéma* 38 (April 1969):21.

22. John Simon, "*Z*," *Movies into Film* (New York: Dial Press, 1971), p. 89.

23. Mikis Theodorakis, *Journal of Resistance* (New York: Coward, McCann, and Geoghegan, 1973).

24. Flatley, "Movies Are Passions," p. 15.

25. Theodorakis, *Journal of Resistance*, p. 183.

26. Georgakas, "*Z*," p. 34.

27. Ibid.

28. Simon, "*Z*," p. 87.

29. Claude Veillot, "Le Premier grand film politique français," *L'Express* 921 (3–9 March 1969):79.

30. Melton S. Davis, "Agent Provocateur of Films," *New York Times Magazine*, 21 March 1971, p. 34.

31. Flatley, "Movies Are Passions," p. 15.

32. Gilbert Salachas, "*Z*," *Télérama* 1304 (8 January 1975):31.

33. Flatley, "Movies Are Passions," p. 15.

34. Yvonne Baby, "Entretien avec Costa-Gavras," *Le Monde*, 27 February 1969, p. 23.

35. Grelier, "Entretien avec Costa-Gavras," p. 64.

36. From the Cinema V publicity materials.

37. This speech is found in the *L'Avant-Scène* script on page 28 and in Vassilikos's novel on page 93.

38. Vassilikos, *Z*, p. 93.

39. Stanley Kauffmann, "*Z*," *New Republic*, 13 December 1969, p. 22.

40. Simon, "*Z*," p. 87.

41. From the Cinema V publicity materials.

42. Ibid.

43. Ibid.

44. Lawrence Loewinger, "*Z*," *Film Quarterly* 2 (Winter 1969–1970):64.

45. Jean Collet, "A propos de *Z*, ou les pièges du fascisme," *Projets*, February–March 1969, p. 29.

46. Georgakas, "*Z*," p. 33.

47. Simon, "*Z*," p. 89.

48. Pauline Kael, "Exiles," *New Yorker*, 13 December 1969, p. 168.

49. Charles W. Brooks, "*Z*: Politics on Film," *Commentary*, May 1970, p. 28.

50. Simon, "*Z*," p. 90. For further reading on the subject of military repression in Greece, see James Beckett, *Barbarism in Greece* (New York: Tower Publications, 1970); and "Athenian," *Inside the Colonel's Greece* (New York: W. W. Norton, 1972), written by an anonymous distinguished Greek

living in Greece at the time of the military regime. Following two requests and an appeal concerning clarification of the CIA's involvement in the coup of the colonels in 1967, the government agency did not offer us any information. By their refusal they neither confirm nor deny any collaboration.

51. Katia D. Kaupp, "Z: La vraie suite," *Le Nouvel Observateur* 327 (15 February 1971):32–33.

52. Steven V. Roberts, "Greece Sees *Z* and Gets Excited," *New York Times*, 13 January 1975, p. 6.

Chapter Five

1. For a study and bibliography of the Stalinist period recommended by Lise and Artur London, see Roy Medvedec, *Let History Judge: The Origins and Consequences of Stalinism*, trans. Colleen Taylor (New York: Alfred A. Knopf, 1971). It was written by Medvedec with access to government documents in the Soviet Union.

2. In this five-hour session with Lise and Artur London, the couple furnished us with extensive, firsthand material on the political events of the 1930s, 1940s and 1950s in Eastern Europe in which they participated. Artur London offered innumerable details about the making of the film *The Confession*. We will gratefully rely upon London's observations throughout this chapter.

3. For one view of the Prague trial, see Eugen Loebl, *Stalinism in Prague: The Loebl Story* (New York: Grove Press, 1971).

4. Artur London, *The Confession*, trans. Alastair Hamilton (New York: William Morrow and Company, 1970), p. 260.

5. Ibid., p. 153.

6. Ibid., p. 19.

7. For one study of the brainwashing process, see Edgar Schein with Inge Schneier and Curtis Barker, *Coercive Persuasion: A Sociopsychological Analysis of the "Brainwashing" of the American Civilian Prisoners by the Chinese Communists* (New York: W. W. Norton, 1961).

8. For a good journalistic overview of this period in retrospective, consult the series on Stalin in *Le Matin* (Paris), 17–22 November 1979, especially 22 November, p. 18, on "Le Culte."

9. Flora Lewis, *The Man Who Disappeared: The Strange History of Noel Field* (London: Arthur Barker, 1965), pp. 151 ff. [Lewis notes that Field was temporarily a member of the Swiss Communist party. During the Alger Hiss trial he appeared to be a Soviet spy, and during the Slansky and Rajk trial, an American agent.] For a more partisan perspective on the Noel Field case, see the German Communist party view of Field and his peers—"bandits," "conspirators," "elite spies," "capitalist agents," and so on—in Hermann Matern, *Uber die Durchführung des Beschlusses des ZK der SED: Lehren aus dem Prozess gegen das Verschwörerzentrum Slansky* (Berlin: Dietz Verlag, 1953), especially pp. 71–90.

10. Expression of Etienne Fajon during the Slansky trial. See also Pavel Tigrid, *Le Printemps de Prague* (Paris: Editions du Seuil, 1968), p. 42.

11. Consult Nathan Leites and Elsa Bernaut, *The Ritual of Liquidation* (Glencoe, Ill.: The Free Press, 1954).

12. For details of the trial, read London, pp. 265–316. For a synthesis of testimonies to the Prague trial, see Neal Ascherson, "Rebirth and Death in Czechoslovakia," *New York Review of Books* 16 (2 September 1971):11–13.

13. The poet Yevgeny Yevtouchenko writes about Stalin's tomb:

> "And I ask my government
> Double, triple the guard before this marble slab,
> So that Stalin does not arrive, resurrect
> And with him, the past."

(Quoted in French by Pierre Feydel in *Le Matin*, 22 November 1979, p. 18.)

14. Robert Grelier, "Entretien avec Costa-Gavras, Jorge Semprun, et Artur London: L'Aveu," *La Revue du Cinéma: Image et Son* 240 (June–July 1970):107.

15. For the chronology of production problems, see Gérard Langlois, "Costa-Gavras: L'Aveu," *Les Lettres Françaises* 1331 (22 April 1970):91.

16. Ginette Gervais, "Entretien avec Costa-Gavras," *Jeune Cinéma* 48 (June–July 1970):3–4.

17. Antonin Liehm, *Le Passé présent: Le Socialisme oriental face au monde moderne* (Paris: J. C. Lattes, 1974), pp. 47–48.

18. Grelier, "Entretien avec Costa-Gavras," p. 106.

19. Melton S. Davis describes the actual filming process of *The Confession* in the *New York Times Magazine*, 21 March 1971, pp. 32–47 (passim).

20. Pavel Tigrid, in *Le Printemps de Prague* (p. 42), includes a sad parallel to this action in a letter from a child of one of the accused published by an organizer of the trial. The child asks for capital punishment for the father, "this monster who does not deserve the name man."

21. Albert Knobler's film *Le Bonheur dans 20 ans* (1971) on the Prague political climate from 1948 to 1968, shows Slansky at the microphone saying, "I am a criminal unworthy of pardon."

22. Stanley Kauffmann, "*The Confession*," *New Republic*, 19 December 1970, p. 16.

23. Alain Rémond, *Montand* (Paris: Editions Henri Veyrier, 1977), p. 137.

24. Simone Signoret, *Nostalgia Isn't What It Used To Be* (London: Granada Publishing, 1979), p. 379.

25. Ibid.

26. Henry Hart, "*The Confession*," *Films in Review* 1 (January 1971):42.

27. David Denby, "Stalinism on Film: *The Confession*," *Atlantic Monthly*, February 1971, p. 124.

28. Joan Mellen, "The Politics of *The Confession*," *Cineaste* 3 (Winter 1970–1971):31.

29. See Chris Marker's script for *Le Fond de l'air est rouge* (Paris: François Maspero, 1978).

30. Glenn O'Brien, "Inter/VIEW with Costa-Gavras, Yves Montand and Jorge Semprun," *Interview* 12 (March 1971):19.

31. Semprun's scenario for Pierre Granier-Deferre's *Une Femme à sa fenêtre* also called for newsreels, as did his own documentary film *Les Deux Mémoires*. With newsreels the screenwriter and director stimulate our memories and put us in touch with a very concrete sociopolitical moment in our history.

32. Mellen, "The Politics of *The Confession*," p. 31.

33. Grelier, "Entretien avec Costa-Gavras," p. 105.

34. Resnais discussed at length this cinematic tool—equivalent to psychological meanderings and impulses—in the course of our interview on location for the filming of *Mon Oncle d'Amérique* in Paris, 23 November 1979.

35. O'Brien, "Inter/VIEW with Costa-Gavras," p. 20.

36. London, *The Confession*, p. 316.

37. Grelier, "Entretien avec Costa-Gavras," p. 106.

38. Vincent Canby, "Montand and Signoret Star in *Confession*," *New York Times*, 10 December 1970, p. 58.

39. Colin L. Westerbeck, Jr., "*The Confession*," *Commonweal*, 5 March 1971, pp. 548–49.

40. Grelier, "Entretien avec Costa-Gavras," p. 111.

41. "*L'Aveu*," *Unifrance Film* 391 (1970):2297.

42. Guy Braucourt, "Costa-Gavras: Mon Témoignage," *Les Nouvelles Littéraires*, 30 April 1970, p. 14.

43. Jorge Semprun. *France Soir*, April 1970.

44. Denby, "Stalinism on Film," p. 122.

45. Hannah Arendt, *The Origins of Totalitarianism* (New York: Harcourt, Brace, Jovanovich, 1973), p. xxxix.

46. Grelier, "Entretien avec Costa-Gavras," pp. 107–8.

47. Bernard Féron, "*L'Aveu* réflète le témoignage d'Artur London," *Le Monde*, 2 May 1970, p. 1.

48. Jean-Louis Comolli, in "Film/Politique (2)—*L'Aveu*: 15 Propositions," *Cahiers du Cinéma* 224 (October 1970):48–51, takes a structural approach in discussing the relationship of the text to the film, especially in terms of the political implications of both.

49. Mark Goodman, "Dialectic Inferno," *Time*, 4 January 1971, p. 59.

50. Patrick McFadden, "*The Confession*," *Film Society Review* 5 (January 1971):39.

51. Goodman, "Dialectic Inferno," p. 59.

52. McFadden, "*The Confession*," p. 40.

53. Mellen, "The Politics of *The Confession*," p. 32.

54. Thierry Maulnier, "*L'Aveu* et les complexes de la droite," *Le Figaro*, 17 June 1970, p. 1.

55. Judith Crist, "The Stuff and Stuffing of Heroes," *New York,* 15 December 1970, p. 70.

56. Mellen, "The Politics of *The Confession,*" p. 27.

57. McFadden, "*The Confession,*" p. 40.

58. Hart, "*The Confession,*" p. 41.

Chapter 6

1. PierNico Solinas, "Article, Interview, Filmography—*State of Siege,* " *Cinema* (U.S.A.) 34 (1974):38. See also Costa-Gavras and Franco Solinas, *State of Siege* (New York: Ballantine Books, 1973).

2. David Philips, director of Western Hemisphere activities of the CIA, discussed the agency's involvement in this change of administration in the televised documentary, *Return of the CIA,* 14 June 1980, Channel 7 (Boston).

3. A. J. Langguth, *Hidden Terrors* (New York: Pantheon Books, 1978), p. 40.

4. Costa-Gavras and Solinas, *State of Siege,* p. 144.

5. Ibid., p. 141.

6. Judy Klemesrud, "Costa-Gavras: I'm Not Anti-American," *New York Times,* Arts and Leisure, 22 April 1973, p. 9.

7. See, for example, the collaboration of Resnais and Robbe-Grillet discussed in detail in *Etudes Cinématographiques* 100–103 (1974).

8. From the press release of the AID Office of Public Affairs for 10 August 1971.

9. For a discussion of the use of torture in interrogation, read Maria Esther Gilio, *The Tupamaro Guerrillas* (New York: Saturday Review Press, 1972, pp. 145–78. See also the documentation in the *State of Siege* text, pp. 198–202.

10. Alan Riding, "Cuban 'Agent' Says U.S. Police Aides Urged Torture," *New York Times,* 5 August 1978, p. 3. This allegation also appears in Allan Francovich's documentary on the CIA, *On Company Business* (1980). This torture is confirmed in a letter to us from former Uruguayan Senator Enrique Erro January 1980. Senator Erro appears as Deputy Fabbri in the film. In his letter of 11 January 1980 Erro stated that Mitrione gave practical lessons on torture using derelicts as guinea pigs. Several of them died, he maintained.

11. Interview with a Leader of Uruguay's National Liberation Movement (Tupamaros)," *NLF: National Liberation Fronts 1960–1970* (New York: William Morrow, 1972), p. 284, originally published in *Granma* (Havana), 13 October 1970. When questioned about their structure, one guerrilla told Costa-Gavras, "Just read about the Jewish resistance of 1948."

12. Alain Labrousse, *The Tupamaros: Urban Guerrillas in Uruguay* (Hamondsworth, England: Penguin, 1973), pp. 24–31. For other works on the Tupamaros, see José Guerrero Martin, *Los Tupamaros segundo poder de Uruguay* (Barcelona: Ediciones Clio, 1972); Carlos Nuñez, *The Tupamaros* (New York: Times Change Press, 1972); Antonio Mercader and Jorge de Vera, *Tupamaros: estrategia y acción* (Mexico City: Editorial Omega, 1971); Carols Suarez, *Los Tupamaros* (Mexico City: Editorial Extemporaneos, 1971); and Carlos Wilson, *The Tupamaros: The Unmentionables* (Boston: Branden Press, 1974).

13. Photos of these cards can be found in the *State of Siege* dossier between pages 104 and 105.

14. Langguth, *Hidden Terrors,* p. 243. Much of Langguth's materials for this section of his text comes from confidential data that he received through the Freedom of Information Act, from the documents of Miguel Angel Bénitez Seguria (a double agent), and from interviews with AID director Byron Engle and former CIA agent Phillip Agee *(Inside the Company).*

15. The guerrillas sent the inscription on the watch to the government to prove that they held Mitrione hostage. A photo of the Brazilian reception can be found in the *State of Siege* dossier between pages 104 and 105.

16. Robert Grelier, "Entretien avec Costa-Gavras et Franco Solinas," *La Revue du Cinéma: Image et Son* 271 (April 1973):92–93.

17. Costa-Gavras and Solinas, *State of Siege,* pp. 153–54.

18. Tom Shales, "Gavras: Artisan or Partisan?" *Washington Post,* Section B, 6 April 1973, p. 13.

19. Costa-Gavras and Solinas, *State of Siege*, pp. 17–18.

20. Hans Ehrmann, "Solinas Shows Script to Chile's Reds Who Thereupon Rap Costa-Gavras," *Variety*, 21 June 1972, p. 3.

21. Klemesrud, "Costa-Gavras: 'I'm Not Anti-American,'" p. 31.

22. Grelier, "Entretien avec Costa-Gavras," p. 96.

23. Langguth (*Hidden Terrors*, p. 129) recalls a film shot in Panama called *The First Line of Defense* and used in the IPA training. The instructor's introduction in Spanish begins: "The events you will see take place in the mythical Latin American republic of San Martin. But they are not fictious events; they 'really happen.'"

24. According to the telegram sent from the American embassy in Uruguay to the United States State Department, the Uruguayan government did not want to negotiate with the guerrillas. The American government did not insist and only asked that the Latin American government "do all that is practical, but not all that is possible."

25. Costa-Gavras and Solinas, *State of Siege*, p. 139.

26. Ibid., p. 100.

27. Penelope Gilliatt, "The Poor Don't Care What They Look Like," *New Yorker*, 14 April 1973, p. 141.

28. The journalist Ducas is patterned on the elderly former legislator Carlos Quijano who once held a chair at the School of Law and Social Sciences. He was the founder and director of the weekly *Marcha*, which published the special issue on torture.

29. Costa-Gavras and Solinas, p. 153.

30. Former Senator Enrique R. Erro, 11 January 1980; personal communication. We are very much indebted to Senator Erro for offering many of the nuances about Uruguayan politics in the late 1960s and early 1970s.

31. Gilliatt, "The Poor Don't Care,", p. 142.

32. Costa-Gavras and Solinas, *State of Siege*, pp. 99–100.

33. Ibid., p. 130.

34. Ibid., p. 181. Nelson Bardesio stated that he followed orders from the Ministry of the Interior to bomb the homes of Doctors Maria Esther Gilio, Arturo Dubra, Liberoff, and Artuccio.

35. Theodore C. Sorensen, "'State of Siege' Speaks 'A Warning to Us All,'" *New York Times*, 24 June 1973, p. 15. For an overview of the controversy, see Sonia Paslawsky, "The Scandal of *State of Siege*," *Macguffin* (University of Illinois), May–June 1973, pp. 21–22

36. PierNico Solinas, "Article, Interview, Filmography," p. 35.

37. Vincent Canby, "'Siege': An Angry Muckraker," *New York Times*, 22 April 1973, p. 11.

38. Peter Biskind, "*State of Siege*," *Film Quarterly* 5 (Fall 1973):53.

39. David Denby, "Guerrillas Without Ideas," *Dissent*, Fall 1973, p. 482.

40. For the sound track from the film comprised of nine selections of instrumental music, see Mikis Theodorakis, *Etat de siège*, played by Los Calchakis, CBS-70079.

41. PierNico Solinas, "Article, Interview, Filmography," p. 43.

42. Costa-Gavras and Solinas, *State of Siege*, p. 142.

43. Stanley G. Eskin, "High Level Politics in the Cinema," *Midstream* 7 (August /September 1973):67.

44. Harold Kalishman and Gary Crowdus, "A Film Is Like a Match, You Can Make a Big Fire or Nothing at All," *Cinéaste* 1 (1973):4.

45. Jean-Louis Tallenay, "*Etat de Siège*: Pourquoi les Tupamaros ont-ils enlevé cet Américain bien tranquille?" *Télérama*, 10 February 1973, p. 68. Costa-Gavras especially appreciates Claude Julien's study of American involvement in Latin America, *L'Empire américain* (Paris: Grasset, 1968).

46. Costa-Gavras and Solinas, *State of Siege*, p. 149.

47. From the telegram of 10 August 1970 from the State Department to the American Ambassador in Montevideo subsequent to Spokesman McCloskey's briefing on the "assassination." The presently declassified material was furnished to us by the State Department. When asked if Mitrione had any kind of diplomatic or official status, McCloskey stated in the conference that Mitrione had an official passport, but perhaps not a diplomatic one.

48. Marcel Niedergang, "Un Entretien avec Costa-Gavras: Les raccourcis historiques de l'*Etat de Siège*," *Le Monde*, 2 February 1973, p. 13.

49. Alain Rémond, *Montand* (Paris: Editions Henri Veyrier, 1977), p. 160. Although positive about the Tupamaros in 1973, he referred to the Italian Red Brigade as "crazy" in 1982.

50. Donald C. Hodges, trans. and ed., *Philosophy of the Urban Guerrilla: The Revolutionary Writings of Abraham Guillén* (New York: William Morrow, 1973), p. 271. For another global view of the urban guerrilla movement, including the Tupamaros, see Claire Sterling, *The Terror Network: The Secret War of International Terrorism* (New York: Holt, Rinehart & Winston, 1981).

51. Quoted in Jean Rochereau's article, "*Etat de Siège:* Le sang appelle le sang," in *La Croix* for 18 February 1973, p. 18.

52. "Costa-Gavras' *State of Siege*," *Films and Filming* 11 (August 1973):19.

53. Omar Costa, *Los Tupamaros* (Mexico City: Ediciones Era, 1971), pp. 210–19. Jackson also appears in Jan Lindqvist's fifty-minute documentary *Tupamaros!* (1972), which contains actual footage of the Tupamaros, interviews, and a glimpse of the "Death Squad." Mitrione's case is mentioned here as the reason for the elaborate crackdown on guerrillas.

54. Costa-Gavras and Solinas, *State of Siege*, p. 108.

55. Grelier, "Entretien avec Costa-Gavras," p. 94.

56. Louis Chauvet, "*Etat de Siège*," *Le Figaro*, 11 February 1973.

57. Canby, "'Siege': An Angry Muckraker," p. 11.

58. Kalishman and Crowdus, "A Film Is Like a Match," p. 4.

59. "Rogers Among Mourners as Mitrione is Buried," *New York Times*, 14 August 1970, p. 3.

60. William Safire, *Safire's Political Dictionary* (New York: Ballantine, 1978), p. 116.

61. Labrousse, *The Tupamaros*, pp. 102–3.

62. PierNico Solinas, "Article, Interview, Filmography," p. 41.

63. Gilliatt, "The Poor Don't Care," p. 141.

64. The exchange of letters and telephone conversations between George Stevens, Jr., at the American Film Institute and Rugoff's office at Cinema V were unfortunately impossible to document. Stevens's office stated that the letters were unavailable, and Rugoff was just leaving the presidency of Cinema V and was thus unable to produce them at that time.

65. James T. Wooten, "Capital Film Festival Opens to Dispute," *New York Times*, 4 April 1973, p. 34.

66. Hugh Bernard, "*State of Siege*," *Films in Review* 6 (June–July 1973):373.

Chapter 7

1. Jean-Pierre Jeancolas, "Fonction du témoignage: Les Années 1939–1945 dans le cinéma de l'après-guerre," *Positif*, June 1975, pp. 45–60. For another view of the Vichy regime which contrasts with that of Costa-Gavras in *Special Section*, see *Les Cahiers de la Cinémathèque* 8 (Winter 1973). In pro-Vichy films one generally observes a paternal image of the country and government; a litany of the values of the past; a romantic nostalgic search for national grandeur; and a desire for decentralization. Continually enforced censorship helped promote films with the ideals of "*Travail, Famille, Patrie*" (Work, Family, Country). These films were in the service of the bourgeois and fascist traditions. For still another view of French film production during World War II, see the collected essays of André Bazin, *Le Cinéma de l'Occupation et de la Résistance* (Paris: Union générale d'éditions, 1975).

2. Glenn O'Brien, "Inter/VIEW with Costa-Gavras, Yves Montand and Jorge Semprun," *Interview* 12 (March 1971):19.

3. Robert O. Paxton, *Vichy France: Old Guard and New Order, 1940–1944* (New York: Alfred A. Knopf, 1972).

4. Hervé Villeré, *L'Affaire de la Section Spéciale* (Paris: Arthème Fayard, 1973). The political situation in France from 1940 to 1945 was even more nuanced and complex than Paxton, Villeré, and Costa-Gavras make it out to be. We will of necessity only treat those aspects of the government's action which touch on the film narrative.

5. Ibid., pp. 173–74.

6. Ibid., p. 185.

7. Ibid., p. 292.

8. Ibid., PP. 224–25.

9. Ibid., p. 227.

10. Thierry Levy, "The Affair," Universal Studio publicity notes for *Special Section*.

11. Georges Conchon, "*In Connection with Special Section*," Universal Studio publicity notes.

12. Villeré, *L'Affaire de la Section Spéciale*, p. 17.

13. Paul Deglin, "*Section Spéciale*," *Ciné Revue* 17 (24 April 1975): 10–11.

14. Betty Jeffries Demby, "Costa-Gavras Discusses 'Special Section,'" *Filmmakers Newsletter* 4 (February 1976: 29.

15. Jorge Semprun, in the Universal Studios publicity notes.

16. Demby, "Costa-Gavras Discusses 'Special Section,'" p. 29. The crew was given permission to shoot at the Palais de Justice on a weekend, when the court was not in session. They filmed on 15 August 1974 on the rue St. Denis when traffic could be blocked off. Then Costa-Gavras and company moved to Vichy for eleven weeks.

17. Ibid.

18. Jack Kroll, "Kangaroo Justice," *Newsweek*, 15 December 1975, p. 95.

19. Demby, "Costa-Gavras Discusses 'Special Section,'" p. 31.

20. Vincent Canby, "*Special Section* by Costa-Gavras Arrives," *New York Times*, 8 December 1975, p. 42.

21. Jay Cocks, "Blind Injustice," *Time*, 8 December 1975, p. 72.

22. Nancy Schwartz, "Diplomatic Pouches in Kangaroo Courts," *Soho Weekly News*, 11 December 1975, p. 31.

23. Pauline Kael, "Political Acts," *New Yorker*, 15 December 1975, p. 89.

24. Schwartz, "Diplomatic Pouches," p. 31.

25. Kroll, "Kangaroo Justice," p. 95.

26. Demby, "Costa-Gavras Discusses 'Special Section,'" p. 29.

27. Ibid.

28. Jeancolas, "Fonction du témoignage," p. 60.

29. Demby, "Costa-Gavras Discusses 'Special Section,'" p. 30.

30. Villeré, *L'Affaire de la Section Spéciale*, p. 287.

31. Demby, "Costa-Gavras Discusses 'Special Section,'" p. 30.

32. Ibid.

33. Schwartz, "Diplomatic Pouches," p. 31.

34. Demby, "Costa-Gavras Discusses 'Special Section,'" p. 31.

35. From the grand-opera libretto, *Boris Godunov* (New York: Edwin F. Kalmus, n.d.), p. 45.

36. Ann Powell, "Costa-Gavras: Beyond Journalism," *Soho Weekly News*, 11 December 1975, p. 30.

37. Claude Benoît, "*Section Spéciale*," *Jeune Cinéma* 87 (May–June 1975): 32.

38. Guy Hennebelle, "A propos d'Yves Boisset et de Costa-Gavras," *Ecran '75* 38 (July–August 1975): 14.

39. Alain Rémond, "De bons mots en répliques cinglantes on oublie l'essentiel," *Télérama*, 23 April 1975, p. 67.

40. Michel Marmin, "*Section Spéciale:* Film de Costa-Gavras," *Valeurs Actuelles*, 21 April 1975, p. 59.

41. "Critique ouverte sur *Section Spéciale*," *Jeune Cinéma* 89 (September–October 1975): 30.

42. Thérèse Fournier, "Costa-Gavras: Pour moi le Festival est une tribune," *France-Soir*, 13 May 1975.

43. Frank Rich, "Costa-Gavras, Vichy, and Watergate," *New York Post*, 13 December 1975, p. 14.

44. Ibid., p. 40.

45. Cocks, "Blind Justice," p. 72.

46. Ibid.

47. Canby, "*Special Section* by Costa-Gavras," p. 42.

48. Ibid.

49. Schwartz, "Diplomatic Pouches," p. 31.

50. Kael, "Political Acts," p. 89.

51. John Simon, "Overblown, But Not Blown Over," *New York*, 8 December 1975, p. 107.

52. Ibid., p. 108.

53. Kroll, "Kangaroo Justice," p. 95.
54. Ibid.

Chapter 8

1. Peter S. Greensberg, "Arts, Lies and Realities: An Interview with Costa-Gavras," *Rolling Stone,* 13 May 1982, p. 17. Ted Koppel on ABC's "Night Line" (27 May 1982) studied disappearances in Argentina over the past five years and came to similar conclusions.

2. Robert Garrett, "Costa-Gavras: A Game Between Hope and Death," *Boston Herald American,* 14 February 1982, p. B4.

3. Thomas Hauser, *The Execution of Charles Horman: An American Sacrifice* (New York: Harcourt, Brace, Jovanovich, 1978), reprinted as *Missing* (New York: Avon, 1982). All references will be to the recent paperback edition.

4. Michael Wood, "In Search of the Missing," *American Film,* March 1982, p. 42.

5. Dan Yakir, *"Missing* in Action," *Film Comment,* March–April 1982, p. 58.

6. Hauser put together this section from countless documents dealing with Chile and the disappearance of Charles Horman which he obtained through the Freedom of Information Act.

7. Statistics from U.S. Agency for International Development in *Overseas Loan and Assistance from International Organizations,* 1 July 1945–30 June 1973.

8. Part Three of Allan Francovich's documentary on the CIA, *On Company Business* (1980), deals with American intervention in the Chilean elections, with the justification that it would help stop the cancerous growth of Communism in Latin America. David Cusack in *Revolution and Reaction: The International Dynamism of Conflict and Confrontation in Chile* (University of Denver, 1977), maintains that after the 1964 Frei elections, Chile became the showplace for the Alliance for Progress and Frei's Christian-Democratic government was "tailor-made for the expressed ideals of the Alliance" (p. 106). Cusack also states that following the coup, "The Junta loudly proclaimed its identification with the U.S.-directed world-wide struggle against Communism, and held itself up as a defender of 'Western' and U.S. economic and cultural values" (p. 118).

9. Hauser, *Missing,* pp. 67–68. For the police report of the incident on 22 October 1972 and the official interpretation of it, see Robinson Rojas Sandford, *The Murder of Allende and the End of the Chilean Way to Socialism* (New York: Harper and Row, 1976), pp. 50–51.

10. The account of physicist Jim Ritter in *Chilean Days of Terror* (1974) shows what he knew of the situation:

> I was finally released on Wednesday, September 26, because of pressure from the U.S. A deal had been made, as I found out later. But all I know is that all Americans were taken to a section and they had a list, including three names who were not there—Frank Teruggi, Charley Horman, and a woman named Rodriguez. These were the names the American Embassy had of those Americans who had been arrested and sent to the stadium. They said Frank Teruggi had been released the previous Friday and that Charley Horman never came to the stadium. Both these men I found out later had been shot. Rodriguez, they said, was being held in the South, which I later found out was true. (p. 40)

11. Virginia Lucier, "Z Director Back with Another Gripping Story," *Middlesex News* (Framingham, MA), 31 January 1982, p. 10 B.

12. Franz-Olivier Giesbert and Jean-François Josselin, "L'Amérique, sans peur, avec reproche," *Nouvel Observateur,* 15–21 May 1982, p. 97. I am grateful to Professor William Richardson for all the French documentation on *Missing.*

13. Henri Behar, "Un film politique doit être populaire," *Première* 62 (May 1982):56.

14. Larry Hart, "Another Controversy for Film's Nonaggressive Good Guy," *Chicago Tribune,* 14 March 1982, Section 6, p. 5.

15. Lucier, "Z Director Back," p. 11 B.

16. For aesthetic equivalents see Pablo Picasso's white horse in panic in his anti-fascist painting recalling the bombing of Guernica. Sergei Eisenstein also uses the same symbol in *October* to repre-

sent the people; the closing drawbridge cutting off the workers' districts from the center leaves the corpse of the white horse dangling.

17. One insensitive American official actually suggested to Joyce that Charles left in order to get away from her.

18. Greensberg, "Arts, Lies and Realities," p. 18.

19. For greater detail, see Lester A. Sobel (ed.), *Chile and Allende* (New York: Facts on File, 1974), especially pp. 140–53. To reflect several sides of the complex Chilean question, Francisco Orrego Vicuña has published *Chile: The Balanced View* (Santiago: University of Chile, 1975).

20. Almost as an aside, Costa-Gavras told Peter Greensberg in *Rolling Stone:*

> I know that Horman's father thinks the American government knew what really happened to his son. I'm not convinced that the government knew. I think some people down there knew and others covered up the whole thing. (p. 18)

In a sense, this statement would deflate the director's apparent thesis of full American complicity which is implied in the film.

21. James Petras and Morris Morley, *The United States and Chile: Imperialism and the Overthrow of the Allende Government* (New York: Monthly Review Press, 1975), p. xii.

22. For revealing studies of American multinational power in Latin America, see Anthony Sampson's *The Sovereign State of ITT* (New York: Stein and Day, 1973), and Stephen Schlesinger and Stephen Kinzer's, *Bitter Fruit: The Untold Story of the American Coup in Guatemala* (New York: Doubleday, 1982).

23. Hauser, *Missing,* p. 245.

24. Michael Blowen, "My Politics are Simple," *Boston Globe,* 7 February 1982, p. 55.

25. Andrew Kopkind, " 'Missing': Cultural Battlefield," *Nation,* 17 April 1982, pp. 467–68.

26. Nathaniel Davis, "What Costa-Gavras' *Missing* Misses is the Truth," *Boston Herald American,* 23 April 1982, p. 28. At one point Davis and other American officials contemplated suing the director and producers for defamation of character.

27. This was underlined in *State of Siege* with the International Police Academy in Washington.

28. Peter Kaplan, "*Missing:* The Search and the Sorrow—The Political Drama Behind the Screen," *Washington Post,* 7 March 1982, p. G 6.

29. Flora Lewis, "New Film by Costa-Gavras Examines the Chilean Coup," *New York Times,* Arts and Leisure, 7 February 1982, p. 26. During the Cannes Film Festival preparations for the screening of *Missing,* Costa-Gavras criticized her critique for being "*profondément malhônnette*" (utterly dishonest).

30. Professor Richard Fagen of Stanford's Political Science Department knew Frank Teruggi, Charles Horman, and Dave Hathaway when they served as his translators in 1972–73 in Santiago. In a letter to Sen. Fulbright in October 1973, published as "An Accusation Against the American Embassy in Santiago," in Laurence Birns's *The End of Chilean Democracy* (New York: Seabury Press, 1974), pp. 164–75, Fagen offered a chronology of events. He said he knew on 23 September through a graduate student in Santiago that Charles had been arrested by the police on 17 September. (The Embassy said it had no trace of him when Ed Horman arrived on 5 October.)

31. Alan Berger, "Were US hands dirty in Chilean murder?" *Boston Globe,* 28 February 1982, p. A 35.

32. Kopkind, " 'Missing': Cultural Battlefield," p. 466.

33. Gerald Clark, "Missing: Fact or Fabrication?" *Time,* 8 March 1982, p. 96.

34. Hauser (*Missing,* p. 142) treats this event as a turning point for Ed's decision to come to Santiago in search of Charles. Professor Richard Fagen in his letter to Fulbright questions why it took more than eight days to establish the identity of Teruggi's body since he was registered at the Embassy and had been fingerprinted there. He also asks why David Hathaway was shown a body which was not that of his dead roommate. In essence, Professor Fagen points out the inefficiency, blunders, and possible cover-up by the American mission.

35. Hauser, *Missing,* p. 224.

36. Ibid., p. 221.

37. Ibid., p. 253.

38. Ibid., p. 255.

Conclusions and Epilogue

1. Jean-Pierre Jeancolas, "Fonction du témoignage," *Positif,* June 1975, p. 60.
2. Ibid.
3. Ann Powell, "Costa-Gavras: Beyond Journalism," *Soho Weekly News,* 11 December 1975, p. 30.

Filmography

The Sleeping Car Murder (Compartiment tueurs)
Producer: Julien Derode (Productions et Editions Cinématographiques Françaises)
Director: Costa-Gavras
Screenplay: Costa-Gavras with Sébastien Japrisot
Source: Le Compartiment tueurs, Sébastien Japrisot
Photography: Jean Tournier
Music: Michel Magne
First Assistant: Bernard Paul
Editor: Christian Gaudin
Sets: Rino Modellini
Cast:
  Simone Signoret (Eliane Darrès)
  Yves Montand (Inspector Grazzi)
  Pierre Mondy (Police Commissioner)
  Cathérine Allégret (Bambi)
  Pascale Roberts (Georgette Thomas)
  Jacques Perrin (Daniel)
  Michel Piccoli (René Cabourg)
  Jean-Louis Trintignant (Eric)
  Charles Denner (Bob)
  Claude Mann (Jean-Lou)
  Nadine Alari (Mme Grazzi)
  And: Daniel Gelin, Claude Dauphin, Françoise Arnoul, André Valmy, Maurice Chevit, Jacques Dynam, Jean Lefebvre, Jean-Pierre Périer, Tanya Lopert, Bernadette Laffont, Christian Marin, Serge Rousseau, Paul Pavel, Albert Michel, Jenny Orléans, Marcel Bozzufi, Georges Géret, Clément Harari, B. Paul, R. Sabatier, J. Steiner
Release Date (Paris): 17 November 1965

Shock Troops (Un Homme de trop)
Producer: Harry Saltzman: Franco-Italian Co-production—Terrafilm, Artistes Associés (Paris); Sol Produzioni, Compagnia Cinematografica Montoro (Rome)
Director: Costa-Gavras
Screenplay: Costa-Gavras and Jean-Pierre Chabrol
Source: Un Homme de trop, Jean-Pierre Chabrol
Dialogue: Daniel Boulanger
Photography: Jean Tournier
Music: Michel Magne
First Assistant: Bernard Paul
Editor: Christian Gaudin
Sets: Maurice Collasson
Sound: Guy Villette

Cast:
Michel Piccoli ("Robert"/"The Man")
Bruno Cremer (Cazal)
François Perier (Moujon)
Pierre Clementi (Fascist sniper)
Jacques Perrin (Kerk)
Claude Brasseur (Groubac)
Gérard Blain (Thomas)
Charles Vanel (Passevin)
Jean-Claude Brialy (Jean)
Julie Dassin (Jeanne)
Release Date (Paris): 5 April 1967.

Z

Producers: French-Algerian Co-production: Jacques Perrin (Reggane
    Films, Paris) and Hamed Rachedi (National Film Office, Algiers)
Director: Costa-Gavras
Screenplay: Jorge Semprum (with Costa-Gavras)
Dialogue: Jorge Semprun
Source: Z, Vassilis Vassilikos
Photography: Raoul Coutard
Music: Mikis Theodorakis (arranged by Bernard Gérard)
First Assistant: Philippe Monnier
Editor: Françoise Bonnot
Sets: Jacques D'Ovidio
Cast:
Yves Montand (Deputy "Z")
Irene Papas (Hélène)
Jean-Louis Trintignant (Examining Magistrate)
Jacques Perrin (Reporter/Photographer)
François Perier (Public Prosecutor)
Charles Denner (Manuel)
Pierre Dux (General)
Julien Guiomar (Colonel)
Bernard Fresson (Matt)
Renato Salvatori (Yago)
Marcel Bozzufi (Vago)
Jean Bouise (Deputy Georges Pirou)
Georges Géret (Nick)
Clotilde Joano (Shoula)
Jean Dasté (Coste)
Magali Noël (Nick's Sister)
Jean-Pierre Miguel (Pierre)
Guy Mairesse (Dumas)
Bob de Bragelonne (Undersecretary of State)
Gérard Darrieu (Baroné)
R. Van Doude (Hospital Director)
Maurice Baquet (Mason)
José Arthur (Newspaper Editor)
Steve Gadler (English Photographer)
Hassan Hassani (General's Chauffeur)

Eva Simonet (Niki, Public Prosecutor's Daughter)
Gabriel Jabbour (Bozzini)
Andrée Tainsy (Nick's Mother)
Jean-François Gobbi (Jimmy-the-Boxer)
Release Date (Paris): 26 February 1969

The Confession (L'Aveu)
Producers: Robert Dorfmann and Bertrand Javal
Director: Costa-Gavras
Screenplay: Jorge Semprun
Source: The Confession (L'Aveu), Artur (and Lise) London
Dialogue: Jorge Semprun
Photography: Raoul Coutard
Cameraman: Chris Marker
First Assistant: Alain Corneau
Sound: William Sivel
Editor: Françoise Bonnot
Sets: Bernard Evein
Cast:
Yves Montand (Gérard)
Simone Signoret (Lise)
Gabriele Ferzetti (Kohoutek)
Michel Vitold (Smola)
Jean Bouise (Factory Boss)
Jacques Rispal (Otto Sling)
Release Date (Paris): 26 April 1970.

State of Siege (Etat de siège)
Producers: Jacques Perrin and Max Palevsky
Director: Costa-Gavras
Screenplay: Franco Solinas (with Costa-Gavras)
Photography: Pierre William Glenn
Sound: André Hervée
Music: Mikis Theodorakis (Interpreted by Los Calchakis)
First Assistant: Christian de Chalogne
Editor: Françoise Bonnot
Sets: Jacques D'Ovidio
Cast:
Yves Montand (Philip Michael Santore)
Renato Salvatori (Captain López)
O. E. Hasse (Carlos Ducas)
Jacques Weber (Hugo)
Jean-Luc Bideau (Este)
Evangeline Peterson (Mrs. Santore)
Maurice Teynac (Minister of Internal Security)
Yvette Etiévant (Woman Senator)
Harold Wolff (Minister of Foreign Affairs)
Némésio Antunes (President of the Republic)
André Falcon (Deputy Fabbri)
Mario Montilles (Fontana)
Jerry Brouer (Lee)
Jean-François Gobbi (Journalist)
Eugénio Guzman (Spokesman for Internal Security)
Maurice Jacquemont (Dean of the Law Faculty)
Roberto Navarette (Romero)

Gloria Lass (Student)
Alejandro Cohen (Manuel)
Martha Contreras (Alicia)
Release Date (Paris): 8 February 1973

Special Section (Section Spéciale)
Producers: Jacques Perrin and Giorgio Silvagni
A French-Italian-German Co-production: Reggane Films, Artistes Associés
  (Paris); Goriz Films (Rome); Janus Film (Frankfurt)
Director: Costa-Gavras
Screenplay: Jorge Semprun (with Costa-Gavras)
Dialogue: Jorge Semprun
Source: L'Affaire de la Section Spéciale, Hervé Villeré
Photography: Andreas Winding
Sound: Harald Maury
Music: Eric Demarsan (Magnetic Music—Takis)
First Assistant: Jean-Michel Lacor
Editor: Françoise Bonnot
Sets: Max Douy
Cast:
Louis Seigner (Minister of Justice Barthélemy)
Michel Lonsdale (Secretary of the Interior Pucheu)
Ivo Garrani (Admiral)
François Maistre (Deputy General)
Roland Bertin (Secretary General of the Justice Department)
Henri Serre (Deputy of the Secretary of the Interior of the Occupied Zone)
Pierre Dux (Attorney General)
Jacques François (State Prosecutor)
Claudio Gora (First President of the Court of Appeal)
Julien Bertheau (Lawyer, Head of the Central Service of the Prosecutor's
  Chamber)
Claude Pieplu (President of the Special Section Benon)
Hubert Gignoux (Judge "in Black")
Jacques Ouvrier (Counsellor)
Alain Nobis (First Counsellor Larricq)
Jean Bouise (Counsellor Linais)
Jean Champion (Lawyer Guyenot)
Julien Guiomar (Deputy Public Prosecutor Tétaud)
Maurice Teynac (Deputy Public Prosecutor Guillec)
Jacques Spiesser (Frédo)
Heinz Bennent (Major Beumelburg)
Michel Galabru (President Cournet)
Guy Rétoré (Bréchet)
Yves Robert (Bastard)
Jacques Rispal (Trzebrucki)
Eric Rouleau (Friedmann)
Guy Mairesse (Redondeau)
Bruno Cremer (Sampaix)
Jacques Perrin (Lawyer Lafarge)
Release Date (Paris): 23 April 1975

Clair de Femme
Producer: Georges-Alain Vuille
Director: Costa-Gavras
Screenplay: Costa-Gavras

Source: Clair de Femme, Romain Gary
Photography: Ricardo Arnovich
First Assistants: Umberto Angeluci, Renald Calcagni
Sound: Pierre Gamet
Music: Jean Musy
Editor: Françoise Bonnot
Sets: Mario Chiari, Eric Simon
Cast:
  Romy Schneider (Lydia)
  Yves Montand (Michel)
  Romolo Valli (Galba)
  Lila Kedrova (Sonia)
  Heinz Bennent (Georges)
  Roberto Benigni (Bartender, Clapsy's)
  Dieter Schidor (Sven)
  Cathérine Allégret (Prostitute)
  François Perrot (Alain)
  Daniel Mesguich (Police Commissioner)
  Gabriel Jabbour (Sacha)
  Hans Verner (Klauss)
  Pierre Cheremetieff and "Runge" (Russian Musicians)
  And: Jean-Claude Bouillaud, Eliane Borras, Gabriel Dussurget, Isabelle Bucaille, Jean-François Gobbi, Béatrice Costantini, Fanny Delbrice, André Dumas, Jacques Dynam, Michèle Lituac, Philippe Manesse, Jean-Pierre Rambal, Jean Reno, Michel Robin, Katia Romanoff, Jacques Sempey, Mireille Pame, Bob Castella, Guiliana Calandra, Margherita Ciboldi, Miranda Campa, Antonio Berkov, Ibrahim Seck
Release Date (Paris): 29 August 1979

Missing
Producers: Edward and Mildred Lewis (Universal)
Director: Costa-Gavras
Screenplay: Costa-Gavras and Donald Stewart
Source: The Execution of Charles Horman: An American Sacrifice (reprinted as *Missing),* Thomas Hauser
Photography: Ricardo Arnovich
Music: Vangelis
First Assistant: Elie Cohn
Editor: Françoise Bonnot
Sets: Linda Spheeris
Cast:
Jack Lemmon (Ed Horman)
Sissy Spacek (Beth Horman)
John Shea (Charles Horman)
Melanie Mayron (Terry Simon)
Charles Cioffi (Captain Ray Tower)
David Clennon (Consul Phil Putnum)
Richard Venture (U.S. Ambassador)
Jerry Hardin (Colonel Sean Patrick)
Richard Bradford (Carter Babcock)
Joe Regalbuto (Frank Teruggi)
Keith Szarabajka (David Holloway)
Janice Rule (Kate Newman)
John Doolittle (David McGeary)
Martin Lasalle (Paris/Perez)
Robert Hitt (Peter Chernin)
Release Date (Boston, New York, etc): 12 February 1982

Bibliography

Chapter 1

Barnouw, Erik. *Documentary: A History of the Nonfiction Film.* New York: Oxford University Press, 1977.

Bazin, André. *Le Cinéma de l'occupation et de la résistance.* Paris: Union générale d'éditions, 1975.

Benayoun, Robert, et al. "Débat: Le cinéma dans la politique." *Positif,* February 1970, pp. 11–27.

Braucourt, Guy. "Entretien avec Costa-Gavras et Jorge Semprun." *Cinéma '70,* December 1970, pp. 38–51.

Burton, Julianne, ed. *The New Latin American Cinema: An Annotated Bibliography of English-Language Sources, 1960–1976. Cinéaste* (Pamphlet) No. 4 (1976).

Chanan, Michael, ed. *Chilean Cinema.* London: British Film Institute, 1976.

"Cinéma Militant." (Special Issue) *Cinéma d'Aujourd'hui* 5/6 (March–April 1976).

"Le Cinéma politique français." *Le Cinéma Français* 12 (1977): 19–23.

Cockburn, Alexander. "The Uses of Hersh." *Village Voice,* 10–16 February 1982, p. 10.

Collet, Jean. "Blue Collar." *Etudes,* January 1979, pp. 51–53.

Douin, Jean Luc and Christine. "Quand le cinéma français parle politique." *Télérama,* 26 August 1972, pp. 48–50.

Duval, Roland. "Causons politique." *Ecran '74,* July 1974, pp. 14–15.

Esnault, Philippe. "Cinema and Politics." *Cinéaste* 3 (Winter 1969/1970), pp. 4–11.

Furhammar, Leif, and Isaksson, Folke. *Politics and Film.* New York: Praeger Publishers, 1971.

Gevaudan, Frantz. "Le Cinéma politique face à son public." *Cinéma '73,* January 1973, pp. 84–93.

Grenier, Richard. "The Curious Career of Costa-Gavras." *Commentary* 4 (April 1982):61–71.

Guidez, Guylaine. "L'Aurore d'un cinéma ouvrier." *Cinémonde,* 16 June 1970, pp. 8–10.

———. "Rencontre avec Pontecorvo." *Cinémonde,* 16 June 1970, pp. 20–25.

Hennebelle, Guy. "Z Movies or What Hath Costa-Gavras Wrought?" *Cinéaste* 2 (1974):28–31.

———, and Serceau, Daniel. "L'Irrésistible Ascension du Cinéma Militant." *L'Ecran '74,* December 1743, pp. 44–54.

Hull, David Stewart. *Film in the Third Reich: Art and Propaganda in Nazi Germany.* New York: Simon and Schuster, 1973.

Kael, Pauline, "Politics and Thrills." *New Yorker,* 19 November 1973, p. 236.

Kliment, Jan. "The Film Goes Political." *Young Cinema and Theatre* 1 (1974): 22–25.

Kovacs, Katherine S. "Miguel Littin's *Recurso del Metodo:* The Aftermath of Allende." *Film Quarterly,* Spring 1980, pp. 22–29.

Lafond, Jean Daniel. "Les paradoxes de la fiction politique." *La Revue du Cinéma,* December 1977, pp. 37–42.

Lane, John Francis. "Film and Politics in Italy: Francesco Rosi's Example." *Films and Filming,* May 1976, pp. 16–17.

Lebel, Jean-Patrick, *Cinéma et idéologie.* Paris: Editions Sociales, 1971.

———. "Cinéma Militant? Cinéma Politique? De Quoi s'agit-il?" *Ecran '74,* December 1974, pp. 55–57, 92.

Leyda, Jay. *Kino: A History of the Russian and Soviet Film.* New York: Collier Books, 1973.

Lionet, Gérard. "Retard politique du cinéma français." *Jeune Cinéma,* May–June 1975, pp. 17–19.

MacBean, James Roy. *Film and Revolution.* Bloomington, Ind.: Indiana University Press, 1975.

Manvell, Roger. *Films and the Second World War.* New York: Dell Publishing Co., Inc., 1974.

Marshall, Herbert, ed. *The Battleship Potemkin.* New York: Avon Books, 1978.

Marty, A. "Un contresens idéologique sur l'oeuvre de Costa-Gavras." *La Revue du Cinéma,* December 1977, pp. 43–55.

Mellen, Joan. "*Executive Action:* The Politics of Distortion." *Cinéaste* 2 (1974), pp. 8–12.

———. "Hollywood's 'Political' Cinema." *Cinéaste,* 2 (Spring 1972), pp. 26–31.

"Politics and the American Cinema" (Special Issue). *The Velvet Light Trap* 4 (1972).

"La politique et le cinéma, et la politique." *Positif,* November 1971, pp. 59–62.

Restif, Henri. "Cinéma et politique." *La Revue du Cinéma,* December 1970, pp. 63–67.

Russell, Sharon A., ed. *Revolutionary Films/Chicago '76.* Chicago: Film Center, School of the Art Institute of Chicago, 1976.

Sarris, Andrew. *Politics and Cinema.* New York: Columbia University Press, 1978.

Sauvaget, Daniel. "A propos de Costa-Gavras." *La Revue du Cinéma,* December 1977, pp. 30–36.

Schnitzer, Luda and Jean, and Martin, Marcel, eds. *Cinema in Revolution.* New York: Hill and Wang, 1973.

Seguin, Louis. "Le cinéma dans la politique." *Positif,* February 1970, pp. 2–12.

Solinas, PierNico, ed. *Gillo Pontecorvo's "The Battle of Algiers."* New York: Charles Scribner's Sons, 1973.

Vogel, Amos. *Film as a Subversive Art.* New York: Random House, 1974.

White, David Manning, and Averson, Richard. *The Celluloid Weapon: Social Comment in the American Film.* Boston: Beacon Press, 1972.

Zimmer, Christian. *Cinéma et Politique.* Paris: Seghers, 1974.

Chapter 2

Auric, Yan. "Françoise Bonnot: Monteuse." *Cinémonde,* 18 June 1970, p. 30.

Austen, David. "Pointing out the Problems." *Films and Filming,* June 1972, pp. 32–35.

Berman, Bruce. "A Conversation with Costa-Gavras." *Take One,* December 1973, pp. 23–26.

Bouteiller, Jean-Pierre, and Offroy, Denis. *"Section Spéciale." Cinématographe,* May–June 1975, pp. 35–37.

"Costa-Gavras: Article/Interview/Filmography—*State of Siege." Cinema* (USA), 1974, pp. 34–43.

Davis, Melton S. "Agent provocateur." *New York Times Magazine,* 21 March 1971, p. 32.

Fournier, Thérèse. "Costa-Gavras: un cinéaste qui croît en l'homme." *France Soir,* 6 February 1973.

Georgakas, Dan, and Crowdus, Gary. "Costa-Gavras talks about *Z." Cinéaste* 3 (Winter 1969–1970): 12–16.

"A German Cinema for a German People." An Interview with Heinz-Dieter Rauchendorf. *Cinéaste* 2 (1974): 40–42.

Giannaris, George. *Mikis Theodorakis: Music and Social Change.* New York: Praeger Publishers, 1972.

Hémeret, Georges. "Montand-Signoret Story." *Euro-Cinéma* 42 (March 1977).

"Des intellectuels communistes s'interrogent sur leur fonction dans le parti." *Le Monde,* 9 June 1978, p. 10.

"Des intellectuels communistes s'interrogent sur leur fonction dans le parti." *Les Nouvelles Littéraires,* 8–15 June 1978, p. 18.

"Mai '68" (Special Issue). *Impact,* May 1978, pp. 38–39.

Moritz, Charles, ed. "Costa-Gavras (Henri)." *Current Bibliography.* New York: H. W. Wilson Co., 1972, pp. 90–92.

———. "Mikis Theodorakis." *Current Bibliography.* New York: H. W. Wilson Co., 1973, pp. 409–12.

Rémond, Alain. *Yves Montand.* Paris: Editions Henri Veyrier, 1977.

Stokes, Geoffrey. "Costa-Gavras: It's Art, But Is It Politics?" *Village Voice,* 8 December 1975, pp. 103, 106.

Theodorakis, Mikis. *Journal of Resistance.* Translated by Graham Webb. New York: Coward, McCann, and Geohegan, 1973.

Urbez, Luis. "El cine político de Costa-Gavras." *Razón y Fe* 973 (February 1979): 208–13.

Yates, Penny. "Costa-Gavras: An Interview." *1000 Eyes,* December 1975, pp. 8, 20, 24.

Chapter 3

Sleeping Car Murder

Ajame, Pierre. "Premiers (faux) pas." *Les Nouvelles Littéraires,* 15 November 1965.

Billard, Pierre. "Corde raide: *Compartiment tueurs* de Costa-Gavras." *L'Express,* 15 November 1965, pp. 116–18, 121.

Bolduc, Albert. *"Compartiment tueurs." Positif,* May 1966, p. 144.

"Bonne chance à Costa-Gavras." *Cinéma '65* 94 (1965): 16–18.

Bory, Jean-Louis. *"Compartiment tueurs." Arts,* 24 November 1965.

Capdenac, Michel. "Du bon travail sur un scénario prétexte." *Les Lettres Fran-çaises,* 25 November 1965, p. 24.

———. "Yves Montand fait sa rentrée." *Les Lettres Françaises,* 18 November 1965, p. 22.

"Cathérine Allégret voyage dans le train de la mort." *Cinémonde,* 19 January 1965, p. 15.

Chapier, Henry. *"Compartiments tueurs* de Costa-Gavras." *Combat,* 19 November 1965, p. 10.

Chauvet, Louis, *"Compartiments tueurs." Le Figaro,* 18 November 1965, p. 26.

Chazal, Robert. *"Compartiment tueurs:* Couchettes surprises." *Paris-Presse,* 18 November 1965.

Clarens, Carlos. *Crime Movies: From Griffith to the* Godfather *and Beyond.* New York: W. W. Norton and Co., 1980.

"Compartiment tueurs." Cinémonde, 16 March 1965, pp. 16–17

Crowther, Bosley. *"The Sleeping Car Murder." New York Times,* 8 March 1966, p. 45.

Davis, Richard. *"The Sleeping Car Murder." Films and Filming,* December 1966, p. 52.

de Bongnie, Jean. *"Compartiment tueurs." Les Amis du Cinéma et Télévision,* January 1975, p. 40.

Earley, Steven C. "Film Noir, or Black Cinema." *An Introduction to American Movies.* New York: Mentor Books, 1978, pp. 138–45.

Emerson, William. *The Detective in Film.* Secaucus, N.J.: Citadel Press, 1972.

Eustache, Jean. *"Compartiment tueurs." Cahiers du Cinéma,* November 1965, p. 128.

Garson, Claude. *"Compartiments tueurs." L'Aurore,* 18 November 1965.

"Grace à la bande Signoret-Montand: *Compartiment tueurs." Cinémonde,* 9 November 1965, p. 21.

Grand, Odile. "Dans *Compartiment tueurs* Montand retrouve l'accent de son enfance." *L'Aurore,* 20 November 1965.

Guérif, François. *Le Film noir.* Paris: Editions Henri Veyrier, 1979.

Japrisot, Sébastien. *Compartement tueurs.* Paris: Ed. Noël, 1962.

Lachize, Samuel. "Un train rapide: *Compartiment tueurs* de Costa-Gavras." *L'Humanité,* 20 November 1965.

Leguebe, Eric. *"Compartiment tueurs." Le Parisien Libéré,* 20 November 1965, p. 6.

Martin, James Michael. *"The Sleeping Car Murder." The Film Quarterly* 3 (Spring 1968): 44–76.

Martin, Marcel. *"Compartiment tueurs." Cinéma '66,* p. 125.

Moellet, Luc. "Réussite mineure." *Cahiers du Cinéma,* July 1965, p. 67.

Paris, André. *"Compartiments tueurs." Le Soir,* 2 November 1965.

Quinson, René. "Yves Montand et Simone Signoret ont pris place dans le *Compartiments tueurs." Combat,* 21 December 1964.

Rampell, Ed. "The Politization of Film Noir." *1000 Eyes,* December 1975, p. 8.

Rochereau, Jean. *"Compartiments tueurs." La Croix,* 27 November 1965, p. 7.

Smith, Lily N. L. *"The Sleeping Car Murder." Films in Review* 4 (April 1966): 252–53.

Tuska, Jon. *The Detective in Hollywood.* Garden City, N.Y.: Doubleday & Co., 1978.

Shock Troops

Chabrol, Jean-Pierre. *Un Homme de trop.* Paris: Gallimard, 1958.

Chapier, Henry. *"Un Homme de trop* de Costa-Gavras." *Combat,* 6 April 1967, p. 8.

Charensol, Georges. *"Un Homme de trop* de Costa-Gavras." *Les Nouvelles Littéraires,* 13 April 1967.

Chauvet, Louis. *"Un Homme de trop." Le Figaro,* 7 April 1967, p. 30.

Chazal, Robert. *"Un Homme de trop." France Soir,* 8 April 1967.

de Baroncelli, Jean. *"Un Homme de trop." Le Monde,* 8 April 1967, p. 17.

de Bongnie, Jean. *"Un Homme de trop." Les Amis du Cinéma et la Télévision,* October 1967, p. 26.

Degliame-Fouche, Marcel. *Histoire de la Résistance en France.* Vol. 4. Paris: Laffont, 1976.

Deglin, Paul. *"Un Homme de trop." Ciné-Revue,* 6 April 1967, p. 29.

Ferjac, Pierre. *"Un Homme de trop." L'Information,* 15 June 1967.

Garson, Claude. *"Un Homme de trop." L'Aurore,* 6 April 1967.

Grand, Odile. "L'Homme de trop c'est Piccoli." *L'Aurore,* 11 October 1966.

Jameson, Richard T. *"Shock Troops." Film Quarterly* (Fall 1969): 55.

Lachize, Samuel. "Celui qui manque. . . . *Un Homme de trop* de Costa-Gavras." *L'Humanité,* 12 April 1967, p. 8.

Leguebe, Eric, *"Un Homme de trop." Le Parisien Libéré,* 7 April 1967, p. 6.

Nogueres, Henri (in collaboration with Marcel Degliame-Fouche). *Histoire de la Résistance.* Vols. 3 and 4. Paris: Laffont, 1972, 1976.

Paris, André. *"Un Homme de trop." Le Soir,* 25 August 1967.

Quinson, René. "Costa-Gavras tourne son second film." *Combat,* 26 September 1966, p. 9.

Rochereau, Jean. *"Un Homme de trop." La Croix,* 16 April 1967, p. 7.

Thompson, Howard, "Action Twin-Bill: *Shock Troops* [and *A Twist of Sand*]." *New York Times,* 22 February 1969, p. 36.

Tournès, Andrée. "Entretien avec Costa-Gavras." *Jeune Cinéma,* April 1969, pp. 25–29.

Vielzeuf, Aimé. *On les appellait "les bandits."* In *Histoire Veçue de la Résistance.* Geneva: Famot, 1977.

Winsten, Archer. *"Shock Troops* Bows." *New York Post,* 22 February 1969.

Yates, Penny. "Costa-Gavras." *1000 Eyes,* December 1975, pp. 8, 20, 24.

Chapter 4

Acot-Mirande, Pierre, et al. *"Z." Télécine,* March–April 1969, pp. 4–16.

Baby, Yvonne. "Entretien avec Costa-Gavras." *Le Monde,* 27 February 1969, p. 23.

Beckett, James. *Barbarism in Greece.* New York: Tower Publishing, Inc., 1970.

Bory, Jean-Louis. "*Z:* La Majusule de l'espoir." *Le Nouvel Observateur,* 10 March 1969.

Braucourt, Guy. "*Z:* Main base sur l'Etat." *Cinéma '69,* April 1969, pp. 114–16.

Brooks, Charles W. "*Z:* Politics on Film." *Commentary,* May 1970, pp. 26–30.

Canby, Vincent. "Screen: Greek Symbols." *New York Times,* 9 December 1969, p. 69.

Capdenac, Michel. "Grèce, heure Z." *Les Lettres Françaises,* 5 March 1969, p. 15.

Chapier, Henry. "Z de Costa-Gavras." *Combat,* 27 February 1969, p. 13.

Charensol, Georges. "La Machine infernale: Z par Costa-Gavras." *Les Nouvelles Littéraires,* 6 March 1969, p. 14.

Collet, Jean. "A propos de Z ou les pièges du fascisme." *Projets,* February–March 1969, pp. 29–32.

———. "Le Vrai Cinéma politique est-il un cinéma de catacombes?" *Télérama,* 29 June 1969, pp. 53–56.

Costa-Gavras (and Jorge Semprun). Z (script). *L'Avant-Scène du Cinéma,* October 1969.

Curtiss, Thomas Quinn. "Z Leaves Its Mark as Able Political Allegory." *Herald Tribune,* 1 March 1969.

d'Yvoire, Jean. "*Z.*" *Télérama,* 16 March 1969, pp. 50–52.

Elliott, Janice. "*Z.*" *New Statesman,* 28 February 1969, p. 302.

Flatley, Guy. "Movies Are Passions and My Great Passion Is Politics." *New York Times,* 11 January 1970, p. 15.

Flynn, Charles. "*Z.*" *Focus,* Spring 1970, pp. 45–46.

Galande, Olivier. "*Z.*" *Panorama Aujourd'hui,* May 1969, p. 50.

Garson, Claude. "*Z.*" *L'Aurore,* 27 February 1969.

Georgakas, Dan. "Costa-Gavras Talks." *Take One,* May–June 1969, pp. 12–13.

———. "*Z.*" *Film Society Review,* December 1969, pp. 28–35.

——— and Crowdus, Gary. "Costa-Gavras talks About Z." *Cinéaste* 3 (Winter 1969–1970): 12–16.

Gow, Gordon. "*Z.*" *Films and Filming,* December 1969, pp. 38–39.

Grelier, Robert. "Entretien avec Costa-Gavras." *La Revue du Cinéma: Image et Son,* May 1969, pp. 60–65.

Kael, Pauline. "Exiles." *New Yorker,* 13 December 1969, pp. 168–75 (passim).

Kauffmann, Stanley. "*Z.*" *The New Republic,* December 1969, pp. 22, 32.

Kaupp, Katia D. "*Z:* la vraie suite." *Le Nouvel Observateur,* 15 February 1971, pp. 32–33.

Lacarrière, Jacques. "L'Affaire Gregorios Lambrakis Qui A Inspiré le Film Z." *Journal du Show Business,* Cannes May 1969.

Lachize, Samuel. "L'Assassinat d'un deputé: Z de Costa-Gavras." *L'Humanité,* 26 February 1969, p. 8.

Langlois, Gérard. "Costa-Gavras et Jacques Perrin parlent de Z." *Les Lettres Françaises,* 26 February 1969, pp. 19–20.

Loewinger, Lawrence. "*Z.*" *Film Quarterly,* Winter 1969–1970, p. 64.

Mauriac, Claude. "*Z.*" *Le Figaro Littéraire,* 9 March 1969, pp. 10–11.

Mian, Pauline A. "Greece Since the Coup d'Etat." Foreign Affair Divisions (U.S. Government), 26 July 1972, pp. 34–35.

Millar, Gavin. "*Adalen '31* and *Z.*" *Sight and Sound,* Winter 1969–1970, pp. 47–48.

Narboni, Jean. "Le Pirée pour un homme: *Z.*" *Cahiers du Cinéma,* March 1969, pp. 54–55.

"Le nouveau film de Costa-Gavras: *Z.*" *Cinémonde,* 11 March 1969, pp. 14–15.

Passek, Jean-Loup. "Mécanisme d'un meurtre: Costa-Gavras parle de *Z.*" *Les Nouvelles Littéraires,* 27 February 1969.

Roberts, Steven. "Greece Sees Z and Gets Excited." *New York Times,* 13 January 1975, p. 6.

Salachas, Gilbert. "*Z.*" *Télérama,* 8 January 1975, pp. 10–11.

Sarris, Andrew. "Films in Focus." *Village Voice,* 11 December 1969, p. 55.

Siclier, Jacques. "*Z.*" *Télérama,* 8 January 1975, p. 31.

Simon, John. "*Z.*" *Movies into Film.* New York: Dial Press, 1971, pp. 86–90.

Sobieski, Monique. "Comment J. Perrin a produit *Z.*" *Journal du Show Business,* Cannes 1969.

Theodorakis, Mikis. *Journal of Resistance.* New York: Coward, McCann and Geoghegan, 1973.

Thirard, Paul-Louis. "Matière à reflexion: *Z.*" *Positif,* May 1969, pp. 63–65.

Tournès, Andrée. "*Z:* un film de notre temps." *Jeune Cinéma,* April 1969, pp. 21–24.

U.S. Congress, Senate Committee on Armed Services. *Nomination of William E. Colby,* 93d Congress, 1st Session, 2, 20, and 25 July 1973.

U.S. Congress, Senate Committee on Foreign Relations. *Greece: February 1971,* 92d Congress, 1st Session, 4 March 1971.

Vassilikos, Vassili. *Z.* Translated by Marilyn Calmann. New York: Ballatine Books, 1968.

Veillot, Claude. "Le Premier grand film politique français." *L'Express,* 3–9 March 1969, pp. 79–80.

Weiner, Judith. "*Z.*" *Paris Presse,* 26 March 1969.

Z. (Publicity Materials). Cinema V Distributing, Inc., New York, 1969.

Chapter 5

Arendt, Hannah. *The Origins of Totalitarianism.* New York: Harcourt, Brace and Jovanovich, 1973.

Ascherson, Neil. "Rebirth and Death in Czechoslovakia." *New York Review of Books* 16 (2 September 1961): 11–13.

"*L'Aveu.*" *Unifrance Film* 391 (1970): 2296–98.

Billard, Pierre; Cotta, Michèle; and Derogy, Jacques (Interview). "Yves Montand et Simone Signoret." *L'Express,* 11 May 1970, pp. 116–18, 121.

Bory, Jean-Louis. "Huis Clos chez Kafka." *Le Nouvel Observateur,* 27 April 1970.

Braucourt, Guy. "An Interview with Costa-Gavras and Jorge Semprun." *Film Society Review,* January 1971, pp. 43–47.

———. "*L'Aveu:* L'Anti-machiavel." *Cinéma '70,* June 1970, pp. 121–23.

———. "Costa-Gavras: Mon Témoignage." *Nouvelles Littéraires,* 30 April 1970, p. 14.

Brice, Jacques. "*L'Aveu* et le P.C." *Le Figaro Littéraire*, 11 May 1970, p. 6.

Canby, Vincent. "Montand and Signoret Star in 'Confession.'" *New York Times*, 10 December 1970, p. 58.

Capdenac, Michel. "Une Operation à coeur ouvert." *Les Lettres Françaises*, 13 May 1970, pp. 15 and 17.

Chapier, Henry. "*L'Aveu* de Costa-Gavras: Une religion trahie." *Combat*, 29 April 1970, p. 13.

Charensol, Georges. "N'Avouez jamais!" *Les Nouvelles Littéraires*, 7 May 1970.

Chatel, Nicole. "*L'Aveu*, du livre à l'ecran." *Le Monde*, 20 May 1970, p. 6.

Chazal, Robert. "*L'Aveu* hallucinant." *France-Soir*, 30 April 1970.

Chirpaz, François. "*L'Aveu* de Costa-Gavras." *Etudes*, July 1970, pp. 81–83.

Collet, Jean. "Un matraquage organisé du public." *Télérama*, 17 May 1970, pp. 54–55.

Comolli, Jean-Louis. "Film/politique (Z)—*L'Aveu*: 15 propositions." *Cahiers du Cinéma*, October 1970, pp. 48–51.

The Confession: Film Publicity. New York: Paramount Pictures, 1970.

Cournot, Michel. "Stroheim, réveille-toi, ils sont devenus fous!" *Cinémonde*, 2 June 1970, pp. 4–5.

Crist, Judith. "The Stuff and Stuffing of Heroes." *New York*, 14 December 1970, p. 70.

Curtis, Thomas Quinn. "Costa-Gavras's New Film—Not Another *Z*." *Herald Tribune*, 2 May 1970.

de Baroncelli, Jean. "*L'Aveu* de Costa-Gavras." *Le Monde*, 2 May 1970, p. 12.

Denby, David. "Stalinism on Film: *The Confession*." *Atlantic Monthly*, February 1971, p. 124.

Douin, Jean-Luc. "Montand ne joue pas." *Télérama*, 7 December 1976, pp. 26–28.

d'Yvoire, Jean. "*L'Aveu* (Dossier)." *Télécine*, May–June 1970, pp. 28–29.

Féron, Bernard, "*L'Aveu* réflète le témoignage d'Artur London." *Le Monde*, 5 February 1970, pp. 1, 12.

Fonveieille-Alquier, F. "Ce terrible *Aveu*." *Combat*, 29 April 1970, pp. 1, 4.

Galande, Olivier. "*L'Aveu*." *Panorama Aujourd'hui*. July 1970, pp. 70–71.

Gervais, Ginette. "Entretien avec Costa-Gavras." *Jeune Cinéma*, June–July 1970, pp. 3–5.

Goodman, Mark. "Dialectic Inferno." *Time*, 4 January 1971, p. 59.

Grelier, Robert. "Entretien avec Costa-Gavras, Jorge Semprun et Artur London." *La Revue du Cinéma: Image et Son*, June–July 1970, pp. 101–11.

Haquet, Charles. "Un Film intervient dans les débat." *Le Figaro*, 11 May 1970, p. 7.

Hart, Henry. "*The Confession*." *Films in Review*, January 1971, pp. 41–42.

Haustrate, Gaston, "*L'Aveu*: Un film." *Témoignage Chrétien*, 7 May 1970.

Kael, Pauline. "Stalinism." *New Yorker*, 12 December 1971, pp. 172–77.

Kauffmann, Stanley. "*The Confession*." *The New Republic*, 19 December 1970, pp. 16, 24.

Langlois, Gérard. "Costa-Gavras: *L'Aveu*—un film sans 'carré blanc.'" *Les Lettres Françaises*, 22 April 1970, pp. 16–17.

Leites, Nathan, and Bernaut, Elsa. *The Ritual of Liquidation.* Glencoe, Ill.: The Free Press, 1954.

Lewis, Flora. *The Man Who Disappeared: The Strange History of Noel Field.* London: Arthur Barker, 1965.

Liehm, Antonin. *Le Passé présent: Le socialisme oriental face au monde moderne.* Paris: J. C. Lattes, 1974.

Limoursin, Jean. "*L'Aveu* de Costa-Gavras." *Valeurs Actuelles,* 18 May 1970, pp. 52–53.

Loebl, Eugen. *Stalinism in Prague: The Loebl Story.* New York: Grove Press, 1971.

London, Artur, *L'Aveu.* Paris: Gallimard, 1968.

―――. *The Confession.* Translated by Alastair Hamilton. New York: William Morrow, 1970.

McFadden, Patrick. "*The Confession:* Con." *Film Society Review,* January 1971, pp. 35–40.

Marengo, Jacques. "*L'Aveu.*" *Cinéma* 8 (1970): 29–30.

Marker, Chris. *Le Fond de l'air est rouge.* Paris: François Maspero. 1978.

Matern, Hermann. *Uber die Durchführung des Beschlusses des ZK der SED: Lehren aus dem Prozess gegen das Verschwörerzentrum Slansky.* Berlin: Dietz Verlag, 1953.

Maulnier, Thierry. "'L'Aveu' et les complexes de la doite." *Le Figaro,* 17 June 1970, p. 1.

Mauriac, Claude. "*L'Aveu* de Costa-Gavras: une machine broyeuse d'hommes." *Le Figaro Littéraire,* 18–24 May 1970, pp. 36–37.

―――. "Les films et la politique de 'l'Aveu' à 'l'effet Z' . . ." *Le Figaro Littéraire,* 17–23 August 1970, pp. 30–31.

Maurin, François. "*L'Aveu* de Costa-Gavras." *L'Humanité,* 29 April 1970, p. 8.

Mazars, Pierre. "*L'Aveu.*" *Le Figaro,* 4 May 1970, p. 30.

Medvedec, Roy. *Let History Judge: The Origins and Consequences of Stalinism.* New York: Alfred Knopf, 1971.

Mellen, Joan. "Artur London and Costa-Gavras: The Politics of *The Confession.*" *Cinéaste,* Winter 1970–71, pp. 25–32.

Mohrt, Michel. "Au paradis des bourreaux." *Carrefour,* 13 May 1970, p. 20.

O'Brien, Glenn. "Inter/VIEW with Costa-Gavras, Yves Montand and Jorge Semprun." *Interview,* March 1971, pp. 18–20.

Prokosch, Mike. "*The Confession.*" *Film Quarterly,* Summer 1971, pp. 54–56.

Reguilhem, Marcel. "*L'Aveu:* tardif." *Réforme,* 9 May 1970.

Rémond, Alain. *Yves Montand.* Paris: Editions Henri Veyrier, 1977.

Rochereau, Jean. "*L'Aveu:* Le Stalinisme en question." *La Croix,* 10–11 May 1970, p. 13.

Rubenstein, Len. "*The Confession:* Background." *Film Society Review.* January 1971, pp. 25–27.

Signoret, Simone. *Nostalgia Isn't What It Used To Be.* London: Granada Publishing, 1979.

Sragow, Michael. "*The Confession:* Pro." *Film Society Review,* January 1971, pp. 27–35.

Suffert, Georges. "*L'Aveu* gène le P.C." *L'Express,* 11 May 1970, p. 53.

Sweeney, Louise. "An Interview with Costa-Gavras, Director of *The Confession.*" *Christian Science Monitor,* 26 January 1971, p. 9.

Tallenay, Jean-Louis. "Des Faits garantis par un témoin." *Télérama,* 17 May 1970, pp. 54–55.

P. L. Thirard. "*L'Aveu.*" *Positif,* September 1970, pp. 60–63.

Tigrid, Pavel. *Le Printemps de Prague.* Paris: Editions du Seuil, 1968.

Vigo, André. "Le Terrible *Aveu* de Costa-Gavras." *L'Aurore,* 29 April 1970.

Westerbeck, Colin L. "*The Confession.*" *Commonwealth,* 5 March 1971, pp. 548–49.

Wilson, David. "*L'Aveu.*" *Sight and Sound,* Winter 1970–1971, pp. 49–50.

Chapter 6

Allombert, Guy. "*Etat de Siège.*" *La Revue du Cinéma,* April 1973, pp. 118–19.

Arnold, Gary. "AFI Bars Screening of 'Siege.'" *Washington Post,* 30 March 1973, Section C, pp. 1 and 7.

———. "AFI: New Home, No 'Siege.'" *Washington Post,* Section M, pp. 1–2.

Baumbach, Jonathan. "Medium and Message: *State of Siege.*" *Partisan Review* 3 (1973):445–47.

Bechtold, Claude. "*Etat de Siège* de l'honnêteté." *Cinématographe,* April–May 1973, p. 11.

Bernard, Hugh. "*State of Siege.*" *Films in Review,* June–July 1973, pp. 373–74.

Biskind, Peter. "*State of Siege.*" *Film Quarterly,* Fall 1973, pp. 51–54.

Bonitzer, Pascal and Toubiana, Serge. "*Etat de siège.*" *Cahiers du Cinéma,* April–June 1973, pp. 49–54.

Bory, Jean-Louis. "Un bourreau bien tranquille." *Nouvel Observateur,* 19 February 1973.

Canby, Vincent. "'Siege': An Angry Muckraker." *New York Times,* 22 April 1973, p. 11.

———. "*State of Siege.*" *New York Times,* 14 April 1973, p. 39.

Chauvet, Louis. "*Etat de Siège.*" *Le Figaro,* 10 February 1973, p. 29.

Chew, Peter T. "Dan Mitrione's Legacy." *National Observer,* 2 August 1971.

Cluny, Claude Michel. "*Etat de Siège.*" *Cinéma '73,* March 1973, pp. 152–53.

Cocks, Jay. "Spurious Suspense: *State of Siege.*" 23 April 1973, p. 69.

Costa, Omar. *Los Tupamaros.* Mexico: Ed. Era, 1971.

Costa-Gavras and Solinas, Franco. *State of Siege.* Translated by Brooke Leveque and Raymond Rosenthal. New York: Ballantine, 1973.

———. *Etat de Siège.* Paris: Stock, 1973.

"Costa-Gavras' *State of Siege.*" *Films and Filming,* August 1973, pp. 18–19.

Crist, Judith. "Production Politic." *New York,* 16 April 1973, pp. 86–87.

"Dan A. Mitrione," *Weekly Compilation of Presidential Documents,* Week Ending Saturday, 15 August 1970, p. 1044.

de Baroncelli, Jean. "*Etat de Siège* de Costa-Gavras." *Le Monde,* 10 February 1973, p. 25.

Declassified Telegrams: Correspondence between U.S. Government (Department of State) and U.S. Embassy in Montevideo, 1–10 August 1970.

Denby, David. "Guerrillas without Ideas." *Dissent,* Fall 1973, pp. 480–82.

Ehrmann, Hans. "Solinas Shows Script to Chile's Reds, Who Thereupon Rap Costa-Gavras." *Variety*, 21 June 1972, p. 3.

Eskin, Stanley G. "High Level Politics in the Cinema." *Midstream*, August–September 1973, pp. 67–71.

"*Etat de Siège:* Dossier." *Télécine*, March 1973, pp. 4–10.

Etat de Siège. Unifrance Dossier, no. 458 (March 1973).

Flacon, Michel. "Les vrais dossiers de l'écran." *Le Point*, 5 February 1973, pp. 62–63.

Fournier, Thérèse. "Costa-Gavras: un cinéaste qui croît en l'homme." *France-Soir*, 6 February 1973.

Gilliatt, Penelope. "The Poor Don't Care What They Look Like." *The New Yorker*, 14 April 1973, pp. 141–44.

Gilio, Maria Esther. *The Tupamaro Guerrillas*. Translated by Anne Edmondson. New York: Saturday Review Press, 1972.

Gilson, Gary. "Interview with Costa-Gavras." *Film and History*, May 1973, pp. 11–20.

Grelier, Robert. "Entretien avec Costa-Gavras et Franco Solinas." *La Revue du cinéma: Image et Son*, April 1973, pp. 92–99.

Gussow, Mel. "Costa-Gavras Elaborates on Politics and Violence." *New York Times*, 14 April 1973, p. 39.

Hardt, Hubert. "*Etat de Siège.*" *Amis du Film et de la Télévision*, May–June 1973, pp. 8–9.

Herman, Rick. "*State of Siege.*" *Movietone News*, April 1974, pp. 27–32.

"Human Rights in Uruguay and Paraguay." *Hearings before the Subcommittee on International Organizations of the Committee on International Relations, House of Representatives*, 17 June, 10–27, 28 July and 4 August 1976.

Isaacs, Stephen, and Zito, Tom. "The Continuing 'Siege' of AFI." *Washington Post*, 4 April 1983, Section E, pp. 1 and 5.

Jeancolas, Jean-Pierre. "Fonction du témoignage (les années 1939–1945 dans le cinéma de l'après-guerre)." *Positif*, June 1975, pp. 45–60.

Julien, Claude. *L'Empire américain*. Paris: Grasset, 1968.

Kalishman, Harold. "*State of Siege:* Persuading the Already Persuaded." *Cinéaste* 2 (1974): 36–39.

————, and Crowdus, Gary. "A Film Is like a Match, You can Make a Big Fire or Nothing At All." *Cinéaste* 1 (1973): 2–7.

Kauffmann, Stanley. "*State of Siege.*" *New Republic*, 5 May 1973, p. 24.

Kelly, Kevin. "*State of Siege;* Frightening—But Should Not Be Missed." *The Boston Globe*, 4 May 1973.

"Kennedy Center Drops Disputed Film." *New York Times*, 30 March 1973, p. 33.

Klemesrud, Judy. "Costa-Gavras: 'I'm Not Anti-American.'" *New York Times*, 22 April 1973, Section D, pp. 9, 31.

Kopkind, Andrew. "Which State? Which Siege?" *Ramparts*, August–September 1973, pp. 45–46.

Labrousse, Alain. *The Tupamaros*. Harmondsworth, England: Penguin, 1973.

Landau, Jon. "Disappointing Sequel to Z." *Rolling Stone*, 21 June 1973, pp. 70–71.

Langguth, A. J. *Hidden Terrors*. New York: Pantheon Books, 1978.

Lefever, Ernest W. "Hypnotic Lies about Terrorists." *Sunday Star and Daily News,* 1 July 1973.

Loeb, James L. "'Siege'—McCarthyism from the Left." *New York Times,* 6 May 1973, Section 2, pp. 1 and 13.

Mader, Julius. *Who's Who in the CIA.* Berlin: Mader, 1968.

Martin, Marcel. *"Etat de Siège." Ecran '73,* March 1973, pp. 59–60.

————. "Le Géometre et le poète: *Etat de Siège." Cinéma Pratique,* April 1973, pp. 68–69.

Mauriac, Claude. "Costa-Gavras en Amérique du Sud." *L'Express,* 5 February 1973, p. 56.

Max, Alphonse. *Tupamaros—A Pattern for Urban Guerrilla Warfare in Latin America.* The Hague: International Documentation and Information Center, 1970.

Mayans, Ernesto. *Tupamaros, Antología documental.* Cuernavaca, Mexico: Centro Intercultural de Documentación, 1971.

Mercader, Antonio, and de Vera, Jorge. *Tupamaros: estrategia y acción.* Mexico City, Editorial Omego, 1971.

Mitrione News Items 1–10 August 1970 in *El Diario* and *El Día.* (Montevideo).

Montaigne, Pierre. "Costa-Gavras: Un film-regard sur l'Amérique latine." *LeFigaro,* 17 March 1972, p. 30.

Niedergang, Marcel. "Un Entretien avec Costa-Gavras: Les raccourcis historiques de l'*Etat de Siège." Le Monde,* 2 February 1973, p. 13.

Nuñez, Carlos. *The Tupamaros.* New York: Times Change Press, 1972.

Paslawsky, Sonia. "The Scandal of *State of Siege." Macguffin* (University of Illinois). May–June 1973, pp. 21–22.

Riding, Alan. "Cuban 'Agent' Says U.S. Police Aides Urged Torture." *New York Times,* 5 August 1978, p. 3.

Rochereau, Jean. *"Etat de Siège:* Le Sang appelle le sang." *La Croix,* 18 February 1973, p. 18.

"Rogers among Mourners as Mitrione Is Buried." *New York Times,* 14 August 1970.

R.T.J. *"State of Siege." Movietone News,* March 1973, pp. 29–30.

Safire, William. *Safire's Political Dictionary.* New York: Ballantine, 1978.

Sarris, Andrew. *"State of Siege." Politics and Cinema.* New York: Columbia University Press, 1978.

Shales, Tom. "Gavras: Artisan or Partisan?" *Washington Post,* 6 April 1973, Section B, pp. 1 and 13.

Solinas, PierNico. "Costa-Gavras: Article, Interview, Filmography—*State of Siege." Cinema* (USA) 34 (1974):34–43.

Sorensen, Theodore C. "'State of Siege' Speaks 'A Warning to Us All.'" *New York Times,* 24 June 1973, p. 15.

State of Siege. Press Material from Cinema V (New York), 1973.

"State of Siege Termed 'Unjust?'" *New York Times,* 19 April 1973, p. 48.

Sterling, Claire. *The Terror Network: The Secret War of International Terrorism.* New York: Holt, Rinehart & Winston, 1981.

Tallenay, Jean-Louis. *"Etat de Siège:* Pourquoi les Tupamaros ont-ils enlevé cet Américain bien tranquille?" *Télérama,* 10 February 1973, pp. 68–69.

Tallmer, Jerry. "Costa-Gavras: After 'Z' Comes . . ." *New York Post*, 14 April 1973, p. 15.

Unifrance: Dossiers Portraits—Costa-Gavras, no. 453 (December 1972).

United States Government Manual 1978–1979. (Washington, D.C.: Office of the Federal Register, 1978.)

Weinstein, Martin. *The Politics of Failure.* Westport, Conn.: Greenwood Press, 1975.

Westerbeck, Colin L. "The Screen." *Commonwealth,* 25 May 1973, pp. 228–89.

Wilson, Carlos. *The Tupamaros: The Unmentionables.* Boston: Branden Press, 1974.

Wilson, David. *"State of Siege." Sight and Sound.* Autumn 1973, p. 238.

Wooten, James T. "Capital Film Festival Opens to Dispute." *New York Times,* 4 April 1973, p. 4.

Yglesias, José. "Did Sorensen Face Facts?" *New York Times,* 15 July 1973, p. 9.

Zimmerman, Paul. "Dirty Yankees." *Newsweek,* 23 April 1973, p. 106.

Zito, Tom. "AFI and the Aftermath of *'Siege.'*" *Washington Post,* 3 April 1973, Section B, pp. 1–2.

———. "AFI Dedication: Warner Absent." *Washington Post,* 5 April 1973, Section B, pp. 1 and 17.

Chapter 7

Annaud, Monique. "Jacques Perrin: Pour une participation financière des réalisateurs." *Film Français,* 4 April 1975, pp. 8–9.

Batifoulier, Christian. "Les hermines tachées de sang." *Télérama,* 29 December 1976, pp. 20–21.

Bazin, André. *Le Cinéma de l'Occupation et de la Résistance.* Paris: Union Générale d'éditions, 1975.

Béhar, Henri. *"Section Spéciale." La Revue du Cinéma.* June–July 1975, pp. 112–16.

Benoît, Claude. *"Section Spéciale." Jeune Cinéma,* May–June 1975, pp. 30–32.

Bernet, Philippe. *"Section Spéciale:* Costa-Gavras divise la magistrature." *L'Aurore,* 21 April 1975.

Bory, Jean-Louis. "Performance en cascade." *Nouvel Observateur,* 21 April 1975.

Boucher, Philippe. "L'équation de la raison d'Etat." *Le Monde,* 24 April 1975, p. 19.

Bouteillier, Jean-Pierre, and Ofroy, Denis. "Costa-Gavras." *Cinématographe,* June 1975, pp. 35–37.

Canby, Vincent. " 'Special Section' by Costa-Gavras Arrives." *New York Times,* 8 December 1975, p. 42.

Chapier, Henry. *"Section Spéciale:* Un vaudeville politique." *Quotidien de Paris,* 24 April 1975.

Chazal, Robert. *"Section Spéciale:* La déraison d'Etat." *France Soir,* 24 April 1975.

Cocks, Jay. "Blind Injustice: *Special Section." Time,* 8 December 1975, p. 72.

Colpart, Gilles. *"Section Spéciale." Télécine,* June 1975, pp. 16–17.

"Critique ouverte sur *Section Spéciale." Jeune Cinéma,* September–October 1975, pp. 28–33.

de Baroncelli, Jean. "*Section Spéciale* de Costa-Gavras." *Le Monde*, 25 April 1975, p. 33.

de Bolzer, Guy. "*Section Spéciale:* Est-ce encore possible?" *Le Figaro*, 13 April 1975, p. 32.

Deglin, Paul. "*Section Spéciale.*" *Ciné Revue*, 24 April 1975, pp. 10–11.

Demby, Betty Jeffries. "Costa-Gavras Discusses 'Special Section.'" *Filmmakers Newsletter*, February 1976, pp. 28–32.

Douin, Jean-Louis. "*Section Spéciale*—L'Occupation Vue par Costa-Gavras." *Télérama*, 29 January 1975, pp. 60–62.

Fournier, Thérèse. "Costa-Gavras: 'Pour moi le festival est une tribune.'" *France Soir*, 13 May 1975.

Gallo, Max. "Costa-Gavras face à Vichy." *L'Express*, 24 April 1975, pp. 26–28.

Gauteur, Claude. "Semprun: *Section Spéciale* est un film anti-rétro." *Film Français*, 4 April 1975, p. 9.

Gevaudan, Frantz. "*Section Spéciale.*" *Cinéma '75*, May 1975, pp. 117–18.

Grisolia, Michel. "*Section Spéciale.*" *Nouvel Observateur*, 28 April 1975.

Grosser, Alfred. "L'Evocation du passé." *Le Monde*, 24 April 1975, pp. 1 and 15.

Hennebelle, Guy. "A propos d'Yves Boisset et de Costa-Gavras." *Ecran '75*, July–August 1975, pp. 14–15.

Kael, Pauline. "Political Acts." *New Yorker*, 15 December 1975, pp. 89–90.

Kroll, Jack. "Kangaroo Justice." *Newsweek*, 15 December 1975, pp. 94–95.

Marmin, Michel. "*Section Spéciale*, film de Costa-Gavras." *Valeurs Actuelles*, 21 April 1975, p. 59.

Martin, Marcel. "Degoûts et des couleurs." *Ecran '75*, May 1975, pp. 12–13.

Mohrt, Michel. "*Section Spéciale* de Costa-Gavras: Une tragédie sobre." *Le Figaro*, 25 April 1975, p. 28.

Mosk. "*Special Section.*" *Variety*, 14 May 1975, p. 27.

Moussorgsky, Modeste Petrovich. *Boris Godunov* (Libretto). New York: Edwin F. Kalmus, n.d.

Paxton, Robert. *Vichy France: Old Guard and New Order, 1940–1944.* New York: Alfred A. Knopf, 1972.

Powell, Ann. "Costa-Gavras: Beyond Journalism." *Soho Weekly News*, 11 December 1975, p. 30.

Rémond, Alain. "De bons mots en répliques cinglantes on oublie l'essentiel." *Télérama*, 23 April 1975, p. 67.

Rich, Frank. "Costa-Gavras, Vichy and Watergate." *New York Post*, 13 December 1975, pp. 14, 40.

Rochereau, Jean. "*Section Spéciale:* La Honte et le chagrin." *La Croix*, 3 May 1975, p. 10.

Schwartz, Nancy L. "Diplomatic Pouches in Kangaroo Courts." *The Soho Weekly*, 11 December 1975, pp. 30–31.

Section Spéciale. Unifrance Dossier. no. 506 (May 1975).

Simon, John. "Overblown, But Not Blown Over." *New York*, 8 December 1975, pp. 107–9.

Special Section. Press Material from Universal Studios (California).

Tallenay, Jean-Louis. "Le rappel nécessaire d'une arithmétique funèbre." *Télérama*, 23 April 1975, p. 66.

Toubiana, Serge. ". . . mais qui raisonne: *Les Ordres, Section Spéciale.*" *Cahiers du Cinéma,* July–August 1975, pp. 42–47.

Villeré, Hervé. *L'Affaire de la Section Spéciale.* Paris: Arthème Fayard, 1973.

Chapter 8

Ansen, David. "A Partisan Director." *Newsweek,* 22 February 1982, p. 69.

———. "Politics on Celluloid." *Newsweek,* 22 February 1982, pp. 68–70.

Berger, Alan. "Were US hands dirty in Chilean murder?" *Boston Globe,* 28 February 1982, pp. A 32–35.

Birns, Laurence, ed. *The End of Chilean Democracy.* New York: Seabury Press, 1973.

Blowen, Michael. "'My politics are simple.'" *Boston Sunday Globe,* 7 February 1982, Arts & Films, pp. 49, 55.

Bonomo, Jacques. "Choc au festival: le film qui a secoué l' Amérique," *Le Figaro Magazine,* 161 (15–21 May 1982): 98–100.

Boorstein, Edward. *Allende's Chile: An Inside View.* New York: International Publishers, 1977.

Canby, Vincent. "Costa-Gavras's Striking Cinematic Achievement." *New York Times,* 14 February 1982, Arts & Leisure, pp. D19, 42.

———. "Screen: 'Missing' by Costa-Gavras." *New York Times,* 12 February 1982, p. C14.

Clarke, Gerald. "*Missing:* Fact or Fabrication?" *Time,* 8 March 1982, p. 96.

Cockburn, Alexander. "The Uses of Hersh." *Village Voice,* 10–16 February 1982, p. 10ff.

Connelly, Christopher. "Sissy Spacek and Jack Lemmon: Actors Playing Real-life Roles." *Rolling Stone,* 13 May 1982, pp. 16–17.

Cortazar, Julio. "*Missing:* Porté disparu. . . ." *Il Faut Lire* (Québec), 1 May 1982, pp. 8–9.

"Costa-Gavras: *Missing.*" Publicity material in *Universal News,* 5 January 1982.

Cusack, David. *Revolution and Reaction: The Internal Dynamics of Conflict and Confrontation in Chile.* Monograph Series in World Affairs, vol. 14. Denver: University of Colorado, 1977.

Devarrieux, Claire. "La gloire discrète de Costa-Gravas," *Le Monde,* 13 May 1982, pp. 16–17.

Garrett, Robert. "Costa-Gavras: 'A game between hope and death.'" *Boston Herald American,* 14 February 1982, p. B4.

Giesbert, Franz-Olivier and Josselin, Jean-François. "L'Amérique sans peur, avec reproche: Un entretien avec Costa-Gavras." *Nouvel Observateur,* 914 (15–21 May 1982): 96–99.

Gleiberman, Owen. "Innocents Abroad." *Boston Phoenix,* 16 February 1982, Section 3, pp. 4, 14.

Globe Wire Service. "U.S. Shares Cannes Prize." *Boston Globe,* 27 May 1982, p. 34.

Greensberg, Peter S. "Arts, Lies and Reality: An Interview with Costa-Gavras." *Rolling Stone,* 13 May 1982, p. 15.

Hall, Carla. "The Debate Over 'Missing.'" *Washington Post,* 11 February 1982, pp. D1, 16.

Hatch, Robert. *"Quest for Fire, Missing."* Nation, 20 February 1982, pp. 218–20.

Hauser, Thomas. *Missing.* New York: Avon, 1982.

Kael, Pauline. "Carry Your Own Matches." *New Yorker,* 8 March 1982, pp. 114–27.

Kaplan, Peter W. "'Missing': The Search & the Sorrow." *Washington Post,* 7 March 1982, pp. G1, 5, 6.

Kart, Larry. "Another Controversy for Film's Nonaggressive Good Guy." *Chicago Tribune,* 14 March 1982, Section 6, pp. 5–7.

Kauffmann, Stanley. "What's Missing is Costa-Gavras." *New Republic,* 10 March 1982, pp. 24–26.

Kernan, Michael. "Jack Lemmon's Carefully Packaged Pandemonium." *Washington Post,* 7 March 1982, pp. G1, 4, 5.

Kopkind, Andrew. "'Missing': Cultural Battlefield." *Nation,* 17 April 1982, pp. 466–69.

Kouchner, Bernard. *"Missing* ou le refus de l'oubli." *Le Matin Magazine,* 15 May 1982, p. 11.

Lewis, Flora. "New Film by Costa-Gavras Examines the Chilean Coup." *New York Times,* 7 February 1982, Arts and Leisure, pp. 1, 26.

Lucier, Virginia. "'Missing' one of year's best films." *Middlesex News* (Framingham, MA), 12 February 1982, p. 6B.

———. "'Z' director back with another gripping story." *Middlesex News* (Framingham, MA), 31 January 1982, pp. 10B, 11B.

Maillet, Dominique. "Un film politique doit être populaire: Une Interview de Costa-Gavras." *Première,* May 1982, pp. 55, 56, 127, 128.

Montaigne, Pierre. *"Missing:* l'événement attendu." *Le Figaro,* 19 May 1982, p. 28.

Orrego Vicuña, Francisco. *Chile: The Balanced View.* Santiago: University of Chile, 1975.

Petras, James and Morely, Morris. *The United States and Chile: Imperialism and the Overthrow of the Allende Government.* New York: Monthly Review Press, 1975.

Rojas Sandford, Robinson. *The Murder of Allende and the End of the Chilean Way to Socialism.* Translated by Andrée Conrad. New York: Harper & Row, 1975.

Sarris, Andrew. "The Father, the Son, and the Holy Revolution (I)." *Village Voice,* 23 February 1982, p. 45.

Sobel, Lester A., ed. *Chile & Allende.* New York: Facts on File, 1974.

Stern, Alan. "Costa-Gavras Covers Up." *Boston Phoenix,* 16 February 1982, Section 3, pp. 4, 16.

White, Judy, ed. *Chile's Days of Terror.* New York: Pathfinder Press, 1974.

Wood, Michael. "In Search of the Missing." *American Film,* March 1982, p. 39.

Yakir, Dan. "'Missing' in Action." *Film Comment,* March–April 1982, pp. 57–59.

Clair de Femme, Conclusions and Epilogue

Gary, Romain. *Clair de Femme.* Paris: Gallimard, 1977.

Hatch, Robert. *"Clair de Femme, Hide in Plain Sight, A Small Circle of Friends."* Nation, 5 April 1980, p. 410.

Insdorf, Annette, "Costa-Gavras Explores the Politics of the Heart." *New York Times,* Arts and Leisure, 27 May 1979, pp. 13, 19.

McCabe, Bruce. "Costa-Gavras presents: A Romance." *Boston Globe,* 23 August 1981, p. 7.

Robelli, Franca. "A Colloquio con Costa-Gavras, un regista scomodo: 'sono contro il potere perché il potere è contro la dignitá.'" *Epoca,* 3 May 1978, pp. 68–71.

Index

ABC Nightline, 252 n.1
Académie Française, 137
Académie Goncourt, 189
Action Française, 198
Adair, Charles W., 148
Advise and Consent, 22
Affaire Dreyfus, L', 22, 138. *See also* Dreyfus Affair
Affaire de la Section Spéciale, L', 188, 190–93, 197–99, 210, 214
Agee, Philip, 173
Agency for International Development (AID): and Alliance for Progress, 174; Costa-Gavras researches, 154; criticism of, 167, 174; in film (*State of Siege*), 158, 164; in Greece, 78; and International Police Academy, 174; in Latin America, 99; 154, 156, 220; locations of offices for, 150, 183; and Mitrione, 148, 149, 152, 179, 182–85, 187; officials, 87, 148, 158, 182, 185, 187, 248 n.14; mentioned, 33–34, 143, 152
Agnew, Spiro, 99, 101
Aims of Education, 237
Ajame, Pierre, 61
Ajar, Emile, 48
Albatross, The, 23
Albee, Edward, 23
Alès (*Shock Troops* location), 68
Alexander Nevsky, 65, 107
Algeria: war in, 19, 36, 153; and Z, 23, 42, 45, 88–89, 98, 113, 245 n.14
Algiers, 89, 104
All the King's Men, 103
All the President's Men, 25, 41
Allégret, Cathérine, 49, 52, 57
Allégret, Yves, 32, 48, 57
Allende, Salvador, 157–58, 220–21, 227. *See also* Chile
Allende Regime (government), 217–20, 225 (in *Missing*), 228–29

Alliance for Progress, 167, 174, 180
Allombert, Guy, 179
Altman, Robert, 222
Amana, Harry, 162
Ambitieuse, L', 32
"America in Insurrection" (*State of Siege* song), 171
American Days, 222
American Film Institute (AFI), 35, 185, 250 n.64
American Health Organization, 163
American Institute for Free Labor Development, 163
American Jewish Point Distribution Committee, 133
Amerikan (original *State of Siege* title), 156
"Amicale" group, 141
Amis du Film et de la Télévision, 170
Amnesty International, 182
Anatomy of a Murder, The, 82
"Anatomy of a Political Assassination" (original Z subtitle), 99
Anderson, Lindsay, 186
Andersson, Bibi, 42
And Justice for All, 25
Andrieu, (French Communist Party), 137
Angel, The, 76
Angèle, 32
Anouilh, Jean, 203
Anti-Semitism, 84, 115; in *Confession*, 113–34, 189; in Z, 85
Antonio das Mortes, 26–27
Appeal of Stockholm, 43, 121
Arab world, 34–35, 89, 185
Aragon, Louis, 43, 88, 137
Arbenz (administration), 144
Areco, Jorge Pacheo, 148, 164
Arendt, Hannah, 133–34
Argentina, 27, 82, 154, 163, 222, 252 n.1

Aristophanes, 98
Armée des ombres, L', 208
Armstrong, John A., 134
Arnoul, Françoise, 113
Arnovich, Ricardo, 222
Artigas, José, 151
Artuccio, Doctor, 249 n.34
Astruc, Alexandre, 72
Athens (Greece), 29–30, 33, 47, 76, 78, 83–84, 89,
    96, 101, 104, 144
Atlantic Monthly, 124
Attentat, L', 146, 203
"Au Clair de la Lune," 204
Auschwitz (concentration camp), 26
Autobiographie de Federico Sanchez, L', 44
Aveu, L'. See The Confession
Aveu: Dans l'engrenage du procès de Slansky, L'
    (book), 112
Avghi (Dawn, Lambrakis's party newspaper), 98
Aymoré, Artur, 152

Baby, Yvonne, 99
Baie des anges, La, 32
Baldwin, James, 242 n.10
Balkan Games, 78
Baltimore Sun, 154
Baptism of Fire, 35
Bardesio, Nelson, 42, 152, 167, 249 n.34
Baroncelli, Jean de, 72, 138, 211
Barrage contre le Pacifique, Un, 45
Barren Lives (Vidas secas), 27
Barthélmy, Joseph (justice minister), 190, 196,
    200, 202
Bastard, Emile/René, 190, 191, 198, 203, 204
Bastard, Pauline, 200
Battle of Algiers, The, 19, 21, 22, 146, 151
Battle of Chile, The, 219
Bay of Pigs, 228
Beatty, Warren, 26
Beauvoir, Simone de, 48
Becker, Jean, 32
Becket, 203
Before the Revolution, 24
Behan, Brendan, 96
Belgium, 43, 170
Belgrade (Yugoslavia), 121
Bellocchio, Marco, 24–25
Belloyannis, Nikos, 89
Belo Horizonte (Brazil), 149, 165
Benjamin, René, 189
Bennent, Heinz, 197
Benoît, Claude, 211
Benon, Michel, 197
Berger, Alan, 232–33
Bergman, Ingmar, 42, 94

Beria, Lavrenty, 41, 107, 110, 115, 120, 124
Berkeley, University of California at, 17
Berlin (Germany), 61
Bernard, Hugh, 181, 186
Bernstein, Carl, 25, 40
Bertolucci, Bernardo, 24, 135
Besançon (France), 19
Beumelburg, Walter (major), 193
Bibault, René, 68, 71–72
Bicycle Thieves, 22
Bideau, Jean-Luc, 160, 166
Bidegain, Raúl, 165
Billancourt Film Studio, 45, 127, 207
Billy Jack, 20
Biskind, Peter, 169, 181
Björnstrand, Gunnar, 42
Black Cinema. *See* Film Noir
Black Panthers, 105
Black September militants, 179
Blain, Gérard, 62, 68
Blood of the Condor, 27
Blue, James, 32, 242 n.7
Blue Collar, 26
Bogart, Humphrey, 37
Bois de la Deule Park (Lille), 116
Boisset, Yves, 23, 44, 83, 146, 203, 212
Bolivia, 27, 42
Bolshevism, 106–8, 190. *See also* Communist
    Party
Bolshoi Ballet, 79, 85, 97
Bond, James (films), 33, 61
Bonitzer, Pascal, 179
Bonnot, Françoise, 47; editing of, 45–46, 95, 104,
    127–29, 136, 170, 206–7, 222–23, 238
Boris Godunov, 196, 199–200, 204, 208
Bory, Jean-Louis, 59, 103–4, 178
Boskakov, Vladimir, 141
Boston (Massachusetts), 29
Boston Globe, 181, 232
Boston Herald American, 231
Bouise, Jean, 49, 87, 114, 119, 123, 137, 194, 198,
    203, 238
Boukarin, Nikolay, 107
Bouquet, Mount (France), 68
Bozzufi, Marcel, 49, 85, 91
Bragelonne, Bob de, 84
Brando, Marlon, 55, 161
Brass Target, 27
Brasseur, Claude, 63
Bray, Charles, 179
Brazil, 82, 104, 146, 149, 152, 155, 158–60, 165,
    170–71, 178, 183–84
Breathless, 48
Bréchet, André, 190–91, 193, 198, 200
Brecht, Bertold, 18, 122, 126, 169, 213, 224, 238

Brel, Jacques, 43
Brezhnev, Leonid, 130
Brialy, Jean-Claude, 67
Bride Wore Black, The, 48, 202
Britain. *See* England
Brno (Czechoslovakia), 141
Broken Blossoms, 185
Brookings Institute (Washington, D.C.), 179
Brooks, Charles W., 103
Brouer, Jerry, 158
Brouze-les-Alès (*Shock Troops* location), 68
Brubaker, 25
Brustlein, Gilbert, 193
Brute Force, 103
B series films, 37, 54
Buchenwald (concentration camp), 44
Bulgaria, 88, 107–8, 112, 141
Bullitt, 55
Burn! (Quemada), 146
Burton, Richard, 161
Butor, Michel, 80

Café Flore, 48
Cagney, James, 37
Cahiers du Cinéma, 60, 103
Calchakis, Los (orchestra), 171–72
Cambridge (Massachusetts), 220
Camus, Albert, 136
Camus, Marcel, 90
Canby, Vincent: criticism of *Confession* by, 128–29; of *Missing,* 234; of *Special Section,* 201, 213; of *State of Siege,* 168–70, 180; of *Z,* 103
Candide, 48
Cannes Film Festival, 23, 34, 104, 113, 114, 212, 253 n.29
Canon, Fraternité, Le, 61
Capa, Robert, 124
Capdenac, Michel, 59, 104, 138
Capelonis (lieutenant), 105
"Capitaine Jean," 68
Capote, Truman, 19
Capra, Frank, 32, 61
Captain Blood, 30
Carabiniers, Les, 48
Cardiff, Jack, 58
Cardinal, Pierre, 31
Car Wash, 222
Cassenti, Frank, 23
Cayatte, André, 23, 52
Cayrol, Jean, 41, 147
Central Committee of the Communist Party (in U.S.S.R.), 44, 107, 109–10
Centre National du Cinéma, 89
Cercle rouge, Le, 208
Cervoni, Albert, 139

César et Rosalie, 43
Cevennes Massif (*Shock Troops* location), 62, 67–69
Chabrol, Jean Pierre, 61–62, 65, 67–72
Chapier, Henry, 60, 72, 104, 173, 212
Chaplin, Charlie, 30
Charensol, Georges, 72
Charter 77 (Prague human rights group), 142
Chatel, Nicole, 142
Chatte rouge, La, 61
Chauvet, Louis, 72, 156, 168, 179
Chazal, Robert, 73
Chekhov, Anton, 98
Cherebusco Studio (*Missing*), 224
Chew, Peter T., 183
"Child Who is Smiling, The" (*Z*), 96
Chile: Costa-Gavras and Solinas in, 140, 145, 154, 227; and filming *State of Siege* in, 43, 46, 157–58, 161, 223; and *Missing,* 221, 223–24, 229, 231, 233, 235, 252 nn. 6, 10; political films in, 27, 227; politics and coup in, 27, 41, 217, 220–22, 225; and U.S. involvement in, 220, 222, 228–29, 232, 235, 252 n.8
China: revolution in, 22
China Syndrome, The, 221
Chinese bath, 149
Chinoise, La, 23, 48, 82
Christian Democrats, 163
Christianity, 35, 112
Christian Science, 233
Christian Science Monitor, 45
Christoper Award (*Z*), 104
Christ Stopped at Eboli, 24
Church, Senator Frank, 220, 232
CIA (Central Intelligence Agency): activities and agents, 39, 173, 233, 248 nn. 2, 14; and film, 25, 231, 248 n.10; and *Missing,* 220, 228, 231–32, 246 n.50; and Mitrione in Latin America, 145, 154, 183–84; and *Z,* 92
Cinéaste, 26, 96, 125, 173, 180–82
Ciné-Club de Jeunes d'Aix-en-Provence, 212
Cinema, 168
Cinéma et idéologie, 17
Cinéma et politique, 17
Cinema V, 157, 250 n.64
Cinema Novo (film group), 26
Cinémathèque (Française), 31, 36
Cinémonde, 46
Cioffi, Charles, 222, 235
Cité Universitaire, 31, 36
Clair, René, 32
Clair de Femme (A Woman's Glow), 27, 34, 39, 41, 49, 50, 215–16, 222
Clément, René, 32–33, 45, 48–49, 52, 203
Clementi, Pierre, 62, 68

Clennon, David, 222, 225
Clockwork Orange, A, 60
Clouzot, Henri-Georges, 61
Cocks, Jay, 180–81, 202, 213
Cohen, Larry, 25
Colby, William, 232
Cold War, 135
Collet, Jean, 26, 102–3, 140
Collins, William, 181
Columbia Pictures, 88
Columbia University, 17
Combat, 104, 141, 173
Combattants Royalistes de l'Occident Chrétien. *See* CROC
Comédie Française, 202–3
Commentary, 103
Comment ça va, 18
Committee of Czech Writers, 130. *See also* Czechoslovakia
Communist parties: and anti-Semitism, 133; in Chile, 252 n.8; and *Confession,* 116–17, 119, 130, 140; and Costa-Gavras, 35, 139, 157, 162; in Czechoslovakia, 107–8, 135, 139; and films, 133, 139, 157; and Germany, 190; in Greece, 242 n.1; and Artur London, 109, 112, 126, 128, 133, 138–39; members of, 44, 99, 109, 147, 242 n.20; and Mitrione, 184, 190; newspaper of, 135; reaction to Moscow, 117; self-criticism of, 119; and *Special Section,* 190, 202; in United States, 135. See also *Confession* and U.S.S.R.
Compartiment tueurs. See Sleeping Car Murder
Compulsion, 53
Conchon, Georges, 191–92
Condé, Un, 23
Condition humaine, La, 22, 215
Condorcanqui, José Gabriel, 151
Confession, The (L'Aveu): 106–42; actors and characterization in, 39, 49, 120–23, 162, 203; adaptation by Semprun and Costa-Gavras, 41, 44–45, 129–31; book and comparisons of, 106–8, 112, 113, 147; comparisons with *Clair de femme,* 216; comparisons with *Shock Troops,* 72; comparisons with *Special Section,* 203, 211; comparisons with *State of Siege,* 171–73, 178; comparisons with *Z,* 125, 128–29, 132, 139, 172; completion and release of, 144–45; criticism of, 35, 134–40; as documentary-type film, 19; editing in, 46, 127–28, 170–71, 207; photographic techniques in 41, 47–48, 124–26, 204–5; political and individual reaction to, 133, 140–42, 157, 214, 238; politics of, 38, 114–15, 122, 131–34, 137, 146–47, 157, 209, 239; purpose and theme of, 38, 115, 121, 131, 142; scenario and production of, 113–20; sound and music in, 116, 128–29, 207–8; tone and

technique of, 35, 39–40, 123, 238–39; mentioned, 33, 34, 37, 236
Conformist, The, 24
Cooper, Gary, 30
Cop, A, 23
Cormoran, 242 n.10
Cornered, 103
Cornu, J., 32
Cosculluela, Manuel Hevia, 150, 184
Costa, Omar, 176
Costa-Gavras: actors in films of, 33, 42–45, 48–49, 52, 57, 68, 89–93, 114, 120–21, 123, 161–62, 164, 201–3, 210, 221–23, 228–30, 238; and audience, 37, 208, 210, 213, 227, 237, 239; cinematic comparisons with, 22–26, 39, 61, 82, 211; cinematic influences on, 22, 27, 30, 32, 33, 37–38, 49–50, 130, 134; collaboration with Giono, 32; collaboration with Japrisot, 52, 54; collaboration with Semprun, 44–45, 81, 113–14, 194–95, 200, 208; collaboration with Solinas, 146–49, 154–55; and Communism, 35, 99, 115, 133, 157, 162; comparison of films of, 19, 211; criticism of, 17, 21, 28, 35, 38–39, 50, 98–100, 104, 234; documentation and historical reality in films of, 38, 62, 65, 81, 83–84, 100, 239; editing of films of, 45–47, 56, 95, 127–28, 170–71, 206–7, 222–23; film training and early career of, 31–33, 40–41, 51–52, 72, 74, 236; funding for films of, 33, 61, 88–89, 113, 157, 195; human and political concerns of, 24, 34–38, 40, 74–76, 82, 99, 135, 143, 156, 163, 216, 237, 239–40; parents of, 30, 44, 47, 77; personal background of, 29–33, 37, 42–45, 61, 141, 156, 186, 227; photographic techniques of, 41–42, 47–48, 94, 125, 169–70, 204–5, 222; and political fiction film, 19, 21–24, 33–37, 57, 60, 113, 131–32, 134, 212, 214, 216, 236–39; and politics of Latin America, 143–45, 157–58, 177, 218–19, 230–31; and politics of U.S., 99, 173–74, 181, 221, 228, 230, 235, 253 n.20; purpose in filmmaking, 22, 83, 100, 103, 115, 122, 142, 155, 236; style of, 40, 54, 56, 92, 168, 204, 239; techniques of, 18, 38, 40, 46–47, 82, 93–95, 125–27, 169, 203–4, 207, 238; themes of, 18, 20–21, 34, 38, 40–42, 100–101, 107, 134, 177–79, 209; travels of, 31, 34, 76, 98, 113, 140–41, 145, 154, 157; and Tupamaros, 147–48, 150–54, 156, 166, 173, 175–77; use of sound and music by, 47–49, 96, 128, 171–72, 207–8; wife of (Michèle Ray), 42, 217
Costa-Gavras films. See *Clair de femme; Confession; Missing; Shock Troops; Sleeping Car Murder; Special Section; State of Siege; Z*
Courage, 203

Cournet (judge), 197

Courrière, Yves, 45

Courts of Special Section Sessions, 190, 206, 214

Coutard, Raoul, 47–49, 94, 124, 127, 169, 203–4, 238

Couteau, David, 128

"Covert Action in Chile: 1963–1973," 232

Cremer, Bruno, 41, 49, 62, 68, 72, 203, 212

Crésus, 32

Creter, Arthur, 231

Crist, Judith, 138–39, 180

CROC (Combattants Royalistes de l'Occident Chrétien), 85–86, 91, 101, 104

Croix, La, 73, 179

Crossfire, 103

Crowdus, Gary, 180

Crowther, Bosley, 57–58, 60

Crucible, The, 121

Cuba, 27, 150, 154, 184

Cukor, George, 58

Curtiss, Thomas Quinn, 103, 136, 139–40

Cusack, David, 252 n.8

Czechoslovakia: Communist party in, 106–9, 133, 135; and *Confession*, 35, 112–14, 129, 135, 141; Costa-Gavras in, 114; film industry in, 113–16, and Artur London, 106, 112–13, 125, 134; occupation of, 34, 106, 130, 137, 188; and politics, 108–9, 122, 130, 135, 138, 142; press and writers of, 106, 112, 128, 134; and Slansky trial, 33, 108, 111, 123, 133

Daix, Pierre, 137–38

Dallas, Texas, 90, 94

Dalle, Herbert, 214

D.A.M. (Daniel A. Mitrione Death Squad), 166. *See also* Death Squad

d'André, Pierre, 98

"Dan Mitrione's Legacy," 183

Darkness at Noon, 107, 113

Darlan, Jean (admiral), 190

Darlan government, 190

Dassin, Jules, 63

Dassin, Julie, 62

Daumier, Honoré, 205

Davis, Angela, 137

Davis, Melton, 34, 48, 98

Davis, Nathaniel, 229, 231–33

Davis, Ray, 229

Davis, Richard, 60

Dawn (Avghi, Lambrakis's party paper), 98

Day and the Hour, The (Le Jour et l'heure), 33, 48–49

Day of the Jackal, The, 25, 26, 202

Dean, John, 162

Death of the President, 97

Death Squad (of Brazil), 42, 152, 160, 166; in *State of Siege*, 250 n.53

Debray, Régis, 43

Deferre, Pierre Granier, 247 n.31

de Gaulle, Charles, 26, 104, 188, 202

Deglin, Paul, 194

Delgado, Humberto, 82

Demarsan, Eric, 208

Demby, Betty Jeffries, 194

Demy, Jacques, 32–33

Denby, David, 124, 133, 170

Denner, Charles, 59, 74, 85, 91

Deputy, The, 182

Derode, Julien, 33, 52

De Sica, Vittorio, 45

Destroy, She Said, 202

Deuxième Mort de Ramon Mercader, La, 44

Deuxième Procès d'Artur London, Le (The Second Trial of Artur London), 125

Deux Mémoires, Les, 44, 247 n.31

Deville, Michel, 23

Día, El, 152

Diable par le queue, Le, 90

Diamandopoulos (commander), 105

Diario, El, 152, 183

Dissent, 170

Djougatchvili, Joseph Vissarionovitch (Stalin), 106

Doctor from Stalingrad, The, 163

Doctor Strangelove, 93

Dominican Republic, 154, 159–60, 171, 179

Dorfmann, Robert, 76, 113–14

"Dormeur du val, Le" (song), 121

"Dossier de l'Ecran" *(Confession)*, 141

Dossier 51, 23

"Dossier Moser" *(Special Section)*, 193

Drach, Michel, 23, 97, 187

Dragnet, 181, 233

Dreyfus Affair, 36, 84, 91, 137, 188

Drieu La Rochelle, Pierre, 194

Drion (judge), 200

Drive, He Said, 20

Dubcek, Alexander, 111, 114

Dubra, Arturo, 249 n.34

Dulles, Allen, 117

Dulles, John Foster, 108

Dupont Lajoie, 23

Duras, Marguerite, 41, 147, 242 n.20

Dux, Pierre, 49, 84, 105, 202, 238

EAM (Ethniko Apeleftherotiko Metopo), 30, 47, 151

Eboli (Christ Stopped at Eboli), 24

Echappement libre, 32

Echols, Lee, 172

Ecran, 179, 212

Ecumenical Program of Interamerican Communication and Action, 183

EDA (Union of the Democratic Left), 77–78, 95, 98

Editions Arthème Fayard, 192

Eisenhower, Dwight D., 108

Eisenstein, Sergei: and fascism, 107; films of, 29, 65; film techniques of, 103, 252 n.10; influence on Costa-Gavras, 38, 134; mentioned, 22, 47

Electra, 47

El Salvador, 230, 232

Eluard, Paul, 121–22

Emanouelidis, Emanuel, 79, 105

Enemy Within, The, 242 n.10

England: ambassador to Uruguay from, 152, 176; director in, 58; film in, 60, 222; Film Academy in, 141; and Petain, 188–89; relations of Greece with, 78; relations of Ireland with, 25; and title of *Sleeping Car Murder,* 242 n.5; and Zilliacus, 119; mentioned, 27, 148, 194

Engle, Byron, 174, 248 n.14

Epoca, 34

Erro, Enrique (senator), 163–64, 248 n.10

Eskin, Stanley, 173

Espoir, L', 29, 45

Etat de siège. See State of Siege

Ethniko Apeleftherotiko Metopo. *See* EAM

Etiévant, Yvette, 160, 164

Europe: and *Confession,* 35, 116, 140–41; Costa-Gavras returns to, 154; Eastern, 48, 106, 109, 134; film criticism of, 135; and politics, 17, 22, 109, 125, 236; in *Shock Troops,* 61

Eustache, Jean, 60

Evanouissement, L', 44

Evien, Bernard, 124

Evry (France), 212

Execution of Charles Horman, The, 218. *See also Missing*

Executive Action, 26

Existentialisme, L', 72

Express, L', 98, 137

Extinct Corpses, 24

Face in the Crowd, A, 45

Fagen, Richard, 253 nn. 30, 34

Falcon, André, 160

Family Reunion, 222

Far From Vietnam, 42

Farm Workers, 20, 37

Fascism, 44, 107, 116

FBI (Federal Bureau of Investigation), 25–26, 149, 152–53, 175, 184

Félins, Les, 32

Fellini, Federico, 32

Femme à sa fenêtre, Une, 44, 194, 247 n.31

Femme Flic, 23

Féron, Bernard, 136

Ferreri, Marco, 45

Ferzetti, Gabriele, 119, 123, 137

Field, Noel, 109–10, 116, 117, 119, 246 n.9

Figaro, Le, 72, 156, 168, 179

Figaro Littéraire, Le, 139

Film Comment, 219

Film Français, 33, 194, 215

Filmmakers Newsletter, 47–48, 194

Film Noir, 22, 37, 49, 54

Film Quarterly, 60, 73, 102, 139, 169, 181

Films and Filming, 60, 93

Films in Review, 139, 181, 186

Film Society Review, 96, 103, 136

Fils, Le, 33, 49, 76–77, 113

FIN (*Source of North American Information* newsletter), 220, 225, 228

Final Solution, 189

First Circle, The, 107

First Line of Defense, The, 249 n.23

Flatley, Guy, 90, 96

Florence (Italy), 43

Fly, Claude, 146

Flynn, Charles, 103

Flynn, Errol, 30

Focus, 103

Focus on Film 47

FOI. *See* Freedom of Information Act

Fond de l'air est rouge, Le, 125

Fontaine, Joan, 30

Ford, Gerald, 228

Ford, John, 32, 43

Ford Foundation, 224, 226

Foreign Service Institute, 158

Forman, Milos, 113

Forsythe, Frederick, 26

Fort Wayne, Indiana, 185

For Us (Für Uns), 63

Fournier, Thérèse, 212

Fous de Dieu, Les, 61

France: actors of, 59, 90; anti-Semitism in, 189; archives of, 192; cinéastes/directors of, 23, 45, 61, 81, 97, 130, 146–47; Communist Party in, 35, 37, 111, 115, 117, 119, 135, 137–38, 141, 214; critics in, 18, 21, 26, 61, 103, 173; critics' reactions to *Confession* in, 132, 134–35; critics' reactions to *Day of the Jackal* in, 26; critics' reactions to *Sleeping Car Murder* in, 60; and Costa-Gavras, 24, 31–32, 34–35, 37, 42, 209, 211, 217; film and theatre in, 48, 91, 121, 129; film audiences in, 19, 61, 211; film production in, 45, 127, 204; Institute of Public Opinion in,

214; and Artur London *(Confession)*, 109, 112–15, 125, 135–36; lycées of, 49, 80; and Yves Montand, 43, 121, 162–63; National Film Center in, 45; poets and novelists of, 22, 80, 188; political fiction film in, 18–19, 23, 27, 30, 61, 132, 141, 187–88; politics in, 23, 36, 89, 97, 189–90, 199, 242 nn.7, 10; 250 n.4; press and television in, 34, 138, 141, 235; Resistance in, 30, 33, 62, 68, 72, 135; and Semprun, 44, 146; and *Shock Troops*, 61, 68, 72–73; SLON (Société de Lancement des Oeuvres Nouvelles) film collective in, 18; and *Special Section* (book), 188, 192–93, 196, 209; and *Special Section* (film), 188, 193–98, 202–3, 211–13; and *State of Siege*, 158, 161–63, 164, 178–79; and Vichy government in, 19, 61, 211; and World War I, 189; and *Z*, 79, 88–89, 98, 100, 102–4

France Nouvelle, 139

France Soir, 212

Franco, Francisco (general), 44, 82, 116, 140, 193

Franco-Prussian War, 196

Francovich, Allan, 154, 248 n.10, 252 n.8

Francs Tireurs et Partisans (FTP), 30, 39, 190. *See also* France, Resistance in

Frankenheimer, John, 218

Frédo *(Special Section)*, 193, 196, 203, 205, 208

Freedom of Information Act, 228, 231, 248 n.14, 252 n.6

Free Zone of Southern France, 74. *See also* France, Resistance in

Frei government (Chile), 157, 220, 252 n.8. *See also* Chile

Freire, Paolo, 42

French Connection, The, 55

French Conspiracy, The, 23, 44, 83

Frente Amplio, 163

Fresson, Bernard, 85

Freud, Sigmund, 224

Fribourg-am-Breisgau, 193

Friedkin, William, 49

Friedmann, Bernard, 210

Friends of Peace *(Z)*, 78, 84–85, 91–92

Fulbright, J. William (senator), 253 nn. 30, 34

Fuyons, 203

Galabru, Michel, 197

Galande, Olivier, 103

Galileo, 238

Galkin (Soviet advisor), 128

Gallimard (publisher), 112–13, 135

Gangster films, 55. *See also* Film Noir

Garabit (France), 72

Gary, Romain, 49, 215

Gaudin, Christian, 56, 69

Gaullists, 196. *See also* de Gaulle

Gaumont Films, 88

Gautherot, Henri, 190, 196, 200

Gavaroc (procurator general), 206

Gavras, Alexandre, 42

Gavras, Harry, 29

Gavras, Hélène, 42

Gavras, Konstantinos (Costa), 29. *See also* Costa-Gavras

Gavras, Michèle (Ray), 42, 217

Gavras, Panayotis, 29–30

Gavras, Roman, 42

Gavras, Tolis, 29, 76

Geneva (Switzerland), 109, 116–17

Gentleman Jim, 30

Georgakas, Dan, 96–97, 103

George II (king of Greece), 36

Georgetown University, 152

Gérard. *See* London, Artur

Géret, Georges, 92

Germany, East, 112, 183

Germany, West: anti-Semitism in, 189; birthplace of S. Signoret, 48; Communist party of, 246 n. 9; and *Confession*, 141; and occupation of France, 188–91, 193–94, 196; and occupation of Greece, 30; political film in, 27; and presence in wars, 97, 107, 196; and *Shock Troops*, 69; and *Special Section* (book and film), 188, 190–91, 193–200, 203, 213; and *State of Siege*, 161, 163, 180

Gérminal, 57

Gervais, Ginette, 115

Gestapo, 109–10, 117

Giannini, Giancarlo, 25

Gilio, Maria Esther, 249 n.34

Gilliatt, Penelope, 163–64

Giono, Jean, 32, 68

Girl Friends, 222

Glenn, Pierre William, 169–70

Godard, Jean-Luc, 18, 23, 32, 42, 48, 82, 124

Godfather, The, 36

Godunov, Boris (tsar), 208

Goebbels, Joseph, 133, 190

Goin, Lauren, 174, 179, 183

Golden Palm Award *(Missing)*, 235

Goldstücker, Eduard, 130

Gomide, Días (Brazilian consul), 146, 152

Gonzalez, Rafael, 231–32, 234–35

Goodbye Land, The, 180

Goodman, Mark, 136–37, 140

Goriz Productions, 195

Gottwald, Klement, 41, 110–11, 124

Gotzamanis, Spyros, 79, 105

Gow, Gordon, 93

Grace, George, 45

Grajales, Jorge Candal, 165

Gramsci, Antonio, 121

Grands Chemins, Les, 57
Grand Voyage, Un, 44, 113
Granier-Deferre, Pierre, 33, 44, 49, 77, 194
Grant, Cary, 93
Grapes of Wrath, 32
Great Britain. *See* England
"Great Cameramen," 47
Great Terror (in Russia), 107, 109
Greece: and Nikos Belloyannis, 89; Communist party of, 30, 242 n.1; Costa-Gavras in, 30, 32, 36, 44, 76, 99, 144, 194; Costa-Gavras's father in, 29, 44; government and political situation in, 18, 32, 34, 36, 76–77, 82–83, 89–90, 96, 98–99, 101, 132, 141–42, 164, 187, 239, 245–46 n.50; historical background of, 30, 35–37, 77–78, 83, 98, 103–4, and Montand, 43; Orthodox Catholic Church in, 30; Parliament of, 76, 78; and John Peurifoy, 144; reaction to *Z* in, 18, 23, 35, 41, 76, 80–82, 89, 99, 103–5; Theodorakis in, 47, 96, 171; U.S. involvement in, 78, 88, 99; Vassilikos in, 80, 101–2
Green Berets, 153
Greenland, 33
Greensberg, Peter, 253 n.20
Grelier, Robert, 100, 112, 116, 134, 154, 158, 178
Griffith, D.W., 185
Gringoire, 48
Guatemala, 144, 145, 233
Guernica, 252 n.10
Guerre est finie, La, 23, 43–44, 48–49, 56, 72, 81, 121, 123
Guevara, Ché, 42
Guillén, Abraham, 175
Guilty of Treason, 135
Guiomar, Julien, 85, 91
Guitry, Sacha, 212
Gulag Archipelago, 107
Gutierrez, Alea Tomas, 27
Guzmán, Jacobo Arbenz, 144
Guzman, Patricio, 219

Hackman, Gene, 161
Hajdu, Vavro, 108, 111
Hamilton, Alastair, 112
Hammett, Dashiel, 37
Hands over the City, 22, 24
Hangmen Also Die!, 142
Hannah, John, 182
Hanoi, 217
Hardt, Hubert, 170
Harold and Maude, 218
Harris, Douglas, 158
Harry and Tonto, 222
Harvard University, 17, 220
Hasse, O. E., 41, 158, 202

Hatch, Robert, 215
Hathaway, David, 253 nn. 30, 34
Hauser, Thomas, 218–21, 225, 228, 233–35, 252 n.6
Haustrate, Gaston, 140
Helms, Richard, 233
Hennebelle, Guy, 18, 25, 27, 212
Henriot, Philippe, 176
Herald Tribune, 103, 136, 139–40
Heritage of Michael Flaherty, The, 25
Hersh, Seymour, 232–33
Hidden Terrors, 152, 154, 173–74
High School, 19
Hiroshima, mon amour, 126
Hiss, Alger, 246 n.9
Histoire simple, Une, 203
Hitchcock, Alfred, 57, 61, 88, 93, 169
Hitler, Adolf, 133, 205
Hitt, Robert, 226
Hoa Binh, 48
Hochhuth, Rolf, 182
Hoffmann, Dustin, 26
Hoffmann, Stanley, 208
Hollywood, 18, 20, 104, 127, 204, 234, 237
Hollywood on Trial, 108
"Hollywood's Political Cinema," 20
Holmes, Robert, 158, 167
Homme à femmes, L', 32
Homme de trop, Un. See Shock Troops
Horman, Beth/Joyce, 39–40, 217, 220–22, 225, 228–29, 253 n.10
Horman, Charles, 40–41, 54, 215, 217, 220–34, 252 nn. 6, 10, 17.; 253 nn. 30, 34
Horman, Ed, 40, 217, 221–22, 225–35, 253 nn. 30, 34
Hospital, 19
Hour of the Furnaces, The, 27
House of Chanel, 42
Hugo, Victor, 37
Humanité L', 41, 49, 60, 73, 115, 136, 138, 140, 147, 196, 200, 203
Humphrey, Hubert, 183
Hungary, 36, 107, 108, 110–12, 116–17, 119, 133, 138
Hussak regime (Czechoslovakia), 141
Huston, John, 32
"Hypnotic Lies about Terrorists," 179

I Choose Freedom, 112–13
Ici et ailleurs, 18
I . . . comme Icare, 24, 43
IDHEC. *See* Institut des Hautes Etudes Cinématographiques
Immigrant Workers (Main d'Oeuvre Immigré), 109

Incas, 151
In Cold Blood, 19
India, 104
Indiana. *See* Richmond, Indiana
Indian revolt (Peru), 151
Indochina, War in, 121
Inheritor, The, 23
Insdorf, Annette, 32, 46
Inside the Company, 173, 248 n.14
Institut des Hautes Etudes Cinématographiques (IDHEC), 31–32, 36, 42, 51, 61
Institut d'Etudes Politiques, 81
Institute of Political Science (Paris), 192
International Brigade (in Spain), 41, 109, 116, 135, 193
International Communist Party, 193. *See also* Communist Party
"Internationale," 196
International Police Academy (IPA), 152–53, 155, 160, 171; in *State of Siege*, 174, 184, 249 n.23
International Red Cross, 109
Interview, 187–88
Investigation of a Citizen Above Suspicion, 24
IPA. *See* International Police Academy
Iphigenia, 47
IRA (Irish Republican Army), 25
Iron Curtain, 134, 140
Irwin, John N., 148
Is Paris Burning?, 48, 72, 90, 203
Italy: Bonnot edits in, 45; and *Confession*, 114; embassy of, in *Missing*, 231, 234; film genres in, 18, 22, 25–26; and film influence on Costa-Gavras, 22, 32; and Mitrione family, 149, 183; and Montand family, 43, 121; Jaques Perrin in films of, 90; political films of, 22, 24–25, 91, 132, 236; Red Brigade in, 250 n.49; Sacco and Vanzetti from, 24; Solinas in, 146; and *State of Siege*, 161, 195; and *Z*, 88
Ivens, Joris, 42
Ivo Livi (Montand's given name), 43
Izvestia (Communist paper), 135

Jackal of Nahueltoro, The, 27
Jackson, Geoffrey, 152, 176
Jacquemont, Maurice, 160
Jameson, Richard, 69, 73
Jancsó, Miklós, 134
Janus Films, 195
Japrisot, Sébastien, 51–56
Jeancolas, Jean-Pierre, 187, 205, 237
Jefferson, Thomas, 117
Jetée, La, 125
Jeune Cinéma, 94, 115, 211–12
Jewison, Norman, 25
Jews, 91, 117, 128, 133–34, 188, 190, 193, 196, 198, 207, 210
Joe, 20
Johnny Got His Gun, 20, 25
Jornal do Brasil, 150, 152, 183
Jour et l'heure, Le (The Day and the Hour), 32–33
Journal of Resistance, 95
Jouvet, Lous, 59
Juge Fayard dit "le Sheriff", 23
Jules and Jim, 48
Jung, Carl, 39
Juquin, Pierre, 141
Jury Prize (*Z*), 104

Kael, Pauline, 103, 139, 202, 214, 234
Kafka, Franz, 106, 135
Kalishman, Harold, 180
Kamenev, L. B., 107
Kaminker, 48. *See also* Signoret, Simone
Kamoutsis, Efthimios (colonel), 79, 105
Kanapa, Jean, 141
Kapò, 22, 146
Karamanlis, Constantine (president), 77, 79, 105, 144
Kauffmann, Stanley, 39, 120, 124–25, 234
Kawalerowicz, Jerzy, 97
Kazan, Elia, 32, 45
Kelly, Kevin, 181
Kennedy Center, 185–86, 231
Kennedy family: 82, 185; Jacqueline, 90; John F., 24–26, 76, 83–84, 90, 94, 167, 174, 180; Robert, 84, 101, 242 n.10
Kent State University, 17
Kessler, Judd, 231
King, Martin Luther, Jr., 25
Kissinger, Henry, 226, 230, 232
Klein, William, 42
Kline, Richard, 185
Klivia (Greece), 29
Koestler, Arthur, 107
Kohoutek, V. (captain) 130, 137
Koldeje castle, 109–10. See also *Confession*
Kollias, Constantine (prosecutor-general), 79
Kopkind, Andrew, 230, 233
Koppel, Ted, 252 n.1
Korea, 110
Kostov, Traicho, 108
Kravchenco, Victor, 112
Kroll, Jack, 201–2, 213–14
Krushchev, Nikita, 43, 111
Kubrick, Stanley, 60, 93

Labro, Philippe, 23
Labrousse, Alain, 176
Lachize, Samuel, 60, 73
Lacombe, Lucien, 187, 211

Lady L, 49

Lafarge, Roger, 198, 200–1

Lambrakis, Gregory, 23, 38–40, 47, 60, 77, 79–80, 83–84, 90, 95–96, 98–103, 162, 242 n.1

Lambrakis Youth Movement, 80, 95, 97

Lang, Fritz, 142

Langguth, A. J., 145, 152–54, 173

Langlois, Gérard, 89, 140

La Paz (Bolivia), 222

Laruschi, Tony, 222

Last Hurrah, The, 22

Last Supper, The (film), 27

Last Year at Marienbad, 48, 126

Latin America: AID in, 99, 154, 156; CIA involvement in, 154; and Costa-Gavras, 27, 34–35, 145, 147, 150; melodies of, in films, 171–72; and *Missing*, 223, 228, 230; and Mitrione, 145, 149, 239; political films of, 17, 26–27; political and revolutionary movements in, 27, 142–43, 151, 157, 167–68, 230, 233, 249 nn. 23, 24; religion in, 167, 178; and *State of Siege*, 40, 147, 158, 163–64, 169; U.S. involvement in, 42, 144–45, 148, 154, 156, 167, 172–73, 179, 181, 227; and *Z*, 35

Latin Quarter (Paris), 18

Laval, Pierre, 188

Lebel, Jean-Patrick, 17–18, 25, 27

Left: and *Confession*, 132, 135; and Costa-Gavras, 101; in Greece, 47, 77–78, 83; and Mitrione, 182–84; and political film, 28; and *Special Section*, 189, 212; and *State of Siege*, 152, 157, 168, 181; in U.S., 156; and *Z*, 81, 84, 89–90, 105

Legion of French Volunteers, 190

Legion of Honor, 206

Légion saute sur le Kolwezi, La, 49, 203

Leguebe, Eric, 73

Leinster, Colin, 25

Lelouch, Claude, 42

"Le Mas perdu," 68

Lemmon, Jack, 221–22, 225, 235

Lenin (Vladimir Ilitch), 37, 106–7, 109, 120, 126, 130, 133–34

Leo XIII (pope), 178

Leone, Serge, 27, 45

Leopold-Loeb case, 53

Lettres Françaises, Les, 59, 89, 104, 138, 140

Levi, Carlo, 24

Levy, Thierry, 190–91

Lewis, Edward, 218–19

Lewis, Flora, 232–33

Lewis, Jerry, 154, 183

Lewis, Mildred, 218

Libération de Paris, La, 187

"Liberators" (song), 171

Liberoff, Doctor, 249 n.34

Liehm, Antonin, 115

Lille (France), 46, 116, 120, 129

Limoursin, Jean, 138

Linais, René, 194, 198, 203

Littin, Miquel, 27

Litvak, Anatole, 58

"Lives of Men, The" (*Special Section* book), 193

Loeb, James L., 180

Loebl, Eugen, 108, 111

Loewinger, Lawrence, 102

Logereau, Edouard, 31

London, Artur, 49; and authenticity of *Confession* film adaptation, 116, 122–23, 126, 130, 135–36, 138–39, 142; and Communist Youth activities, 139; and *Confession* (book) as literary testimony, 33, 108, 112–13, 132, 134–36, 140, 142; in Czechoslovakia, 108–9, 112–13, 130, 141; family of, 39, 138; and Noel Field, 109, 116; and Milos Forman, 113; and French television, 141–42; imprisonment of, 110–12, 115–17, 123, 128–29; personal interview with, 108, 114, 246 n.2; played by Montand in *Confession*, 40, 120–22; political complications for, 109, 126, 134–35, 141, 187; in Resistance as Gérard, 109–10, 113, 116, 124, 129–30, and Semprun, 113–16; and Slansky trial, 41, 107–10; sympathy for, 121–22, 135, 141; as Undersecretary of Foreign Affairs, 106, 109; and writing of *Confession*, 106–7, 109, 112, 125, 236

London, Françoise, 113

London, Lise, 49, 111–12, 119, 122–24, 135, 141

London (England), 61, 188

Long Blue Road, 22

Lonsdale, Michel, 196, 202

Look, 92

Loren, Sophia, 49

Lorre, Peter, 37

Losey, Joseph, 44

Los Fresnos (Texas), 153

Love and Anarchy, 25

Lozère region, 63

Lucas, Juan Maria, 164

Lucia, 27

Lukács, Georg, 39

Lumet, Sidney, 74, 221

Lumiére, 203

Lumumba, Patrice, 82

Luntz, Edouard, 19

Luraschi, Tony, 25

Lyons (France), 188, 212

Madame Rosa, 48

Made in U.S.A., 23

Mader, Julius, 183

Madrugo, Leopoldo, 176

Mafia, 24, 36
Magne, Michel, 57, 69
Mairesse, Guy, 86, 198
Malcolm X (Malcolm Little), 82
Malfille, Pierre, 31
Malle, Louis, 187
Mal Partis, Les, 52
Malraux, André, 22, 29, 39, 43, 45, 65, 215
Man and a Woman, A, 59, 90
Manicheism, 39, 92, 138, 162, 166
Mann, Claude, 53, 60
Mann, Heinrich, 224
Mann, Thomas, 224
Man's Fate, 22
Man's Hope, 29
Ma Nuit chez Maud, 104
Marathon March (to Athens), 47, 78
Marcha, 149, 249 n.28
Maréchal et son peuple, Le, 189
Marker, Chris, 18–19, 42, 125
Marmin, Michel, 212
Marquand, Christian, 57
"Marseillaise, La," 196
Marseilles (France), 52, 59, 116
Martin, James Michael, 60
Martin, Marcel, 99, 179, 212
Marx, Karl/Marxism, 23–24, 37, 44, 47, 67–68, 112, 132, 172, 179, 224
Mattei, Enrico, 82
Matteoti Affair, The, 24
Maulnier, Thierry, 137
Mauriac, Claude, 43, 139
Maurin, François, 136, 138, 147
Mauthausen (concentration camp), 44, 109, 134, 141
Mayron, Melaine, 222, 225
McCarthy, Eugene (senator), 183
McCarthy, Joseph (senator)/McCarthyism, 26, 31, 43, 48, 103, 108, 121, 180, 183
McCloskey, Robert, 249 n.47
McFadden, Patrick, 136–37, 139
McGeary, Dave, 233–34
McNally, Donald, 233
Mekas, Jonas, 186
Méliès, Georges, 22
Mellen, Joan, 20, 25–26, 125–26, 129, 135, 137
Mélodie en sous-sol, 57
Melville, Jean-Pierre, 45, 199, 208
Memories of Underdevelopment, 27
Memory of Justice, 32
Mendes-France, Pierre, 43
Mexico, 27, 46, 104, 107, 144, 223–24
Mian, Pauline A., 78
Michel, Jacqueline, 120, 136
Michelini, Zelmar, 163

"Middle European Great Economic Region," 189
Midstream, 173
Miller, Arthur, 48, 121
Miller, David, 26
Millgram, Stanley, 24, 191, 210
Mills, Donia, 156
Mimi the Metallurgist (Seduction of Mimi), 25
Mindzenty (cardinal), 135
Minton, Robert, 156, 183
"Minute, A," 193
Miquel, Jean-Pierre, 85
Missing: actors and characterization in, 39, 41, 238; at Cannes, 235; criticism of United States foreign policy in, 228–29, 231, 233; editing of, 46, 236; historical background to production and filming of, 217, 223, 227–28, 235; as political fiction film, 34, 215, 234, 239; purpose of, 235; reaction of United States government officials to, 231–34, 253 n.10; screening of, 222, 230, 253 n.29; technique in, 35, 40, 54; United States Embassy and ambassadors in, 224–29
Missouri, 179
Mr. Smith Goes to Washington, 22
Mitrione, Dan A.: AID involvement and image of, 149, 182; case of, 152, 158, 173, 175; Death Squad named after, 166–67; defense of, by U.S., 148, 179, 182–84; documentation about, 153–55; first anniversary of death of, 148, 183; his function in South America, 145, 149–50, 152, 172, 174, 184, 247 n.47; judgment by Costa-Gavras of, 144, 155, 184–85; kidnapping and execution of, 40, 146, 152, 156, 171, 175–76, 187; and martial law in Uruguay, 179; papal nuncio's views of, 155–56, 167, 178; personal background of, 143, 148–49, 154, 166; protrayal of, in *State of Siege* 40, 147, 157, 162, 173, 229; as symbol of American imperialism, 148, 155, 162, 183–84; tapes of, 153–54, 168; and torture techniques, 150, 184, 248 n.10; and Tupamaros, 175–76, 223, 250 n.53; viewed by Left, 182–84
Mitrione, Dan A., Jr., 183
Mitrione, Ray, 154
Mitsou, Constantine (general), 79, 105
Mitterand, François, 242 n.10
MLN (Movimiento de Liberación Nacional), 151, 158, 248 n.10. *See also* Tupamaros
Mockey, Jean-Pierre, 23
Moellet, Luc, 60
Monde, Le, 80, 136, 138, 142, 146, 211
Mondy, Pierre, 53, 59
Mon Oncle d'Amérique, 126, 247 n.31
Monsumano Alto (Italy), 43
Montaldo, Guido, 24
Montand, Yves: in *Clair de femme,* 215; compared

to Humphrey Bogart, 59; in *Confession*, 40, 114, 116, 120–22, 136–37, 141; and Costa-Gavras, 43; film career of, 42–43, 58, 76–77, 90, 114; in films of Costa-Gavras, 40, 42–43, 120–21, 162, 201, 203, 238; and Alfred Hitchcock, 88; personal background of, 43; political concerns of, 43–44, 112; and Simone Signoret (wife), 48; in *Sleeping Car Murder*, 53–54, 58; in *State of Siege*, 40, 120–21, 156, 158, 162–63, 175, 179; visit to United States of, 48; in *Z*, 23, 85, 88, 90

Monte Carlo (Monaco), 117, 123, 126–27, 137, 140

Montesquieu, Baron de, 197

Montevideo (Uruguay), 146, 148–50, 152, 154, 158, 174, 178, 183–84, 249 n.47

Montilles, Mario, 153, 160

Moreau, Jeanne, 203

Morocco, 104

Moscow, 43, 48, 61, 107, 109, 111, 115, 117, 121–22, 123, 135, 139, 142, 175, 177. *See also* U.S.S.R.

Moser, Alfons, 193, 200, 205, 207, 210

Mother Courage, 238

Movement of Peace (France), 121

Movietone, 163

Movimiento de Liberación Nacional, 151, 158

Mucchielli, Hercule, 89

Muriel, 48

Murmur of the Heart, 202

Muskie, Edward, 231

Mussolini, Benito, 24–25

Mussorgsky, Modest 196

Nahum, J., 32

Nantes (France), 190

Narboni, Jean, 103

Nation, 215, 230, 232

National Liberation Front (Greece). *See* EAM

National Liberation Movement (Movimiento de Liberación Nacional), 151, 158, 248 n.10

National Observer, 183

National Public Radio, 230–31

Nativity, The, 222

NATO, 78, 89

Navarette, Robert, 160

Navy (U.S.), 149

Nazis: and *Confession*, 116, 119, 125; and films, 20, 22, 26, 35, 65, 187; in *Shock Troops*, 61–63, 67, 69, 74; in *Special Section*, 196, 198–99, 210; and U.S.S.R., 107, 125, 134, 190; and Vichy government, 48, 77, 187–89, 194; and *Z*, 97; mentioned, 126, 224

Neame, Ronald, 20

Neue Bremme (labor camp), 109

Neuman, Kate, 234

New Day Films, 186

Newman, Paul, 49

New Republic, 39, 124, 234

Newsweek, 180–81, 189, 201, 213–14

New Wave (in France), 31–32, 48, 51, 94, 126, 242 n.4

New York (N. Y.), 60, 76, 84, 113, 121, 225

New York (magazine), 138–39, 180–81, 214

New Yorker, 103, 139, 163, 202, 214, 234

New York Film Critics, 104, 186

New York Post, 73, 213

New York Times, 36, 43, 60, 73–74, 98, 129, 159, 168, 179–80, 185, 213, 232–34

New York Times Magazine, 34

Nicaragua, 17

Nichols, John, 219

Nicita, Wally, 222

Night and Fog, 19, 48, 191

Nîmes (France), 63, 68

1984, 117

1900, 24, 135

Nirvana Blues, 219

Nixon, Richard, 80, 174, 183, 185, 213, 221, 230

Noël, Magali, 92

North America, 143, 168, 172–73. *See also* U.S.

North by Northwest, 93

Nouvelles Littéraires, Les, 61, 72

Nouvel Observateur, Le, 103–4, 178–79

Nuñez, Carlos, 176

Nykvist, Sven, 42, 94

Objectif 500 Million, 68

Objective Burma, 30

O'Brien, Glenn, 125

Occupation (by Nazis), 36, 74, 188, 198

October, 252 n.10

October Revolution, 125

Octypus, 203

Odéon (Théâtre National), 203

Odessa (Russia), 29–30

O.D.E.S.S.A. File, The, 20, 41

Oiseau rare, L', 68

"Old Man Milon," 196, 200

Olympic Airlines, 89

On a Clear Day You Can See Forever, 114

On Company Business, 154, 248 n.10, 252 n.8

One Flew Over the Cuckoo's Nest, 113

One Man Too Many. *See Shock Troops*

1000 Eyes, 74

On les appelait "les bandits," 63

On the Waterfront, 32, 45

"Opération Centrale" *(Shock Troops)*, 63

"Operation Cleanup" *(Missing)*, 220

Ophüls, Marcel, 32–33, 187

OPR (anarchist guerrillas), 33, 42
Order of the Republic (Czechoslovakia), 141
Orengo, Charles, 192
Origins of Totalitarianism, 133
Oscar Awards, 45–46, 48, 95, 104, 113, 127
Otero, Alejandro, 150, 152, 175, 183–84
Outsider, The, 25, 222

Pacific Steel Film Collective, 18–19
Pagnol, Marcel, 32
Paine, Thomas, 117
País, El, 152, 183
Pakula, Alan, 25–26, 97
Palais de Justice (Paris), 195–96, 251 n.16
Palance, Jack, 162
Palestine, 18
Palevsky, Max, 157, 185
Panic in Needle Park, 20
Panorama Aujourd'hui, 103
Papadopoulos, George, 79
Papandreou, George, 79–80
Papas, Irene, 38, 85, 88, 90, 103, 122
Papillon, 76
Parallax View, The, 26, 97
Paris (France): American western films shown in,
    73; "Amicale" group in, 141; and Ben Barka
    Affair, 76, 83; Centre National du Cinéma in,
    89; and *Clair de femme*, 215–16; and *Confession*,
    109, 113, 136, 141–42; film studies in, 45, 49,
    89; German troops in, 188, 190; Institute of
    Political Science in, 192; intellectual and polit-
    ical life in, 36, 217; personal interview with
    Bonnot in, 206; Semprun in, 81; and *Shock
    Troops*, 74; Signoret in, 48; and *Sleeping Car
    Murder*, 52–53, 55, 58; Soviet cinema in, 141;
    and *Special Section*, 190, 193, 195–97, 211, 214;
    and *State of Siege*, 42, 46, 186; Vassilikos in, 77;
    and *Z*, 81, 102, 104
Paris/Perez (*Missing*): 225, 231–32, 234
Partelli (bishop), 156
Particular Day, A (American title: *A Special Day*),
    205
Partido Nacional, 163. *See also* Uruguay
Passager de la pluie, Le, 52
*Passé présent: Le socialism oriental face au monde
    moderne, Le*, 115
Passionara, La, 111
Patton, George (general), 27
Pauker, Ana, 133
Paul VI (pope), 183
Paul I (king of Greece), 36
Paul, Bernard, 19
Paxton, Robert, 188–90, 192, 209–10, 250 n.4
Peau de banane, 32
Peckinpah, Sam, 146

Pedagogy of the Oppressed, 42
Pelikan, Jiri, 141
Peling, Maurice, 212
Peloponnesus (Greece), 29–30, 96
"People in a Struggle, A" (song), 171
People's Prison (*State of Siege*), 153, 155, 159–60,
    171, 176
Pereira dos Santos, Nelson, 27
Périer, François, 63, 85, 88, 91
Peronism, 27
Perrin, Jacques, 41, 45, 48, 53, 59, 62, 68, 85, 88–
    90, 96, 157, 195, 198, 203
Perrot, François, 215
Peru, 151, 180
Pétain, Henri Philippe, 62, 74, 188–91, 196–97,
    204, 209
Peter the Great, 98
Petit Soldat, Le, 48
Petri, Elio, 24
Peurifoy, John 144, 155
Philadelphia Inquirer, 181
Philadelphia Story, The, 41
Philadelphia Tribune, 162
Philips, David, 248 n.2
Philips Exeter Academy, 220
Philosophy of the Urban Guerrilla, 175
Piatakov, G. L., 107
Picasso, Pablo, 252 n.16
Piccoli, Michel, 53, 59, 68
Piège pour Cendrillon, Un, 52
Pieplu, Claude, 197
Pinochet regime (Chile), 217, 227
Pinoteau, Jack, 32
Piraeus (Greece), 29, 95–96
Piroukas (deputy), 79
Pius IX (pope), 178
Place Maurice Audin (Algiers), 89
Plant, The, 76
Platero, Luis Martínez, 165
Plaza del Toros (*Missing*), 224
Poland, 27, 97, 107–9, 112, 188, 193, 207, 230
Polanski, Roman, 45
Police Python 357, 43
Pollock, Sydney, 25
Pontecorvo, Gillo, 19, 21, 22, 146, 236
Portugal, 104
Positif, 103, 137, 187
Potemkin, 22, 29, 103
Powell, Ann, 208, 239
Prague (Czechoslovakia): and *Confession*, 114,
    116, 120, 128–30, 141, 205; Noel Field in, 116;
    and invasion of 1968, 125, 142; Artur London
    in, 109–10, 112–13, 120, 130, 141, 187; and
    Yves Montand, 43, 121; political climate in,
    112, 119, 142, 247 n.21; Slansky trials in, 106,

128, 139
Pravda, 180
Preminger, Otto, 82
Prisoner, The, 135
Projets, 102
Prokosch, Mike, 139
Promised Land, The, 27
Providence, 126
Pucheu, Pierre, 190, 193, 196, 200, 202, 211
Pull-Over Rouge, Le, 97
Purdy, Fred, 229, 232
Puro Chile, 157

Quai de Brest (Algiers), 89
"Quand un soldat" (song), 121
Question, La, 23
Quijano, Carlos, 149, 249 n.28
Quotidien de Paris, Le, 212

Radek, K. B., 107
Radical Socialist Party (France), 97. *See also* France
Radio Prague, 141
Raison d' Etat, La, 23
Rajk, Laszlo, 108, 110–11, 116–17, 133, 246 n.9
Ramona, 157
Rampell, Ed, 37
Ranucci, Christian, 97
R.A.S. (film), 23, 203
Rauchendorf, Heinz-Dieter, 35–36
Ray, Michèle, 42, 217
Reason of State, the, 199–200, 202, 209
Recurso del Metodo (Viva el Presidente!), 27
Red Army, 107. *See also* Trotsky
Redford, Robert, 25
Redonneau, Léon, 198
Red Poster, The, 23
Red Sweater, The, 23
Regain, 32
Regalbuto, Joe, 225
Reggane Films, 88, 195
Reichert, Julia, 186
Rémond, Alain, 43, 212
Renoir, Jean, 32
Representatives, U.S. House of, 183. *See also* U.S.
Rerum Novarum, 178
Reseau d'Organismes Culturelles, 98
Resistance: and *Special Section*, 190; and *Z*, 97
Resnais, Alain: and actors, 203; and collaboration with Semprun, 41, 44, 81, 94, 126, 147, 194; and collaboration with Sacha Vierny, 48; and comparisons with Costa-Gavras, 23, 32; and documentary film, 19, 42, 191; and *La Guerre est finie*, 23, 49, 56, 121; and new wave of political fiction film, 23, 247 n.31

Retore, Guy, 198
Reuters: cable, 152; correspondent, 154
Revolution and Reaction: The International Dynamism of Conflict and Confrontation in Chile, 252 n.8
Revue du Cinéma, La, 46, 171, 178–79
Rich, Frank, 213
Richardson, Tony, 58
Richard III, 182
Richmond, Indiana (home of Mitrione), 148–49, 154, 156, 183–84
Riefenstahl, Leni, 35
Right: and *Confession*, 132, 137; Costa-Gavras's description of, 166; against Left, 157; literary weekly of, 48; Mitrione's view of, 182; and *Special Section*, 212; and *State of Siege*, 157, 168, 177–79; and *Z*, 77, 84, 90, 105
Rimbaud, Arthur, 121
Rio de Janiero (Brazil), 149, 183
Rispal, Jacques, 119, 123, 198, 203
Ritter, Jim, 252 n.10
Rivette, Jacques, 186
"Roads of Honors, The" (*Special Section* book), 193
Roballa, Dr. Alba, 164
Robbe-Grillet, Alain, 41, 147
Robert, Yves, 198, 203
Roberts, Pascale, 52, 59
Robinson et le triporteur, 32
Rocha, Glauber, 26–27
Rochereau, Jean, 73, 179
Rogers, William B. (secretary of state), 182
Rolland, Romain, 37
Rolling Stone, 253 n.20
Roman Catholic Church: and Catholics, 163; and newspaper *La Croix*, 179; in *State of Siege*, 156, 166–67, 177–78, 183; and Theology of Liberation, 178
Rome (Italy), 77, 146, 205
Romeo and Juliet, 85, 95, 222
Room at the Top, 48
Rosenberg, Julius and Ethel, 37, 43, 121
Rosenberg, Stuart, 25
Rosenfeld, Stephen, 181
Rosi, Francesco, 24–25, 32, 68, 146, 236
Ross, Adolphe, 63
Rossi, Jean-Baptiste, 52. *See also* Japrisot, Sébastien
Routes du Sud, Les, 43–44
Rovelli, Franca, 34
Royal Combatants of the Christian West. *See* CROC
Rue St. Denis (Paris), 195
Ruguff, Donald, 157, 186, 250 n.64
Rule, Janice, 222, 225

Rumania, 88, 107–8, 133
Rusk, Dean, 183
Russia. *See* U.S.S.R.
Ruzyn prison, 109, 128. See also *Confession*
Ryan, Patrick, 228–29
Rykov, A. I., 107

Sabu the Indian, 30
Sacco, Nicola (and Bartolomeo Vanzetti), 119, 125–26, 201
Sacco and Vanzetti, 24
Safire's Political Dictionary, 184
Saigon (Vietnam), 217
Saint-Flour (France), 68
Saint mène la danse, Le, 32
St. Paul-de-Vence (France), 48
Salamandre, La, 166
Salicetti, Ange-Marie, 63
Salonika (Greece), 78, 80, 83–84, 101
Saltzmann, Harry, 61
Salvatore Giuliano, 22, 24, 146
Salvatori, Renato, 49, 85, 91, 159, 164
Sampaix, Lucien, 198, 200–3, 210, 212
Sanchis, Abrundio, 63
San Francisco Newsreel, 19–20
Sanjines, Jorge, 27
Santiago (Chile), 158, 223, 225, 253 nn. 30, 34. *See also* Chile
Sarlande Prison, 63
Sarrebruck (labor camp), 109
Sarris, Andrew, 101, 103, 140, 234
Sartre, Jean-Paul, 43, 48, 72, 88, 124
Sartrean Marxist (Costa-Gavras), 35, 132
Sartzetakis, Christos, 79, 105
Sauer, Rémy, 63
Sauvage, Le, 43
Sauvaget, Daniel, 171
Schatzberg, Jerry, 20
Schlesinger, James, 228
Schneider, René, 220
Schneider, Romy, 215
School of Law and Social Sciences (Uruguay), 249 n.28
Schrader, Paul, 26
Schulberg, Budd, 45
Scola Ettore, 205
Scott, George C., 161
Scwartz, Laurent, 141
Scwartz, Nancy, 202, 207, 213
Seconds, 218
Second Trial of Artur London, The, 125
Secret Files of J. Edgar Hoover, The, 25
Secret Service (U.S.), 24
Seduction of Joe Tynan, The, 20
Seduction of Mimi, The, 25

Seguin, Louis, 21, 35
Seigner, Louis, 196, 202
Semprun, Colette, 114
Semprun, Jorge: and collaboration with Costa-Gavras, 41, 44–45, 81, 113–14, 146, 194; and collaboration with Resnais, 41, 81, 147, 194; and *Confession,* 114–16, 122, 132, 134, 140, 141; criticism and response to works of, 137, 139, 202, 211, 213, 214; interview with, 114; novels and plays of, 113; personal and political ideology of, 36, 44, 99, 113, 130, 132, 135, 238; and purpose of *Confession,* 115, 122, 132–33, 142; scenarios and adaptations by, 81–82, 115–16, 127, 136, 138, 193, 194, 199–201, 247 n.31; and Solinas text, 45; and *Special Section,* 194–95, 201, 208, 210; and *State of Siege,* 21; technique and style of, 82, 91, 94, 125–26
Sendic, Raúl, 151, 165, 175–76
Sepinski, Augustín, 167
Serceau, Daniel, 18, 25, 27
Serpico, 74
Servan-Schreiber, Jean-Jacques, 97
"Settling of Accounts, The" (*Special Section* book), 193
Seven Beauties, 25
Seven Days in May, 218
Seznec Affair, 76
Shakespeare, William, 182; festival, 222
Shea, John, 222, 225
Ship of Fools, 48
Shlardemann, Harry, 228
Shock Troops (Un Homme de trop), 61–75; actors and characters in, 45, 49, 68, 90, 238; Costa-Gavras discusses purpose of, 51, 70, 74; as early Costa-Gavras film, 33, 74, 76, 143; scriptwriting and filming of, 41, 61, 68, 83, 124
Shoot the Piano Player, 48
Siberia: labor camps in, 137
Sierra de Teruel, 45
Sieverina, Alejandro, 160
Siglo, El, 140, 157
Signoret, Simone: and *Confession,* 114, 116, 122, 141; and Costa-Gavras, 33, 52; critics view of, 137; films of, 48, 52, 114, 121, 238; and Montand and politics, 43–44, 49, 112; personal background of, 48–49, 57; visit to United States of, 48, 122
Silence de la mer, Le, 199
Silvagni, Giorgio, 195
Simenon, Georges, 61
Simon, John, 60, 94, 97–98, 101, 103–4, 214
Simon, René, 49
Simon, Terry, 225, 229, 231
Sinatra, Frank, 154, 183
Singe en hiver, Un, 32, 57

Sivel, William, 128

Slansky, Rudolf: 111, 119, 123, 204, 247 n.21

Slansky Trial: and defendants, 106, 111; editing of, in *Confession*, 207; and Artur London, 33, 108, 123, 141; and Montand, 121; and Noel Field, 246 n.9; public awareness of, 111, 113, 133, 135

Slap the Monster on Page One, 24–25

Sleeping Car Murder (Compartiment tueurs): 51–61; actors in, 45, 49, 90–91; compared to *Z*, 93; as Costa-Gavras's first film, 60, 143; criticism of, 60, 61; English and American title of, 244 n.5; film compared to novel, 147; and importance for Costa-Gavras, 51–52, 60, 74, 238; Montand in, 43, 58; the novel, 52; plot of, 33, 51; scriptwriting, filming, and editing of, 41, 56–57, 69, 94, 171, 205

Sling, Otto, 123, 126, 203

SLON (Société de Lancement des Oeuvres Nouvelles), 18

Société des Réalisateurs Français, 141

Socrates, 88, 90

Soho Weekly News, 202, 207–8, 213

Soir, un train, Un, 90

Sokolnikov, G. I., 107

Solanas, Fernando, 27–28

Solas, Humberto, 27

Solinas, Franco: and collaboration with Costa-Gavras, 41, 146–49; and documentation and research for *State of Siege*, 36, 147, 149, 153–54, 173, 177, 193; interviews with and comments by, 42, 146, 156, 163, 168, 174; political ideology of, 146–47, 155, 157, 163, 173, 177; and presentation of Church in *State of Siege*, 167, 178; and purpose and work on *State of Siege*, 146, 154–55, 168, 170, 172–73, 178; and research on Mitrione, 150, 152–54, 182; as scriptwriter, 19, 146; and Semprun text, 45; and Tupamaros guerrillas, 151, 153–54, 156, 176; work of, compared to *Hidden Terrors*, 152

Solinas, PierNico, 168

Sollers, Philippe, 18

Solo, 23

Solzhenitsyn, Alexander, 107

Sophocles, 88, 98, 192

Sorbonne, 31, 36, 41–42

Sorcerer, The, 49

Sorcières de Salem, Les, 48. *See also* Montand, Yves; Signoret, Simone; *Witches of Salem*

Sorenson, Theodore, 167, 173, 179–80

Sorrow and the Pity, The, 32, 211

South America, 145, 148, 158

Spacek, Sissy, 39, 222, 225

Spain: Civil War in, 22, 29, 41, 44–45, 109, 111, 116, 189, 193; Communist party in, 44, 114;

Costa-Gavras and Montand in, 43; history of, 82, 148, 151; and International Brigade, 135, 193; language of, 117, 222, 224; London/Gérard in, 109, 117, 119; reaction to Costa-Gavras's films in, 104, 140; and Semprun, 44, 81, 114

Special Section (Section Spéciale): 187–214; actors and characterization in, 39, 45, 49, 123, 201–3, 238; compared to other Costa-Gavras films, 202, 204, 211; criticism of, 211–14, 234, 236; as documentary style film, 19, 194; and documents, 192–93; editing of, 206–7; music and sound in, 207–8; narrative and plot of, 34, 187–88, 196–99, 210; photography in, 204–6; politics in, 187, 191, 208–10; prejudiced leftist slant in, 74, 99, 191–92, 208, 210; production and filming of, 45, 195–96, 205; screenings of and reaction to, 208, 210, 213–14; scriptwriting and scenario of, 44–45, 194–95, 199–201, 237; technique and tone of, 34, 46, 195, 203–4, 238–39. *See also* L'Affaire de la Section Spéciale

Special Sections, 190

Speidel, Hans (colonel), 190, 193

Spider's Strategem, The, 24

Spiesser, Jacques, 196, 203

"Springtime of Prague," 130–31

SS officers *(Shock Troops)*, 69

Stalin, Joseph: anti-Semitism of, 125, 133–34, 139; and *Confession*, 117, 122–24, 126, 132, 178; and enemies of, 106–8, 135; in power, 107, 109, 133; significance and death of, 111, 119–20, 131, 246 n.13; and Trotsky, 107, 110; mentioned, 41, 139, 142

Stalinism: abuses of power of, 108, 112, 130, 133, 238; and *Confession*, 38, 112, 115, 125, 132, 137, 142, 147, 209; and Costa-Gavras and *Confession* seen as anti-Stalinist, 34, 138, 147, 157; criticism of, 111, 121, 140; regime of, 41, 106, 131–32

"Stalinism on Film," 133

Stanford University, 253 n.30

State of Siege (Etat de siège): 143–86; actors and characterization in, 41, 43, 49, 161–68, 202, 238; and American Film Institute festival at Kennedy Center, 35, 185, 231; compared to other Costa-Gavras films, 39, 201–3, 207, 211, 219, 227, 229; as Costa-Gavras's challenge, 144, 173; documentation in, 19, 21, 38, 42, 168, 182, 193, 206; editing of, 46, 170–72, 207; genre and technique of, 33, 35, 40, 46, 168–69; music and sound in, 47, 171–72, 208; narrative scenes in, 158–61, 168, 172, 206; as part of Costa-Gavras trilogy, 143; photographic techniques in, 41–42, 45, 169–70; politics in, 144, 172–74, 177–79, 189–90, 229, 239; production and filming of, 157–61, 195; reaction of United States government officials to, 42, 143, 148–49, 152–54, 156, 179, 183; and research into AID, 99, 154, 176, 184; reviews of, 21, 28, 168, 171, 173, 178–82, 238; and Tupamaros, 149, 175–77, 223; United States government in, 156, 181; United States presence in, 41, 155, 158, 160, 175

Stavisky, 44, 194, 203

Stavisky file, 194, 200, 210

Steinbeck, John, 37

Sternberg, Jacques, 41, 147

Stevens, George, Jr., 176, 179, 185–86, 250 n.64

Stewart, Donald, 219

Stockholm (Sweden), 43

Stokes, Geoffrey, 39

Streisand, Barbara, 114

Strike, 103

Studio de Saint Maurice, 60

Stulpnagel, Otto von, 193

Sunshine Grabber, The, 220

Sweet, Sweetback's Baadasssss Song, 20

Swept Away, 25

Switzerland, 83, 119; in *Confession,* 246 n.9

Swoboda, Ludvik (president), 141

Syndicat de la Magistrature (lawyers' union), 214

Taking Off, 114

Takis (musician), 208

Tall Blond Man with One Black Shoe, The, 203

Tanguy, Rol, 68

Tarter, Linda, 148

Taxi Driver, 26

Taylor, Gene (congressman), 179

Télérama, 103, 140, 174, 212

Télé Sept Jours, 120, 136

Tel Quel, 18

Témoignage Chrétien, 149

Teruggi, Frank, 225, 252 n.10, 253 nn. 30, 34

Texas, 153, 160, 171

Teynac, Maurice, 158

Thaelmann, Ernst, 124

Thailand, 144

Théâtre National, 203

Themelio Press, 80

Theodorakis, Mikis, 47, 77, 80, 85, 88, 90, 95–97, 171–72

Theology of Liberation, 178

Thirard, Paul-Louis, 103, 137

Third International, 190

Third Reich, 107

Third World: cinema, 22, 26; and politics, 17, 27, 149, 153, 174, 230

This Angry Age (Un Barrage contre le Pacifique), 45

Thompson, Howard, 73

Thorez, Maurice, 111, 115, 138

Three Brothers (Tre Fratelli), 68

Three Days of the Condor, 25

Three Women, 222

Time, 136–37, 140, 180, 202, 213

Titicut Follies, 19

Tito (Josif Broz)/Titoism: 39, 107, 110, 117; in *Confession,* 135, 139

Todo Modo, 22

Tolstoy, Leo, 88, 98

Topaz, 88

Toubriana, Serge, 179

Toulouse (France), 212

Tournès, Andrée, 94

Tournier, Jean, 57, 69

Tout l'or du monde, 32

Trans-Europ-Express, 90

Tre Fratelli (Three Brothers), 68

Trial, The, 106, 124

"Trial in the Eastern European Bloc: A Socialist Malady, The," 141

Trials of Alger Hiss, The, 108

Tribute, 221

Trintignant, Jean-Louis, 53, 59, 85, 88, 90, 104

Triumph of the Will, 35

317ème Section, 68

Trotsky, Leon/Trotskyism, 88, 107, 110, 117, 119, 139

Truffaut, François, 186

Truman, Harry, 78

Trumbo, Dalton, 25–26

Trzebrucki, Abraham, 190–91, 193, 198, 203

Tupac Amaru I, 151. *See also* Tupamaros

Tupamaros (guerrillas): and Costa-Gavras, 38, 146, 150–51, 154, 156, 166, 173, 176; ideology and organization of, 40–42, 151–52, 175–76; and Mitrione, 143, 146, 149, 152–53, 158, 162, 168, 176, 182, 184, 187; reactions to, 147, 154, 163, 167, 177, 179, 183, 250 n.49; in *State of Siege,* 46, 153, 155, 156, 159–62, 165, 169, 171, 175–78; works on, 248 n.12, 250 n.53

Turkey, film in, 235

Turner, Stanfield, 231

Twentieth Century Fox, 88

Twentieth Division headquarters (Communist party), 167

Twentieth Party Congress, 111–12, 138

Tyszelman, Samuel, 190, 196, 200

Ullmann, Liv, 42

UNESCO, 44

Unifrance, 131

Union of the Democratic Left (EDA), 77–78, 80

U.S.S.R.: and anti-Soviet propaganda, 30, 139;

birthplace of Costa-Gavras's father, 29; cinema classics of, and effect on Costa-Gavras, 22, 30, 32, 141; and *Confession,* 129, 133, 135, 139; in *Confession,* 115, 119, 120, 125–26; Czech invasion by, 107, 113, 120, 127, 129–32, 135, 137; and Greece, 78, 88, 98; and Lenin, 106; and Artur London, 109–11; and Nazi Germany invasion, 107, 189–90; regime and policies of, 48, 107, 112, 116, 128, 130, 133–35, 230; and satellite countries, 35, 38, 107, 142; secret service of, 115, 138, 246 n.9; and Stalin, 123, 133; and *Z,* 88, 91, 98

Unión Popular, 163

Unitarian Relief Service Committee, 109, 116

United All-Greek Youth Organization, 47

United Artists, 81, 88, 195

United Fruit Co., 144

United Nations Prize *(Confession),* 141

U.S., 24, 37, 117, 142, 146, 161, 230

U.S. cinema, 43, 46, 185; cinema/television and relations to Costa-Gavras, 29–31, 32, 93, 154, 237–38; film genres in, 22, 25, 37, 52, 54–55, 60, 72–73, 103, 132; film production in, 25–26, 38, 47, 114, 124

U.S. film criticism: of *Clair de Femme,* 216; compared to France and Europe, 26, 135, 211; of *Confession,* 132, 134–35, 163; of *Shock Troops,* 73; of *Special Section,* 211; of *State of Siege,* 173, 179–81, 212, 214; of *Z,* 83, 97, 102–4, 134–35

U.S. government, 174, 249 n.24; and Allende government, 220, 228; and the Catholic Church, 156, 177; censorship in, 186; criticism of, 21, 27, 37, 99, 157, 167, 171, 173–74, 178–81, 185, 227–28, 230; embassy and ambassadors of, 144–45, 174, 185, 220–21, 224, 228, 232, 235, 249 nn. 24, 47; 253 n.30 (see also *Missing*); and historic parallels, 140, 213; involvement in torture, 149–53, 155–56, 167; and NATO, 78; policy, 48, 143, 174, 221, 227; Public Health Service, 163; State Department, 40, 74, 116, 148–49, 174, 179, 182, 228, 231, 249 nn. 24, 47; Senate, 17, 228. See also Missing; State of Siege

U.S. producers and directors: 18, 24–25, 32, 127, 157, 180, 186, 211, 219

U.S. public reaction to: *Clair de femme,* 216; *Confession,* 140; *Day of the Jackal,* 26; *Eboli,* 24; films and politics, 17, 36, 76, 108, 174, 180, 204, 227, 229, 235, 238; *Missing,* 228, 230, 235; *Shock Troops,* 61, 73; *Sleeping Car Murder,* 60–61; *Special Section,* 202, 213; *State of Siege,* 35, 162, 173, 185; *Z,* 83–84, 90, 105

U.S. relations with: Chile, 220, 225, 228, 229, 235, 252 n.8, 253 nn. 20, 34; Greece, 78; Latin America, 26, 34, 144–45, 148, 154, 156, 173,

227, 229, 230, 232; Uruguay, 132, 134, 144, 148–49, 153, 167, 172, 174–75, 178

U.S. and socio-political mood, 17, 83, 156, 179, 235–36, 242 n.10

Universal Studios: and *Missing,* 34, 219; and *State of Siege,* 192, 195, 211–12, 214

Uruguay: AID in, 33–34, 148, 174–75; British ambassador to, 152, 176; Costa-Gavras in, 146, 154; Death Squad in, 167; embassy of, 148, 157, 185; film representation of in *State of Siege,* 148, 157–58, 223, 227; government of, in *State of Siege,* 156, 175; history of, 148; mass for Mitrione in, 148, 156; Mitrione's presence in, 146, 148–50, 153, 155, 172, 182, 184; and National Liberation Front (*see* Tupamaros); Parliament of, 158, 160, 163, 182; political scene in, 148, 151, 167, 179; Michèle Ray in, 42, 148, 164; Senate in, 164, 248 n.10; Solinas in, 154; Tupamaros in, 146, 149, 151, 154, 248 n.11; and United States government, 144, 149, 167, 174, 249 n.24

Valéry, Paul, 188, 208

Valeurs Actuelles, Les, 138, 212

Valoria Films, 89

Valparaiso (Chile), 158

Vancini, Florestano, 24

Vanel, Charles, 62, 68

Vanzetti, Bartolomeo, 119, 125–26, 201. *See also* Sacco, Nicola

Varda, Agnès, 42

Variety, 140, 157

Vassilikos, Vassilis: authenticity of *Z* (novel), 81, 96, 100–2; and film *Z,* 44–45, 81–84, 98, 102; and novel *Z,* 33, 76, 80, 94; and politics, 77, 98, 242 n.7

Vatican, 167, 178. *See also* Roman Catholic Church

Vecchiali, Paul, 46–47

Veillot, Claude, 98

Veliantis (general), 96

Venezuela, 223

Venture, Richard, 222, 225

Verdun (France), 198

Verneuil, Henri, 23–24, 32, 45, 57

Veterans of Foreign Wars, 185

Vichy: films on, 187, 250 n.1; government, 34, 188–94, 209, 211, 213, 214; in *Special Section,* 195–97, 200–2, 206, 210, 212, 251 n.16

Vichy France: Old Guard and New Order, 1940–1944, 188

Victory in the West, 35

Vidas Secas (Barren Lives), 27

Vie c'est comme un train, La, 146

Vie devant soi, La, 48

Vielzeuf, Aimé, 63, 72

Vienna (Austria), 141

Vierny, Sacha, 48

Viet Cong, 42, 217

Vietnam, 42, 110, 142, 217, 220

Vietnam War, 17, 36, 153, 235, 242 n.10; and films, 20, 48, 225

Village Voice, 103, 140, 234

Villeré, Hervé: comparison of book (*Special Section*) and film, 190, 192–94, 199–201, 206, 210 and documentation of Special Sections, 192–93, 208; and politics in France, 188, 192, 209, 250 n.4

Villette, Francis, 206

Viña del Mar (Chile), 224, 228

Violins at the Ball, 187

Vitold, Michel, 119, 123, 137

Vitti, Monica, 23

Viva el Presidente!, 27

Vivre la nuit, 90

Vogel, Amos, 20, 23

Volets clos, Les, 68

Volk, Steve, 233

Von Sydow, Max, 42

Vus, (Yugoslavia weekly), 141

Wall, The, 76

Walsh, Raoul, 32

War Game, The, 19

Warner, Jack, 186

Warner Brothers, 88, 140

Warren Commission, 26, 94

Warsaw (Poland), 121. *See also* Poland

Warsaw Pact, 112–13, 130

Washington, D.C.: AID in, 152–53, 183; Brookings Institute in, 179; Costa-Gavras researches in, 154; International Police Academy in, 155, 160, 184; and *Missing*, 228, 235; Mitrione and, 148–49; and *State of Siege*, 35, 84, 181, 185–86, 228

Washington Post, 40, 155, 179, 181, 183, 186, 231

Washington Sunday Star and Daily News, 179

Watergate affair, 17, 25, 40, 76, 162, 186, 213, 230

Watkins, Peter, 19

Wayne, John, 43, 73

Weathermen, 179

Weber, Jacques, 159, 165

Weekend, 23

Wehrmacht, 189

Weinstein, Martin, 176

Welles, Orson, 124

Wertmüller, Lina, 25

Westerbeck, Colin, 130

Western agents, 142

Western European Affairs, 78

Western films, 55

Western Hemisphere, 110, 113, 134, 248 n.2

Wheaton, Rev. Philip E., 183

White Angel, The, 26

Whitehead, Alfred, 237

White House, 182

Who's Who in the CIA, 183

Why We Fight Series, 61

Wiesbaden (Germany), 48

Wild One, The, 55

Winding, Andreas, 204

Wiseman, Fred, 19

Witches of Salem, The (Les Sorcières de Salem), 48, 57

Without Apparent Motive, 23

Woman's Glow, A. 215. See also *Clair de femme*

Woodward, Bob, 25, 40

Working Class Goes to Heaven, The, 24

World War I, 25, 76, 158

World War II: and effect on Costa-Gavras, 30–31; and films, 22, 25, 33, 61, 116, 187, 211; and history, 22, 30, 62, 72, 77–78, 107, 109; Lise and Artur London during, 111; Mitrione in, 149; and Theodorakis, 47, 95

Wyler, William, 61

Yale University, 24, 191, 210

Yentl, 222

Yevtouchenko, Yevgeny, 246 n.13

Yglesias, José, 180

Yol, 235

Yugoslavia, 88, 107, 110, 135, 141

Yvoire, Jean d', 103

Z: 76–103; actors in, 49; Bouise in, 123; characters in, 38–39, 92, 122, 163, 222, 238; compared to other films, 23, 37, 39, 157–58, 171, 201, 203, 208, 211, 220; consequences of, 97–98, 104–5, 140; and Coutard, 94, 124, 204; criticism of, 21, 28, 39, 72, 101–4, 134, 139–40; Denner acts in, 60, 91; Dux acts in, 202; editing of, 45–46, 128, 207, 223; epilogue of, 97–98, 129, 172; and evolution of Costa-Gavras as director, 34, 113, 143, 187, 237; filming of, 23, 42, 77, 89; funding for, 89, 195; and *La Guerre est finie*, 23; Montand acts in, 43, 88, 90, 121, 162; as novel, 33, 76–77, 80, 102; Perrin acts in, 41, 45; photography in, 41–42, 47; as political film, 23, 36, 98–100, 104, 236; politics in, 35, 47, 78, 82–83, 98–102, 132–33, 139, 151, 230; purpose of, 18, 83, 99–100, 104, 131; Salvatori in, 164; screenings of, 35, 96–97, 104–5, 141; and Semprun, 21, 38, 44–45, 113; sound track of, 47, 96, 129, 171, 207; style of, 35, 38, 93, 206, 238–39; success of, 19, 33, 102, 114, 236;

technique in, 46, 94–95, 114, 125, 127; Trintig-
  nant acts in, 59, 90
Zagreb (Yugoslavia), 141
Zapruder, Abraham, 94
Zatouna (Greece), 96
Zavattini, Cesare, 45
Zavrodosky, Osvald, 126
"Z effect," 18

Ziegler, Ronald, 182
Zilliacus, Konni, 119
Zimmer, Christian, 17
Zimmerman, Paul, 181
Zinnemann, Fred, 25–26
Zinoviev, G. E., 107
Zionism, 39, 134
Zorba the Greek, 47, 96